Multinational Management

Rien T. Segers
Editor

Multinational Management

A Casebook on Asia's Global Market Leaders

 Springer

Editor
Rien T. Segers
Hanze University
Groningen, The Netherlands

ISBN 978-3-319-23011-5   ISBN 978-3-319-23012-2 (eBook)
DOI 10.1007/978-3-319-23012-2

Library of Congress Control Number: 2015960797

Springer Cham Heidelberg New York Dordrecht London
© Springer International Publishing Switzerland 2016
This work is subject to copyright. All rights are reserved by the Publisher, whether the whole or part of the material is concerned, specifically the rights of translation, reprinting, reuse of illustrations, recitation, broadcasting, reproduction on microfilms or in any other physical way, and transmission or information storage and retrieval, electronic adaptation, computer software, or by similar or dissimilar methodology now known or hereafter developed.
The use of general descriptive names, registered names, trademarks, service marks, etc. in this publication does not imply, even in the absence of a specific statement, that such names are exempt from the relevant protective laws and regulations and therefore free for general use.
The publisher, the authors and the editors are safe to assume that the advice and information in this book are believed to be true and accurate at the date of publication. Neither the publisher nor the authors or the editors give a warranty, express or implied, with respect to the material contained herein or for any errors or omissions that may have been made.

Printed on acid-free paper

Springer International Publishing AG Switzerland is part of Springer Science+Business Media (www.springer.com)

Preface

In this book, we want to emphasize that hundreds of emerging Asian companies will reach out to the world and enter the global market in the next decade. At this moment, these new companies are rather unknown in the West. The message of this book is that this will rapidly change. After they have firmly established themselves in their vast home markets in China, India, Japan, South Korea and other Asian countries, they will be knocking at many Western doors. And then the central question arises: are we in the West ready for this development unprecedented in economic history?

This book, with its case studies of 13 Asian companies and its explanation of their hidden strategies and successes, contains an incitement to prepare ourselves in the West for the coming era dominated by East Asia. These preparations should consist of serious attempts to understand the cultural identity of major Asian countries. In addition, we should study the corporate culture and business strategies of those Asian companies which will appear in the Western market rather soon. We have selected the most relevant and important companies in this respect.

This book results from a research project completed by members of the research group belonging to the chair *Asian Business Strategies* of the International Business School of Hanze University of Applied Sciences (Groningen, The Netherlands).

The editor wishes to thank all institutions and persons who made this book possible. First of all, I would like to thank the members of my research team for their great investment in time and thinking. Filip Vedder and Karen Prowse again have proven to be excellent assistants. The Investment and Development Agency for the Northern Netherlands (NOM) financially facilitated the research done by the members of the research group. The International Business School of Hanze University made the publication of this book possible. I am also grateful to the International Business School and the Institute of Marketing and Management of Hanze University for having granted me a leave of absence to serve as visiting professor at UMBC (University of Baltimore). I thank my colleague Professor Constantine Vaporis for his invitation to teach and do research at his Asian Studies Program and for his warm hospitality during a cold winter semester in Baltimore.

Baltimore, MD   Rien T. Segers
Groningen, The Netherlands
April 2015

Acknowledgment

The editor thanks the following institutions, which made the publication of this book possible.

Contents

Introduction 1
Rien T. Segers

Part I China

Alibaba: A Case Study on Building an International Imperium
on Information and E-Commerce. 13
Marieke Havinga, Martijn Hoving, and Virgil Swagemakers

Geely: A Case Study on the Trend Following Volvo-Owner 33
Gero von Bismarck and Yunyao Zheng

Haier: A Case Study on How One of China's First Global Brands
Keeps Expanding 55
Florian Pallas

Huawei: A Case Study on a Telecom Giant on the Rise 75
Michelle Haveman and Jeroen Vochteloo

Lenovo: A Case Study on Strengthening the Position in the European
Market Through Innovation. 95
Franz Josef Gellert

Tencent: A Case Study on Expanding Through Micro-Innovation
and Strategic Partnerships. 111
Filip Vedder

Part II India

Dr. Reddy's: A Case Study on Conquering the World with Affordable
Medicine for the Masses. 133
Maximilian Egender and Irina Rotari

Infosys: A Case Study on Becoming a Global Brand in Consulting
Technology and Outsourcing Solutions. 149
Mariusz Soltanifar

Part III Japan

Panasonic: A Case Study on Constant Change and Reinvention of a World Brand 173
Uli Mathies

Rakuten: A Case Study on Entering New Markets Through an Innovative Business-to-Business-to-Consumer Strategy 203
Thomas S. Willenborg

Uniqlo: A Case Study on Creating Market Share with Affordable and Timeless Designs 221
Frederike Schulz-Müllensiefen and Aenne Stöckmann

Part IV South Korea

Lotte: A Case Study on Market Entries Through Acquisition 239
Manuel Schlothauer and Denise Wilhaus

Part V Vietnam

Vinamilk: A Case Study on Partnering Up to Expand on the World Market 257
Kim Nguyen

Part VI Underlying Strategies and Success Factors of Emerging Asian Multinationals

Corporate Enterpreneurship and Triple Helix 275
Mariusz Soltanifar

Asian Human Resource Management and Intercultural Competence 301
Marcel H. van der Poel

Branding Trends in Asian Markets 311
Diederich Bakker

Part VII Conclusion

Conclusions: Why and How Asian Businesses Will Conquer the World 331
Rien T. Segers and Filip Vedder

List of Contributors

Diederich Bakker International Business School, Hanze University OAS, Groningen, The Netherlands

Gero von Bismarck The Honor's Program of the International Business School, Hanze University OAS, Groningen, The Netherlands

Maximilian Egender The Honor's Program of the International Business School, Hanze University OAS, Groningen, The Netherlands

Franz Josef Gellert FOM University OAS for Economics and Management, Bremen, Germany

International Business School, Hanze University OAS, Groningen, The Netherlands

Michelle Haveman The Honor's Program of the International Business School, Hanze University OAS, Groningen, The Netherlands

Marieke Havinga School of Marketing Management, Hanze University OAS, Groningen, The Netherlands

Martijn Hoving The SBRM program of the School of Marketing Management, Hanze University OAS, Groningen, The Netherlands

Uli Mathies International Business School, Hanze University OAS, Groningen, The Netherlands

Kim Nguyen The Honor's Program of the International Business School, Hanze University OAS, Groningen, The Netherlands

Florian Pallas Iskander Business Partner, Düsseldorf, Germany

Marcel H. van der Poel International Business School, Hanze University OAS, Groningen, The Netherlands

Irani Rotari The Honor's Program of the International Business School, Hanze University OAS, Groningen, The Netherlands

Manuel Schlothauer The Honor's Program of the International Business School, Hanze University OAS, Groningen, The Netherlands

Frederike Schulz-Müllensiefen The Honor's Program of the International Business School, Hanze University OAS, Groningen, The Netherlands

Rien T. Segers International Business School, Hanze University OAS, Groningen, The Netherlands

Clingendael Netherlands Institute of International Relations, The Hague, The Netherlands

Mariusz Soltanifar International Business School, Hanze University OAS, Groningen, The Netherlands

Aenne Stöckmann The Honor's Program of the International Business School, Hanze University OAS, Groningen, The Netherlands

Virgil Swagemakers The SBRM program of the School of Marketing Management, Hanze University OAS, Groningen, The Netherlands

Filip Vedder International Business School, Hanze University OAS, Groningen, The Netherlands

Jeroen Vochteloo The Honor's Program of the International Business School, Hanze University OAS, Groningen, The Netherlands

Denise Wilhaus The Honor's Program of the International Business School, Hanze University OAS, Groningen, The Netherlands

Thomas S. Willenborg Datatrans AG, Zurich, Switzerland

Yunyao Zheng The Honor's Program of the International Business School, Hanze University OAS, Groningen, The Netherlands

Abbreviations

ADS	American Depositary Shares
AIS	Automotive & Industrial Systems Company (Panasonic)
AMNC	Asian Multinationals
AP	Appliance Company (Panasonic)
API	Active Pharmaceutical Ingredients
ATHS	Asia Triple Helix Society
AVC	AVC Networks Company (Panasonic)
B2B	Business-to-Business
B2B2C	Business-to-Business-to-Consumer
B2C	Business-to-Consumer
BP	Business Performance
BPO	Business Process Outsourcing
C2C	Consumer-to-Consumer
CAGR	Compound Annual Growth Rate
CE	Corporate Entrepreneurship
CEAI	Corporate Entrepreneurship Assessment Instrument
CEO	Chief Executive Officer
CERN	European Organization for Nuclear Research
CMO	Chief Marketing Officer
CPG	Consumer Packaged Goods
CR	Corporate Renewal
CSR	Customer Social Responsibility
CV	Corporate Venturing
EC	European Commission
EO	Entrepreneurial Orientation
ES	Eco Solutions Company (Panasonic)
FCF	Free Cash Flow
FDA	Food and Drug Administration (US)
FDI	Foreign Direct Investment/Investor(s)
FY	Financial Year
Hanze UAS	Hanze University of Applied Sciences
HR	Human Resources
HRM	Human Resource Management

ICT	Information and Communication Technology
IHRM	International Human Resource Management
IPO	Initial Public Offering
IS	Innovation System
ISP	Internet Service Provider
IT	Information Technology
ITHA	International Triple Helix Association
KBE	Knowledge Based Economy
KBS	Knowledge Based Society
M&A	Merger and Acquisition
M2M	Machine-to-Machine
MEI	Matsushita Electric Industrial Co. Ltd. (Panasonic)
MIDH	Mobile Internet and Digital Home Business Group (division of Lenovo)
MNE	Multinational Enterprise
NFIA	Netherlands Foreign Investment Agency
NVC	New Venture Creation
NYSE	New York Stock Exchange
O&M	Operations and Maintenance
O2O	Online-to-Offline
ODM	Original Design Manufacturer
OECD	The Organization for Economic Co-operation and Development
OEM	Original Equipment Manufacturer
OP	Operating Profits
OPCE	Organizational Preparedness for Corporate Entrepreneurship
OPM	Operating Profit Margin
PR	Public Relations
R&D	Research and Development
RoE	Return on Equity
SE	Strategic Entrepreneurship
SR	Strategic Renewal
TH	Triple Helix
TMS	Top Management Support
UHT	Ultra High Temperature
VAS	Value Added Service(s)
VC	Venture Capital
YoY	Year-on-Year
ZZJYT	Zi Zhu Jing Ying Ti (self-managed teams from Haier)

Introduction

Rien T. Segers

Abstract

Asia will soon reshape the global economic landscape. This undoubtedly will result in a change in the global power center—both soft and hard—from the West to the East. In global business, interactions between Asia and the West will most likely intensify. The West will encounter Asian values more than before in a working environment. In this book, we want to emphasize that hundreds of Asian companies will reach out to the world and enter the global market. At this moment, most of these new companies are relatively unknown in the West. The message of this book is that this will rapidly change. By choosing to highlight rather recently-established, multinational, companies, we hope to show what kind of strategies these exemplary companies have developed to become successful not only in their home market, but also in the world market and thus become strong competitors to their Western rivals. We have selected at least one company to analyze from the key countries of China, India, Japan, South Korea and Vietnam, with a focus on its strategies and endeavors to become a global multinational.

1 The Rise of Asia

After the current financial-economic crisis, the world will have a completely different outlook. Three developments will be decisive in this respect. First of all, the leadership of the United States, the undisputed leader of the second half of the twentieth century, will no longer be self-evident. In addition, the integration process of the European Union and especially that of the Eurozone has come to a standstill,

---

R.T. Segers (✉)
International Business School, Hanze University OAS, Groningen, The Netherlands

Clingendael Netherlands Institute of International Relations, The Hague, The Netherlands
e-mail: m.t.m.segers@pl.hanze.nl

and maybe worse, is on the brink of destruction. Finally, yet importantly, the global economic center of gravity is shifting more rapidly than expected from the West to the East. All of this means that the twenty-first century may very well be the Asian century.

If that is the case, then Asia will soon reshape the global political-economic landscape. This undoubtedly will result in a change in the global power center—both soft and hard—from the West to the East. In global business, interactions between Asia and the West will most likely intensify. In the West, we will encounter Asian values more than before in our working environment: business cultures and conventions that are so different from ours, based as they are on a completely different philosophy and another outlook on life. Is the West prepared for these encounters that are going to happen on a more frequent basis?

Many members of the Asian elite have given negative answers to this question. For example, the former top diplomat and current dean of the Lee Kuan Yew School of Public Policy at the National University of Singapore, Kishore Mahbubani, recently mentioned that no country has done more than the United States "to spark the rise of Asia. But paradoxically, America is among the countries least prepared to handle the rise of East Asia."

High growth, rapid industrialization, economic reforms and the gradual opening of domestic markets to foreign competition characterize the economic development path of emerging Asian economies. Asia's high growth combined with its vast market potential and large diversified labor pool has made it a favored investment location for Western companies. The influx of FDI has generated positive spillover effects in Asian economies. Asian firms were quick to absorb knowledge, technology and best practices from foreign firms to enhance their own operational capacities and build up their domestic market share. In addition, Asian firms have increased their ability to read trends in global markets and make the most of the endowments provided by their domestic environment to climb up the global ranks. Many Asian governments actively require and stimulate outbound activities of companies and are gradually cutting away the red tape that (formerly) impeded cross-border investments.

During the economic downturn in 2008, many Asian economies demonstrated great resilience, quick recovery and stable economic growth. Furthermore, the volume and global share of Asian cross-border investments continued to grow despite the dominant downward trend in global OFDI. Although the overall share of Asia in global OFDI is still relatively small, predictions are that it will increase based on Asia's current economic growth levels and a possible upcoming recession in Europe and North America.

2 Growth in the Asian Hemisphere

2.1 China

The most eye-catching feature of Asia's economic ascent is the rise of China. Since the gradual opening up of the Chinese economy in 1978, economic growth rates have averaged nearly 10 % per year. According to forecasts, economic growth levels in China will persist, be it at levels significantly less than 10 %, and China could overtake the United States as the world's largest economy (by GDP) by 2020.

Although market forces have entered China, the government still exerts great influence on the economy. The initial economic success of China lies primarily in using economies of scale to their advantage. A large and diversified labor pool and considerable inward investment have been important factors for China in becoming a powerful source of low-cost manufacturing and industrial exports in the world. The Chinese government intends to diversify its economy and develop more knowledge- and technology-intensive economic activities. Chinese exports and outward FDI have grown explosively, especially after China joined the WTO in 2001. Government incentives have assisted Chinese companies in establishing a global footprint. Large greenfield investments of State-owned enterprises (SOEs) have sprouted in Central Asia, Latin America and Africa to safeguard resources and energy supplies for China's industries. The number of Chinese companies (mainly SOEs) acquiring European and North American targets in high-tech, manufacturing and raw materials has grown exponentially to secure intangible assets, knowledge and technology.

2.2 India

Although still a poor country with vast socio-economic problems, India has managed to become the ninth largest economy in the world since economic liberalization in 1991. Between 1990 and 2010, the annual average growth rate of the Indian economy was 6.6 %. For an emerging economy, India has well-developed services and ICT industries which have showcased remarkable growth over the years. Indian ICT companies have been quick to embrace overseas clientele and business opportunities and have created a low-cost niche in the global ICT market. They derive the majority of revenues from services and software exports to developed markets.

Although service exports are booming, India has a trade deficit due to large importation of commodities. To improve its trade situation, India is negotiating various free trade agreements. Indian OFDI and M&A have surged since restrictions on outward investment and cross-border acquisitions have been loosened. Indian OFDI is mainly concentrated in the manufacturing sector followed by services and wholesale/retail activities. Favored investment destinations are Singapore, the Netherlands, United Kingdom, United States, various tax havens and the Middle East.

Indian greenfield investment mainly concerns mining, construction and heavy manufacturing activities in developing nations, often resource-rich countries. Indian outbound M&A has skyrocketed. Conglomerates have been especially keen to acquire foreign firms to gain market access and intangible assets. Indian outbound M&A activity is concentrated in developed nations' manufacturing sector and, to a lesser extent, in services.

2.3   Japan

Japan was the first country in Asia to industrialize. In the latter half of the 19th century, foreign expertise and technologies were borrowed to create a solid industrial base. The main objective was to catch up with the West. After WWII, Japan's industry evolved quickly from light industrial production to heavy manufacturing. By the 1970s, Japanese industry had upgraded to mass-production of consumer goods. Japanese companies were successful and out-competed Western manufacturing by developing efficient lean production processes and thorough quality control systems. In the 1980s, Japan's industrial catch-up process was finalized when industries started to focus on innovation-driven activities. Since the end of WWII, Japan experienced continuous economic growth.

However, since 1989, when the economic bubble started to go bust, Japan has been in an on-going recession. The Japanese economy has been plagued by deflation, an ageing workforce and a banking crisis for two decades. Furthermore, Japan is still recovering from 3/11, the Fukushima triple disaster (earthquake, tsunami and nuclear meltdown). Japanese firms have seen their labor productivity, export revenues, domestic sales and production volume drop. International competition has increased and, in many industries, Japanese firms have lost market share. Therefore many Japanese multinationals are trying to reinvent themselves.

These factors have re-invigorated Japanese OFDI. In recent years, Japanese outbound investments have increased. Surprisingly, non-manufacturing FDI flows have overtaken manufacturing investment since 2007. Japanese overseas affiliates are mainly active in wholesale trade, transport equipment, various services, machinery and electrical equipment. Japanese companies have established a global footprint and are now strengthening and expanding their overseas production networks through investment. The scale and scope of activities of overseas subsidiaries have increased to build global market share. Many Japanese companies are globalizing their R&D base to enhance firm competence and international competitiveness. Many of these recent expansion efforts have been carried out through cross-border M&A.

2.4   South Korea

In South Korea, we witness that industrialization with close state monitoring, development of industrial conglomerates (chaebol), domestic market protection and export promotion has fueled high economic growth. Growth levels were high until the Asian Crisis in 1997 hit South Korea hard. Drastic reforms in the labor market and in the corporate and financial sectors were undertaken to avert total economic collapse. The chaebol, the main pillars of the South Korean economy, were forced to downsize and switch course from labor intensive production to capital- and technology-intensive production.

The South Korean economy quickly recovered and chaebol have become worldwide household names in handsets, LCD devices and automobiles. Chaebol dominate South Korea's outbound economic activity, accounting for a large share of manufacturing exports and 80 % of outbound investment. South Korea's prominent outward economic activity is rooted in export. It is the seventh biggest exporter and eighth largest importer in the world in terms of value. Many South Korean industrial companies choose to maintain production facilities in the home market, hence the large volumes of commodities flowing into South Korea.

Numerous FTAs are being negotiated to facilitate intensified trade flows. South Korean OFDI has grown substantially over the years. The majority of investments is concentrated in China, South East Asia, North America and Europe, in that order. Electronic equipment, shipbuilding, motor vehicles and petrochemicals are the main industries in which South Korean companies hold foreign assets. Greenfield investments are preferred over M&A deals, but the number of cross-border acquisitions is on the rise. Even though foreign assets of South Korean companies have grown, export will not be substituted for outward investment anytime soon.

3   Building Globally-Competitive Firms Which Will Conquer the World

Asian companies are gaining competence and becoming competitive in the global economy. Cost advantages have been essential for them to break into international markets. Factors such as government support, internalization of best practice in manufacturing, and economies of scale have also been instrumental to the growth of Asian firms. Some firms have adapted to tough business conditions at home and created new opportunities in other emerging economies with similar market conditions. Although the growing success of Asian corporate internationalization is evident, capability constraints, such as the lack of international experience, brand names, innovation, management competence and quality products, can hinder international competitiveness of Asian firms (with the exception of South Korean and Japanese firms).[1]

In this book, we want to emphasize that hundreds of Asian companies will reach out to the world and enter the global market. At this moment these new companies are relatively unknown in the West. The message of this book is that this will

---

[1] The previous pages of this chapter are taken and adapted from Segers and Stam (2013), pp. 29–33.

rapidly change. After they have firmly established themselves in their vast own Chinese, Indian, Japanese, South Korean and other Asian markets, they will be knocking at many Western doors. In China, the government has given orders to a large number of companies to also become a brand outside China itself; this became known under the term *go out strategy*.

By choosing to highlight rather recently-established, multinational, companies in this book, we hope to show what kind of strategies these exemplary companies have developed to become successful not only in their home market, but also in the world market and thus become strong competitors to their Western rivals. We have selected companies from Asian countries that are promising as future economic giants. Right now, Japan and South Korea are already among the most sophisticated and competitive nations in East Asia, followed by China (among others) and at a bit larger distance, by India and Vietnam. From all these countries, we have chosen at least one company to analyze with a focus on its strategies and endeavors to become a global multinational.[2]

3.1 China

In China, we have selected six companies, large and powerful in their home market, while relatively unknown in the West, but definitely on their way to become a world brand.

Alibaba is a giant e-commerce company, established only in 1999 by Jack Ma; in September 2014 its market value was 25 billion US$. Alibaba became known in the West by its spectacular IPO.

Geeley is another Chinese company this book focuses upon; it is an automotive manufacturing company. The company became somewhat known in the West by buying up the Swedish car maker Volvo in August 2010.

We further concentrate on *Haier*, a multinational consumer electronics and home appliances company; its products include air conditioners, mobile phones, computers, microwaves ovens, washing machines, refrigerators and TV sets; its revenues were 2.45 billion US$ in 2014, earned with 70,000 employees.

Another multinational company producing networking and telecommunications equipment and services is *Huawei*, headquartered in Shenzhen, Guangdong province. Founded in 1987 by Ren Zhengfei, it now has over 140,000 employees.

Lenovo is a computer technology company with headquarters in Beijing. It designs and manufactures tablets, computers, smartphones, work stations and servers. Together with Huawei, Lenovo is undoubtedly China's most well-known company in the West with many branches and products sold in the world. The company was founded in 1984 and has now more than 54,000 employees.

---

[2] The description of the following 13 companies is selectively taken from Wikipedia (>*Wikipedia.org*), in combination with facts taken from the 13 analyses in this book.

Tencent is the sixth Chinese company in this book. It is an investment holding company whose subsidiaries provide mass media, entertainment, internet, and mobile phone value-added services. Those services include social networks, web portals, e-commerce and multi-player online games. It is the fifth-largest internet company in the world after Google, Amazon, Alibaba and Ebay (figures as of October 2014). Its market value is now about 150 billion US$.

3.2   India

We focus on two promising Indian companies: Dr. Reddy's and Infosys.

Dr. Reddy's Laboratories is a pharmaceutical company based in Hyderabad. Dr. Reddy's has developed 190 medications and started exporting them to non- or less-regulated markets. The profitability from these unregulated markets enabled the company to get approval from drug regulators in more developed economies in Europe and the US. In 2012, the company had revenues of 2.1 billion US$ and 16,300 employees.

Infosys provides business consulting, information technology, software engineering and outsourcing services. Its headquarters can be found in Bangalore. The company was founded in 1981 and has over 165,000 employees. It already has a clear global presence with 72 offices and 94 development centers in India, the US, China, Australia, Japan, the Middle East and in Europe.

3.3   Japan

Japan has a large number of companies which have enjoyed world brand status for a long time, including Canon, Honda, Mazda, Mitsubishi, NEC, Panasonic, Sony, Suzuki, Toyota, Yamaha, etc. These are all large and prestigious companies, well-established for a long time at home as well as on the global market. Often these companies are threatened by the new emerging Asian multinationals and many of them see their revenues dropping. Most of these well-established and brand companies are trying to reinvent themselves to stop the downturn. In this sense, they will also become 'new' companies entering the world market with a new strategy. From these companies we selected one example: the famous company Panasonic.

Panasonic, formerly known as Matsushita Electric Industrial Co., was founded in 1918 and has grown to become one of the largest Japanese electronics producers together with Sony. Its total revenues in 2014 were 64 billion US$ and it has over 300,000 employees and some 580 subsidiaries. Panasonic is now trying to get its own house in order. Consumer electronics were once the basis for Panasonic's and Japan's economic miracle after World War II. But in recent years South Korea (e.g. Samsung) and Silicon Valley (e.g. Apple) have moved to the fore in technological innovation. That means it was necessary for Panasonic and other established Japanese companies to reinvent themselves. In Panasonic's case, it meant providing less visible but more profitable industrial technologies (International New York Times 2013). Panasonic focuses now on two areas: homes and cars. In homes, it no longer sells only individual products (refrigerators, TV-sets, etc.) but sells systems which integrate all home products. In the automotive market, it supplies battery cells to makers of electric cars, like Tesla motors.

But in Japan there also exists a large number of rather recent and globally unknown companies which are going to enter the global market rather soon or have done so recently. From those companies, we selected Rakuten and Uniqlo, respectively.

Rakuten is a relatively unknown e-commerce and internet company, established in 1997 and based in Tokyo, providing online shopping. In 2013, Rakuten's revenues were over five billion US$, providing work for over 11,000 employees. In 2005, Rakuten started expanding outside Japan, mainly through acquisitions and joint ventures.

Uniqlo (a contraction of "unique clothing") is a casual-wear designer, manufacturer and retailer, founded in 1949. Only at the end of the 1990s did Uniqlo became a successful brand in Japan. At that time, Uniqlo opened its first urban stores in Tokyo, offering good and cheap clothing which was a hit in recession-stricken Japan. After 500 stores were in operation in Japan, Uniqlo decided to establish itself abroad, first of all in China in 2002. After that year, many stores in many countries were opened, including one flagship store in the SOHO fashion district of Manhattan in 2006.

3.4 South Korea

In South Korea we focused on the Lotte conglomerate.

Lotte is a multinational food and shopping company with headquarters in South Korea and Japan, established in Japan in 1948. The Lotte Group consists of over 60 business units employing 60,000 people in very diverse industries such as candy manufacturing, beverages, hotels, fast food, financial services, entertainment, etc. The Lotte Group is relatively old, which means it has to reinvent itself constantly to survive the attacks from newly-emerging multinationals in East and West. So far, Lotte's strategy to affect all parts of its customers' lives (not only in South Korea but also in the rest of Asia) has proven to be very successful. Lotte is now a conglomerate company that is broadly engaged in food, retail, tourism, petrochemicals/construction/manufacturing, service/study and finally also finance. That means the company is able to compensate any losses in one particular domain by its gains in another.

3.5 Vietnam

In Vietnam, our research has dealt with Vinamilk.

Vinamilk was founded in 1976 and is the biggest dairy company in Vietnam. The major activities of the company are to produce and distribute condensed milk, powdered milk, fresh milk, soya milk, yoghurts, ice cream, cheese and other products derived from milk. Revenues are 1.3 billion US$ and headquarters are located in Ho Chi Minh City.

3.6   Underlying Strategies and Success Factors of Emerging Asian Multinationals

The above 13 companies are analyzed in detail in this study. From these analyses, an intriguing question arises: how is it possible that these newly emerged Asian multinationals (as well as the 'old' companies reinventing themselves now) are set to become so successful in the world market that they will become strong competitors to existing prestigious Western companies? In part VI "Underlying Strategies and Success Factors of Emerging Asian Multinationals", we describe a number of underlying strategies and success factors of these multinationals. It concerns factors such as Asian corporate entrepreneurship and the strong phenomenon of the so-called Triple Helix system: the close collaboration between governmental and educational institutions with the business community. In addition, there are success factors such Asian human resource management, intercultural competence and branding.

The overall message of this book is that we in the West should prepare ourselves for a business world which is going to be increasingly dominated by Asian companies. These companies have enjoyed great successes in their home market, but are relatively unknown so far in the West, except for many Japanese and, to a lesser extent, South Korean companies. Our research reported in this book makes it evident that many of those companies will become household brands in the West in the near future. This might seem unbelievable to many, but recent history has shown us a similar development of other companies.

Some fifty years ago, the Japanese Sony's and Toyota's were completely unknown in the West, but 15 years later—around 1980—they became well-known and well-respected companies in the world, and moreover, also strong competitors for Western companies. Most of the Japanese multinationals became very successful in the West. We call this phenomenon the first wave of Asianization, mostly coming from Japan during the years 1970–1990.

The second wave of Asianization gradually became visible since the turn of the century. This second wave has a much broader and stronger character. The current second Asianization process concerns more Asian countries and thus much more companies than in the first wave which was only Japan-based. But the tempo and scale in which the new Asian companies will conquer the world is much faster and larger than in the case of the first wave.

That means that this book implicitly contains an incitement to prepare ourselves in the West for the coming Asian era. These preparations should consist of serious attempts to understand the cultural identity of the several Asian countries and the corporate culture and business strategies of the Asian companies which will appear in the Western market rather soon. In this book, we have selected the most important companies in this respect.

References

Segers, R. T., & Stam, T. (2013). *Asia reshaping the global economic landscape*. Maastricht: Shaker Media.
International New York Times. (2013, December 28–29). Business Asia. *International New York Times*.

Part I
China

Alibaba: A Case Study on Building an International Imperium on Information and E-Commerce

Marieke Havinga, Martijn Hoving, and Virgil Swagemakers

Abstract

The Alibaba Group is a group of internet based businesses with a mission to make it easy for anyone to buy or sell anything, anywhere in the world, but especially to make Chinese businesses more open and accessible for the world. The revenue of the Alibaba Group is running high, since they achieve more sales than their competitors Ebay and Amazon.com together. Alibaba is the first company to make market information and data available for free to all the users, all over the world. Customers/providers of goods can expand the reach of their business quickly. In addition, the connection system of Alibaba and how they connect business people with suppliers is fascinating. Their business strategy has made them both well-known and successful in Asia already. Alibaba's international interest is to get more access to popular Western brands, especially high-end and luxury brands, given the huge unmet demand among Chinese consumers for products that are not yet available in China. For that matter, it is likely that Alibaba will become a successful brand for retailers all over the world for selling their products and since the world is getting smaller, perhaps even for B2B or C2C markets.

M. Havinga (✉)
School of Marketing Management, Hanze University OAS, Groningen, The Netherlands
e-mail: r.s.havinga@pl.hanze.nl

M. Hoving • V. Swagemakers
The SBRM program of the School of Marketing Management, Hanze University OAS, Groningen, The Netherlands

1 Introduction

Once upon a time there was a large and successful company in China called the Alibaba Group, a large internet and e-commerce company ready to conquer the world. The company is already well known in many countries all over the world and is getting more attention in every European country. This is especially true now that Alibaba has applied for its initial public offering (IPO) in the New York Stock exchange market, and it is expected that Alibaba will make history with the largest IPO ever and make a fairytale come true.

The Alibaba Group is a group of internet based businesses with a mission to make it easy for anyone to buy or sell anything, anywhere in the world, but especially to make Chinese businesses more open and accessible for the world. The Alibaba Group consists of many subsidiaries. One of them is Alibaba.com. By offering online web portals for the Business-to-Business market and online retailing, companies are able to purchase and contact the suppliers. The revenue of the Alibaba Group is running high, since they achieve more sales than their competitors Ebay and Amazon.com together.

Alibaba is the first company to make market information and data available for free to all the users, all over the world. Customers/providers of goods can expand the reach of their business quickly. In addition, the connection system of Alibaba and how they connect business people with suppliers is fascinating. Their business strategy has made them both well-known and successful in Asia already, and it is interesting to see how this was accomplished. It also raises the question if it is possible for Alibaba to become a successful player on the B2B, B2C or C2C world market.

2 Company Profile

2.1 History

In 1999, Jack Ma (Yun Ma) and 17 others founded Alibaba Group. Mr. Ma visited the city of San Francisco in 1999 and got the idea to set up a company named Alibaba. The name Alibaba comes from the story "Alibaba and the 40 thieves". This online selling and buying place was set up to open an international business world. The name Alibaba can also be linked to the saying of Alibaba, "Open, Sesame". Jack Ma used this saying to refer to the fact that the world would become open for China. The company started in the Business-to-Business market. However, in 2003, the consumer e-commerce website Taobao was founded, and Alibaba expanded with the online payment system Alipay. In 2002, Alibaba.com became profitable, but after 2005, Alibaba Group began to grow quickly. The strategic partnership with Yahoo Inc and taking over the operation of China Yahoo, seems to have been a successful strategy for generating growth. In 2006, the group makes a strategic investment in Koubei.com, and in June 2008, Koubei.com merges with China Yahoo to form Yahoo Koubei.

From 2007 onwards, many new services are generated. First, Alisoft, an internet-based business software company, is launched in January, followed by Alimama, an online advertising exchange company, in November. In this same month, Alibaba.com Limited is listed on the Hong Kong Stock Exchange. In April 2008, the Taobo Mail (currently known as Tmall.com) is introduced, and Alimama is integrated in Taobao in September of 2008. Alibaba groups continued to set up new services, including Alibaba group R&D Institute in September 2008 and Alibaba Cloud Computing in September 2009, thus making Alibaba a real virtual empire, serving business customers and private customers but also offering every imaginable multimedia service. Also in 2008, Alibaba.com Japan is founded as a joint venture between Alibaba.com and Softbank and its first international steps are taken.

Mergers then follow: Alisoft merges with Alibaba Group R&D Institute (July 2009); Alisoft's Business Management Software division is injected into Alibaba.com (August 2009); and Koubei.com is injected into Taobao as part of the "Big Taobao" strategy. The "Big Taobao" strategy positions Taobao as a one-stop e-commerce service provider to promote wider use of e-commerce among consumers. In March 2010, Alibaba Group creates a cross-business team comprising senior managers from Taobao, Alipay, Alibaba Cloud Computing and China Yahoo to execute a full scale roll-out of this "Big Taobao" strategy. In 2011, Alibaba Group expanded its consumer market and announces its plan to build a network of warehouses across China.

Alibaba takes a new direction in 2010 by wanting to contribute to society. This initiative started with the announcement that it will begin to earmark 0.3 % of annual revenues to fund efforts designed to spur environmental awareness and conservation in China and around the world (Alibaba 2014a).

To better adapt to China's fast growing e-commerce environment, Alibaba Group reorganizes the company in 2011 with lots of new business groups. As of now and beginning in 2013, the company is divided into 25 business units. New business initiatives, such as mobile platforms and financing small businesses, show that Alibaba envisions changes in the e-commerce world and the broader international business world. They know how to pool market information, how to identify future opportunities, and how to develop innovative projects.

Recently, Alibaba bought stakes in four major online media giants in China, the Chinese Twitter lookalike Sina Weibo (2013), ChinaVision (March 2014), Wasu Media and the Chinese Youtube lookalike Youku Tudou (April 2014), to boost their consumer-facing non-e-commerce business.

Investments have been made to improve their position in the international e-commerce market by purchasing ShopRunner in September 2013, which is the biggest competitor of Amazon.

2.2   The Founders

The main founder Jack Ma (Yun Ma) founded Alibaba Group with 17 other people in 1999. Jack Ma is a Chinese internet entrepreneur, the first Mainland Chinese entrepreneur to appear on the world's billionaires ranking list. Jack Ma was born in Hangzhou, China. In 1988, Ma graduated with a bachelor's degree in English from the Teacher's Institute. He failed twice for the entrance exam. After graduating, Ma became a Teacher in English and International Business.

In 1995, Ma founded China Pages, China's first internet-based company. It was his first time to get in touch with the internet and he found that there was astonishingly little online information about Chinese businesses. He decided that this should change and he put some information about Chinese companies online, which became a real success: Ma founded The Alibaba Group. Previously, he was leading an information technology company in a department of Ministry of Foreign Trade and Economic Cooperation. Now, Ma is one of the "Top 10 most-valued entrepreneurs of China", as the American Business magazine Business Week published in 2009. In 2010, Forbes depicted him as being one of the "heroes in philanthropy".

2.3 Employees

With more than 25,000 employees, the company has grown to be one of the largest companies in China. All of these employees work in different departments for the company all over the world. The company has more than 70 offices in cities in China, Singapore, India, Japan, Europe and the USA.

When new employees join the Alibaba group, they attend a heavy team-building program in the headquarters. This program is based on the strong focus of the mission and vision of the company: the market and the clients. It is expected that employees should be deeply committed to Alibaba's culture of trust, teamwork, dedication, and professionalism. Both the training exercises and company events create a strong company culture. In addition, there is a degree of competition between the business units where the managers are rewarded (through autonomy/decision rights) to achieve "the best in their business". At the same time, compensation systems (incentive design) are geared to achieving coordination across business units (Wulf 2012). Every business unit has its own board of directors. The business units, especially Taobao, are very effective at communicating with users and responding quickly to market developments. Jack Ma uses a corporate center to encourage its business units to share best practices and information, and in this way Alibaba controls some of the group's internal competition and encourages cooperation. Alibaba's manager rotation program is a tool used to broaden the experience of its leaders and build group-wide social networks. Group-level meetings, annual retreats and management training programs provide some benefits to the managers (Fig. 1, Table 1).

Fig. 1 Hierarchic structure of Alibaba Group (Alibaba 2014b)

Table 1 Alibaba Group's major businesses and affiliated entities (Alibaba 2014c)

Company name	Description
Tao Bao	China's most popular C2C marketplace
Tmall.com	China's leading B2C shopping destination for quality, brand-name goods
Juhuasuan	Comprehensive group shopping platform in China
Etao	Comprehensive shopping search engine in China
Alibaba.com	Leading global e-commerce platform for small businesses
Aliexpress	Leading global e-marketplace for consumers
Alibaba Cloud Computing	Developer of platforms for cloud computing and data management
AliPay	Most widely used third-party online payment platform in China
1688.com	Leading e-commerce platform for domestic China trade among small businesses

2.4 Product Range

Alibaba doesn't sell any physical products themselves, but instead offers many kinds of services. Alibaba.com provides services for businesses in more than 240 countries all over the world to easily get in contact with each other and trade with each other. For buyers, it's possible to buy almost everything on Alibaba.com.

Besides Alibaba.com (international B2B and national B2B) and Taobao (C2C), there's a third platform called Tmall. Tmall is a business to consumer (B2C) platform where companies and brands can set up an online store (storefront). Tmall is so popular now amongst consumers that even competitors from Alibaba opened a digital shop on it (Sander 2013). Originally, Tmall was set up for Chinese companies but recently also foreign companies are allowed to step in, as long as they offer customer care in Mandarin and are able to offer a return service within China. Aliexpress is an international version of Taobao.

The services of Alibaba extend to more than platforms for e-commerce only. They offer also AliFinance (low rent "kickstarter" loans to entrepreneurs who like to do business on the platforms and have difficulties getting loans from Chinese banks); Aliyun (cloud computing, mobile OS and e-commerce data mining); Juhuasuan (Taobao's daily deals); eTao (search engine for products); and Yuebao (personal finance).

The Alibaba Group also offers a payment service called Alipay. It's a well-known payment service in Asia, but it's small in the Western world. Alipay provides a user-friendly and transaction- guaranty model for business partners to make and receive online payments.

2.5 Revenues

The revenues are mainly derived from the payments of suppliers. Every single supplier needs a membership to take part in the Alibaba website. The vendors come to alibaba.com for their licenses, which are in the form of a member card. There are two different kind of memberships: "Gold Supplier Lite Package" and "Gold Supplier Standard Package". The costs for a Lite Package for small businesses, are 299 US$ each year. For the Standard Package, vendors pay a total amount of 2999 US$ each year. Other revenues are generated from advertising income, from games, and from offering extra services for clients such as web design and translations.

When comparing the revenue streams of Alibaba.com from 2006 through 2010, one sees a steady increase. In 2006, the revenue of Alibaba.com was only 1,363,863 RMB, but in 2007, they achieved revenues of 2,162,757 RMB which amounts to a doubling within 1 year. In 2010, Alibaba.com has generated revenues of 5,557,600 RMB.

Sales for 2014 are estimated at 420 billion US$. In 2012, sales were 170 billion US$. This dwarfs Amazon, its closest competitor, with reported sales of 74.4 billion US$ for fiscal 2013 while EBay reported sales for fiscal 2013 of 16 billion US$, less than one-tenth of Alibaba's 2012 sales (Forbes 2014).

2.6 Business Strategies

Alibaba is a company with a unique selling point of sharing a massive amount of market information and data. They are the first company to make market information and data available for free to all users, all over the world. Customers can expand the reach of their business very quickly.

Besides sharing market information, the Alibaba group strives to be the company with the highest employee satisfaction. The company established a strong company culture based on their mission and vision. Their business success and quick growth is built on the spirit of entrepreneurship, innovation, and an unwavering focus on meeting the needs of their customers. New and current employees join the Alibaba team-building training program which is based on communication, mission, and vision. In this way, the company creates a common company culture and community system (Slideshare 2014).

Big Bao Strategy. In order to meet the needs of the customers in the whole e-commerce market, Alibaba Group expanded by buying competitors and integrating them in their own system. Alibaba has been using the "Big Taobao strategy" for this. This strategy focuses on positioning Taobao as a central e-commerce platform, providing consumers and businesses with a broad range of e-commerce services. This strategy was the starting point for not only establishing Alibaba in the field of B2B, but also in the fields of B2C and C2C, enabling them to become a large player in the e-commerce scene (Wu 2013).

The Gold Supplier Strategy. The Gold Supplier strategy is Alibaba's main strategy for its international market on alibaba.com. The service was introduced in 2000 and with it the suppliers could buy a premium membership offering them a large range of services. In 2007 and 2008, the service was also made available to suppliers in Hong Kong and Taiwan. On the website, Gold Suppliers are displayed with a golden icon, demonstrating their authenticity and trustworthiness for the buyers and allowing them to be ranked higher in the search results. This kind of "seal of approval" helped expand the trust of their suppliers and thus generated growth in the Asian market.

2.7 Quality and Innovation of the Product Range

As Alibaba states on its website: "Alibaba will continue to develop the quality of products." The company indicates it will remain open if there are questions or complaints. They made rules to control the quality of services and goods rendered (Alibaba 2014d). After a fraud incident in 2011, Alibaba is very keen to authenticate its members. Alibaba is trying to solve the problems by performing factory audits for Chinese suppliers, or by providing a safe-trading class on one of its websites providing the readers with information on how to distinguish genuine traders from scammers. The C2C marketplace is still prone to fraud due to lack of control over the credibility of sellers.

Alibaba Group will expand their product range by offering a service for game developers. The company will ensure that the games are distributed and become famous. Twenty percent of sales are for the company and an additional 10 % will be spent on charity. The remaining 70 % is for the game developers (South China Morning Post 2014).

The latest development is the purchase of Autonavi. This enables Alibaba to become a huge player in navigation systems, but also gives them the possibility to advertise locally all over the world. Alibaba already has 28 % of the market shares, and recently (April, 2014) bought this mapping and navigation system company for 1.5 billion US$ (NRC 2014a).

3 The Rise of the Company

3.1 Growth Development

By the end of December 2013, China had a total of 302 million online shoppers, a growth of 59.87 million, or 24.7 %, over the previous year, and the utilization ratio rose from 42.9 to 48.9 %. With 242 million online buyers, the e-commerce transactions volume is growing steadily by 60 % every 12 months (CNNIC 2014).

Alibaba is growing fast as well. In 2012, Alibaba is showing an annual revenue of 4083 million US$ (see Fig. 2). In China, Alibaba has now the biggest share of the e-tailing market (Economist 2014), but they can gain ground all over the rest of the world. When one looks at the gross merchandise volume, Alibaba is the largest in the world (see Table 2) and is still growing.

Alibaba's growth was enabled because Mr. Ma had two good insights into what makes marketplaces work in China. Many Chinese people are tight-fisted. Therefore, Alibaba has made all their basic services free for their customers. Alibaba earns a lot with advertisements from other companies and with offering extra services for clients such as web design (Economist 2014). Alibaba has also given small loans to merchants trading on its platforms (average size 8000 US$). Alibaba's total amount of loans to merchants was 200 million US$ in 2012. Alibaba is expanding its loans to individuals and into the insurance market, in which it has announced a joint venture with Tencent and Ping An (Economist 2014).

Alibaba consolidated their position in the home market by some very clever actions. They purchased the music portal Xiami, the travel portal Qyer.com, and app developer Umeng, which facilitated Alibaba to advertise and make Alibaba's services better known. They also removed and even forbade services from competitors. They also removed Tencent's WeChat from Taobao, because, as they say, some salesmen bothered customers with it. They do not allow the use of QR-codes from other payment systems from Alipay on the Taobao platform.

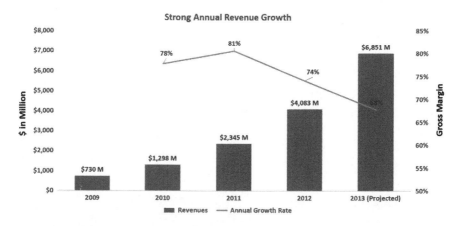

Fig. 2 Strong annual revenue growth (Privco 2014)

Table 2 Three ways to win (based on Economist 2014)

	Revenue (2012, $bn)	Net profit/loss (2012, $bn)	Gross merchandise volume (2012, $bn)
Alibaba	4.1[a]	0.5[a]	**171.2**
Amazon	**61.1**	−0.04	87.8
eBay	41.1	**2.6**	67.8

[a]Year to September
Bold = largest/biggest

Besides these market actions, they also took measures in their own offices, such as forbidding Tencent's popular communication tools QQ and WeChat, probably out of fear for company espionage (Sander 2013).

What contributes to the success of Alibaba is the fact that they know exactly what the Chinese customer wants. E-commerce in China really started growing when they met two basic conditions in Chinese sales: reliability and haggling. In China, people are mistrustful of sales, often for a very good reason. Chinese people see well-known brands as good and reliable (Doctoroff 2013). The fact that Taobao is China's largest e-commerce website with small retailers but which has more than 800 million items and more than 80 million visitors a day, gives the Chinese people faith and trust. This grants a reliability necessary for becoming an important player in the Chinese e-commerce market. In addition, Taobao insists that their entrepreneurs offer conditions for returning goods without cost, which makes the website even more reliable. The system of Taobao also includes that customers can judge the providers with "small crowns", which contributes to their reliability. The introduction of Alipay offers security and reliability since the buyer can pay after he was satisfied with the product he bought on the site. Alipay claims to have over 500 million registered accounts and offers credit card and bank account payments. The company also provides the ability to pay for basic home utilities such as water, electricity, mobile bills, etc.

The second precondition for the success of Alibaba is the possibility to bargain for the best buy. Chinese people love to haggle and are historically the best hagglers. With a search engine on the Taobao website and a large offer of products, it is possible for consumers to obtain the best buy. Taobao even offers a possibility of chatting, so the consumer can get in contact with the provider to obtain more information but also to bargain the price down. Tmall, also a subsidiary of Alibaba, every year offers a mega promotion, when 10,000 online salesmen offer their products for half price. This promotion day is in November every year and was set up to attract more Chinese people to the online web shop. In 2013, Alibaba recorded sales of 5.6 billion US$ on that single day. By comparison, in the United States, 2013 on-line sales on Cyber Monday were about 1.7 billion US$ (Forbes 2014).

Alibaba made their position strong by launching their own search engine called Aliyun and performed a big update to their mobile payment system, called Alipay Wallet, thus offering more services. They also work together with China's number two in search engines, Qihao 360. More than 60 % of buying searches by Chinese internet users starts directly on the Taobao homepage.

Other ways to keep the company growing are to make huge investments and spread the risks. Therefore, Alibaba is making more investments in other markets. Recently, Alibaba bought the Chinese map and navigation system Autonavi, a big competitor of the Dutch system TomTom (NRC 2014a), thus opening up new opportunities in a new market.

For the future, Alibaba is looking for a growth opportunity in the telecom market. Mr. Ma has ordered a large number of engineers to work on the mobile division (Economist 2014). There is a big market overseas in Africa and Latin-America. Alibaba is also working on a 24-h delivery service in which the distance between the seller and buyer doesn't matter. The expectation is that the delivery network will be launched in 2020 (Breemen 2013).

3.2 Becoming a Brand

Alibaba started in 1999 and is now the world's largest online business-to-business marketplace. With approximately 60 million visitors every day and more than 500 million registered users, Alibaba has more and more influence in this market. In 2005, the Alibaba Group started a cooperation with the company Yahoo. Yahoo took a 40 % stake in Alibaba. In 2010, the company continued a healthy growth in the user base of the international marketplace. At the end of December, they had 18,024,993 registered users, representing a 55.7 % year-on-year growth in the international marketplace. By constantly enhancing user experience and providing a safer e-commerce environment, they continued to reinforce their position as the leading marketplace company (Nu Zakelijk 2013).

Alibaba did market research in order to improve the company very quickly. For Mr. Ma, the name of the company is very important for their success. The name Alibaba reminds many people of the story of Alibaba. All the people he asked knew the story of Alibaba and all of them told him "Open Sesame". Alibaba does indeed "open sesame" for small- to medium-sized companies. The name is a provocation and that's exactly the reason Mr. Ma called his company Alibaba. This is called "negative messaging" and people tend to process negative messages positively (Worldlab 2007). The company also registered the name Alimama. Nowadays, 80 % of all online shopping in China goes through a webshop of the Alibaba Group. The fact that part of the name, "baba", means 88 in Chinese is also very effective since 8 is the lucky number and stands for good fortune in China.

Investment in other internet sites, such as social media site Sina Weibo, is giving Alibaba huge opportunities to consolidate their name by making online advertisements on Taobao for example.

3.3 Position in the Home Market

Alibaba operates primarily in the People's Republic of China. The headquarters are located in Hangzhou, China, and the international headquarter is located in Hong Kong. Alibaba has a strong company culture based on a mission and vision.

Tmall	50,7%
Jingdong	17,1%
Tencent	5,6%
Suning	5,0%
Amazon China	2,2%
VIPshop	2,0%
Gome	1,9%
Dangdang	1,8%
Yihaodian	1,4%
Vancl	0,7%
Others	11,6%

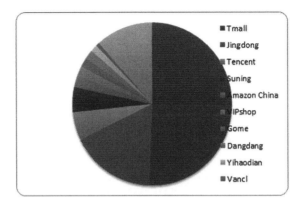

Fig. 3 Revenues on the Chinese B2C market, Q1 2013 (Sander 2013)

Their business success and fast growth is built on the spirit of entrepreneurs, innovation, and the focus on the needs of their customers.

The top ten of China's B2C e-commerce sites, based on the revenues in the first semester of 2013, can be seen in Fig. 3.

Tmall is Alibaba's B2C-platform. Jingdong (formerly known as 360buy.com) is an online warehouse with great assortment. Tencent principally sells virtual goods in online games. Suning and Gome are originally brick-and-mortar retail chains in white goods and electronics. Amazon China and Dangdang are online bookstores. VIPshop is an online discounter. Yihoudian is a food e-tailer. Vancl is a garment e-tailer with its own brands.

The numbers in Fig. 3 are percentages of a B2C-market covering 25.6 billion US$. The consumer-to-consumer market (mostly formed by Alibaba's Taobao) represents the rest of the 71 billion US$ e-commerce market in the second quarter of 2013. The B2C-share of the total market shows a huge growth however: from 29.5 % in the second quarter of 2012 to 36.9 % in 2013.

Amazon, a big player in the international e-commerce market, can't compete with Alibaba in China, because the major focus of Alibaba is on the Chinese market. This focus will not change any time soon after its IPO (Zhu 2014). Alibaba has dominated all aspects of e-commerce in China since it was founded in 1999. In addition to this point, Alibaba is not a retailer, but just a mediator, offering a platform for free, whereas eBay, for example, asks sellers to pay a commission to eBay. The extreme growth of the company is also because of the popularity of the platforms Taobao and Tmall in China. These two platforms were responsible for a one billion RMB turnover in 2012. The biggest competitor Amazon accounted for less than 2 % after 10 years of operating in China (FTM 2014).

3.4 Position in the Global Market

Alibaba Group has specialized marketplaces for its international market. The international marketplace is divided into alibaba.com and alibaba.com.cn, where the first one is mainly for suppliers who export their products to the world and the last one is for suppliers exporting their products to China or trading within China. The majority of members on this platform, 24 % of the 4.4 million registered members, are from the USA (Wu 2013). Furthermore, Alibaba provides a special website for customers in the Japanese market, called alibaba.co.jp. Aliexpress offers a transaction-based global wholesale marketplace in China and an international version of Taobao.

Tmall was set up for Chinese companies but recently also foreign companies are allowed to step in, as long as they offer customer care in Mandarin and are able to offer a return service within China. Alipay is already having conversations with MasterCard and is aiming to expand its reach globally in the following years (E-commercefacts 2013).

Despite efforts to go global, Alibaba.com's storefronts and paying members in international markets have been growing at a slower pace than those in China. From 2006 to 2010, the portion of its international storefronts dropped from 24.8 to 19.9 %, and the portion of its paying members dropped from 4.9 to 1.3 % (Tao 2011).

Alibaba invested 206 billion US$ in Shoprunner in September 2013. Shoprunner is the biggest competitor of Amazon and therefore Alibaba is now also competing in the international world (Allthingssd 2013).

3.5 Alibaba's Competitors

> I agree with Jeff Bezos (Amazon.com): spend more time on customers, not on competitors.
> —Jack Ma (Tao 2011)

Because of the wide diversification of the Alibaba group, its competitors and potential competitors cover every aspect of internet business. Major competitors in the international world of B2C are Baidu, Tencent, and eBay. They all have their specialism, respectively search, social networking and online games and e-commerce, but since the last three years they taking interest in each other's fields.

eBay was first a competitor in the Chinese market. eBay had a larger marketing budget, but did not have the advantages a Chinese company like Alibaba has: Taobao was a specific Chinese made website with the focus on the Chinese customers whereas eBay had a translated version of its international site; Alibaba has its own Alipay, whereas eBay had no such payment system recognized by the Chinese government that the Chinese people trusted. The introduction of Paypal took a long time and was not so accessible to and popular with Chinese people because of the credit card system. People using Alipay did not have to pay for transactions as on eBay; in contrast to eBay, Alibaba's business model was not based on a percentage of the revenues of the transactions, but on offering services for salesmen, such as helping to set up English sites, storefronts, and authentication and verification of salesmen (Trustpass). In 2006, eBay left China and Alibaba had won due to winning the trust of the Chinese people and its large marketing campaigns.

3.6 Stock Market Development

In November 2007, Alibaba.com successfully made its first IPO at the Hong Kong Stock exchange. In September 2013, speculations about the New York listing began when the Alibaba Group abandoned plans for a stock offering in Hong Kong after talks with regulators broke down. Alibaba's management structure fell afoul of Hong Kong's listing rules. Alibaba Group has now announced plans for a flotation in the US. In this way, they will become a more global company. The revealed plan for entering the US stock market is, according to analysts, the biggest share offering by a tech firm since Facebook in 2012. This will make the company more global and enhance the company's transparency as well. The company decided to list its shares in the US rather than Hong Kong since the US stock market brings them more freedom and they have a say in shares (NRC 2013).

Alibaba wants to go global and this is the perfect way. The two major US stock exchanges typically compete aggressively for marquee IPO's, offering discounts and certain fees (Fig. 4). Representatives from NYSE and NASDAQ have been courting Alibaba CEO Jack Ma since the middle of last year. The Chinese e-commerce giant is almost certain to offer public shares worldwide in June or July 2014. The process has already started in the US with a 15 billion US$ IPO. Analysts have estimated that Alibaba is worth more than 140 billion US$ in the home market. The working model is a combination of PayPal, Google, and eBay and is not based on retail activities (BBC 2014). With entering the US stock market, Alibaba will become the largest internet company in the world, after Google.

A special case is the cooperation with Yahoo in the stock market. Yahoo bought a 40 % share in 2005. Alibaba wants to buy these shares back and agreed upon this in 2012 with the right to buy back half of Yahoo's remaining 23 % stake before the IPO. Yahoo then could choose to sell its remaining Alibaba stock after the shares begin trading. Alibaba currently has a market value of about 40 billion US$, based on the prices paid for the stock that the company recently sold to raise enough money to finance the Yahoo deal. Yahoo, in contrast, has a market value of less than 20 billion US$ (Yahoo 2012).

Currently, Yahoo owns 24 % of Alibaba shares, Softbank 37 %, Jack Ma, the founder and Joe Tsai, the Taiwan born executive vice president, own about 10 % together. There are about 17 smaller investors and officials that hold the rest, about 29 %, of the shares (Forbes 2014).

Fig. 4 IPO's listed on US exchanges (WSJ 2014)

3.7 Triple Helix

The focus of the Chinese government in recent years is on the third sector, and services are freely developing in China, as is the e-commerce market as well. China has only just begun with the process to develop from an industrial economy into an economy with a large service sector. This growth of the service sector is very much supported by the growth of a middle class. Old state-owned companies (Baosteel, Roncheng shipyards, Shanxi Mines) are being replaced by new companies and international companies like Alibaba, Baidu, or Huawei. For Alibaba, the government was not directly beneficial to the rise of the company, but indirectly by making the internet possible for the majority of Chinese people and allowing the e-commerce market to develop itself. With a free market and no limitation on advertising, Taobao became a well-known brand. Alibaba has good contacts with the government, which, amongst others, supported the introduction of the Alipay systems (FTM 2014).

The employees of Alibaba management are all Chinese natives. They were all raised with traditional values of Confucianism. Education, personal development, and virtuous conduct are basic Confucian values in China. Chief Ma wants his company to be of high moral standards. In an email to his Aliren (Alibaba's employees), as an answer to a fraud case, Ma wrote:

> The world does need another internet company, much less another company that can make money; What this world needs is a company that is more open, more transparent, more sharing, more responsible, more global; What this world needs is a company that is grounded in society, serves the interest of society, and accepts the responsibilities of society; What this world needs is a culture, a soul, a belief and an acceptance of obligation...Only through holding onto our ideals and our principles will we be able to become the pride of this era! (Allthingssd 2011)

4 Future Developments

With a growing middle class in China, more and more people are able to own a computer and are able to purchase online. More and more people see the possibilities of becoming an entrepreneur and are stepping into e-trade.

Although e-commerce is growing, they are also facing problems. Price wars are the game of the day in the world of e-commerce. In 2012, almost all of the top ten e-tailers had promotions with huge price discounts. In 2013, e-tailers Suning and Gome promised huge discounts on social media. However, a inspection commission found out that the original prices were not as high as they said in the advertisements but instead were made up, so the discount was not as high as was told, and the goods were not in stock. For Jack Ma and his employees, it is a priority to keep promises and a challenge to hold the providers to their principles.

Another problem of e-commerce is the delivery of the products. The cost of delivery in China is exceptionally low, which is a stimulant to buy online. However, the real delivery of a package is a problem in China: people who can afford a computer and have enough income to purchase online are working at the time of delivery, and they are living in huge apartment complexes where packages are hard to deliver and a lot of packages get lost. Tmall, therefore, started pick-up services in five big cities in Mainland China and in Hong Kong at 2500 locations (Sander 2013).

To keep up with the growing market of e-commerce, Alibaba made huge investments. Alibaba found itself in a minor position in the social and mobile field and therefore bought an 18 % share of Sina Weibo in April 2013 and in that way found a way to practice social commerce. With a partnership in China Telecom, they made sure that on all telephones sold by China Telecom apps from Alibaba (Taobao and the message app Laiwang) are installed. The investment in Autonavi seems to indicate plans for location-based commerce. It seems also that Alibaba is going to invest in online streaming video and has recently announced it will deliver smart TV set-top boxes and a compatible operating system. These set-top boxes will be integrated in Alibaba's daily deals platform Juhuasuan, but according to the company, Taobao and Tmall will follow in the future (Sander 2013).

Investments and expanding its territory will make Alibaba more powerful in time. With the control over a lot of services in the e-commerce and social media, they can afford to bring new services and devices to the market without paying for external marketing. Most of the investments are still in China, although Alibaba is now showing interest in foreign companies.

4.1 Possibilities Abroad

Global coverage in every sector is a big job. But still, Alibaba does not want to be known as only a Chinese company. They like to expand and know this will not be an easy job. India was one of the first markets Alibaba entered successfully. India shares a lot of characteristics with the Chinese market, including extensive domestic trading by local members. In 2010, Alibaba entered the US market with Aliexpress. It has also acquired two US-based B2B firms, Vendio and Auctiva. com, which have been integrated with Alibaba.com. But Alibaba has little management know-how or business integration experience in this new market. Alibaba. com is already an essential link between Chinese small businesses and retailers and more than 75 million foreign buyers in Africa, the Middle East, and Latin America (NRC 2013).

Alibaba is strong in the Chinese market since it knows what Chinese people want and knows how to market this. Perhaps Alibaba will see international chances, but it needs to acquire know-how on the specific foreign markets. A lot of Chinese companies find it difficult to adapt to non-Chinese ways of doing international business and therefore also miss out on the chances. There are chances however. Jack Ma has shown optimism and idealism with innovative ideas and is managing in a more Western way that represents a new generation of entrepreneurs in China. He can shift between Western and Chinese cultures with ease. The future will tell if he will be able to use his optimism and knowledge of Western ways of marketing, and his US corporate strategies in incentive managing, to have a bright international future.

In Europe, many people are engaged in sales and are always looking for good prices. In China, European businessmen can find many products for low prices relatively easily on websites such as Alibaba (two others, a little smaller, are Global Sources and Made in China) (Klantenscores 2014). Alibaba is a fine starting point for European businessmen who touch ground in China for the first time. The large number of providers who are clearly segmented are easy to contact. There are some risks involved in importing goods from sites like Alibaba. First, there is the minimum purchase, which can be quite a bit higher than we are used to. Then, there is the quality issue. Chinese people will never say no to a large order and will never say they are not able to produce it. In particular, "good" means something else then we are used to. For foreigners, it is best to perform an inspection of the production location and ask for detailed descriptions first. On the other hand, Western brands can become popular in China using Alibaba.com or Aliexpress. New opportunities are emerging for Western brands to gain greater access to

Chinese consumers, providing them with new channels to fulfill the voracious appetites of China's emerging middle class. Alibaba had approximately 500 million registered users, including 60 million daily visitors on its Taobao marketplace in June 2013. The company is now eager to open its extensive user base to Western brands which can try to cash in by meeting the Chinese hunger for overseas brands. In addition to attracting Western brands to its domestic platforms like Tmall, Alibaba recently launched a new site—Tmall International—that exclusively targets brands and merchants outside China and allows them to sell directly to Chinese online shoppers from their home counties.

5 Conclusions

5.1 Why Did This Company Become so Successful?

Alibaba is a good example of how to grow and expand quickly, and become a popular business in Asia, especially in China. Alibaba first of all had a clear goal and held to it: to make market information and data available to all users all over the world, and had a mission to make it easy for anyone to buy or sell anything, anywhere in the world. For that reason, they wanted to make Chinese business more open and accessible for the world.

Becoming so successful was mainly because they knew how to meet the needs of the Chinese market. Chinese people like to haggle, so they offered them the service to do this (WangWang). Chinese people need products and services to be reliable, so they offered Alipay and asked preconditions to new salesmen. Chinese people like to get services for free and so they offered them, but also delivered services the Chinese provider needs to generate more business (website building, English translations, etc.). To make online business more available to all Chinese, they provided loans.

The third reason for being so successful was the generation of new services and investing in new markets while keeping an eye on its competitors (for example, Yahoo). Expanding by buying competitors and integrating them in their own system was a successful strategy. Others were bought to get free promotion of their big platform Taobao (the Taobao strategy), like Xiami, Qyer, Umeng, all providing free possibilities to advertise with their services, but also to make new services well known without having the costs of a huge marketing project. Buying a stake in Sina Weibo (Chinese Twitter), one can only imagine what power they bought. Using this same strategy, investments in search engines, (Sugou) and media giants, such as the recent the investment in the Chinese Youtube, Yukou Toudu, also brought huge advantages.

5.2 Becoming a World Brand?

Alibaba Group operates Alibaba.com, an online trading site focused on international B2B sourcing and wholesale. In addition, its AliExpress website allows international visitors to buy products directly from Chinese vendors, and is a new competitor for eBay. The last few years demonstrates Alibaba's interest in foreign companies. They are successfully investing in companies like Shoprunner and expanding their horizon by talking now with MasterCard. What will make them a real international player will be their entrance into the New York Stock Exchange and NASDAQ. The whole world will get to know Alibaba and what they do, and it will of course generate tremendous media exposure and recognition from the business community in the USA and the rest of the world.

But will they be successful in the international market? Does Alibaba's IPO mean that the Chinese e-commerce giant will conquer the international e-tailing market, challenging established players like Amazon and eBay? Only if they invest in good market research and find local employees and advisors to meet the needs of the local markets. Alibaba's core business is Taobao and Tmall, two leading companies in the Chinese market, that know very well how to act on the Chinese market, which was the reason why eBay failed in China. Alibaba needs to understand local consumers, characteristics of the retail sector, and have the resources of adjacent supporting industries such as payment processing and logistics. The focus on the Chinese market will probably remain after its IPO, but companies like Amazon, eBay or Zalando in Europe, or Kobo in India, have to be aware that Alibaba will contribute to an even more competitive environment in the world's e-commerce market.

Alibaba's international interest is actually to get more access to popular Western brands, especially high-end and luxury brands, given the huge unmet demand among millions of Chinese consumers for products that are not yet available in China. For that matter, it is likely that Alibaba will become a successful brand for retailers all over the world for selling their products and since the world is getting smaller, perhaps even for B2B or C2C markets. However, these markets ask for a lot more local know-how and require thorough market research before entering this market. A good path to follow will be to buy stakes in foreign e-commerce companies to gain market shares, like eBay did with Marktplaats.nl. However, this will not give them a well-known brand name, since names stay attached to the old well-known brand in this country.

5.3 Update October 10th, 2014

On September 19th, 2014 the fairytale of Alibaba became true. Its IPO was expected to gain 21.8 billion US$, but reached that amount already the day before. The stock "Baba" exploded after the initial IPO from 68 to 93 US$ at the end of the day, with some rising now and then up to 100 US$. It is expected that they will collect between 25 billion and 29 billion US$. With this result being the largest IPO so far.

With this exploding result it is said that Alibaba is bigger than Amazon (150 billion) and eBay (67 billion) together, worth 231 billion US$ (NRC 2014b).

Alibaba's revenues are rising and with its IPO it is expecting even more revenue. Last quarter the turnover was about 2.5 billion US$ (Dagblad van het Noorden, 2014).

The world fame of the brand Alibaba is huge nowadays and everyone heard of the company since September 19. Already a dozen Dutch entrepreneurs are doing business in China through accounts on alibaba.com, and from now on more and more small and medium Dutch enterprises will follow them (NRC 2014c).

They will not only find the Chinese market on the site but also meet enterprises from all over the world. Alibaba.com will become the world leader in E-commerce if more and more companies all over the world will join the site of alibaba.com and especially the global site Tmall.com.

Consultancies in Holland are taking advantage of this explosion of E-commerce in China and are helping Dutch entrepreneurs to step into the Chinese market by helping them to set up an account on Tmall global (CRTV 2014).

References

Alibaba. (2014a). *History and milestones, company overview, integrity*. Retrieved February and March, 2014, from http://news.alibaba.com/specials/aboutalibaba/aligroup/index.html.
Alibaba. (2014b). *Executive team*. Retrieved April 16, 2014, from http://news.alibaba.com/specials/aboutalibaba/aligroup/executive_team.html.
Alibaba. (2014c). *About Alibaba*. Retrieved April 16, 2014, from http://news.alibaba.com/specials/aboutalibaba/aligroup/index.html.
Alibaba. (2014d). *Integrity compliance*. Retrieved April 16, 2014, from http://news.alibaba.com/specials/aboutalibaba/aligroup/integrity_compliance.html.
Allthingssd. (2011). Chairman Jack Ma's Internal Email on Alibaba.com Management Shakeup, February 21, 2011. Retrieved from http://allthingsd.com/20110221/alibaba-group-jack-mas-internal-email-on-alibaba-com-management-shakeup/.
Allthingssd. (2013). ShopRunners Scott Thompson: We are building so much more than an Amazon prime competitor, October 12, 2013. Retrieved from http://allthingsd.com/20131012/shoprunners-scott-thompson-were-building-so-much-more-than-an-amazon-prime-competitor/.
BBC. (2014). Alibaba reveals plan for US stock market listing, March 17, 2014. Retrieved from http://www.bbc.com/news/business-26601056.
China Internet Network Information Center (CNNIC). (2014). *33rd Statistical report on the Internet development in China*. Retrieved April 25, 2014, http://www1.cnnic.cn/IDR/ReportDownloads/201404/U020140417607531610855.pdf.
CRTV. (2014). Chinese Radio & TV, October 5, 2014.
Dagblad van het Noorden. (2014). Beursgang Alibaba is doorslaand succes. September 20, 2014.
Doctoroff, T. (2013). *What Chinese want, culture, communism and China's modern consumer*. New York, NY: Palgrave Macmillan.
E-commercefacts. (2013). Alibaba Group signs MOU with MasterCard, April 5, 2013. Retrieved from http://www.e-commercefacts.com/news/2013/04/alibaba-mastercard-agreem/index.xml.

Economist. (2014). Alibaba, the world's greatest bazaar, March 23, 2013. Retrieved from http://www.economist.com/news/briefing/21573980-alibaba-trailblazing-chinese-internet-giant-will-soon-go-public-worlds-greatest-bazaar.
Forbes. (2014). W. Loeb, '10 reasons why Alibaba blows away Amazon and eBay', April 11, 2014. Retrieved from http://www.forbes.com/sites/walterloeb/2014/04/11/10-reasons-why-alibaba-is-a-worldwide-leader-in-e-commerce/.
FTM. (2014). Follow the Money, 'Het geheim van China's alleenheerser Alibaba', March 20, 2014. Retrieved from http://www.ftm.nl/exclusive/het-geheim-van-chinas-alleenheerser-alibaba/.
Klantenscores. (2014). *Chinese import sites Alibaba, Global Sources en Made-in-China.* Retrieved April 3, 2014, from http://blog.klantenscores.nl/chinese-import-sites-alibaba-global-sources-en-made-in-china.
NRC. (2013). NRC Handelsblad 'Chinese internetgigant mijdt beurs Hongkong', September 27, 2014.
NRC. (2014a). NRC Handelsblad 'Alibaba koopt concurrent TomTom', April 11, 2014.
NRC. (2014b). NRC Handelsblad 'De nieuwe rijken van Alibaba', September 20, 2014.
NRC. (2014c). NRC Handelsblad 'Nederlandse bedrijven over handelen via Alibaba', September 11, 2014.
Nu Zakelijk. (2013). 'Alibaba benoemt nieuwe topman', March 11, 2013. http://www.nuzakelijk.nl/e-business/3365302/alibaba-benoemt-nieuwe-topman.html.
Privco. (2014). Alibaba's pre-IPO financials revealed. Retrieved April 27, 2014, from http://www.privco.com/alibabas-pre-ipo-financials-revealed.
Sander. (2013). Ed Sander, 'China Talk: De digitale revolutie'. E book: Bravenewbook.nl.
Slideshare. (2014). 'Alibaba culture', March 20, 2014. http://www.slideshare.net/WongSookYen/alibaba-culture.
South China Morning Post. (2014). 'Alibaba game plan to benefit top developers', January 10, 2014.
Tao, Z. (2011). *Yahoo: Relationship crisis with Alibaba in China. The Asia Case Research Center.* Pokfula: University of Hong Kong.
Van Breemen, D. (2013). *Online verkopen in China: Lokalisatie op het internet.* Retrieved April 27, 2014, from http://china2025.nl/online-verkopen-china-lokalisatie-op-het-internet/.
Worldlab. (2007). 'Where did Alibaba, the brand name, come from?', October 15, 2007. Retrieved from http://www.wordlab.com/2007/10/where-did-alibaba-the-brand-name-come-from/.
WSJ. (2014). Wall Street Journal, 'New York Stock Exchange Is Front-Runner to Land Prized Alibaba Listing', March 18, 2014. Retrieved from http://online.wsj.com/news/articles/SB10001424052702303563304579447271784600840.
Wu, X. (2013). Alibaba: Facing its thieves. In P. Haghirian (Ed.), *Case studies in Asian management* (pp. 33–53). Singapore: World Scientific Publishing Company.
Wulf, J. M. (2012). *Teaching note Alibaba Group.* Boston, MA: Harvard Business School.
Yahoo. (2012). 'Yahoo closes $7.6 billion deal with Alibaba Group. September 18, 2012', September 18th, 2012. Retrieved from http://finance.yahoo.com/news/yahoo-closes-7-6-billion-deal-alibaba-group-161614948-finance.html.
Zhu, J. Q. (2014). What Alibaba's IPO means for e-tailing in the US, April 8, 2014, Retrieved from http://thenextweb.com/asia/2014/04/08/alibabas-ipo-means-e-tailing-us/.

Geely: A Case Study on the Trend Following Volvo-Owner

Gero von Bismarck and Yunyao Zheng

Abstract

This chapter focuses on Geely, a Chinese car manufacturer, who is not even a leading player in its domestic market, but has recently become the largest exporter of cars from China. This has been done through both acquisitions and fast technological development. Geely follows a clear strategy and aims to become a leading global player through its quality products, great safety standards, and excellent sales and after sales services, as well as through competitiveness in pricing. Strategic investments worldwide, acquisitions of renowned companies such as Volvo, and continuous development of its human capital, its know-how and product range all place Geely into a position where they should be considered as a serious competitor, certainly in the next decade. The reason for Geely's success can be summarized in the following points: good enterprise culture and philosophy, the right time and right place, and "Go with the trend": good strategies for different times. Building upon its strength, it is very likely that Geely will become a world brand.

1 Introduction

That China is a growing market with enormous resource and human potential has been common knowledge over the past years. However, that some of the largest corporations worldwide are Chinese companies is a little less well known, especially as these companies have not made international appearances but rather built on their own local market potential.

G. von Bismarck • Y. Zheng (✉)
The Honor's Program of the International Business School, Hanze University OAS, Groningen, The Netherlands
e-mail: yu.zheng@st.hanze.nl

In recent years, some of these companies have started on a mission to conquer international markets as well. Since China is being flooded by international companies, why should Chinese companies not also flood the world? The emergence of Chinese corporations on the European market could have been noticed by the careful spectator in recent years. Huawei and Lenovo are two examples which have successfully made a name for themselves in the European market. These two examples are electronic companies but the Chinese industry in not limited to this. This chapter focuses on Geely, a Chinese car manufacturer, who is not even a leading player in their domestic market, but has recently become the largest exporter of cars from China. This has been done through both acquisitions and fast technological development.

Geely follows a clear strategy and aims to become a leading global player through its quality products, great safety standards, and excellent sales and after sales services (Geely 2014), as well as through competitiveness in pricing. Strategic investments worldwide, acquisitions of renowned companies such as Volvo, and continuous development of its human capital, its know-how and product range all place Geely into a position where they should be considered as a serious competitor, certainly in the next decade.

Shufu Li, the founder of Geely, founded the company based on clear corporate principles which include: teamwork, study, innovation, diligence, practicality, and perfection (Daxueconsulting 2014). One can see that these are principles designed toward long term growth and quality, not low cost, copy-paste production which may still be a very common image when one thinks of Chinese manufacturing.

The following chapter will present Geely's background/profile, its corporate development and its development potential for the future. One will see the prevalent prejudices toward Chinese companies are outdated. China is not only catching up economically but its companies are performing the same in terms of professionalism, technology, and quality.

2 Company Profile

2.1 History

In order to understand Geely as it currently exists and to be able to make predictions about its future, we must first look at its development up to the present to obtain a comprehensive understanding of the company.

Geely was founded on November 6th, 1986, originally producing refrigerators and decoration materials. In 1994, it began manufacturing motorized vehicles by producing motorcycles. Geely also produced the first scooter in China, selling 60,000 items in its year of release. Two years later in 1996, sales figures had reached 200,000 (Autoevolution 2014). Due to its success in the motorcycle manufacturing industry, founder Shufu Li, decided in 1997 to enter the automobile industry (Autoevolution 2014).

In 1998, the first Geely car rolled off the production line. The Geely cars were sold with mediocre success in the local market and the young car manufacturer had to overcome numerous governmental obstacles (Xu 2014) as it was the first private car manufacturer facing numerous, established, state-owned competitors (Wan 2014). From the beginning, Li had planned to internationalize his company, but at first without concrete plans. However, by 2003, the first batch of Geely cars were exported overseas (Histomobile 2014). In 2003, Geely had produced a total of 34,360 cars and gained a domestic market share of 3.8 % (Autoevolution 2014).

The year 2005 marked another milestone in Geely's development; it went public and was listed on the Hong Kong stock exchange. This was the beginning of a period of fast development, in which Li pushed forward the company's internationalization. By then, Geely had exported large quantities of cars to the Middle East, Africa, Eastern Europe, and South and Central America. Furthermore, it had established extensive trading networks in over 50 countries (Histomobile 2014).

The years 2007 and 2008 included some vital elements to Geely's development. First, in 2007, Li publicly announced a strategy shift from competing solely on price to competing on quality, technology, and safety. To do this, it strived to form international partnerships to catch up to its international competition (Chinacartimes 2013).

In the depth of the crisis, Geely had plenty of cash and thus found many valuable partnership opportunities. In 2008, it reached an agreement with British Manganese Bronze on the production of Taxis, which was a first foothold in Europe. More importantly, in 2009, Geely completed its acquisition of Drivetrain Systems International Pty Ltd, and through this closed the gap on high-end transitions. This would later prove instrumental for Geely's global competitiveness (Andrews 2014). In 2010, it pushed forward its internationalization efforts and enlarged its stand in Europe by completing its acquisition of Volvo Car Corporation, making it the first Chinese car multinational. This deal was followed by a "technology transfer agreement further enabling Geely to close the technological gap to international competitors" (Geely 2014).

In 2013, Geely exported cars to 26 countries. Striving to enter the European market with its brands (and Volvo) and with production facilities planned in Eastern Europe (Wan 2014), Geely's sales were nearly 550,000 cars (without Volvo) (Bloomberg 2014).

Today, Geely has a total of 18,000 employees worldwide, of which 2300 are engineers. Furthermore, Geely's staff currently (2014) includes three academicians, a dozen foreign professors, and hundreds of senior engineers who contribute in different fields to spur Geely's further development (Daxueconsulting 2014).

Now, Geely is a well-functioning international company, poised to make the most of its potential.

2.2 The Founder

Founder Shufu Li can best be described as a self-made man. Coming from humble beginnings, he has made his fortune through refrigerators, motorcycles, and finally, cars, and he has recently been called the "Henry Ford of China" (The Economist 2014).

Growing up in the small mountain village of Taizhou in Zhejiang province, his experiences of hardship and poverty endowed him with initiative and a hard-working spirit. In an interview, he stated that "when I was young, I was not afraid of hardship and being poor because I knew I will work hard to make a fortune" (World of CEOs 2014). Throughout his career, Li has proven many times that he is able to recognize and make the most of the business opportunities that he is presented with (World of CEOs 2014).

In managing his business, Li is said to be energetic and highly goal driven. On top of that, he is a creative problem solver with an intrinsic flair for innovation. This is combined with financial consciousness and measured risk taking. When making a decision, it is reported that Li listens carefully to his advisors, scholars, or other members of his management team, and takes into account the in depth market research and feasibility studies (World of CEOs 2014). Thus, it can be said that the founder of Geely is not one for rash action. However, once a path has been decided upon, he is strong willed and will not give up until success is reached (World of CEOs 2014).

Li's journey toward success started when he graduated from high school; he received 100 RMB (16.50 US$) from which he bought a camera and a bicycle and started his first photography enterprise. Within 6 months, he had made a tenfold return on his investment. In 1984, he began producing spare parts for refrigerators and his career as an industrialist began (China's Tycoons 2014). His business expanded from refrigerators to aluminum bending boards to motorcycles, scooters, and finally cars, through the different opportunities Li saw and seized.

Li's current net worth is 1.7 billion US$ (Forbes 2014). The "Hurun" rich list ranks him at 63rd with a total of 16 billion RMB in total assets (China's Tycoons 2014). The founder of Geely is not only concerned with his business success but is also one of China's most popular philanthropists who has invested 800 million RMB into the nation's largest private university (Beijing Geely University), and who has donated large amounts of money to help Chinese earthquake victims after the Wenchuan earthquake in 2008 (China's Tycoons 2014).

Altogether, it can be said that Shufu Li has proven that he possesses the entrepreneurial and managerial skills to run Geely and continue its success story. His talent for innovation and for picking talented managers plus his positive image in the Chinese population will help to develop Geely into a global brand.

2.3 Employees

In 1997, when Geely first entered the auto-producing field, it had about 1000 employees. The number grew to 13,000 by 2009. Until 2012, Geely had 18,512 employees, and other sources stated the number as "above 18,000" (Fortunechina 2013). Geely believes employees are their "first resource". They use a "人本" (RenBen) management method, which means "people are the base of every activity and every activity should be conducted in consideration of people" (Wenku 2014). The management takes care of its employees to make them motivated to create value for the company. They respect employees and trust them to have a sense of responsibility and to work proactively, which creates more value and means the value of human resource grows.

Geely offers training opportunities to employees, as they believe training is the best bonus for employees, and this company now has a well-organized training system. Geely also focuses on offering employees the room for future development, both from a professional facet as well as a financial facet (Wenku 2014).

In its daily running, the management always tries to make employees feel "at home". Accordingly, the devotion of its employees is very high; they feel they are a member of their home (Geely), they are willing to work hard and work overtime to make their home better, and they feel very proud of Geely's development. There is an emotional connection between the employees and the company (Enorth 2010).

The building of human resource in Geely is in concert with their strategic transformation. First, Geely sets up their own universities and colleges to cultivate professionals and technical personnel to suit their needs and the society's need. Second, Geely introduces talents globally; highly qualified personnel with international experience are their focus. And last but not least, Geely encourages employees to find their potential in practice. Geely doesn't take the level of diploma very seriously; they find talents among their frontline staff during everyday manufacturing (163blog 2010).

2.4 Product Range

In its early days, Geely competed solely on price and attempted to produce a "people's car". The result was the Geely HQ (first released in 1998), a car that even at its release could on no account be called a modern car (Andrews 2014), demonstrating the cut price technique envisioned by Shufu Li. Sales were few and Geely began gaining market share very slowly.

In 2005, however, new products with much improved quality, such as the Jin Gang (King Kong) and the Yuan Jing, were developed and proved instrumental to getting Geely to where they are today and especially to their establishment in the domestic market (Chinacartimes 2013). These cars were also the first to be exported in large quantities.

However, the quality of these models especially in comparison to those of other multinational competitors, was trailing badly, and even the English names were laughable. They included the "Beauty Leopard", the "King Kong" and the "Shanghai Maple". Most of the early cars were based heavily on the Citroën ZX, making them not exactly cutting edge technology (Andrews 2014). Thus, the vision that Li had of entering the European and North American market was not possible with these models.

In 2010, this changed, however, and a new model, the EC7, became the first of Geely's products to pass the European safety test with four stars (Xu 2014). In 2012, it was launched in the UK market as a cut-price rival to its counterparts such as Hyundai and Kia (Whatcar 2014).

Currently, in accordance with Geely's multi-brand strategy, it has various models of different brands made for the varying consumer needs on the international market. At the Shanghai Auto show in 2010, Geely released six new models and 20 model variances for its three sub brands (Autocar 2014). These include:

Gleagle (affordable saloons and SUVs): Gleagle presented two different electric car models, the IG, a very small and convenient two-door car, and the EK 2, a five-door electric saloon with "Toyota Argo dimensions". Since 2010, Geely tries to impress and show off its new technological capabilities by presenting its new electrical car developments at international motor shows. This is reflected in the Gleagle developments (Wiwo 2014).

Emgrand (sporty and prestigious models): The EX285, a grand luxury SUV, and the Emgrand GT (Geely Tiger).

Shanghai Englon (for "heritage' models"): The Shanghai Englon GE is a luxury saloon with clear styling references to the Rolls Royce Phantom. Also under the Englon brand is a TX4 London cab, which will soon be put into production in China.

Altogether, it can be said that Geely features models of nearly every category of car and can therefore reach nearly every consumer segment just like other large, car multinationals with whom it is competing. Since 2010, Geely has presented itself as an R&D company capable of designing and producing cars of international quality by themselves. As can be seen from this section, Geely has progressed hugely in the last ten years from producing a few, low quality (but low cost) models to manufacturing a wide variety of brands and models with a qualitative standard that (together with a low price) makes them a real alternative even for Western consumers.

2.5 Revenues

Geely has developed at breathtaking speed in the years following 2007 when their new internationalization strategy was publicly announced. For the following explanation and analysis of Geely's performance, it is important to remember that these figures exclude all sales from Volvo which was acquired in 2010. For a complete picture of the Zhejiang Geely holding group Ltd, sales of Volvo would have to be

Table 1 Basic financial information in RMB 1000 (Annual report 2007, 2008, 2010, 2012)

	2006	2007	2008	2009	2010	2011	2012
Revenue	127.006	131.720	4.289.0.37	14.069.225	20.099.388	20.964.931	24.627.913
Costs of goods sold	110.0.37	116.401	3.637.752	11.528.489	16.399.684	17.144.820	20.069.092
Gross profit	16.970	15.319	651.285	2.540.736	3.699.704	3.820.111	4.558.821
Net profit	214.149	305.767	866.053	1.550.460	1.900.323	1.715.849	2.049.786
EPS	RMB 5.05 cents	RMB 6.14 cents	RMB 15.0 cents	RMB 17.08 cents	RMB 18.59 cents	RMB 20.72 cents	RMB 27.05 cents

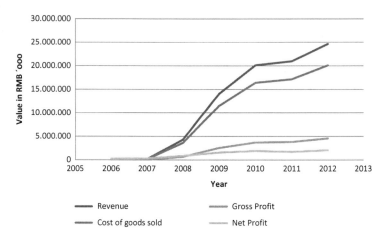

Fig. 1 Basic financial information 2006 through 2012 (Annual report 2007, 2008, 2010, and 2012)

incorporated. However, for the analysis of the Geely brand, only its financial data was examined.

Table 1 clearly shows the impressive development that Geely has taken. Its revenue increased from just 127,000 RMB in 2006 to 24 million RMB in 2012, showing just how much Shufu Li has pushed ahead with his internationalization plans and what substantial success he has had.

Similarly impressive developments can also be seen in gross and net profits (as shown in Fig. 1).

It is noteworthy that in the years 2006–2008, the net revenue was larger than the gross revenue. This means that during this time, Geely relied on external financing to fund its operations, and the 2005 public stock offering offered the external financing needed to make the rapid expansion possible. It is noteworthy that even though external financing was necessary, Li managed to retain a majority stake hold and thus control of his company (Anderson 2011). From 2009 onwards, external finance injections were not necessary anymore and the expansion carried and financed itself. Furthermore, the trend shown above was continued in 2013 with a further increase of revenue from 2,049,000 million RMB net profit, increasing by close to 25 % to 2,680,248 million RMB (Annual Report 2013).

Since it is Geely's pronounced goal to be a multinational car company who is able to take on Western competition, it is interesting to see what the revenue spread of Geely looks like over various regions.

While Table 2 shows an obvious focus on the domestic market in the People's Republic of China, it also shows substantial increases from 2011 to 2012 in foreign sales, especially in the Middle East and Europe. Figs. 2, 3, and 4 clearly illustrate this trend.

As can be seen, the percentage of sales done domestically is continuously reduced and sales abroad, especially in (Eastern) Europe and the Middle East, are

Table 2 Revenue from external customers (Annual Report 2012, 2013)

Revenue from external customers	2011	2012	2013
Hong Kong, place of domicile			
PRC	18.923.680	19.304.515	21.962.293
Middle East	179.139	2.051.605	1.834.877
Europe	595.012	1.779.001	3.072.291
Korea	803.571	684.684	604.903
Central and South America	230.548	305.887	386.888
Africa	144.360	215.318	514.177
Australia	75.950	25.053	5.436
Other countries	12.671	261.850	326.706
Total	20.964.931	24.627.913	28.707.571

Fig. 2 Revenue from external customers 2011 (Annual report 2012)

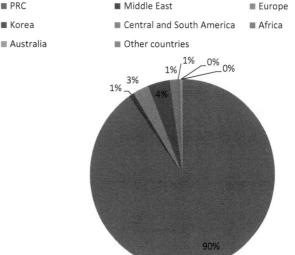

increasing. This shows that the internationalization strategy of Geely is running with some success and, particularly in slightly less developed markets, that Geely cars are already established. Li's dream of selling cars in the USA and Western Europe, however, is still some steps away (China's Tycoons 2014). Another important conclusion that can be drawn from these figures is that Geely is becoming less and less dependent on its domestic market. Its drive to diversification may pay off in the future when the Chinese market discontinues its current rapid growth. Due to its international sales, Geely would, should the Chinese market weaken, be in a much stronger position then its local competitors, such as Great Wall.

It is one thing to look at revenue increases, but to complete the picture we must also look at the unit sales. Table 3 shows these figures from 2008 through 2013.

Visually, Fig. 5 shows that the total unit sales have increased constantly in line with revenue increases. While this could be regarded as obvious, it is nevertheless

Fig. 3 Revenue from external customers 2012 (Annual report 2012)

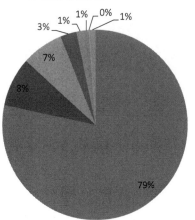

Fig. 4 Revenue from external customers 2013 (Annual report 2013)

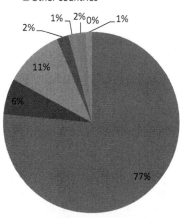

Table 3 Total unit sales (Annual report 2007, 2008, 2010, and 2012)

	2008	2009	2010	2011	2012	2013
Total unit sales	204.205	326.710	415.843	421.611	483.483	549.468

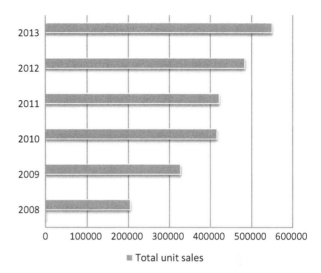

Fig. 5 Total unit sales 2008–2013 (Annual Report 2007, 2008, 2010, 2012, 2013)

noteworthy as it doesn't mean that more expensive models are sold but that market share is constantly increasing.

In the previous section, the different Geely sub brands were briefly introduced and the most common models presented. In this section, it may be interesting to see how these models are received by the market. Table 4 shows the unit sales per model and Fig. 6 visually shows this division. It is interesting to see is that 16 % of sales are still made with the Geely KingKong, an outdated model by today's standards. Presumably it still sells very well on the domestic market in China or other developing markets.

The previously introduced EC7, one of the prides of Geely which has also been launched in the UK and can technologically and in terms of safety hold its own against global competition, amounts to 29 % of unit sales. This proves the importance of the previously-mentioned categories and shows that Geely's efforts to catch up have had some success. Other main sales positions were Free Cruiser, Vision, and Geely Panda.

The sales from very different car models also shows that Geely has managed, with its various sub brands, to establish itself in different demographic markets and with different consumer groups.

If development continues at this rate, Geely will soon be a considerable global competitor for the established companies. Previous development has shown that Geely is capable of rapid growth and can healthily expand without losing its competitive advantages or getting stuck in bureaucracy.

Table 4 Sales by models, 2012 (Annual Report 2012)

Sales by models 2012	Sales volume (unit)
EC7	142.503
Geely KingKong	78.444
Free Cruiser	66.481
SC7	45.569
GX7/SX7	30.793
Vision	33.306
Geely Panda	31.471
GC7	14.948
SC3	12.952
EC8	12.771
SC6	11.377
Others	2.868
Total	483.483

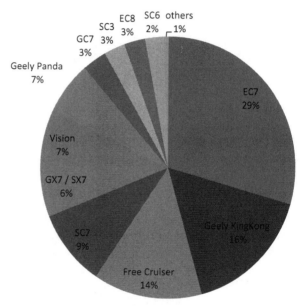

Fig. 6 Sales by models 2012 (Annual report 2012)

2.6 Business (Success) Strategies

Geely's main business strategy is a good example of how China's national business environments influence certain industries and companies. From price to quality, from labor force to technology, the Chinese economy is facing a great industrial transformation and is upgrading. Geely began their strategic transformation process in May 2007. There are three stages of this process (Sina 2010):

First stage (June 2007–2009): Geely becomes a "well-known" brand; the effect of transformation begins to appear.

Second stage (2010–2012): Geely becomes an "influential" brand; transformation is basically done.

Third stage (2013–2015): Geely becomes a "competitive" brand; the enterprise achieves totally transformation, and a "rebirth" of the company is completed.

The strategic goal of Geely is to produce and sell two million cars by 2015, with half of them being sold abroad.

During this process, the mission of the enterprise shifts from "produce good automobiles that people can afford" to "produce the safest, most environmentally-friendly and the most energy-saving automobile".

In 2010, Geely acquired Volvo. This operation gave Geely the opportunity to apply the higher technologies that they received from Volvo to their own brand production. At the same time, Geely made a step to draw attention to their way becoming an international brand (Ifeng 2014).

In April 2014, Geely announced a new branding strategy. At this moment, Geely has three sub-brands: Emgrand, Gleagle, and Englon Automobile. From 2014, on all new models will be under the brand Geely; those three sub-brands will still exist but will return to Geely step by step. All marketing and promotion activities will emphasize the mother brand Geely. This is a measure to integrate resources, enhance competitiveness of the brand, and further promote the brand (China daily, 2014a, b).

2.7 Quality and Innovation of the Product Range

Geely always promotes independent technology innovation as the company's first driving force (Geely 2014).

In the early years of Geely's development, their main business strategy was to produce a "people's car": affordable for people to purchase, and good enough to drive, although the quality of the cars was not expected to be very high (Wenku 2014).

In recent years, price competition became less important in the Chinese market, and Geely also began to make an effort to grow into an international enterprise. Therefore, a strategic transformation was undertaken in 2007. Quality and innovation became the first priorities of this company instead of price (Wenku 2014).

Due to the fact that the Chinese automobile industry didn't have many independent property rights, which resulted in poor quality and limitation on future development, Geely invested huge amounts into research. The company has an enterprise culture where "everyone is an innovator"; this encourages everyone, from the frontline staff to top managers, to innovate and further develop the existing production procedure (Sina 2010).

The new models being released use new technologies to raise the level of safety and environmental protection. The quality of the product range is improving, although compared with Geely's multinational competitors; there is still room for improvement.

3 The Rise of the Company

3.1 Growth Development

"Geely, relying on flexible administration and continuous innovation, has quickly developed into China's leading brand in mid and lower class sedans" (Daxueconsulting 2012). This statement accurately depicts the situation Geely is in and the growth development it has taken.

Since its entry into the car manufacturing industry, Geely has grown swiftly. The vision of founder Shufu Li, that of the above mentioned flexible administration, continuous innovation, and clever fiscal policies and investment, have in ten years created a multinational car company poised to attack the established companies.

One of the most important factors which contributed to the international growth of Geely was the Ningpo agreement in 2007, in which Li publicly announced a change of strategy away from competing solely on price and toward a high tech, high quality company. Following the 2007 Ningpo agreement, Li set new sales goals for the company which were, for Geely to sell 300,000 units in 2008, 500,000 units in 2009, one million in 2012 and two million units by 2015 (Chinacartimes 2013). These goals seemed high at the time, but in combination with the new strategy were more practical and realistic then previously thought. In 2010, Geely had managed to sell 415,000 cars of its three newly-established brands following its new strategy (Chinacartimes 2013). In 2013, this value was 550,000 (Annual Report 2013). Even though these figures miss the previously established targets, they achieve a result which shows the success of the Ningpo agreement. Together with the 427,000 unit sales of Volvo, one could consider the goal of one million unit sales almost met (Annual report Volvo 2013). After 2010, Geely entered a period of slower, more consolidated growth, focusing not only on sales but other factors as well. This is reflected in the excellent performance of some models, such as the EC7, in crash tests (Chinacartimes 2013).

Altogether, it is clearly evident that Geely has grown rapidly, and its growth path has mostly been straight forward and upward especially after the 2007 Ningpo agreement and following the strategy changes. The fact that from 2010 onwards Geely has focused less on sales expansion and more on improving quality and investing in its sales network and R&D has not curbed sales growth. Currently, in 2014, Geely stands on a firmer foundation and there is little reason to doubt its continuing growth.

3.2 Becoming a Brand

Shufu Li has stated that he wanted to turn the company into an international brand from the moment it entered the automobile market (World of CEOs 2014). To achieve this, his company has attempted various strategies and used some remarkable tactics. At the beginning, Geely competed exclusively on pricing in its domestic market, offering a car "for the people": affordable and functioning, but not much more.

The internationalization efforts really started off in 2007 with two different actions. Firstly, Geely introduced a TV show named "Sui Yue Feng Yun", about a car company-owning family, which may or may not be based on Geely, and its development, its rivalries with competitors, and romances between them. The show became a huge hit in the Chinese speaking market (Chinacartimes 2013). Through this show, Geely gained popularity in its domestic market, laying the foundation for further internationalization efforts.

Secondly, also in 2007, Li Shifu signed the Ningpo Agreement, pledging to not only compete on price but to develop models on high qualitative and technological levels. This was a great marketing coup, officially pronouncing his change of strategy and publicly pushing his company into a new era. The agreement was not just a gesture but was followed quickly by change: three old models (HaoQing, Meiri, and YouLiOu) were discontinued along with their production lines. These were replaced with three new models (Yuan Jing, Jin Gang, and Zi You Jian) following an 800 million RMB investment in new production lines (Chinacartimes 2013). Internationally, Li Shifu realized that this shift of strategy would be necessary if Geely was ever to successfully compete with leading multinational companies such as Toyota or GM.

Parallel to these goals, Geely's new multi-brand strategy was launched: three brands would eventually replace Geely as a consumer brand. These were to be Global Eagle brand (2009, affordable saloons and small utility vehicles), Emgrand (2009, sporty and prestigous vehicles) and Shanghai Englon (2010, "heritage" designs) (The Economist 2014). A multi-brand strategy is used by nearly all international car manufacturers thus ensuring themselves a broad customer base in different demographic segments of the target market, without diluting the strength of any one brand. Effective targeting in marketing can only occur with a multi-brand strategy unless the company wishes to remain in a niche market. The current portfolio of cars and the unit sales achieved (as can be seen in the previous sections) show that successful implementation of these strategies has been achieved.

In 2010, new batches of Geely products have been launched in the international market in succession, including EC7, EC8, and GC2. Making high-quality cars and maintaining a high safety standard is now the signature of Geely (2014). This statement made by Geely shows their current approach and that they feel that their strategy shift has been accepted by the international market environment.

It can be classified as a great success of Li that by 2011 Geely was recognized as being one of Chinas most recognized brands (Daxueconsulting 2014).

"In 2014, the group would continue to focus on improving its product quality, after-sales services and average selling price of its products," Geely stated (Bloomberg 2014). Thus, we can expect Geely to continue with the strategy it has embarked upon in 2007 of not only competing in price (even though this will always remain a big selling point) but also through its quality products, great safety standards, and excellent sales and after sales services (Geely 2014).

3.3 Position in the Home Market

In 2013, Geely ranked tenth in the Chinese market with total sales of 549,393 automobiles (Table 5).

In today's Chinese automobile market, the high-end market is mostly dominated by joint venture brands (with capital and technology from foreign brands), while the middle and low-end market are dominated by local brands, such as Geely. Geely is in a leading position among local brands (Wenku 2014).

However, the economic growth of China is slowing down and consumption is experiencing an up-grading. From 2012 onwards, joint venture brands are turning their attention to middle/low-end markets and have introduced more affordable models. All the factors above illustrate a challenging situation towards local brands. In the past, joint venture brands and local brands focused on different markets

Table 5 Chinese car manufacturer passenger car sales ranking 2013 (Autohome 2014)

Ranking	Manufacturer	Sales in total in 2013
1	Shanghai GM	1,542,559
2	Shanghai Volkswagen	1,527,008
3	FAW-Volkswagen	1,526,288
4	Beijing Hyundai	1,030,808
5	Nissan	926,229
6	Changan	682,686
7	Great Wall Motor	627,436
8	FAW Toyota	554,661
9	DPCA	552,073
10	Geely Holding	549,393
11	Shanghai -GM-Wuling	548,984
12	KIA	546,766
13	BYD Auto	506,189
14	Changan Automobile	500,500
15	Chery Automobile	443,944
16	Guangqi Honda	434,828
17	Dongfeng Honda	321,216
18	GAC Toyota	303,088
19	Shanghai Automotive	230,020
20	BMW Brilliance	207,327

which had little intersection, but now the situation has changed, and true competition is just beginning (Ifeng 2014).

In the past 7 months, the sales of local brands have dropped, and Geely actually dropped the most (36.5 %); Geely management claim that this is because of ongoing restructuring of production and branding strategy (China daily, 2014a, b).

3.4 Position in the Global Market

Geely approached internationalization in 2007 with a three-phase plan. The first phase from 2007 to 2009 aimed at increasing Geely's fame and brand recognition. In the second phase from 2010 to 2012, Geely attempted to become an "influential" brand and in the final, third stage from 2013 to 2015, Geely is attempting to achieve competitiveness even against established multinational car giants (Daxueconsulting 2014).

Coinciding with the beginning of Geely's internationalization was the economic crisis which began in 2007 and really struck home in 2008. During this period, many competitors were struggling severely and were trying to weather the storm. Geely, on the other hand, equipped with large amounts of funds from the Chinese government, was looking for partners to invest in (Chinacartimes 2013). This provided a strong position for Geely on its quest for internationalization. This proved to be particularly important as Chinese car manufacturers faced three bottlenecks from 2007 to 2009 when competing internationally. These were gearboxes, engines, and safety.

Geely tried to overcome these problems through R&D and as a kick start through acquisitions, mergers, and strategic partnerships. With the acquisition of Drivetrain Systems (an Australian transmissions manufacturer and one of the leading international suppliers of gearboxes) in the same year, Geely took a huge step toward overcoming the gearbox bottleneck (Andrews 2014).

Geely followed this with the acquisition of Volvo, a brand renowned for its emphasis on safety. Through this, Shufu Li's company took a big step towards overcoming another hurdle to international competitiveness, especially after a technology transfer agreement was signed in the same year (Andrews 2014).

Thus, in the past few years Geely has worked diligently toward overcoming the traditional technological hurdles that Chinese car manufacturers face, through its acquisitions and its own sizable investments in R&D. Geely currently employs 2300 engineers (Daxueconsulting 2014) and founded and funds the largest technological private university of China (China's Tycoons 2014). Geely is now in a position where it has closed the most evident gaps between itself and the international competition.

Since 2013, Geely is China's largest exporter of vehicles (Chinadaily 2013). Geely has set up production facilities in eight countries outside of China, and its products are particularly in demand in markets such as in Iraq, Iran, Vietnam, Turkey, and many African nations: countries which maintain a close economic relationship with China (Chinadaily 2013). By 2015, Geely plans to enlarge its foothold in international markets by adding seven more production facilities (Perkowski 2013). At the end of 2013, the group exported its products to 41 countries through 41 exclusive sales agents and 527 sales and service outlets in these countries (Annual Report 2013).

In February 2013, Geely set up a R&D center in Göteborg in Sweden where it will develop "modular architecture design products" and levy Volvos technological know-how (Chinadaily 2014a).

Geely has said that it plans to start exporting cars that it develops with Volvo Cars to the US in 2016, a decade after founder Shufu Li first set the goal (Bloomberg 2014). These newly-developed products may also help Geely tap the mature Western European market (Chinadaily 2014b). But for now, Geely's global positioning is focused on sales in developing nations which are easier to enter, where Geely may be able to avoid taxes, where assemblers enjoy significant price advantages and where competition is not quite as fierce. In these markets, Geely can say with pride that it is the leader among the Chinese exporters (Perkowski 2013).

4 Future Development

4.1 What Are the Future Challenges/Problems to be Overcome at Home and Abroad?

Geely faces a large number of threats both at home and abroad, some of which are extraordinary and probably unique to the coming years, while others are continuous and Geely's management will have to find long term solutions.

At home, Geely is especially under threat from growing competitive pressures from, in particular, multinational brands such as Volkswagen or GM. These companies constantly increase their presence in the Chinese market and become more and more competitive through establishing new local manufacturing plants, for example. These multinationals with their high-quality products and know-how appeal to the Chinese consumer, and their increasing presence puts considerable pressure on indigenous brands such as Geely (Annual Report 2013).

Furthermore, domestically local car companies face considerable political pressure which results in growing cost pressure, and is something in which Chinese manufacturers still trail behind their international competitors. The Chinese Government is considering new regulatory requirements on environmentability (fuel consumption and emission) and product warranty, product recall, and other consumer protectionist actions. On top of that, due to the huge pollution in Chinese metropolitan areas a limited number of car licenses for these areas are under consideration. These factors would put cost pressures on Geely as they would have to make large investments and could seriously harm sales. However, on the upside, Shufu Li's company is in a much better position than his indigenous competitors, as he has, through the acquisition of Volvo, access to more advanced technological know-how, and therefore has a head start on his competitors. Furthermore, the Chinese government is moving away from foreign cars as official vehicles and is shifting towards domestic brands, something that could help offset the reducing sales figures or even lead to an increase in sales, if the previously mentioned threats don't play out with all their weight (Annual Report 2013).

Abroad, the outlook for the coming years is varied; Geely has many excellent opportunities but also faces a number of threats. In some countries, the demand has decreased and will continue to do so due to political tension such as in Egypt, the Ukraine, or Russia. Additionally, in Russia, the ever-changing legislations and governmental restrictions are a continuing source of volatility making accurate sales predictions and continuous growth difficult (Annual Report 2013).

However, some aspects give a reason for an optimistic outlook towards future sales numbers abroad. The past investments in production plants in Uruguay and Belarus enable a much easier access into the markets, and from the plant in Uruguay, Geely plans to enter the Brazilian market for the first time. Sales there are expected to offset possible decreases in other regions. Thus, in total, one can say that Geely is diversifying its sales regions and expanding its global reach (Annual Report 2013).

Finally, it can be said that the acquisition of Volvo and the partnership agreement are beginning to pay out in other ways and with them Li's company works hard to increase its cost savings in terms of economics of scale and more efficient production. This will give an overall competitive advantage to Geely both at home and abroad (Annual Report 2013).

4.2 Which Companies Are Its Competitors Now and in the Future?

At the moment, Geely's competitors are mostly its Chinese peers, so called "local own brands", including: BYD, Tianjin Xiali, Chery, and Shanghai GM. Other competitors are brands like Toyota and Citroën, but this competition only occurs among certain car models. Most of Geely's products are within the middle and low-end market; the products meet the requirement for a large number of consumers for a daily use and which can be purchased at a relatively low price level. Geely's sales are in a leading position in this competition.

In the future, with the transformation of Geely's production and upgrading of technology, Geely will enter the higher-end market in China and also other foreign markets. The competitors it will meet in the future will be Hyundai, Honda, Volkswagen, and so on.

5 Conclusion

5.1 Why Did This Company Become so Successful?

The reason for Geely's success can be summarized in the following points:

5.1.1 Good enterprise culture and philosophy

Geely is a modern enterprise with a classical Chinese philosophy. It doesn't regard people working there only as employees, but also as family. It doesn't see society as a place to just earn money, but as a company it is a member of the society and is responsible for creating long-term sustainable prosperity for the whole community. The management takes care of its employees not only in regards to their jobs, but also to their needs and difficulties in life. And with the effort from the management to offer employees a happy life in Geely, a homelike atmosphere was created in this enterprise. Everyone feels that they are a member of the family, so they work hard for their family and are proud of the achievements the company makes. When the company seeks innovation and transformation, everyone in the company is invited to make a contribution, not only the group of people working on that task. When people consider themselves to be a part of the whole enterprise, they willingly work hard because if they benefit the company, they also benefit themselves.

Geely believes in its social responsibility and it is proactively leading the research in environmental protection technologies. All the effort is for the goodness of the society in the long run.

5.1.2 The right time and right place

Geely was founded and developed rapidly along with the development of the Chinese economy. The business environment offered opportunities for businesses like Geely to grow. There was no domestic automobile industry for the private car market, and the potential market was huge. A large number of people wanted a car that was cheap but still safe and handy, and the foreign brands were too expensive. Geely caught the opportunity and made a way to survive.

5.1.3 "Go with the trend": good strategies for different times

At the very beginning, most Chinese people only wanted a car which they could drive, and the quality was not as important as the price. So, Geely produced the "people's car" to meet the requirement of the market. However, then people began to look more at the safety and quality, and the time of low-price-winner was coming to an end. Geely began their strategic transformation to suit the new reality of the market. When technology innovation became rather important for the company's future development, Geely invested in research bases and built educational organizations to cultivate their own talent backup. Always go with the trend and survive with changes.

5.2 Is It Likely That This Company Will Become a World Brand?

It is very likely that Geely will become a world brand. First, it is a governmental plan that Chinese car products enter the world market to compete with multinational competitors, and Geely is an important enterprise which is in a leading position in the Chinese local automobile industry. Second, Geely is working hard on new technology innovation and is producing more environmentally-friendly products. Although the quality of their products is still not very competitive in the global market, the gap is shortening. We can expect that in the near future Geely will become a player in the world market. Third, it is a strategic goal of Geely to sell a certain number of its products to foreign markets. Geely has already begun its actions in upgrading its production to meet foreign markets' standards and is drawing international attention by, for example, the acquisition of Volvo.

References

163blog. (2010). *The strategy and goal of Geely Automobile*. Retrieved May 3, 2014, from http://ok10030.blog.163.com/blog/static/128790170201042551519253/.
Anderson, G. (2011). *Who is Li Shufu's "Associate"?*, January 23, 2011. Retrieved May 6, 2014, from http://chinabizgov.blogspot.de/2011_01_01_archive.html.
Andrews, M. (2014). *Geely – The Chinese Skoda*. Retrieved May 3, 2014, from http://www.markeaandrews.com/blog/car-blog/geely-the-chinese-skoda.
Annual Report. (2007). *Geely annual report 2007*. Retrieved May 5, 2014, from http://www.geelyauto.com.hk/core/files/financial/en/2007-02.pdf.
Annual Report. (2008). *Geely annual report 2008*. Retrieved May 5, 2014, from http://www.geelyauto.com.hk/core/files/financial/en/2008-02.pdf.
Annual Report. (2010). *Geely annual report 2010*. Retrieved May 5, 2014, from http://www.geelyauto.com.hk/core/files/financial/en/2010-02.pdf.
Annual Report. (2012). *Geely annual report 2012*. Retrieved May 5, 2014, from http://www.geelyauto.com.hk/core/files/financial/en/2012-02.pdf.
Annual Report. (2013). *Geely annual report 2013*. Retrieved May 6, 2014, from http://www.geelyauto.com.hk/core/files/financial/en/2013-02.pdf.
Annual Report Volvo. (2013). *Volvo annual report 2013*. Retrieved May 6, 2014, from http://www3.volvo.com/investors/finrep/ar13/ar_2013_eng.pdf.
Autocar. (2014). *Geely's new model blitz*. Retrieved May 5, 2014, from http://www.autocar.co.uk/car-news/new-cars/geelys-new-model-blitz.
Autoevolution. (2014). *GEELY models & brand history*. Retrieved May 5, 2014, from http://www.autoevolution.com/moto/geely/history/.
Autohome. (2014). *National car manufacturer passenger car sales ranking 2013*. Retrieved May 3, 2014, from http://club.autohome.com.cn/bbs/thread-c-2980-27470125-1.html.
Bloomberg. (2014). *Geely predicts slower sales growth after missing 2013 target*. Retrieved May 5, 2014, from http://www.bloomberg.com/news/2014-01-14/geely-predicts-slower-sales-growth-after-missing-2013-target.html.
China's Tycoons. (2014). *HSBC*. Retrieved May 5, 2014, from http://www.hsbc.com/news-and-insight/2014/week-in-china-chinas-tycoons-2014.
Chinacartimes. (2013). *Culture / from refrigerators to Volvo part five: The Geely story – Making cheap cars, better*. Retrieved May 2, 2014, from http://www.chinacartimes.com/2013/12/refrigerators-volvo-part-geely-story-making-cheap-cars/.
Chinadaily. (2013). *Geely becomes China's top automobile exporter*. Retrieved May 6, 2014, from http://usa.chinadaily.com.cn/business/2013-08/30/content_16931599.htm.
Chinadaily. (2014a). *One brand strategy to return to Geely*. Retrieved May 3, 2014, from http://usa.chinadaily.com.cn/epaper/2014-03/05/content_17324863.htm.
Chinadaily. (2014b). *Geely and BYD leading the decrease in sales*. Retrieved May 3, 2014, from http://www.chinadaily.com.cn/hqgj/jryw/2014-04-18/content_11609731.html.
Daxueconsulting. (2012). *Market report: Geely in China – Daxue Consulting – Market research China*. Retrieved May 3, 2014, from http://daxueconsulting.com/geely-in-china/.
Daxueconsulting. (2014). *Market research: Chinese Auto – Daxue Consulting – Market research China*. Retrieved May 3, 2014, from http://daxueconsulting.com/chinese-auto/.

Enorth. (2010). *Geely's employees stay at their work to satisfy the need of market during Spring festival*. Retrieved May 5, 2014, from http://auto.enorth.com.cn/system/2010/02/21/004505143.shtml.
Forbes. (2014). *Li Shufu*. Retrieved May 5, 2014, from http://www.forbes.com/profile/li-shufu/.
Fortunechina. (2013). *Geely Automobile Holdings Limited*. Retrieved May 5, 2014, from http://www.fortunechina.com/china500/company/176.
Geely. (2014). *Geely history*. Retrieved May 2, 2014, from http://www.geely.com.sa/geely_milestone.html.
Histomobile. (2014). *Geely history*. Retrieved May 5, 2014, from http://histomobile.com/history.php?id=328333.
Ifeng. (2014). *Geely acquisition of Volvo*. Retrieved May 3, 2014, from http://auto.ifeng.com/topic/shougou/.
Perkowski, J. (2013). *Chinese carmakers go global*. Retrieved May 6, 2014, from http://www.forbes.com/sites/jackperkowski/2013/07/23/chinese-carmakers-go-global/.
Sina. (2010). *Basic description of Geely's strategic transformation*. Retrieved May 5, 2014, from http://auto.sina.com.cn/news/2010-12-29/1452696746_2.shtml.
The Economist. (2014). *The ambition of Geely*. Retrieved May 5, 2014, from http://www.economist.com/node/14140382.
Wan, M. (2014). *Geely*. Retrieved May 5, 2014, from http://www.autozine.org/Manufacturer/China/Geely.html.
Wenku. (2014). Retrieved May 8, 2014, from http://wenku.baidu.com/link?url=4wekmFqTkwzTyy9VvCMWgwbKHQGDrLB3qCuCMzGSBofO5SjujVbx3IOB4ZSPFMzGrjGHotFS2q5lbA993s96ycc5b4q81LW0VxE1IDNMArW.
Whatcar. (2014). *Geely to come to UK in 2012*. Retrieved May 5, 2014, from http://www.whatcar.com/car-news/geely-to-uk-2012/1200162.
Wiwo. (2014). *Geely: Der Volvo-Käufer gefällt sich in der Vorreiterrolle*. Retrieved May 5, 2014, from http://www.wiwo.de/unternehmen/geely-der-volvo-kaeufer-gefaellt-sich-in-der-vorreiterrolle/5640510.html.
World of CEOs. (2014). *Shufu Li, Chairman, Geely automobile*. Retrieved May 5, 2014, from http://www.worldofceos.com/dossiers/shufu-li.
Xu, Z. (2014). *Trace the history of Geely-made refrigerators to build cars*. Retrieved May 3, 2014, from http://softwaretimes.com/kandi/kandi-1.html

Haier: A Case Study on How One of China's First Global Brands Keeps Expanding

Florian Pallas

Abstract

In less than 30 years, the nearly bankrupt Qingdao Refrigerator Factory transformed itself into Haier, one of China's first global brands. With its roots in the consumer appliance market, Haier extended its product portfolio also to the consumer electronic market. The company succeeded in transforming itself from an imitating manufacturer to one of the world's most innovative companies. Using knowledge from several sources, Haier is able to stay up-to-date with consumers' constantly changing needs. Furthermore, Haier is constantly developing and adjusting its business strategies to meet the demands of the changing market environments. Haier refrained from major brand acquisitions to enter developed markets at the beginning of its internationalization process. Instead of purchasing an existing domestic brand to enter international markets, Haier focused on positioning itself as a local brand in the different world markets by using local staff who would build up a market-specific brand. In order to reduce its strong dependency on its domestic market, Haier is likely to extend its global activities in the more mature markets (North America and Western Europe) in the near future.

1 Introduction

Who would have thought that the success story of today's biggest appliance-maker would start with a sledgehammer and 76 refrigerators?

Joining a nearly bankrupt, collectively-owned, local company in Qingdao (China) in 1984, founder and CEO Ruimin Zhang successfully developed the Haier Group into the number one global home appliance brand. To revive the company and to raise quality awareness amongst his employees, Zhang pulled

F. Pallas (✉)
Iskander Business Partner, Düsseldorf, Germany
e-mail: florianpallas@gmail.com

76 defective refrigerators off the line and destroyed them together with his workers. Now, more than 30 years later, Haier has transformed itself from a local Chinese refrigerator manufacturer into a multinational company employing more than 80,000 employees around the world and distributing and expanding its various products in more than 160 countries and regions. Starting as a refrigerator manufacturer, Haier extended its product portfolio and is now actively developing, manufacturing and selling products in the areas of air conditioning, washing machines, mobile phones, televisions, computers or microwave ovens. It manufactures about 16,000 product varieties and is, according to Reuters in 2013, the leading global company for large home appliances for the fifth consecutive year with 9.7 % retail sales market share as well as the "Best Brand of China" (Haier 2013). In the same year, Haier was selected from more than 1200 companies as Forbes Asia's "Fabulous 50" company based on revenue, profits, return on capital, share-price movements and outlook (Forbes 2013).

The emergence from a local refrigerator company into a global player was due to several important strategic decisions made by the CEO Ruimin Zhang. In order to better understand the company's success on the domestic as well as the global market, this case study reviews the business strategies employed by Haier. First, a company overview is given followed by an analysis of the reasons for the company's growth. Second, the study explores the challenges for Haier in the domestic market as well abroad. Last, the possibilities for Haier to establish itself in the (Northern) Netherlands are discussed.

2 Company Profile

2.1 History

Starting in 1984 in Qingdao (China), founder and CEO Zhang[1] took control of a nearly bankrupt, local, collectively-owned company "Qingdao Refrigerator Factory" (renamed into Haier Group in 1992). Inspired by the workmanship of German products, Zhang strived for producing high-quality products, as he saw great potential on the Chinese markets. Turning around the work ethics from the employees, he improved the company's efficiency, discipline, and finally its quality control (Liu and Li 2002). Instead of being solely output oriented, Haier strove for a market and service oriented culture. For example, a customer called the service hotline after his 10-year-old refrigerator broke down (Khannna et al. 2011). He did not expect to receive much help for such an old appliance. Surprisingly, the next day a service man arrived at his door to pick up the old refrigerator and to return it repaired after 2 weeks. By the late 1980s, Haier established itself as being the leading national refrigerator brand in China.

In the late 1990s, Haier started to diversify into new product markets by acquiring several domestic companies with good products and facilities, as well

---

[1] Zhang is pronounced like "jong" and rhymes with "long" (Khanna et al. 2011).

Fig. 1 Haier's Headquarter in Qingdao (Wikipedia 2014)

as distribution channels, but with poor management. This led Haier to expand its core activities into other businesses, such as telecommunications equipment, washing machines and televisions. After Haier expanded on the domestic market, Zhang decided to venture into overseas markets by first exporting as an original equipment manufacturer (OEM) and later investing in manufacturing plants in the USA and other developed countries (Fig. 1) (Liu and Li 2002).

Today, Qingdao Haier Co., Ltd, is a multinational company with four direct subsidiaries that are related to refrigerators: air conditioners, equipment components business, small household electrical appliances, and the Haier Electronics Group Co. In 2013, Haier's achieved a global revenue of 180.3 billion RMB (29.5 billion US$), while the profit hit 10.8 billion RMB (1.76 billion US$) in total. Furthermore, Haier continues to extend its retail volume share to 9.7 %. It also retained the top position in Euromonitor's Global Major Appliances 2012 brand ranking (Haier 2013).

2.2 Founder

Ruimin Zhang (born on January 5, 1949 in Laizhou, Shandong) represents the rise of China's economy towards the biggest global trading power as no other manager could. As a son of a working class family, he became founder of Haier Group and is today Secretary of the Party Committee of the Haier Group, Chairman of the Board of Directors, and CEO (Haier 2014). He holds an MBA from the University of

Science and Technology of China (1995) and is a member of the Chinese Communist Party 16th and 17th Central Committee's alternate committee.

In 1984, Zhang joined Qingdao Refrigerator Factory as a Director. Inspired by his trips to Germany, Zhang realized that "the quality of the goods represented not only a company, but the whole country. I figured I couldn't raise the entire worth of China, but I could raise the worth of this company" (Newsweek 2009). With his focus on high quality and by pursuing a brand strategy, he managed to turn a small state-owned factory into a multinational cooperation. Zhang combines aspects of Chinese traditional culture with Western management concepts to successfully lead the Haier Group. "The good thing about Chinese culture is that it treats something as a whole system, the forest not just the trees" (Day 2013). Thus, Zhang believes that successful enterprises need to move with the times and adapt their management approaches as well as organizational structures to stay user-centered at all times. He introduced several enterprise or business models (e.g., Win-Win Model of Individual-Goal Combination, All-around Optimized Management Approach) that also received great interest among scholars. Zhang has been awarded by the Financial Times (amongst others) as "Asian 25 Most Influential Business Leaders" (2004) as well as "The World's 50 Most Respected Business Leaders" (2005) (see Haier's homepage for an overview of all awards) (Haier 2014).

2.3 Employees

To achieve its current leading market position, Haier organized around small cross-functional teams. These teams are able to respond faster and better to customers' changing needs as well as to identify specific competitive advantages on the markets. The about 80,000 employees are arranged into 2000 "zi zhu jing ying ti" (ZZJYTs) (The Economist 2013). These self-managed teams perform many different roles and typically contain between 9 and 30 members (consisting of at least a leader, four customer managers, and four product managers from the core businesses). Each of the units receives an individual budget and is also responsible for profit and loss, thus functioning almost like an independent company. The ZZJYTs operate in market research, product design, or production and manufacturing. The incentive system is directly related to the units' individual performance (reflected in explicit key performance indicators). The goal of the ZZJYTs is to encourage open innovation as well as entrepreneurial spirit.

Another aim of using ZZJYTs is also to attract, foster, and retain talented employees. Haier's culture offers employees the opportunity to constantly compete and "fight" for the leading position (Khannna et al. 2011). Any employee is free to propose new product or service ideas which are voted on by their colleagues as well as by suppliers and customers. If the decision is positive, the idea provider becomes project leader and is responsible in forming his/her team. Zhang claims that this "unsteady and dynamic environment is the best way to keep everyone flexible" (The Economist 2013) and therefore pushes employees to deliver the best results and constantly improve themselves.

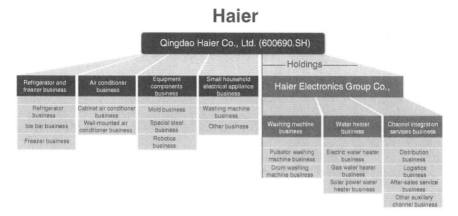

Fig. 2 Haier's Group chart (Haier 2014)

2.4 Product Range

Haier is mainly present in the consumer appliances market in China as well as worldwide, as it possesses a wide product portfolio covering both major[2] and small[3] appliances. Haier possesses a strong product range suitable for smaller homes with price-sensitive budgets (although the products are still priced higher than their domestic competitors) but which nevertheless demand a higher quality. The company's core products include refrigeration appliances, home laundry appliances, air conditioners and water heaters (see Fig. 2 for an overview of Haier's product divisions).

Yet, Haier's product range also includes consumer electronics, which encompass computers and in-home consumer electronics, as well as home video and televisions. In the last years, Haier has transitioned from solely selling products to providing complete smart appliance solutions. The idea of smart appliances is to provide simple and seamless connectivity with the consumers' mobile devices. This way, it allows the consumer to manage and control their appliances from anywhere in the world.

2.5 Revenues

Haier Group's global revenues have been constantly increasing from 2008 to 2013 and accumulated about 180.3 billion RMB in 2013 (see Table 1). Revenues grew on average by 7 % (based on YoY growth), while net profit growths were on average around 6 % (without 2011). Net profit margins grew by 2 % in 2008 and increased up to 6 % in 2012 as well as 2013.

---

[2] Major appliances include: Dishwashers, home laundry appliances, large cooking appliances, microwaves and refrigeration appliances.

[3] Small appliances include: air treatment products, food preparation appliances, heating appliances, irons, personal care appliances, small cooking appliances, small kitchen appliances (non-cooking) and vacuum cleaners.

Table 1 Haier Group approximate revenue and net profit (in RMB billions): 2008–2013 (based on Khannna et al. 2011)

	2008	2009	2010	2011	2012	2013
Revenue	122.0	124.0	136.0	150.9	163.1	180.3
YoY growth (%)	3	2	10	11	8	11
Net profit	2.2	3.5	6.2	n.a.	9.0	10.8

Table 2 Haier Group approximate revenue breakdown (in RMB millions): 2005–2010 (Khannna et al. 2011)

	2005	2006	2007	2008	2009	2010
Domestic sales	83,642	83,453	87,095	89,829	93,771	99,344
As % of total revenue	81	78	74	74	75	72
Exports from China	11,052	14,285	16,467	16,180	16,081	19,186
As % of total revenue	11	13	14	13	13	14
Overseas made and sold	9020	9762	13,847	14,635	14,909	18,562
As % of total revenue	9	9	12	12	12	14
Total revenue	103,714	107,500	117,409	120,644	124,761	137,092

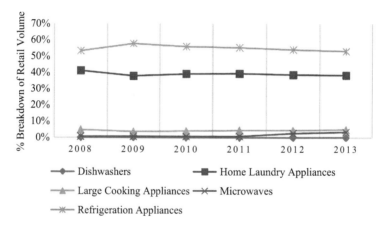

Fig. 3 Haier Group's % breakdown of retail volume by category in major appliances in China 2008–2013 (Euromonitor International 2014a)

Most of Haier's revenues are still made in the domestic market China. In 2010, the domestic sales revenues accounted for about 73 %, whereas the remaining 27 % were achieved via exports (14 %) and overseas manufactured and sold products (13 %) (Khannna et al. 2011). These numbers indicate that Haier still relies heavily on its home market (see Table 2).

Haier's revenues are mainly obtained from the categories home laundry as well as refrigerator appliances. These represent Haier's main sources as both accounted for about 92 % of the total retail volume in 2013 in China (see Fig. 3 for the development from 2008 to 2013).

2.6 Business Strategies

Haier's business strategies have been constantly adapted to the changing market environments in order to meet customer needs and generate continuous revenues. The development of Haier's strategies can be divided into five phases (see Fig. 4 for an overview).

In the first period from 1984 to 1990, Haier's primary objective was to pursue a brand-building strategy. Although many Chinese companies focused on expanding and selling large quantities, Haier made high-quality a priority. Zhang believed that Chinese consumers would be willing to pay a premium price for higher-quality products as well as reliable services. In order to achieve this, Haier signed license agreements with the refrigerator maker Liebherr (Germany), imported advanced technologies and equipment from abroad, and created joint ventures with Mitsubishi (Japan) and Merloni (Italy) (Khannna et al. 2011). These strategic steps helped Haier to better understand the technology of the high-quality products in order to imitate and design a product independently. During this period, although other domestic companies started reducing their prices, Haier stuck to its beliefs and differentiated itself with its high-quality products on the Chinese market.

In the 1990s, Chinese state policies stimulated mergers and acquisitions which led Haier to acquire eighteen domestic businesses to diversify their operations in the appliance market—washing machines, telecommunications equipment, and televisions—and expand their scale. The aim was to acquire "only those firms which have markets and good products but bad management," Zhang said (Xaingwei 1997). These companies were taken over at low prices and brought up to Haier's standards by introducing a new management team as well as implementing a new quality control.

In the early 1990s, Haier also began to export overseas as a contract manufacturer for multinational brands. Starting in Germany, among others, Haier-brand refrigerators were marketed by Liebherr. After beating Liebherr in a blind quality test performed by a German magazine, Haier decided to market its own brands

Fig. 4 Development of Haier's business strategies (Haier 2014)

internationally to establish greater international brand reputation. Using a "three-step strategy" of "going out, going in and going up", Haier started on focusing on difficult, developed markets first. In this way, they met the highest quality standards and were later better able to convince emerging market retailers to carry their products, due to the experience from the US and European markets, and to grow in these markets.

When the internet age began, Haier took the opportunity of customized demand and fragmented marketing. Following a global brand strategy, the company implemented its strategy of international branding. The global brand for the internet era was established by transforming the company from one who solely sells products to one who sells service. Haier focused at positioning itself as a local brand in the different world markets by using local staff who would think and act local. In the USA, for example, they wanted Americans to build up Haier America. The company aimed to localize design, manufacturing and sales processes to create localized mainstream brands which were still different.

To address the new challenges of advanced technologies and the customer's constant access to various information, Zhang initiated Haier's fifth business strategy phase: Networking Strategy. In this phase, Haier focused further on being user-centric and established itself as a networking organization. To achieve this, Haier combined its global resources in R&D, manufacturing and marketing to create a customized home appliance solution for consumers *with* their consumers to meet the customized need for product design, manufacturing and delivery.

2.7 Quality and Innovation

Since the beginning of Haier, Zhang's focus has been always on providing high-quality products as well as services. This aim is supported by the promise to provide a full refund to any dissatisfied customer with a Haier product within 90 days after purchase. This has been recognized by several associations which have awarded Haier for its general high-quality (e.g. China Quality Award in 2013).

Besides the demand for high-quality, Haier constantly searches for innovations/innovative ideas in order to win consumer awareness and to meet their needs in the worldwide marketplace. It is recognized for disruptive innovation with the goal to provide world class products to its consumers. The company is able to foster domestic innovation without the technology transfer from Western companies (Backaler 2010). The company uses an open platform which provides top home appliance solutions to its users. Through strong strategic partnerships with suppliers, research institutions, and prestigious universities, Haier had filed 15,737 patent applications (10,167 granted patents) by the end of 2013, demonstrating its innovativeness. Furthermore, Haier has been recognized as one of the world's most innovative companies (and one of China's top ten leading innovative companies) which is due to its flexible and self-organized employees (ZZJYTs) (Inside Retail Asia 2014). For example, recent product innovations were initiated and developed by a ZZJYT which used knowledge and input from 670,000 internet users via an online engagement program. This form of open innovation ensures that Haier is up-to-date with the changing consumer needs in order to stay ahead of the competition.

3 The Rise of the Company

3.1 Growth Development

On the domestic market, Haier has been growing well ahead of competitors for the past 5 years (see Fig. 5). Compared to its three major competitors (GD Midea Holding Co. Ltd., Galanz Enterprises Group Co., and Hisense Kelon Electrical Appliance Co. Ltd.), Haier retained a strong average growth of 18 % over the period from 2008 to 2013, outperforming them by about 10 %. In 2012, when the crisis also caught up with the industry, Haier managed still to grow by 7 % while its competitors lost major sales (−7 %).

In the global market, Haier has been still heavily relying on the growth (CAGR of 23.5 %) and market size (200 million units) of the Asian Pacific region (see Fig. 6). By acquiring Sanyo in 2011, Haier shifted its activities to more mature markets and reduced its reliance on its home market. Furthermore, Haier was able to establish a strong position behind Electrolux AB in Australasia. Haier's weakest presences are in Eastern Europe and Latin America with only company shares of around 1.5 %. In North America, Haier managed to increase its shares by 2 % points from 2008 to 2013 but is still lagging behind the three biggest competitors

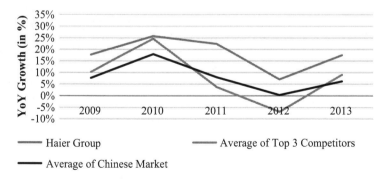

Fig. 5 Development of consumer major appliances market in China (retail volume growth) 2009–2013 (Euromonitor International 2014a)

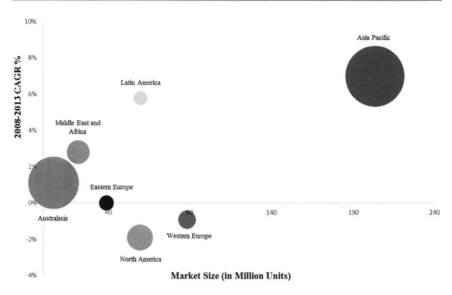

Fig. 6 Haier's major appliance presence in 2013 and growth rates by region 2018–2013 (Euromonitor International 2014a). *Note*: Bubble size shows Haier's company share per region in 2013. Range displayed 1.2–23.5 %

Whirlpool Corp., General Electric Co., and Electrolux AB. In the second biggest market, Western Europe, Haier is still struggling to gain company shares and has less than 2 % volume in this market.

3.2 Position in the Home Market

While Haier remains second in the overall consumer appliance industry behind GD Midea, it constantly grew its retail sales volume by an average of 16 %. Up until 2011, GD Midea posted strong year-to-year sales growth in China by benefiting from the Chinese government's subsidy program for mass appliances. It has the leading position according to retail sales volume and remains the number one competitor for Haier. Lately, GD Midea, however, suffered from decreasing retail volumes and thus Haier was able to reduce the gap to the market leader (see Fig. 7 for an overview).

Regarding the market in major appliances, Haier retains its leading position on the domestic market in 2013 ahead of its Chinese competitors GD Midea and Galanz Enterprises (see Table 3 for an overview). From 2008 until 2013, Haier increased its market share by 11 % points confirming its constant growth.

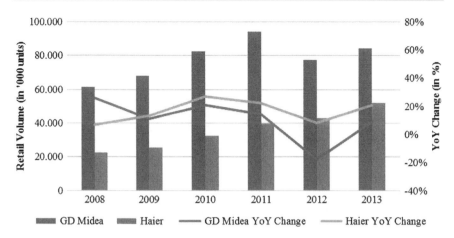

Fig. 7 Haier Group versus GD Midea Holding: Consumer appliance (volume sales) 2008–2013 (Euromonitor International 2014a)

Table 3 Company shares (in %) China: major appliances 2008–2013 (Euromonitor International 2014a)

Companies	Base country	2008	2009	2010	2011	2012	2013
Haier Group	China	19.6	21.4	22.9	25.9	27.7	30.6
GD Midea Holding Co.	China	14.9	15.5	17.6	17.8	13.2	13.8
Galanz Enterprises Group Co.	China	5.3	5.4	5.1	4.4	4.5	4.5
Hisense Kelon Electrical Appliance Co.	China	3.4	3.5	3.8	3.8	4.0	4.1
BSH Bosch & Siemens Hausgeräte GmbH	Germany	2.6	2.6	2.9	3.0	3.3	3.6
Panasonic Corp	Japan	2.7	4.2	4.1	4.0	3.7	3.4
Zhongshan Vatti Gas Appliance Stock Co.	China	2.3	2.3	2.2	2.4	2.8	3.0
Henan Xinfei Electric Appliance Co.	China	4.0	4.1	3.9	3.8	3.0	2.5
Hangzhou Robam Industrial Group Co.	China	1.7	1.6	1.6	1.8	2.1	2.4
Others		43.6	39.2	35.8	33.0	35.8	32.2

3.3 Position in the Global Market

Haier's position in the overall consumer appliance market has been constantly improving. In 2008, Haier still placed 13th in terms of retail volume (measured in '000' units), but only achieved one third of the market leader's retail volume (Philips Electronics NV). In 2013, the company managed to place sixth due to its steady growth in the last 5 years (see Fig. 8). Haier has managed to outgrow its major competitors and is trying to close the gap.

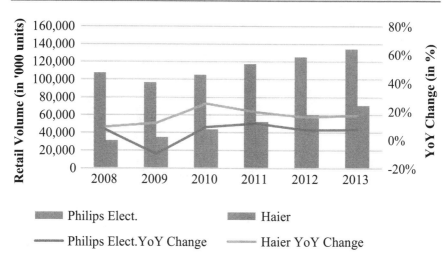

Fig. 8 Haier Group versus Philips Electronic: Consumer appliance (volume sales) 2008–2013 (Euromonitor International 2014a)

In the global major appliances market, Whirlpool lost its first place to Haier in 2012, which has been consistently striving for the leading position in the market (see Table 4).

Haier's strong role in the emerging Chinese market has helped the company to rise in the rankings, while companies from Western countries (e.g., USA, Germany etc.) were losing ground due to the maturity of their home market. In 2013, Haier has increased its company share (based on retail volume) by 5.7 % points compared to 2008 and is supposed to continue with this trend.

3.4 Becoming a Brand?

The Haier Group has adopted a multi-brand strategy and maintains three key home grown brands: Haier, Casarte and Leader (see Fig. 9 for the logos of the three brands). Haier remains the flagship brand which is the most widely distributed and addresses the largest target audience. It is used for the key major appliance categories as well as the consumer market (Euromonitor International 2012). For its premium products, Haier Group has introduced Casarte. It aims to combine the best of European design and link functionality to aesthetics. Combining the best in global design and innovation, Casarte has already won the annual design award from "Business Week" or "Best of the Best Award" from Germany. Leader is considered to be a brand for the household appliances of Haier Group and provides tailor-made household appliances. Consumers are designing for consumers and the products are thus completely based on consumers' demands.

Table 4 Ranking of the top 10 global companies for major appliances (retail volume) 2008–2013 (Euromonitor International 2014a)

No.	Companies	Base country	2008	2009	2010	2011	2012	2013	2013 % company share
1	Haier Group	China	4	2	2	2	1	1	11.6
2	Whirlpool Corp.	USA	1	1	1	1	2	2	9.3
3	Electrolux AB	Sweden	2	3	3	3	3	3	7.2
4	LG Corp.	South Korea	5	5	5	5	4	4	5.9
5	BSH Bosch & Siemens	Germany	3	4	4	4	5	5	5.8
6	GD Midea Holding	China	7	7	6	6	8	6	4.1
7	Samsung Corp.	South Korea	6	8	8	8	7	7	4.1
8	Panasonic Corp.	Japan	10	6	7	7	6	8	3.7
9	Arçelik AS	Turkey	11	11	11	9	9	9	3.3
10	Indesit Co. SpA.	Italy	8	10	9	10	10	10	2.8

Fig. 9 Logos of the three major brands of Haier Group (Haier 2014)

The three main brands of the Haier Group are already well-known on the domestic market. While Haier already gained worldwide recognition, Casarte's and Leader's presence still remain somewhat unimportant on the global market.

3.5 External Driving Forces for Haier's Growth

Several external factors have helped Haier to grow domestically and expand internationally. One of the most important factors enhancing Haier's success was the subsidy program initiated in 2009.

This governmental subsidy program for rural areas (15 billion RMB) supported rural residents to purchase appliances by covering up to 13 % of the occurring costs (Business Insider 2012). The program aimed at increasing domestic consumption to strengthen economic growth as the financial crisis reduced the foreign demand. Ending in 2012, the program was a major success for China's white goods industry with growth rates reaching double and sometimes even triple figures (Business Insider 2012). Mainly due to the subsidy program, Haier succeeded to double its growth within the first quarter of 2010 (Backaler 2010) and to grow on average by about 13 % from 2009 to 2013 (Khannna et al. 2011).

Furthermore, Haier's activities to internationalize were also further encouraged and enhanced by the Chinese government. Introducing the "going out policy", China intended to foster domestic companies to expand into foreign markets (Backaler 2013). This policy advocated Haier's internationalization ambitions by providing access to low (or even free)—interest capital.

4 Future Developments

4.1 What Are the Future Challenges to Be Overcome at Home and Abroad?

There are two major challenges (domestically as well as globally) that Haier needs to overcome in order to ensure the company's success.

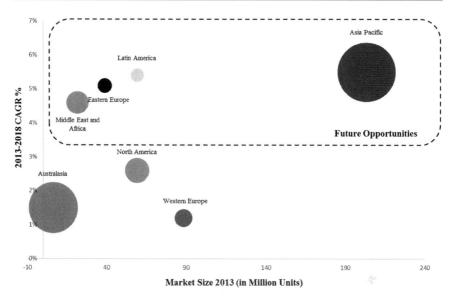

Fig. 10 Haier's major appliance presence in 2013 and assumed growth rates by region 2013–2018 (Euromonitor International 2014a). *Note*: Bubble size shows Haier's company share per region in 2013. Range displayed 1.2–23.5 %.

4.1.1 Reliance on Domestic Market

Although, Haier expanded its international activities, 74 % of its sales volume still takes place in its domestic market, making the company strongly dependent on one region.

In order to reduce this reliance, Haier should expand its activities in particular in Latin America as well as Eastern Europe. At this moment, Haier has only a weak presence in both regions but both regions are expected to grow strongly. With a CAGR of about 5 % over the 2013–2018 period, these regions offer strong opportunities to expand and secure Haier's continuous growth (see Fig. 10).

4.1.2 Government Support and Economic Changes

The Chinese market for consumer appliances, and thus Haier, was heavily reliant on government subsidies and intervention. Thus, any future changes in the Chinese government can have negative as well as positive effects on the company's success. Haier's growth from 2009 to 2013 was greatly enhanced by governmental actions. As the subsidy program expired in 2012, Haier needs now to compete more aggressively to maintain as well as enhance its growth. Furthermore, due to China's economic growth and, as a consequence thereof, a higher pressure on rising wages, Haier's cost advantage might diminish soon. Haier should therefore aim to move to the higher-end markets in China as well as abroad in the long run. In China, the company has already tried moving to the high-end market with its brands Casarte and Leader.

4.2 Current Competitors and in the Future

On the domestic market, the competition for Haier is moderate (see Fig. 11). In the general consumer appliance market (incorporating both small as well as major appliances), Haier is currently ranked second place after GD Midea with about 10 % market share. Although competitors like Philips Electronics NV (the Netherlands) as well as Zhuahai Gree (China) are close behind Haier, Haier with a growth of 15 % from 2012 to 2013 is most likely to close the gap to GD Midea. Looking at the major appliances market, one encounters similar competitors. The market is mainly led by two companies, Haier and GD Midea. The other (mainly Chinese) competitors are rather a minor threat with market shares around 5 %.

The situation on the consumer appliance market worldwide has rather a balanced distribution among the main competitors with Philips Electronics NV as well as Groupe SEB (France) being market leaders (see Fig. 12). Yet, BSH Bosch & Siemens (Germany) (currently placed 11th) is going to be a potential threat in the future with growth rates of 11 % from 2012 to 2013. Haier will probably move closer to the market leaders with growth rates above 13 % within the last 3 years. For major appliances, Haier is the global market leader with 12 % followed by Whirlpool Corp. (USA) as well as Electrolux AB (Sweden). However, similar to the general consumer appliance market, BSH Bosch & Siemens, Samsung (South Korea) as well as LG (South Korea) are potential competitors in the future with growth rates between 6 and 9 %.

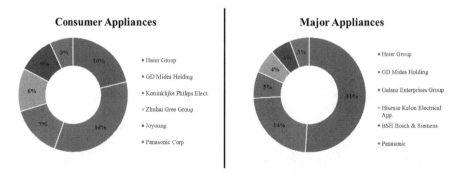

Fig. 11 Overview market share in China (consumer appliances and major appliances): 2013 (Euromonitor International 2014a)

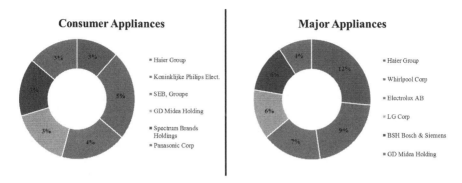

Fig. 12 Overview market share worldwide (consumer appliances and major appliances): 2013 (Euromonitor International 2014a)

4.3 Possibilities for Haier to Establish Itself in the (Northern) Netherlands

Despite the positive expectations, 2013 was another year of recession which impacted consumers' spending and thus led again to a sales decline in the major appliances market (Euromonitor International 2014b). Although, consumers are highly price sensitive, the Dutch consumer appliance market is still dominated by trusted global brands such as Philips Electronics NV, Groupe SEB, or BSH Bosch & Siemens Hausgeräte GmbH. Consumers buy these brands because of their belief in their higher reliability as well as durability. The outlook for the upcoming years is that although the Dutch economy is expected to recover, the consumer sentiment will remain weak for a while longer (Euromonitor International 2014b). Traditional high-quality brands will most likely benefit as consumers tend to purchase these in order to differentiate from the main audience (via new product designs) as well as to reduce purchasing risks. Consumers' changing need for traditional brands might hamper an attempt by Haier to establish itself in the Netherlands as it is still "stigmatized" with the "Made in China" tag, which will undermine its efforts to launch into the higher-end markets.

The Dutch consumer appliance market has stagnated since 2010 and encompassed a total sales volume of around 2200 million €. About 70 % of the total sales volume is still generated through major appliances. Although the sales volume of major appliances have been declining yearly since 2009 (except for 2013), the sales volume of small appliances has been increasing by about 8 % since 2009 (see Table 5 for an overview). This trend indicates that consumers are switching from major to small appliances which are less risky but still satisfy the Dutch consumers' need for design aesthetics. The presented switch from major to small appliances will not facilitate Haier's potential ambitions to extend its activities in the Netherlands, as its strength is the major appliance sector[4].

---

[4] Haier was only placed 18th on the small appliance market worldwide in 2013 (Euromonitor International 2014a).

Table 5 Sales and YoY growth of consumer appliances by category in the Netherlands: 2009–2013 (Euromonitor International 2014b)

Markets	2009	2010	2011	2012	2013
Major Appliances (in mill. €)	1560	1540	1519	1509	1519
YoY Growth (in %)	−8	−1	−1	−1	1
Small Appliances (in mill. €)	667.2	674.5	688.3	701	719
YoY Growth (in %)	0	1	2	2	3
Consumer Appliances (in mill. €)	2228	2215	2208	2210	2238
YoY growth (in %)	−5	−1	0	0	1

Table 6 Overview of Western Europe's Market (Market Size, YoY Change and CAGR) as well as Haier's market share (Euromonitor International 2014a)

Country	2013 Market Size (retail volume in '000 units)	2013 Haier's Share (in %)	2012–2013 YoY Change (in %)	2013–2018 CAGR (in %)
United Kingdom	77,849	–	1.3	0.8
Germany	75,731	0.4	2	−1
France	65,063	0.4	0.3	0.9
Turkey	39,025	–	6.7	6.1
Italy	31,194	0.9	−3	−0.9
Spain	23,956	0.4	−5	−0.6
Netherlands	11,121	–	0	0.7
Sweden	8870	–	−0.3	0.8
Belgium	7427	–	0.2	1.1
Austria	6603	0.2	3.9	4.3
Greece	6275	–	2.6	0
Portugal	6099	–	−8	0.6
Switzerland	6012	–	2.5	0.4
Norway	5335	–	1.7	1.1
Denmark	5296	–	1.8	1.2
Ireland	5213	–	0.3	0.7
Finland	3284	–	−1.4	0

The overall consumer appliance market in the Netherlands is the seventh biggest according to market size in Western Europe representing only 3 % of the total market potential (see Table 6). Although Haier is generally competing in all European countries, the company merely attained 0.5 % of the total market share as well as gained countable shares solely in five countries (Germany, France, Italy, Spain and Austria). The Dutch market's growth is, compared to its neighboring countries, below the average value of 0.3 %. With a CAGR of about 0.7 % over the 2013–2018 period, the Netherlands do not represent an interesting opportunity for Haier to expand and grow. Turkey, with a market size of about 39 million units in 2013 and an expected CAGR of 6.1 % over the 2013–2018 period, seems to be a more viable option for Haier in the future. To better gain ground on the Dutch market, Haier could access the market by acquiring a Dutch small appliances manufacturer. Similar to Sanyo for the Japanese market, this step offers the company the capacity to use an existing distribution network, production plants, and marketing expertise to grow beyond its lower price segments.

5 Conclusions

In less than 30 years, the CEO Ruimin Zhang transformed the nearly bankrupt Qingdao Refrigerator Factory into Haier, one of China's first global brands (Colvin 2011). With its roots in the consumer appliance market, Haier extended its product portfolio also to the consumer electronic market.

Haier's continuous focus on delivering high-quality products and services has ensured its domestic and global success. The company succeeded in transforming itself from an imitating manufacturer to one of the world's most innovative companies. Using knowledge from several sources (suppliers, customers, or research institutions), Haier is able to stay up-to-date with consumers' constantly changing needs. Furthermore, Haier is constantly developing and adjusting its business strategies to meet the demands of the changing market environments. Other success factors are Haier's employees and its management style. Arranging its employees into small self-managed teams with individual budgets and individual performance targets encourages open innovation as well as entrepreneurial spirit.

Against all odds, Haier refrained from major brand acquisitions to enter developed markets, such as Germany or the USA, at the beginning of its internationalization process. Instead of purchasing an existing domestic brand to enter international markets, Haier focused on positioning itself as a local brand in the different world markets by using local staff who would build up a market-specific brand. The company could already demonstrate preliminary success on the US market with its self-branded products.

In order to reduce its strong dependency on its domestic market, Haier is likely to extend its global activities in the more mature markets (North America and Western Europe) in the near future. While the Netherlands might be an interesting location to expand Haier's operations due to its central geographical position, the probability is rather small. Currently, there are five local offices across Europe (Russia, Poland, Germany, Belgium, U.K., France, Spain ($2\times$) and Italy), as well as two R&D Centers (Germany and Italy) and one manufacturing plant in Italy. Several factors might inhibit possible investments in the Netherlands. First, due to the proximity to Belgium and Germany, Haier is not likely to open an additional office in the Netherlands. Furthermore, the growth rates as well as current sales figures for the Western European market are not promising. Regions such as Latin America, Middle East & Africa but also Eastern Europe show greater potential for future investments. Last, other countries in Europe possess greater market volume potential as well as CAGR rates (such as Turkey) which reduce the chance for a potential subsidiary of Haier in the Netherlands.

References

Backaler, J. (2010). *Haier: A Chinese company that innovates.* Retrieved March 23, 2014, from http://www.forbes.com/sites/china/2010/06/17/haier-a-chinese-company-that-innovates/.

Backaler, J. (2013). *Why do chinese companies want to go west?* Retrieved April 15, 2014, from http://www.forbes.com/sites/joelbackaler/2013/12/11/why-do-chinese-companies-want-to-go-west/.

Business Insider. (2012). *China launched a massive subsidy program to get people to buy appliances.* Retrieved April 15, 2014, from http://www.businessinsider.com/chinas-successful-appliance-subsidies-at-an-end-2012-1.

Colvin, G. (2011). *Zhang Ruimin: Management's next icon.* Retrieved April 23, 2014, from http://management.fortune.cnn.com/2011/07/15/zhang-ruimin-managements-next-icon/.

Day, P. (2013). Smashing way to start a global business. Retrieved March 23, 2014, from http://www.bbc.com/news/business-24622247.

Euromonitor International. (2012). *Haier Group in consumer appliances (world) – Global company profile.* Retrieved April 15, 2014, from http://www.euromonitor.com.

Euromonitor International. (2014a). *Information about industry figures etc.* Retrieved April 15, 2014, from http://www.euromonitor.com.

Euromonitor International. (2014b). *Consumer appliances in the Netherlands – Industry overview.* Retrieved April 22, 2014, from www.euromonitor.com.

Forbes. (2013). *Asia's Fab 50 companies.* Retrieved April 15, 2014, from http://www.forbes.com/fab50/list.

Haier. (2013). *Reuters: Haier's large home appliances rank no.1 worldwide for the fifth time.* Retrieved March 23, 2014, from http://www.haier.net/en/about_haier/news/201402/t20140226_207980.shtml.

Haier. (2014). *CEO profile.* Retrieved March 23, 2014, from http://www.haier.net/en/about_haier/ceo/introduction/.

Inside Retail Asia. (2014). *China's Haier recognized.* Retrieved March 23, 2014, from http://www.insideretail.asia/2014/02/11/chinas-haier-recognised/.

Khannna, T., Palepu, K., & Andrews, P. (2011). *Haier: Taking a Chinese company global in 2011* (pp. 712–408). Harvard Business School Case.

Liu, H., & Li, K. (2002). Strategic implications of emerging Chinese multinationals: The Haier case study. *European Management Journal, 20*(6), 699–706.

Newsweek. (2009). *Business Jack Welch Communists.* Retrieved March 23, 2014, from http://www.newsweek.com/business-jack-welch-communists-118987.

The Economist. (2013). *Haier and higher.* Retrieved March 23, 2014, from http://www.economist.com/news/business/21587792-radical-boss-haier-wants-transform-worlds-biggest-appliance-maker-nimble.

Wikipedia. (2014). *Haier.* Retrieved April 25, 2014, from http://en.wikipedia.org/wiki/file:Haier_Headquarter_in_Qingdao.jpg.

Xaingwei, W. (1997). *Haier Group buys up ailing state firms.* Retrieved March 23, 2014, from http://www.scmp.com/article/211199/haier-group-buys-ailing-state-firms.

Huawei: A Case Study on a Telecom Giant on the Rise

Michelle Haveman and Jeroen Vochteloo

Abstract

For many years, Huawei was only an Original Design Manufacturer (ODM), which means that the company only developed and designed mobile phones for other manufactures. In 2011, the company switched its vision and also decided to produce mobile phones under their own name. Furthermore, since 2012, Huawei is rushing to the European market. Its vision is to become one of the top three world smartphone brands. The focus of Huawei is on continuous innovation that is customer-centric and improving customer service quality. Huawei is also the third largest applicant for patents in the world. The company is capable of offering innovative products for a cheaper price, sometimes even more than 25 % cheaper than similar products of its competitor. Africa's mobile technology progression would not have been as far as it is now without Huawei and its cheaper products. The success of Huawei could also be due to the help that Huawei is accused of receiving from the Chinese government. However, this could also be something that is stopping Huawei from entering markets, as Huawei could represent a national security threat.

1 Introduction

Huawei is a Chinese company which was founded in 1987 by Zhengfei Ren, a former engineer in the Chinese army who was born in 1944 and studied civil engineering. It started off in Shenzhen as a sales agent for a Hong Kong company producing Private Branch Exchange switches. In the next years, Huawei focused more and more on selling equipment for mobile networks, mobile services and

M. Haveman (✉) • J. Vochteloo
The Honor's Program of the International Business School, Hanze University OAS, Groningen, The Netherlands
e-mail: MichelleHaveman95@gmail.com; jeroenvochteloo@live.nl

enterprise services, which made them in 2012 the largest global telecommunications equipment maker. For many years, Huawei was only an Original Design Manufacturer (ODM), which means that they only developed and designed mobile phones for other manufactures. In 2011, they switched their vision and also decided to produce mobile phones under their own name. Furthermore, since 2012, Huawei is rushing the European market. Their vision is to become one of the top three world smartphone brands.

Huawei has recently entered the Dutch market and has a vision to nestle itself in the top of the Dutch smartphone market. For most people in the Netherlands, the brand itself is not very well known, where on the other hand the business sector has been familiar with Huawei for many years. The Telecom providers KPN, Vodafone and T-Mobile have a contract with Huawei to maintain the Dutch Mobile Network. The company is located in Amsterdam, which means that they are very close to two very large ports, the international airport Schiphol, and public transport.

One of the biggest problems for Huawei is their own name. In Europe, people have difficulties to pronounce the name correctly. To make sure the company name is understandable and also pronounceable, Huawei changed the pronunciation per country. This will (most of the time) be done by video with the right pronunciation.

The most important reason for choosing Huawei as a case study is that it is an emerging Asian multinational that is one of the biggest telecom equipment companies in the world (and in 2012, was *the* biggest) with sales over 11.5 billion €. Besides that, as stated above, it has recently entered the Dutch market. This gives us the opportunity to see and experience first hand how a large global company establishes itself in a country and which strategies it will choose to attract customers.

2 Company Profile

2.1 History

In 1987, Zhengfei Ren founded the company Huawei. It started off in Shenzhen as a sales agent for a Hong Kong company producing Private Branch Exchange switches. In 1990, Huawei started its own independent research and commercialization of Private Branch Switches, aiming at hotels and small enterprises. Huawei designed and sold the switches and network machines which make the modern telecommunication "internet" possible. After 1990, Huawei initiated a R&D department and from 1997 until 2001, it opened several R&D centers in i.e. the USA, Sweden and India.

Huawei belongs to the group of companies that were established after the "Open door policy" of Xiaoping Deng in 1978. Deng realized that there was a high need for Western technology and investments and therefore "opened the door" for Western business with his policy (BBC 2014). Due to the fact that Ren has been a member of the Communist Party since 1978, he used the vision of Zedong Mao in his business strategies. One of those strategies, inspired by Mao, is ideological education. The thousands of newly-hired employees have to undergo a six-month course, including a 2-week cultural induction on the campus itself and an internship, to acquire the "wolf spirit" which is said to drive Huawei on (Economist 2011). It stresses innovation with the message "Get on top and stay there." Zhengfei Ren has described the wolf spirit as a blend of three qualities: extreme resilience in the face of failure, a strong willingness to self-sacrifice, and sharp predator instincts.

"In the battle with lions, wolves have terrifying abilities. With a strong desire to win and no fear of losing, they stick to the goal firmly, making the lions exhausted in every possible way," Ren is reported to tell his staff.

The name Huawei means both "China can" and "splendid act". This is in line with Zhengfei's mission: helping China to develop its own telecom technology. Because the big cities already had state-owned telecom equipment, Ren went first to the provinces and applied his business strategy: "using the countryside to encircle and finally capture the cities". By offering cheaper advanced equipment (sometimes even 25 % less than competitors) and hiring a lot of sales people, Ren managed to persuade local operators to buy his products. Due to this success, Ren applied this tactic abroad as well. After he obtained a contract in Russia, contracts in Eastern Europe followed. A nice note here is that the mobile technology progression in Africa might not have happened without Huawei's cheap, but advantaged, equipment strategy (Economist 2011).

2.2 The Founder

Zhengfei Ren was born in 1944 and studied civil engineering. Before Ren founded Huawei, he was an engineer in the Chinese army. When the Chinese government disbanded the entire Engineering Corps in 1987, Ren retired from the army. He founded his Huawei with only 3381 € of his own money. He started to import telephone switches, but then decided to build his own products.

Currently, Ren owns a 1.4 % stake and the remaining part is held by Huawei's employees. Therefore, Huawei is an employee-held company. Ren was ranked number 1 in the Fortune China's list of the "50 most influential Business leaders in China of 2012" (CNN 2012).

Since 2011, Huawei is using a rotating CEO system. This rotating mechanism is one form of Huawei's innovations and a unique management structure adopted by Zhengfei Ren. This rotation system consists of three senior executives, named Guo Ping (finance), Ken Hu (human resources) and Eric Xu (business strategy), who rotate through the chief executive officer position. Each term consist of 6 months. The three rotating CEO's have more influence in decision making during the board meetings then each of Huawei's 13 board directors. At the same time, Zhengfei Ren is also a CEO, but his role is different than the CEO's on the rotation system. Ren has been spending a lot of time coaching and mentoring the three CEO's from the rotation system. Furthermore, he has the right to veto decisions made by the board (Osawa 2013).

Fig. 1 Percentages of employees from different areas worldwide (Huawei 2014b)

Area	Percentage (2012)	Percentage (2011)
China	72.09%	79.81%
Other Asian countries	11.32%	7.56%
Oceania	0.28%	0.21%
Africa	3.84%	2.85%
Europe	6.64%	4.92%
North America	1.95%	1.72%
South America	3.88%	2.93%

Time will tell if the rotation CEO system is the right move or not.

2.3 Employees

The company has over 150,000 employees, with 44 % in research and development (Economist 2012). Huawei has employees from 156 countries and regions across six continents. In their home country China, the Huaweians (employees of Huawei) represent 34 out of the 56 minority ethnic groups, which results in a diversified workforce (Fig. 1) (Huawei 2014b).

This diverse group of employees is very important for Huawei. They believe that the employees are the foundation of the company. By enhancing the employees' capabilities, they ensure that both the individual employees and the company will benefit. In line with that, Huawei provides training programs. Besides these training programs, Huawei also established a benefit system and insurance plans for their employees, consisting of personal accident-, critical illness-, life-, medical-, and business travel insurance. The total investment in global employee benefits in 2012 was 680 million €.

You can see that Huawei prioritizes the health and safety of their Huaweians. They implemented an occupational health and safety management system to prevent accidents in workplaces, manufacturing, fire fighting and employee services. Besides all these points, Huawei focuses on food safety as well, by providing diversified catering services and upgraded cafeterias to make sure the employees get a better experience while eating (Huawei 2014b).

2.4 Product Range

Huawei has its products in the networking, telecommunication and equipment industry. "Our industry-leading products cover all your needs," as Huawei stated on their own website (Huawei 2014e). Huawei divides their products into three different categories: the cloud, the pipe, and the devices. The different categories complement each other.

2.4.1 The Cloud
The cloud is a metaphor for the internet; it relies on sharing computing resources rather than having private devices such as servers and storage to handle applications (Webopedia 2014). Huawei is providing "the building blocks for the cloud such as spanning applications & services, storage & security, and O&M" (Huawei 2014e).

Huawei's Business Support Systems rank No. 1 in the world's emerging markets and is the leader in next generation network innovation. Huawei BSS serves more than 160 operators worldwide, such as China Mobile, Vodafone, MTN, Royal KPN, Etisalat, and Singtel. In the consumer service fields, they offer operators integrated platforms which deliver services and applications. In the enterprise service, they offer products that enable enterprises to handle business affairs automatically and employees to communicate with each other (Huawei 2014a).

Huawei also offers Operational Support Systems that includes software, or occasionally hardware, for e.g. telecom network planning, design, IP maintenance, resource management, provisioning and activation, network diagnosis and monitoring, system architecture, and end-to-end professional service. Huawei does this by using mobile broadband (MBB) and fleet broadband (FBB).

Based on the idea of "intelligence on demand, convergence for future", Huawei has developed a range of products covering enterprise storage, unified storage, solid state drive (SSD), BigData, NAS, data protection, and cloud storage fields (Huawei 2014j).

2.4.2 The Pipe
The pipe stands for the infrastructure that enables operators to build a network. Huawei offers multiple products in radio access and fixed access. For the network, they offer both core networks, energy networks, and transport networks. The final product in the pipe is data communication, which includes routers, network security, and Ethernet switches. Huawei data communication solutions and products serve 35 operators of the top 50, including China Telecom, China Mobile, China Unicom, France Telecom, Deutsche Telekom, British Telecom, Telefonica, SingTel, and Etisalat, etc. (Huawei 2014c).

2.4.3 Devices
Huawei offers devices for personal use, such as mobile phones, mobile broadband and tablets. Currently, Huawei has the Ascend mobile phone series containing over 20 different types and models of mobile phones. The tablet series of Huawei are called the MediaPad, which has approximately six different types of models. For the home, Huawei has home internet and media devices in its product range. Huawei offers routers, connection adapters and fixed wireless terminals in their home internet assortment. For the media devices used at home, they offer set-top

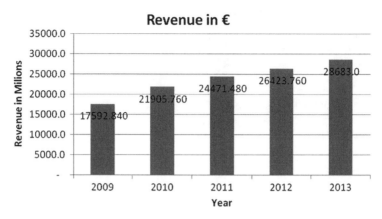

Fig. 2 Revenues of Huawei (euros) 2006–2013 (Huawei 2014l)

boxes and digital photo frames. For enterprises, they offer M2M solutions, and telepresence and video communications.

2.5 Revenues

The revenue of Huawei has grown over the past few years. In 2013, the revenue of Huawei increased with 8 % compared to 2012 (Huawei 2011). As shown in Fig. 2, the revenues of Huawei have grown since 2009 onwards.

2.6 Business Success Strategies

Huawei originally began in China. The past 10 years Huawei have expanded from their home market in China to become global players (Economist 2012). "We have it easier than Samsung did," says Colin Giles, chief marketing officer for its consumer business, because South Korean firms paved the way for global acceptance of Chinese brands (Business Insider 2014).

It is often speculated by critics that Huawei has connections with the Chinese government. "I think it's ridiculous to allow a Chinese company with connections to the Chinese government and the People's Liberation Army (PLA) to have access to a network," says Dmitri Alperovitch of CrowdStrike, a web-security outfit (Economist 2012). When the former head of the United States' Central Intelligence Agency Michael Hayden responded to the question whether Huawei represented an unambiguous national security threat to the USA and Australia, he replied: "Yes, I believe it does" (Business Insider 2013). Due to all these speculations, it has become so difficult for Huawei to market their products in the USA that they may decide to leave this nation.

Huawei states that their rapid growth in both developed markets and emerging markets is due to the fact that their "customer-centric innovation strategy enables us to deliver customized, flexible and secure network solutions that meet the business challenges of operators. This focus on continuous customer-centric innovation is highlighted by the fact that Huawei is the third largest applicant for patents in the world" (Huawei 2014k).

Huawei also indicates that localization is an import part of their strategies in global markets. This means that the product's functional properties and characteristics accommodate the language, cultural, political and legal differences of a foreign country. Therefore, Huawei has a balanced global presence. In 2012, 66 % of the overall revenue came outside of China.

2.7 Quality and Innovation of the Product Range

Huawei has as a company its own quality policy. However, Huawei's quality policy is focused upon customer service. The requirements and needs of the customers are implemented in their products so Huawei also focuses upon the quality of the products. In their quality policy, it is: "ensure[d] that quality is included at all points in our research, development and delivery processes" (Huawei 2014h).

Huawei has over 70,000 product and solution research and development employees, which is more that 45 % of their total workforce worldwide. There are 16 Huawei R&D centers in multiple countries. In the past few years, Huawei has been one of the world's leading generators of intellectual property (Economist 2012), with over 41,948 patent applications in China, 12,453 under the Patent Cooperation Treaty (PCT), and 14,494 outside China. Among these applications, 30,240 patents have been granted as of December 2012 (Huawei 2014i).

3 Rise of the Company

3.1 Growth Development

After the foundation of the company, which took place in 1987, Huawei has been growing. Huawei's revenues have been growing steadily over the past few years. To delineate the development of Huawei, the business life cycle will be used. The business life cycle consists of four stages. The first stage is the start-up, the second stage is the growth stage, the third stage is the maturity stage, and the last stage is the decline stage. For Huawei's development so far, the first two stages are of particular importance.

3.1.1 The start-Up Phase

When Huawei was founded in 1987 by Ren Zhengfei, it was a small startup company. It began as a sales agent and was selling Private Branch Switches produced by another company from Hong Kong. In 1990, Huawei started doing its own independent research and commercialization of the Private Branch Switches. The first target group was hotels and small enterprises. From 1997 until 2001, Huawei opened several research centers globally (Huawei 2014e).

3.1.2 The Growth Phase

After the period where Huawei was doing research, the business was capable of developing its own products. Huawei was able to offer cheaper, more advanced products that were sometimes even 25 % less than what the competitors were charging. Huawei hired a lot of salespeople and soon the local operators were persuaded to buy the products. After the local operators, the businesses abroad became the targets. When Russia signed a contract with Huawei, many countries in Eastern Europe followed. Huawei was about to take over the world with their products. In 2012, Huawei acquired Symantec's 49 % stake in their joint venture, Huawei-Symantec, for 530 million US$. Huawei now retains full ownership of Huawei-Symantec. Also in 2012, Huawei signed an important partnership agreement with Synnex Group. This helped Huawei to successfully enter into the channel network of the US enterprise ICT market. Later, Huawei established a global strategic partnership with Intel for IT products and solutions (Huawei 2014f).

In 2014, Huawei is still in the growth phase. Huawei is still building up its brand in Europe, America, and other parts of the world. They are still expanding and getting new contracts signed. Huawei achieved progress in technological innovation and market expansion in the last few years.

3.2 Becoming a Brand

By achieving these successes and signing these contracts, Huawei is becoming more and more known in ICT. All these positive developments help Huawei to consolidate the company's position as a global leading ICT solutions company, although globally leading does not mean it is a global brand yet. To determine whether Huawei is a brand, the word brand first needs to be defined. A brand is a unique design, sign, symbol, set of words, or a combination of these that creates an image and distinguishes a company or product from its competitors.

By selling mobile phones and other devices where consumers can see the logo and the name Huawei, the consumers become more aware of the company. The logo of Huawei gets easier to recognize and it is increasing in popularity. The logo of Huawei is seen as an extension of the company's core values. The radiating shapes of the icon are focused on the bottom center and they indicate Huawei's commitment to creating long-term value for the customers. The tone and the symmetrical figure stands for harmony and is used as a metaphor for Huawei's open-minded attitude and partnership strategy, indicating that Huawei will maintain its healthy growth and create a harmonious business environment (The-Logo-Quiz 2008).

To see whether Huawei is becoming one of the most well-known brands in the world, there is another company to take into account. This company is called

Interbrand and they create a list every year: a list with the biggest companies on the world. On their main list from 2013, Huawei is not yet present. This means that Huawei is not part of the 100 biggest brands in the world yet (Interbrand 2013).

Besides the Interbrand list of global brands, there is also a list created for regional brands. On the list of China, Huawei is not mentioned as they are a privately-owned brand and do not have their financial data publicly available. However, Huawei is the only company that is mentioned as an exception for not standing on this list, although the "Best China Brand list of 2011" does mention that Huawei would be expected to be on the list. All this means that Huawei most certainly does have a brand value (Interbrand 2011).

3.3 Position in the Home Market/Market Share

In order to determine the size of a company, people look at the market share. Huawei is a Chinese company and that is why the market share of Huawei in China as the home market is important. As mentioned in the product range in the "company/profile" section, Huawei has many different products and therefore operates in multiple markets.

The market share of Huawei on the mobile devices in China in the first quarter of 2012 is 5 %. This ranks Huawei as the fifth biggest company with the most market share on the mobile devices market (SMIA 2012).

Figure 3 shows that Huawei was not the biggest player on the market in 2012. Nokia, Shanzhai, and Samsung are much bigger than Huawei. Apple and HTC are almost of a similar size on the Chinese mobile devices market. In Fig. 4, China's 3G wireless equipment market share from 2009 is displayed. Here ZTE is the biggest player in the market with a 42.2 % of the total market. Huawei is second with 38.2 % and the third biggest Alcatel-Lucent has a mere 16.4 % (IHST 2010). With

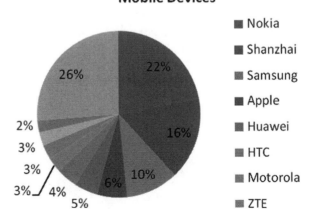

Fig. 3 Market share 2011 Q1 mobile devices (SMIA 2012)

Fig. 4 China's 3G Wireless Equipment Market share (IHST 2010)

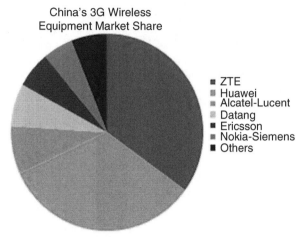

these two examples, it is shown that Huawei is not the biggest player in the Chinese market, although it is also not the smallest.

3.4 Position in the Global Market/Market Share

To determine the size of a company on a global scale, market share is an important item to consider. Again, a few examples will be shown to indicate Huawei's position in the global market. In Fig. 5, the hardware market share in 2012 is shown. Here it becomes clear that Huawei is the ultimate optical network hardware market leader. It leaves all the competitors far behind, including, for example, Alcatel-Lucent and ZTE, who were bigger players in the Chinese market for wireless equipment.

In Fig. 6, the market share of handsets is shown in Q1 of 2012. Here you can see how big the competition from other Asian brands such as Samsung and ZTE. Huawei is, compared to the other bigger Asian players, one of the smaller players with only 3 % of the total market share. In this totally different figure of the global market share, Huawei is again rated differently per product. Therefore, it is difficult to determine the exact market share of Huawei as they are in multiple different markets for different products and have a different position in every market.

Overall, it can be said that Huawei is not an unimportant player in the market in general. In some markets, they have more influence as a market leader than in others where they have a relatively small market share. Especially now, Huawei is trying to expand their global market share on multiple markets.

Fig. 5 Optical Network Hardware Market share leaders (NetworkStatic 2012)

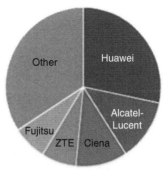

Optical Network Hardware Market Share Leaders

Based on 3Q12 global revenue

Fig. 6 Market share handsets Q1 2012 (FierceWireless 2013)

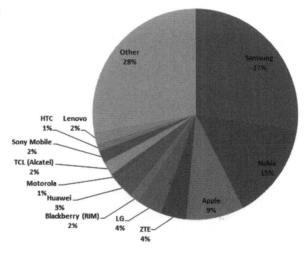

3.5 Stock Market Development

Many big companies have securities (also known as stocks) for sale. The stock market is a place where companies and organizations can sell stocks. People or buyers can buy these stocks and they become partial owners of the company. The buyers can be offered dividends or they may speculate whether they can make a profit when the price of a stock increases after the stock has been bought.

Huawei has issued stocks as well. Their IPO stocks went on the market on the 30th of November in 2010 (Wall Street Journal 2014). The stocks initially sold at 33.04 RMB; this was the highest price the stocks of Huawei have been sold for to date.

After the IPO's were offered, the stocks started dropping slowly, sometimes with small increases but it was dropping steadily. It even came to a point where the Huawei Technology Co. Ltd. A stocks were valued at 8.08 RMB. After this ultimate low, the stocks started to slowly increase again and after a while they even started to increase at a faster pace. The stocks of Huawei were able to reach 31.33 RMB on the 27th of February 2014, which was the closest the stocks came to the launch price. After this price, the value of the stocks dropped again and the stocks of Huawei are currently trading at 21.16 RMB (Wall Street Journal 2014).

The stocks yield dividends at 0.47 %. The latest dividend payment took place on the 19th of July in 2013. The amount of dividend paid on that date is 0.10 RMB. The P/E ratio is 100.76 with a trailing of 12 months.

Overall the yield is pretty low in comparison to other stocks. The dividend payment is also pretty low in comparison to other stock-owning companies.

The total market cap is 2.95 Billion RMB. Huawei has 80.15 million shares outstanding and with a public float of 51.6 million. The stocks of Huawei are not listed in any of the major indexes of the world.

3.6 To What Extent Was the Governmental, Business and Educational System Beneficial to the Rise of This Company?

3.6.1 Governmental

Nowadays the Asian market is booming. The companies of Asia are becoming international and getting bigger and bigger. This is also the case for Chinese companies. The Chinese government is stimulating companies to grow and become global market players. It has often been speculated that Huawei is one of the companies the Chinese government wants to grow bigger. In multiple articles on the web, Huawei is accused of having strong government connections and receiving money from the government. On the one hand, it is positive for Huawei to be part of this booming Asian economy. This enables the company to grow bigger since the circumstances are positive. On the other hand, having connections with the government can be seen as negative. Both the USA and Australia have been debating whether Huawei should be allowed to enter their home market as Huawei could be spying for the Chinese Government.

3.6.2 Business

The business of Huawei has strong core values where people are the central value. They stand for their customers first, as well as teamwork, integrity and dedication. They also stand for transparency, because Huawei tries to have openness. Huawei's values for the products are to continuously improve them by taking the initiative. By conducting research, Huawei tries to get more market expertise. They are buying other companies to increase their capital. Huawei is also sponsoring events etc. For example, they signed a sponsorship deal with the English football club Arsenal. They also try to be sustainable and participate in multiple charity projects.

3.6.3 Education

The Chinese educational system has four different levels. The primary school and junior middle school are compulsory. The senior high school and university degree are not compulsory. Most of the times, people who do have an university degree have high grades and are seen as top students. Huawei itself also has multiple possibilities for people who want to learn more while developing the company. The program is called: "grow with Huawei".

4 Future Development

4.1 What Are the Future Challenges/Problems to Be Overcome at Home and Abroad?

As stated on the website of Huawei: "There are obviously cultural differences between China and the West, but Huawei treats this as an advantage: it has combined the Western professional management style with the Eastern culture".

Huawei has recruited a number of Western executives with the aim of helping Huawei better understand the overseas markets and provide solutions that satisfy their operator customers. But besides the cultural differences between China and the West, there are some other challenges, and occasionally problems, that Huawei has to overcome. In this section, we will cover two of those challenges: the company name, and the suspicion of spying.

4.1.1 Company Name

Huawei has some major challenges to overcome if they want to expand more and more abroad. One of the biggest challenges is the name of the company itself: Huawei. Other Chinese companies often have names that are easier to pronounce for foreigners. Some examples are China Mobile and ZTE. But Huawei is a "difficult" name for foreigners.

The Chinese people, obviously, have no problems pronouncing Huawei. As maintained by Huawei: "The character 华 means "splendid" or "magnificent", but can also mean "China". The character 为 means "action" or "achievement". The two characters combined (Huáwéi) can be variously translated as "achievement", "splendid act", or "China is able"".

To make sure the company name is understandable and also pronounceable, Huawai changes the pronunciation per country. This will (most of the time) be done by video with the right pronunciation.

The right pronunciation is "Wah Way". In the USA, most of the people pronounce it like Hawaii, Hua Way, Whoo Whee, or How Wee. In the Netherlands, the most used "name" is Hoe-ah-wei.

As indicated by the Wall Street Journal, about two years ago, Huawei was really considering changing their brand name because of the struggles with pronouncing it correctly. The company eventually decided to stick with its name, despite the problem, after coming to the conclusion that it was a well-established brand, with a strong reputation in the telecom-equipment sector. But, Huawei did not rule out the firm's fast growing consumer group using another brand name at some point in the future (Wall Street Journal 2013).

4.1.2 Suspicion of Spying

Another challenge for Huawei is maybe the most important one: the suspicion that the company is spying because of the company's perceived links with the Chinese government. As stated by the Wall Street Journal, this perception has long been a bugbear for the company, causing problems in the USA (Wall Street Journal 2013).

In the end of 2013, Huawei officially gave up on the US market. As the executive vice president of Huawei stated in the Financial Times, "We are not interested in the US market anymore." As reported by The Diplomat, it was not really a big surprise, because Huawei has struggled to gain entrance to the USA for years due to security concerns. The company has been blocked several times from bidding on projects to purchase or partner with U.S. technology and telecommunications firms. The most devastating setback came in October 2012, when a House Intelligence Committee Report encouraged US companies not to partner with Huawei. Huawei officials have repeatedly denied the accusation of espionage, and demanded that their accusers show hard proof. In addition to that, the company tried with an aggressive PR campaign to clear the negative image in the USA. This was done by hiring lobbyist and staff members of the congress to visit Huawei factories during their official trips to China. But all those attempts did not reach the goal they were hoping for. So in the end of 2013, they gave up on the USA (Tiezzi 2013).

In 2012, the Australian government prevented Huawei from rolling out the 38 billion US$ high-speed broadband network which aimed to connect 93 % of the Australian homes and workplaces with optical fiber. The government was concerned about cyber-attacks originating in China and rejected a bid by Huawei to take part in the rollout of the National Broadband Network, Australians largest nation-building project in history. A spokesman for Attorney-General Nicola Roxon said in a statement that: "The Australian government have the responsibility to do their utmost to protect its integrity and that of the information carried on it." The Australian government arrived at the decision to reject the bid under the guidance of the Australian Security Intelligence Organization (Winning 2012).

4.2 Which Companies Are Its Competitors Now and in the Future?

Huawei is facing strong competition from companies such as Ericsson, Alcatel-Lucent, Cisco, and Nokia Siemens.

As stated on Huawei's website: "One of Huawei's strategies is to help develop the global telecom industry together with our partners and competitors in order to share the benefits of the industry value chain".

The policy that Huawei has, is "to compete openly and fairly in every market where we operate and to also ensure that our contribution to those economies

Fig. 7 Global Network Infrastructure Market share 2010 (Prasso 2011)

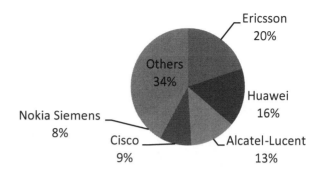

Global Network Infastructure; Market Share 2010

includes not just significant investment in those regions, but also the recruitment of local staff, and, where appropriate, the localization of R&D operations" (Huawei 2014d).

To compare Huawei's current competitiveness with that of its most important peers (Ericsson, Alcatel-Lucent, Cisco, and Nokia Siemens), their performance is shown in Fig. 7.

After 2010, Huawei took the title "largest telecom infrastructure maker in the world" from Ericsson. These two companies are neck and neck and one new contract or just a fluctuation in currency could see these two companies changing places again. To compare: Huawei had revenues of 16.1 billion US$ for the first 6 months of 2012. Ericsson, which is originally from Sweden, brought in 15.25 billion US$ in the first 6 months of 2012, which is 850 million US$ less than Huawei. Consider here that the currency exchange rates have a really big impact on this amount.

Since Huawei has their biggest industry in the sizable handset and enterprise business, Ericsson is still by far the biggest cellular infrastructure maker in the world. Both companies are growing really fast, despite the poor global economy and the economic recession around the year 2008 (Fitchard 2012). Comparing the telecom equipment revenue by region (2011), Ericsson has better revenues compared with Huawei. The biggest difference is in North America, but one of the reasons for that is the suspicion of spying by the US government against Huawei (see section "Future Development"—Suspicion of spying) (Economist 2012).

The past few years, especially from 2006 until 2010, Huawei spent less than all of their peers. This applies to R&D as a percentage of revenue, but also to the total R&D spending (Figs. 8 and 9). In 2011, Huawei exceeded Alcatel-Lucent in the total amount of R&D spending. But, according to Reuters, Huawei is planning to increase the total amount of R&D to 4.5 billion US$, which makes the gap between Cisco and Ericsson even smaller (Ahrens 2013).

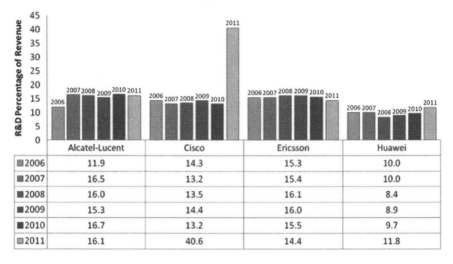

Fig. 8 Research and development percentage of revenue (Ahrens 2013)

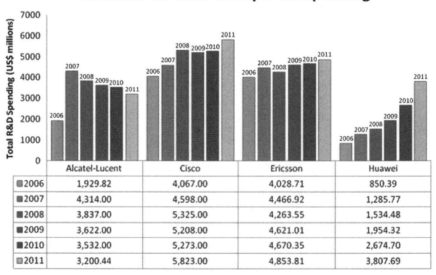

Fig. 9 Total research and development spending (Ahrens 2013)

As Ahrens stated, Huawei has focused on research and development as their core business. Therefore, Huawei tries to allocate 10 % of their annual revenue to the R&D sector. Due to the low-cost center of China, Huawei has a substantial marginal cost advantage over its competitors (Ahrens 2013).

4.3 From Asia to Europe

As stated on their own website; Huawei wants to expand their activities more and more into Europe. To achieve this, Huawei opened a new exhibition center in Amstelveen (south side of Amsterdam), the Netherlands. This center underscores the fact that Huawei is a fast-growing and innovative company in the enterprise market. The company plans to hire 5500 employees in Europe during the next 5 years, and together with the current 7500 employees, that will make a total of 13,000 European employees. "Western Europe remains the key target market for Huawei Enterprise. Our global success as a company will be measured against our achievements here," said Leon He, President of Huawei Enterprise in Western Europe (Huawei 2013).

Huawei's success in Europe will be measured by its ability to help enterprise and channel partners successfully navigate the current major IT challenges and opportunities, which include: increasing the mobility of employees, as well as increasing customers and applications; the deepening role of cloud computing; the real-world utilization of big data; and the impact of social media on the success of enterprises. In order to be successful, the company is committed to working closely with its local European partners to meet the unique needs of customers in each distinct European market it serves.

Huawei has already made its mark in Europe as a valuable partner for public and private sector clients. Its cloud storage system passed the performance test of the European Organization for Nuclear Research (CERN), enabling CERN to extend its capabilities in preparation for a huge increase in data volume. Its corporate networking solutions power the networks of many hospitals, schools, enterprises, and ISPs throughout Europe. Huawei is also proud to be the wireless (WIFI) solutions provider for the stadiums of two major European football clubs, Glasgow Rangers in Scotland and Borussia Dortmund in Germany (Huawei 2013).

As indicated by the China Daily, the exhibition center in the Netherlands is a milestone in its expansion in Europe, particularly in the Benelux countries. "By opening this new exhibition center I believe Huawei is demonstrating its commitment to long-term development in the Netherlands," says Fei Li, Economic Counselor of the Chinese embassy in the Netherlands. "It also demonstrates the Netherlands' favorable investment environment" (Jing 2013).

Europe is like a second home market for the company, Zhang says. Nevertheless, the enterprise business in Europe has not been all plain sailing, given the highly competitive market. But, if Huawei can succeed in Europe, it can achieve more globally, Zhang says (Jing 2013).

5 Conclusion and Recommendation

5.1 The Company's Successes

Huawei is growing bigger every year. The revenue is constantly increasing. There are multiple reasons to attribute to the successes of Huawei. First of all, Samsung had previously entered the global market before Huawei. This means that the South Koreans paved the way for Chinese brands such as Huawei.

Huawei states that their rapid growth is due to their customer-centric innovation strategy and customer focus. The focus of Huawei is on continuous innovation that is customer-centric and improving customer service quality. Huawei is the third largest applicant for patents in the world. Huawei also has a quality policy for customer service.

Huawei is capable of offering innovative products for a cheaper price, sometimes even more than 25 % cheaper than the competitors. Africa's mobile technology progression would not have been as far as it is now without Huawei and its cheaper products.

The success of Huawei could also be due to the help that Huawei is accused of receiving from the Chinese government. However, this could also be something that is stopping Huawei from entering markets, as Huawei could represent a national security threat.

5.2 Becoming a Brand

Huawei is already a market leader in multiple markets, such as the optical network hardware market. The markets that Huawei is a market leader in are mostly the pipe and cloud products market. Both the pipe and the cloud are mostly unknown to the end consumers. This means that Huawei probably did not establish a brand name because of these products.

In other markets, such as the smartphone market, Huawei is trying to establish a bigger market share. End consumers recognize smartphone brands more easily, because they will see it in their daily lives. If Huawei is getting a bigger market share in their devices product range, they will have a greater possibility to become a world brand. Judging on the continuous growth in the devices industry, we can conclude that it is likely that Huawei is becoming a world brand.

5.3 The Possibilities for Other Companies

Huawei is already established in Amsterdam. It has multiple campaigns running in the Netherlands to get more brand recognition. Huawei has contracts with several Dutch companies to maintain the Dutch Mobile Network. That Huawei is present and expanding its market share on the Dutch smart phone market is a fact. By increasing the number of campaigns about their new smartphones and also by sponsoring several events and sports teams, Huawei is trying to increase their market share. Other companies should enhance the possibility that Huawei become well established in the Netherlands.

Ignoring that Huawei is operating in their market could be the worst option that a company takes. Huawei can produce cheap products that are very innovative, and has many resources and technology patents. This enables Huawei to have a large influence on other companies. Cooperating to get the best results is most likely the best option for both parties. If both companies are willing to work together towards one objective, growth and profit maximization should result.

References

Ahrens, N. (2013). *China's competitiveness*. Washington, DC: CSIS.
BBC. (2014). *Open door policy*. available via World Wide Web: http://news.bbc.co.uk/2/shared/spl/hi/in_depth/china_politics/key_people_events/html/8.stm.
Business Insider. (2013). *Huawei Spies for China says Micheal Hayden*. Retrieved February 14, 2014, from http://www.businessinsider.com/huawei-spies-for-china-says-michael-hayden-2013-7#ixzz2tIDedtEa.
Business Insider. (2014). *Chinese consumers doing it their way*. Retrieved February 14, 2014, from http://www.businessinsider.com/chinese-consumers-doing-it-their-way-2014-1#ixzz2tHr0UowI.
CNN. (2012). *10 most powerful businesspeople in China*. Retrieved February 4, 2014, from http://money.cnn.com/galleries/2012/news/world/1205/gallery.china-most-powerful-businesspeople.fortune/.
Economist. (2011). *The long march of the invisible Mr Ren*. Retrieved February 5, 2014, from http://www.economist.com/node/18771640.
Economist. (2012). *The company that spooked the world*. Retrieved February 7, 2014, from http://www.economist.com/node/21559929.
FierceWireless. (2013). *Analyzing worlds 12 biggest handset makers*. Retrieved March 31, 2014, from http://www.fiercewireless.com/europe/special-reports/analyzing-worlds-12-biggest-handset-makers-q1-2013.
Fitchard, K. (2012). *Making T-Mo's MyTouch is just step 1 of Huawei's master plan*. Retrieved March 27, 2014, from http://gigaom.com/2012/07/24/huawei-knocks-off-ericsson-as-worlds-biggest-telecom-vendor/.
Huawei Technologies Co., Ltd. (2011). *2010 Corporate social responsibility report*. Retrieved February 13, 2014, from http://www.huawei.com/en/ucmf/groups/public/documents/attachments/hw_093033.pdf.
Huawei. (2013). *Huawei expands activities in Europe with Enterprise Exhibition Centre*. Retrieved March 30, 2014, from http://www.huawei.eu/press-release/huawei-expands-activities-europe-enterprise-exhibition-centre.
Huawei. (2014a). *Application & software*. Retrieved February 4, 2014, from http://www.huawei.com/en/products/software/index.htm.
Huawei. (2014b). *Caring for employees*. Retrieved February 14, 2014, from http://huawei.com/en/about-huawei/sustainability/win-win-development/caring-employees/index.htm.
Huawei. (2014c). *Data communication*. Retrieved February 13, 2014, from http://www.huawei.com/en/products/data-communication/index.htm.
Huawei. (2014d). *How does Huawei cooperate with Western partners and competitors? Why do so many of the major European operators choose to work with Huawei?* Retrieved March 27, 2014, from http://www.huawei.eu/how-does-huawei-cooperate-western-partners-and-competitors-why-do-so-many-major-european-operators.

Huawei. (2014e). *Huawei products*. Retrieved February 2, 2014, from http://www.huawei.com/en/products/index.htm.

Huawei. (2014f). *Milestones*. Retrieved March 26, 2014, from http://enterprise.huawei.com/en/about/about-intro/index.htm.

Huawei. (2014h). *Quality policy*. Retrieved February 14, 2014, from http://www.huawei.com/en/about-huawei/corporate-info/quality-policy/.

Huawei. (2014i). *Research and development*. Retrieved February 14, 2014, from http://www.huawei.com/en/about-huawei/corporate-info/research-development/index.htm.

Huawei. (2014j). *Storage*. Retrieved February 4, 2014, from http://www.huawei.com/en/products/storage/index.htm.

Huawei. (2014k). *What is Huawei's strategy for international markets*. Retrieved February 13, 2014, from http://www.huawei.com/what-huawei-s-strategy-international-markets.

Huawei. (2014l). *Financial highlights*. Retrieved May 6, 2014, from http://www.huawei.com/en/about-huawei/corporate-info/financial/index.htm.

IHST Technology. (2010). *ZTE Holds Off China Competition*. Retrieved March 31, 2014, from https://technology.ihs.com/393747/zte-holds-off-china-competition.

Interbrand. (2011). *Best China brands 2011*. Retrieved March 31, 2014, from http://issuu.com/interbrand/docs/2011_bcb_cn-single_0914/1?e=o.

Interbrand. (2013). *Best global brands 2013*. Retrieved March 31, 2014, from http://www.interbrand.com/nl/best-global-brands/2013/Best-Global-Brands-2013.aspx.

Jing, F. (2013). *Up, up, Huawei finds new friends in Europe nations*. Retrieved March 30, 2014, from http://usa.chinadaily.com.cn/business/2013-09/30/content_17003779.htm.

NetworkStatic. (2012). *Programming the NSP: Vendors on SDN for SP operators*. Retrieved March 31, 2014, from http://networkstatic.net/programming-the-nsp-vendors-on-sdn-for-sp-operators/#!prettyPhoto.

Osawa, J. (2013). *Huawei innovates with rotating CEO system*. Retrieved February 13, 2014, from http://blogs.wsj.com/digits/2013/10/14/huawei-innovates-with-rotating-ceo-system/.

Prasso, S. (2011). *What makes China telecom Huawei so scary?* Retrieved March 27, 2014, from http://tech.fortune.cnn.com/2011/07/28/what-makes-china-telecom-huawei-so-scary/.

Social Media in Asia. (SMIA). (2012). *Social media and mobile in China*. Retrieved March 31, 2014, from http://socialmediainasia.blogspot.nl/2012/05/baidu-published-report-of-chinese.html.

The-Logo-Quiz. (2008). *Logo meaning: Huawei logo*. Retrieved March 31, 2014, from http://thelogoquiz.blogspot.nl/2008/03/logo-meaning-huawei-logo.html.

Tiezzi, S. (2013). *Huawei officially gives up on the us market*. Retrieved March 27, 2014, from http://thediplomat.com/2013/12/huawei-officially-gives-up-on-the-us-market/.

Wall Street Journal. (2013). *Huawei mulled changing its name as foreigners found it too hard*. Retrieved March 27, 2014, from http://blogs.wsj.com/tech-europe/2013/09/04/huawei-mulled-changing-its-name-as-foreigners-found-it-too-hard/.

Wall Street Journal. (2014). *Huawei Technology Co. Ltd. A*. Retrieved March 31, 2014, from http://quotes.wsj.com/CN/XSHE/002502/interactive-chart#All.

Webopedia. (2014). *Cloud computing*. Retrieved February 2, 2014, from http://www.webopedia.com/TERM/C/cloud_computing.html.

Winning, D. (2012). *Huawei barred from NBN rollout*. Retrieved March 27, 2014, from http://www.theaustralian.com.au/technology/huawei-barred-from-nbn-rollout/story-fn4iyzsr-1226309888516#.

Lenovo: A Case Study on Strengthening the Position in the European Market Through Innovation

Franz Josef Gellert

Abstract
Lenovo is a Chinese company operating in the computer and ICT area with great success in its domestic market. The product range is spread over computers (laptops) as well as smartphones for private and for professional users. Lenovo's strengths are the high quality of electronic devices, ease of use, and selling the devices for an acceptable and fair price. The supply chain of Lenovo is very strong and effective as well as efficient. Lenovo and its specific product segments can become a world brand. The increase in sales and market shares was achieved by mergers and acquisitions which are limited by nature. So, it might be a challenge for Lenovo, when the time is ripe, to further develop its business with its own resources.

1 Introduction

We can observe that Chinese companies are entering the European markets in various business fields. Lenovo is a Chinese company operating in the computer and ICT area with great success in its domestic market. The product range is spread over computers (laptops) as well as smartphones for private and for professional users. Lenovo organizes its worldwide operations with the view that a truly global company must be able to quickly capitalize on new ideas and opportunities from anywhere. By foregoing a traditional headquarters model and focusing on centers of excellence around the world, Lenovo makes the maximum use of its resources to create the best products in the most efficient and effective way possible. In addition, the dispersed structure keeps them closer to customers, enabling Lenovo to react

F.J. Gellert (✉)
FOM University OAS for Economics and Management, Bremen, Germany

International Business School, Hanze University OAS, Groningen, The Netherlands
e-mail: f.j.gellert@pl.hanze.nl

quickly to local market requirements (Lenovo 2014). Lenovo is a 34 billion US$ personal technology and a Fortune Global 500 company that serves customers in more than 160 countries globally. Lenovo is therefore the largest PC Company in the world and an emerging PC Plus leader. Major research centers are in Yamato in Japan; Beijing, Shanghai and Shenzhen in China, and Raleigh, North Carolina in the USA. PC manufacturing and assembly facilities are in Beijing, Chengdu, Hefei, Huiyang, Shanghai and Shenzhen in China; Pondicherry in India; Monterrey in Mexico; Itu in Brazil; and Whitsett, North Carolina in the USA, with contract manufacturing and OEM worldwide.

Lenovo's culture is what has enabled them to consistently raise the bar on delivering break-through innovations, award-winning designs and strong financial performances. Being a successful Chinese company raises the question how can Lenovo strengthen its position in Europe. The first steps of Lenovo in Europe have been already taken, but what are the success and failure, factors Lenovo might be confronted with in the future and what can make Lenovo a strong IT B2C and B2B company in a very competitive European market? How can Lenovo's business in Europe become sustainable? In this chapter, we want to examine how Lenovo can position itself in Europe. Desk research by analyzing secondary data will give an overview of opportunities and threats for developing a European strategy in an interesting but very competitive market (Fig. 1).

Fig. 1 Lenovo (Lenovo 2014)

2 Company Profile

2.1 History

Lenovo got its start in Beijing in 1984 as the New Technology Development Company (NTD Co). "The company was considered as the first company in China that was working in the science and technological sectors of the Chinese Market Reform" (Ahrens and Zhou 2013).

In 2004, Lenovo became an Olympic worldwide partner (International Olympic Committee). It was the first Chinese company to become a computer technology equipment partner of the IOC. Furthermore, Lenovo decided to develop the rural market by launching the "Yuanmeng" PC series designed for township home users. Later on, Lenovo and IBM announced an agreement in which Lenovo acquired IBM's Personal Computing Division, its global PC (desktop and notebook computer) business. The acquisition forms a top-tier (third-largest) global PC leader (Lenovo 2014). In 2005, Lenovo completed the acquisition of IBM's Personal Computing Division, making it a new international IT competitor and the third-largest personal computer company in the world. Lenovo announced the closing of a 350 million US$ strategic investment by three leading private equity firms: Texas Pacific Group, General Atlantic LLC and Newbridge Capital LLC. Lenovo established a new Innovation Center in the Research Triangle Park, N.C., to enable customers, business partners, solution providers and independent software vendors to collaborate on new personal computing solutions. Lenovo introduced the industry's thinnest, lightest and most secure Tablet PC, the ThinkPad X41 Tablet. From that moment on, Lenovo developed as a specialist for ICT home users as well as for professionals. The current situation in 2014 is that according to the German Handelsblatt and Reuters "Lenovo bought an important IBM component as well as Motorola Smart phone components and therefore ranks now at number 4 in the world in that particular business" (Handelsblatt 2014; Reuters 2014).

2.2 Position at the Home Market

Lenovo was incorporated in Hong Kong in 1988, has been listed on The Stock Exchange of Hong Kong since February 1994, and has currently been included as a constituent stock of the MSCI China Free Index, MSCI Information Technology Index, Hang Seng Main Board Index, Hang Seng Composite Index, Hang Seng Mainland Comp Index, Hang Seng Freefloat Comp Index, Hang Seng China-Aff Corp Index, and Hang Seng Corporate Sustainability Index. Ordinary shares are distributed over the following shareholders: Public shareholders, 60.25 %; Legend Holdings Limited, 32.45 %; Mr. Yuanqing Yang (CEO of Lenovo), 7.05 %; and other directors, 0.25 % (Fig. 2).

Lenovo's position in the home market is characterized by dynamic developments in manufacturing IT components for domestic users and for users in the global market. The Chinese PC market represents about 20 % of the global

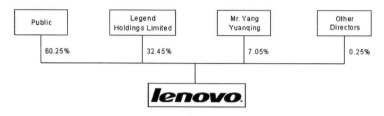

Fig. 2 Lenovo's shareholder structure (Wang et al. 2009)

market volume (Ahrens and Zhou 2013). Lenovo holds 34 % of the large enterprise market in China according to Wu (2012). Since Lenovo concentrates on its strong brands, product portfolio and its distribution advantages, it will get a stronger position in the global market.

2.3 Position at the Global Market

Lenovo's global market strategy was recently in the news when it was mentioned that they will open an additional plant in India as well as in Mexico (People's daily online 2014). Thus, Lenovo applies its global manufacturing strategy: "Think Your Company's Global? This Is Global. Lenovo's top leaders live, sell, manage, and work all over the world" (Fig. 3).

Ask the average American to name top Chinese brands and the list usually starts and stops with Tsingtao beer. As Lenovo CMO David Roman—formerly of Apple and HP—says, "The business is ahead of the brand." Stateside, Lenovo is best known as the outfit that came out of nowhere to buy IBM's PC division and ThinkPad brand in 2005, which is why in 2011, Lenovo launched its largest-ever branding campaign, aiming to become the first global consumer brand to emerge from China.

Lenovo is a company the likes of which we've never seen. It is a product of Communist China (the government still owns 36 % of its parent, Legend Holdings); it is heavily influenced by the democratized West; it boasts an international workforce of 27,000 employees and customers in more than 160 countries. But the story of Lenovo's rise is also a parable for Chinese business: in just 30 years, an enterprise launched in the Beijing equivalent of a garage—by a founder who endured forced relocation and admits he bungled his early attempts at business—has blossomed at a pace no one predicted. Lenovo is redefining "Made in China," producing the industry's highest-quality machines. It ranked No. 1 in the 2011 Computer Reliability Report, ahead of Apple and HP. And the company's culture skillfully blends an Eastern way of thinking with the best of Western business, demonstrating innovation and nimbleness that would impress—and unnerve—the most skeptical Silicon Valley digerati.

In Table 1, we can see how Lenovo is positioned in the global PC market as a company and as a company specialized on specific brands.

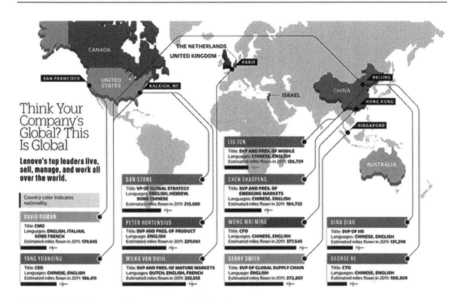

Fig. 3 Global Lenovo (Fastcompany 2014)

Table 1 Preliminary Worldwide PC vendor unit shipments estimates for 2013 (units) (Recode 2014)

Company	2013 shipments	2013 market share (%)	2012 shipments	2012 market share (%)	2013–2012 growth (%)
Lenovo	53,272,522	16.9	52,187,653	14.9	2.1
HP	51,252,229	16.2	56,505,757	16.1	−9.3
Dell	36,788,285	11.6	37,611,247	10.7	−2.2
Acer Group	25,689,496	8.1	35,745,401	10.2	−28.1
Asus	20,030,837	6.3	24,339,951	6.9	−17.7
Others	128,934,147	40.8	144,669,689	41.2	−10.9
Grand Total	315,967,516	100.0	351,059,698	100.0	−10.0

Note: Data includes desk-based PCs and mobile PCs, including mini-notebooks but not media tablets such as he iPad. Data is based on the shipments selling into channels
Source: Gartner (January 2014)

2.4 Extension of Government, Business and Education Support for Company's Rise

"Government support seems to play a very limited role in Lenovo's comparative advantages" (Ahrens and Zhou 2013). However, due to changes in taxes and tariffs for technological companies, Lenovo benefits as foreign companies do when they are investing in China's industry. This allows Lenovo to strengthen their position either in the domestic market or in the global market. For sustainable business development, Lenovo formed a joint venture in Hong Kong to take advantage of the government's preferential policy toward foreign investment and products.

2.5 The Founder(s)/Management

The founder of Lenovo is Chuanzhi Liu who is also known as the "Godfather" of China's Information technology. Liu left China's business leaders' months ago, arguing that leaders should talk business and not politics. Recently, he admitted in a speech that China changed its political environment significantly and that economic reforms are on its way. Furthermore, he stated: "Now if the market is to play a central role and the government only plays the referee, only you will decide if you are going to win the race," urging business leaders to seek new opportunities and make the most out of the new economic environment. Liu, talking to his peers from the elite Zhisland online club in Hainan, also admitted that his "don't talk politics" speech made months ago was only meant for a private audience. He said he had not expected his comment to be taken out of context and "leaked" to the media.

The current board of Lenovo consists of Yuanqing Yang and Dr. Peter Hortensius. Yang, 48, is Chief Executive Officer and an executive director of the company and has been appointed as the Chairman of the Board on November 3, 2011. He is also a director and a shareholder of Sureinvest Holdings Limited which holds interests in the issued share capital of the company. Yang assumed the duties of Chief Executive Officer on February 5, 2009. Prior to that, he was the Chairman of the Board from April 30, 2005. Before taking up the office as chairman, he was the Chief Executive Officer and has been an executive director since December 16, 1997. Yang has more than 20 years of experience in the field of computers. Under his leadership, Lenovo has been China's best-selling PC brand since 1997. He holds a Master's degree from the Department of Computer Science at the University of Science and Technology of China. Yang is also a guest professor at the University of Science and Technology of China and a member of the New York Stock Exchange's International Advisory Committee.

Dr. Peter Hortensius is Senior Vice President of Lenovo and currently President of the Think Business Group which has supply chain and product responsibilities for Lenovo's Think branded product lines. His focus areas include driving leadership in Lenovo's core global commercial business, creating a premium consumer brand across a wide range of products (especially desktops, notebooks and tablets), growing Lenovo's workstation business, and managing Lenovo's global enterprise business in server and related products. Dr. Hortensius has held several key leadership positions in Lenovo including most recently President of the Product Group where he managed both the company's commercial and consumer PC product portfolio, and enterprise business. Prior to this role, he served as Senior Vice President of Lenovo's Think Product Group where he managed the company's commercial product portfolio and was responsible for increasing market share and profitability in enterprise segments and in new growth areas like small-to-medium business by launching the ThinkPad Edge line of laptops. Dr. Hortensius joined

Lenovo in May, 2005 as Senior Vice President for Worldwide Product Development and was appointed Senior Vice President for Lenovo's Notebook Business Unit in October with business and product development responsibilities for all the ThinkPad and Lenovo-branded laptop lines. Before joining Lenovo, he spent 17 years with IBM where he was the Vice President, Products and Offerings, for IBM's PC Division. He has extensive expertise in product and technology research & development. Dr. Hortensius holds a Doctorate degree in Electrical Engineering from the University of Manitoba in Canada.

2.6 Employees

At Lenovo, people share a common aspiration to be the very best. Whether serving their customers, working together as a team or contributing to the community, they are working to build a unique company delivering unparalleled products created and supported by people who represent a wealth of cultures and experiences. Lenovo's strength lies in this diversity. And every day, on every project, people are creating a new language for inclusion and respect for others. People are dedicated to fostering an environment that encourages entrepreneurism and ownership: a workplace where people's talents can be challenged and their efforts recognized and rewarded. Lenovo's success in the past fiscal year is a testament to their leaders, their people and the way they do business. What unifies Lenovo as a company is the commitment to their customers and partners and the vision to become one of the world's leading technology companies. In short, people are Lenovo's greatest strength. Lenovo offers specific trainings for their customers such as introduction to Windows 8, or getting innovation Apps as well as a course for using tablets (Lenovo idea tab).

2.7 Product Range

In Fig. 4, we can see what type of products Lenovo is selling and what the share of each type is from the first quarter in 2012 to the first quarter in 2013.

We can observe that notebooks are decreasing and server as well as other business is increasing. The development is based on the latest acquisition plans of Lenovo which can consequently be considered as logical strategic steps.

2.8 Revenues

Lenovo's revenues in Table 2 show that notebooks are contributing less to revenues than the desktop business or even more importantly the "Other revenues", which includes services as well as the smartphone business sector.

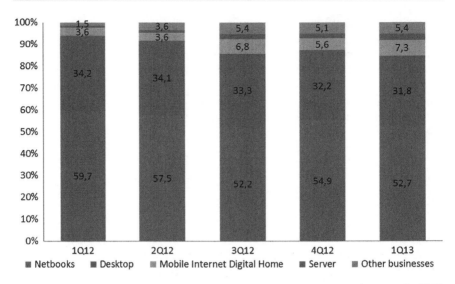

Fig. 4 Overview of products and its share in various quarters of a fiscal year (Based on Wu 2012)

Table 2 Lenovo Group 1Q FY3/13 June quarter results summary (Wu 2012)

Lenovo Group 1Q FY3/13 June quarter results summary
(US$ mn, unless otherwise stated)

	Actual	CS Est.	+/- (%)	Cons.	+/- (%)
Notebook revenues	4,333	4,619	-6.2		
Desktop revenues	2,545	2,327	9.4		
MIDH revenues	587	611	-3.9		
Other revenues	544	376	44.6		
Revenues	**8,010**	**7,934**	**1.0**	**8,124**	**-1.4**

2.9 Business Strategies

For Lenovo, it turned out that the best strategy was to take over companies that match their basic interests as well as extend their portfolio the best. In Fig. 5, we can see how Lenovo positions itself at the moment, bearing in mind that this is related to their global strategy and not narrowed down to product/price/promotion/or placement or even to single products.

We can see from Fig. 5 that Lenovo has achieved a relatively high market share in a competitive global market. In many aspects, Lenovo can be considered a star which has a strong market position. On the other hand, being in such a position requires a high investment in customer satisfaction and business development. The question that needs to be answered is how can Lenovo keep its position or make it sustainable, and even more importantly, how can Lenovo strengthen its position in Europe?

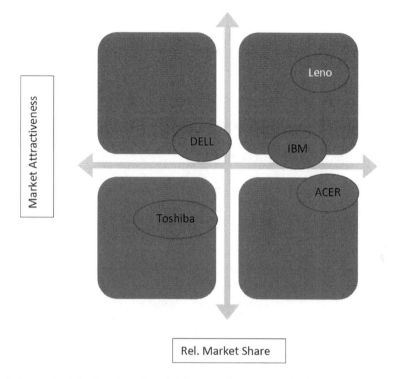

Fig. 5 Lenovo's strategic position in a global PC world (*Source*: author)

2.10 Quality and Innovation of the Product Range

The products of Lenovo are positioned in the middle and high end market. Lenovo produces products where end users can benefit from their use. Machines are well developed to meet customers' needs and wishes: easy to handle and up to the current standards. The price for a laptop is a bit higher than that of comparable ones from Dell, Acer or Toshiba, but the performance is much higher than competitors. The latest development in Thinkpad allows it to have a standalone position compared to other pads.

Just west of the Bird's Nest, that architectural jewel of the 2008 Summer Games in Beijing, lies an electronics district of Olympic proportions. It's called Zhongguancun, and if you need a computer or smartphone or camera or any other digital device when in China's capital, this is the place to go. Hundreds of mostly compact stores crowd the complex's dozen glass towers as tightly as commuters on the subway at rush hour. It's like a year-round Consumer Electronics Show, with every major brand, from Apple to HP to Dell to Sony. But one brand is nearly ubiquitous: Lenovo. The bigger Lenovo locations offer the gamut of products—laptops, desktops, netbooks, notebooks, tablets, smartphones—while the smaller ones cater to niches, such as small-business owners or young consumers. Outside the Zhongguancun towers, a Times Square-sized digital screen continually plays the company's ads. A third of the computers sold in the district are Lenovos, roughly approximating its market share in the whole of China, where it is by far the No. 1 seller of PCs. Its network of 15,000-plus stores reaches into the most remote of villages.

3 The Rise of the Company

3.1 Growth Development

For the past 2 years, Lenovo has been the fastest-growing company in the PC industry. In the third quarter of 2011, it sold a record 13.5 % of PCs worldwide, leapfrogging Dell and Acer to seize the No. 2 spot (only HP sells more). Dominating China has much to do with Lenovo's success; the rising "super economy" became the world's largest PC market this year.

CEO Yang calls Lenovo's strategy "protect and attack," two words you hear repeatedly at the company's headquarters in Beijing and its offices in Raleigh, North Carolina, where Yang spends a third of his time. Lenovo seeks to protect its core business—the Chinese and enterprise (large-scale commercial and public-sector) markets, which generated about 70 % of its $21 billion in revenue last year. On the attack side, he's pumping Lenovo's profits—$273 million in 2010—into emerging markets, new product categories (tablets, smartphones, smart TVs), and, of course, the U.S.

In Figs. 6 and 7, we see the market developments with Lenovo and without Lenovo. It becomes very obvious that Lenovo has a huge impact on market developments in China and around the world.

It is interesting to see how the company's development has influenced China's market development.

3.2 Becoming a Brand?

To own a brand is not difficult, but to establish a brand is very difficult, and to build a brand with worldwide influence is even more difficult. With the acceleration of economic integration, today's world has entered a competitive era of brand internationalization. To an enterprise, a brand does not merely reflect the product itself, but is more a comprehensive embodiment of the enterprise's culture, influence and social value. On Dec. 8, 2004, Lenovo Group officially announced in Beijing that it had completed its acquisition of IBM's PC-making business for 1.25 billion US$, and taken ownership of the gold-lettered signboard "Think", IBM's long-time established trademark. As a leading enterprise in China's IT field, did Lenovo encounter any problems in the course of its brand management? If so, how did it solve these problems if there were any? These issues will be discussed in the following sections.

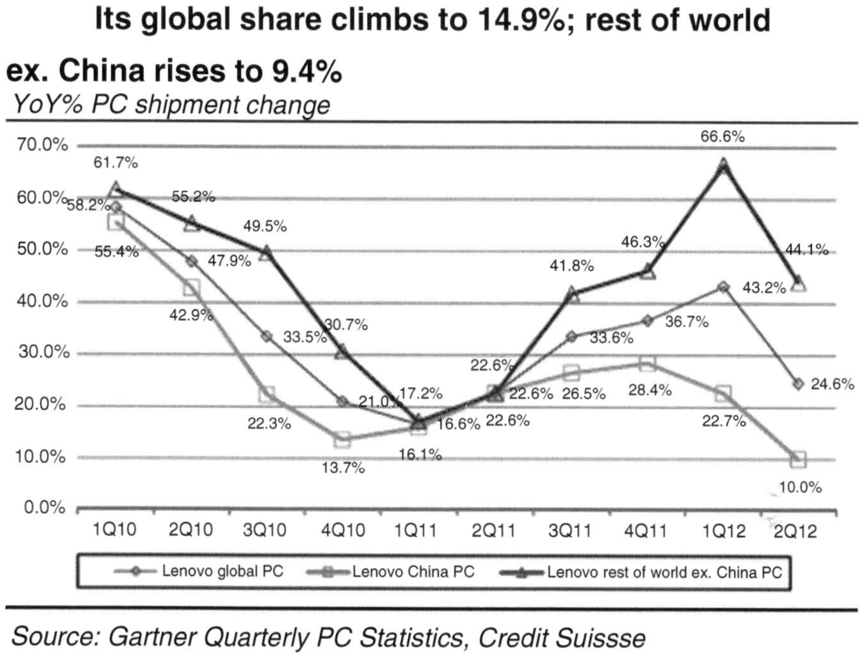

Its global share climbs to 14.9%; rest of world ex. China rises to 9.4%

YoY% PC shipment change

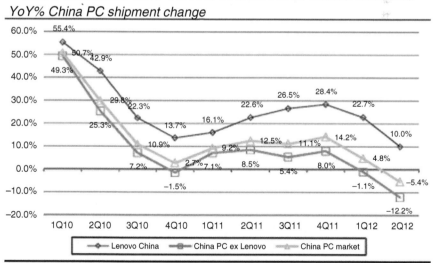

Source: Gartner Quarterly PC Statistics, Credit Suissse

Fig. 6 Lenovo's market development globally, in China, and the rest of the world (Wu 2012)

Without Lenovo, the overall China market would have declined 12% YoY. It drives rural China demand

YoY% China PC shipment change

Source: Gartner Quarterly PC Statistics, Credit Suissse

Fig. 7 Lenovo market development in China, and China market development without Lenovo (Wu 2012)

3.3 The "Four-in-One" Brand Promotion Strategy

Lenovo has relatively sound brand architecture with its sub-brands reaching every level of the market. To be specific, "Lenovo" is the master brand name for Lenovo's products, and under it there are some sub-brands. These sub-brands boast technological highlights or service features, and are developed for a specific consumer group. Meanwhile, Lenovo conducts or participates in a series of activities to strengthen the marketing promotion for its sub-brands. For example, among its desktop sub-brands, "Yangtian", which is targeted at small and medium-sized enterprises, has the function of one-touch restoration and flash scanning of viruses. To publicize these highlights, Lenovo launched a campaign named "Lenovo Yangtian Science and Technology Olympics Express". For the "Fengxing" series designed for computer game players, Lenovo sponsored the International Electronic Sports Tournament. For family users, Lenovo has the "Plan for Family Enjoyment and Dream Realization". For Chinese rural consumers, it has a "Heavenly Pleasure Strategy for a New Countryside". In this way, a solid chain of support is established for the building of its brands.

In the international market, the promotion of Lenovo's brands is mainly focused on the sports field. For example, in 2004, Lenovo signed up as the top sponsor of the 2008 Beijing Olympic Games; in October 2006, Lenovo announced its "Yangtian Tomorrow Superstars Plan", the first plan related to NBA, immediately after it became the top global official PC partner of NBA. In February 2007, Lenovo announced a top sponsorship agreement with the AT&T Williams team competing in the Formula One World Championship. When asked about whether Lenovo would use sports marketing as a way to promote its brands in the international market, Mr. Yan said, "Lenovo has no mature pattern for international market promotion due to such limits as market share and development time. Now we do international market promotion by modeling on the Chinese pattern." (Lenovo 2014)

4 Future Developments

Recently, when Lenovo bought Motorola Mobility from Google, the company announced its plan to become a profitable phone maker without eliminating jobs. That is a strong statement because the investment of the deal was so big that Lenovo announced a 1 Billion US$-a year-loss saying that they were not concerned about it. Regardless of the investment, Lenovo enters another competitive market with the enthusiasm of management and employees who are proud of being better in manufacturing devices than competitors.

4.1 Current Competitors and the Future

The purchase of Motorola and IBM's low-end server business is planned to move Lenovo beyond the shrinking personal computer market to become a broader technology company. Mr. Yang said: "If we only focus on PCs, one to 2 years later we cannot further grow. So we must find a new area, so we can help our shareholders make more money, and see more growth. So I think our choice is the right choice" (SCMP 2014). Furthermore, Yang said: "Improved profitability will come from increased production and sales as the company targets emerging markets. The company will also seek to reduce costs from internal communication and computing services. Motorola's gross margins are already pretty decent" (SCMP 2014).

Looking at current competitors (Wu 2012), we can observe different developments. Lenovo is mainly competing with HP and Acer in the notebook and desktop sector. In the MIDH business (smartphones, tablets, TV business, handset), Lenovo can be considered as a novice fighting for market shares around established companies like Google, Samsung, Motorola etc. The first step in the specific market (based on mergers and acquisitions) brought Lenovo a 173 % increase in sales (Wu 2012). Therefore, new business units shed new lights on profitability for the American Business as well as for the European Business due to the re-organization of four big geographical areas: China, Asia-Pacific/Latin America, North America and Europe-Middle/East Africa. The purpose behind the re-organization is to become stronger, faster, and more focused. One of the countries in Europe-Middle could be the Netherlands. The Dutch market is less segmented than in other European countries which is a great opportunity for Lenovo with its excellent working supply chain management. Lenovo has a strong position in PC's and in so-called Hardcopy Peripherals (Kamann et al. 2012) around the world as we can see in Fig. 8.

Vendor	2Q 2011 Shipments	2Q 2011 Market Share	2Q 2010 Shipments	2Q 2010 Market Share	2Q 2011/2Q 2010 Growth
HP	15,263	18.1%	14,823	18.0%	3.0%
Dell	10,927	12.9%	10,626	12.9%	2.8%
Lenovo	10,276	12.2%	8,363	10.2%	22.9%
Acer Group	9,160	10.9%	10,190	12.4%	-10.1%
ASUS	4,468	5.3%	4,216	5.1%	6.0%
Others	34,320	40.7%	34,070	41.4%	0.7%
Total	84,413	100%	82,289	100%	2.6%

Figure 15: Hardcopy Peripherals Market Share and Growth Rates, 2Q 2010

Source – http://www.idc.com/getdoc.jsp?containerId=prUS22988111

Fig. 8 Hardcopy Peripherals Market Share and Growth Rates (Kamann et al. 2012)

Table 3 Western Europe—PC vendor unit shipment estimates for 2Q13 (thousands of units) (Gartner 2013)

Vendor	2Q13 shipments	2Q13 market share (%)	2Q12 shipments	2Q12 market share (%)	2Q12–2Q13 growth (%)
HP	2,280	20.8	2,76	20.2	−17.40
Acer	1,305	11.9	2,362	17.3	−44.70
Lenovo	1,258	11.5	1,058	7.8	18.90
Dell	1,172	10.7	1,185	8.7	−1.10
Asus	850	7.8	1,458	10.7	−41.70
Others	4,077	37.3	4,82	35.3	−15.40
Total	10,942	100.0	13,643	100.0	−19.80

If we look at recent developments in shipments and shares, Lenovo is number 3 in the concert of world champions in the IT sector after HP, Acer, etc. Lenovo is the only company that increased sales and shares compared to the other companies, as we can see in Table 3.

5 Conclusions

5.1 Why Did the Company Become So Successful?

Our aim was to examine the development of the Chinese IT company Lenovo and how they position themselves in the European market. Lenovo's strengths are the high quality of electronic devices, ease of use, and selling the devices for an acceptable and fair price. The supply chain of Lenovo is very strong and effective as well as efficient.

5.2 Is It Likely that the Company Will Become a World Brand?

Drawing conclusions from what we have found so far, we can summarize that Lenovo and its specific product segments can become a world brand. On the other hand, the increase in sales and market shares was achieved by mergers and acquisitions which are limited by nature. So, it might be a challenge for Lenovo, when the time is ripe, to further develop their business with their own resources.

References

Ahrens, N., & Zhou, Y. (2013). *Chinas Competitiveness. Myths, Reality and Lessons for the United States and Japan.* Case Study: Lenovo, CSIS, Center for Strategic & International studies; Washington.

Fastcompany. (2014). *Fastcompany.* Retrieved February 2014, from http://infographic.fastcompany.com.

Gartner. (2013). *Press Release*. Retrieved March 12, 2014, from http://www.gartner.com/newsroom/id/2570220.

Handelsblatt. (2014). Retrieved January 31, 2014, from http://www.handelsblatt.de.

Kamann, G., Gkill, N., Sen, A. (2012). *The changing dynamics of the global high tech industry.* An analysis of key segments and trends. Retrieved February 2014, from http://www.capgemini.com.

Lenovo. (2014). *Lenovo official website*. Retrieved January 20, 2014, from www.lenovo.com.

Peoples daily-online. (2014). Retrieved February 15, 2014, from http://english.peopledaily.com.cn/.

Recode. (2014). *Lenovo dominated worst-ever world PC market in 2013*. Retrieved January 9, 2014, from https://recode.net/2014/01/09/lenovo-dominated-worst-ever-world-pc-market-in-2013/.

Reuters. (2014). Retrieved February 15, 2014, from http://www. http://de.reuters.com/news/world.

SCMP. (2014). *Business in China*. Retrieved March 3, 2014, from http://www.scmp.com/business/china-business/article/1435357/lenovo-chief-executive-pledges-end-losses-motorola-mobility.

Wang, W., Chu, Y., & Ching, K. (2009). *The strategic marketing management analysis of Lenovo group*. Retrieved February 12, 2014, from http://www.jgbm.org/page/.pdf.

Wu, T. (2012). *Credit Suisse securities research & analytics*. Lenovo Group. Retrieved February 20, 2014, from https://www.credit-suisse.com/global/en/.

Tencent: A Case Study on Expanding Through Micro-Innovation and Strategic Partnerships

Filip Vedder

Abstract Tencent is a Chinese IT company that offers a wide variety of products in the e-commerce, online advertising, online games and social network markets. Most of these services are centered around the central hubs of QQ and Weixin/WeChat. This allows for a spillover of users and a brand name that can be used for a variety of products. Most of Tencent's software products are free to use, but allow users to buy small cosmetic upgrades. For Tencent, these value-added services are the main source of income. This differentiates the company from most of its competitors, which still rely mostly on online advertisements to monetize users of free services. Tencent focuses on 'micro-innovation', taking a proven concept and adjusting it to the Chinese market. The company is very strong in the domestic market, but has had trouble in foreign markets. More recently, Tencent started strategic partnerships with companies in segments where the company cannot become market leader on its own. Perhaps the company could also use this strategy for foreign market entry.

1 Introduction

Since the introduction of the World Wide Web in China in 1994, the user base has grown exponentially. By 2008, there were 253 million internet users in China, making it the largest internet market in the world (Zhang 2008). During the last survey of the China Internet Network Information Center in July 2013, this count was up to 591 million (CNNIC 2013). It will come as no surprise then, that there is a lot of money to be made in this market by companies who know how to approach

F. Vedder (✉)
International Business School, Hanze University OAS, Groningen, The Netherlands
e-mail: filip.vedder@gmail.com

it. Chinese internet-based companies, such as Baidu, Alibaba, and Tencent, have grown quickly and their founders have become billionaires.

Like many of its Western counterparts, Tencent started as a small company founded by a few friends and with little money. Since then, it has grown to become one of the largest internet companies worldwide, and has a revenue that is higher than Western giants such as Facebook. The company offers a variety of services to its customers, mostly centered on their hub of qq.com. Services include instant messaging programs, social networks, online video games and e-commerce, both on PC and mobile platforms. The instant messaging program QQ was at the start of Tencent's success and is the largest such service in China. At the end of 2013, Tencent's instant messaging services had 808 million monthly active accounts and their WhatsApp-like Weixin and WeChat protocols had a combined monthly active user count of 355 million (Tencent 2014e). Unlike most of Tencent's competitors, the company does not monetize this enormous user base with online advertising. Instead, the company concentrates on 'value-added services', small cosmetic features that a user can buy for a small fee. It is hard to find a Chinese PC that does not contain a product from Tencent, and the company is also growing in the mobile market.

So far, Tencent has gotten the vast majority of its revenue from the Chinese market. The company is, however, also looking to expand into various international markets. It already opened offices in South Korea and the USA. Tencent has also invested in a variety of companies in countries such as the USA, South Korea, Thailand, and India. While Tencent has yet to get a firm foothold in any market outside of the domestic one, the company is not planning on giving up anytime soon. One of its long-term goals is to make their services popular in select foreign markets. In this analysis, we will examine Tencent's profile, rise, and expected developments.

2 Company Profile

2.1 History

Tencent was founded in November of 1998 by Huateng Ma (or Pony Ma, as he likes to call himself in English) in Shenzen, Guangdong, China. Originally the company was called OICQ and it developed an instant messenger service of the same name aimed specifically at the Chinese market. The motivation was the deal of AOL, who bought the Israeli developed instant messenger ICQ for 407 million US$ earlier in 1998 (Businessweek 2011). The instant messenger, renamed QQ after complaints by AOL, would quickly grow to become the most popular Chinese instant messenger system. After the launch of QQ, the company (by then renamed Tencent) would diversify its business while still staying focused on the internet market. Between 1999 and 2006, Tencent launched, amongst other things, mobile and telecommunication value-added services, internet value-added services, web portals, casual (computer) games, a social networking service, and an online payment platform

Fig. 1 Substantial shareholders of Tencent as of Q1, 2014 (Tencent 2014a)

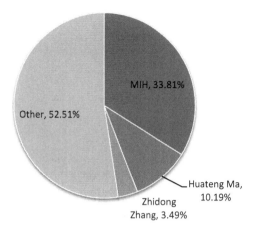

(Tencent 2014a). Initially, it was hard for the company to find investors. These problems seemed solved when, in 2001, MIH, a holding company connected to South African media group Naspers, paid 32 million US$ for a 47 % share in Tencent (Businessweek 2011). MIH has stayed a major shareholder until this day, with 33.81 % of the shares by early 2014. Other major shareholders are Huanteng Ma himself (10.19 %) and Tencent co-founder Zhidong Zhang (3.49 %) (Fig. 1). In June of 2004, Tencent would be listed on the Hong Kong stock Exchange and in June of 2008, the company also became a constituent of the Hong Kong's Hang Seng Index (Tencent 2014a).

2.2 The Founders

The main founder of Tencent is Huateng Ma. Forbes lists him as the fifth richest Chinese citizen (Forbes 2014a). Ma is a native of Chaoyang, in Guangdong. He graduated from Shenzhen University with a bachelor degree in computer science in 1993 (Sun and Quan 2009). Afterwards he started working for China Motion, a telecommunications company. In 1996, he was send to the US by this company, for training at a telecom equipment company in Melbourne. This was where he first discovered the possibilities of the web (Businessweek 2011). Compared to some other Chinese internet billionaires, Ma chooses to keep a relatively low profile. He dislikes public speaking and does not talk with the press often. Internally at Tencent, however, Ma is known as a perfectionist and micromanager (Businessweek 2011). Currently, he is Executive Chairman of the Board and Chief Executive Officer at Tencent.

Tencent cofounder Zhidong Zhang stays away from publicity even more so than Ma. He also, is listed on the Forbes list of richest Chinese, at place 25 (Forbes 2014a). Zhang holds a bachelor degree in computer science from Shenzhen University and a master degree in computer application and system structure from the South China University of Technology. Before he founded Tencent together with

Ma, he worked at the Li Ming Network Group. On March 18, 2014, Tencent announced that Zhang would resign from his position at the board of directors immediately and from his position as chief technology officer after September 20 for "personal reasons" (Forbes 2014b). He will, however, stay connected with the company in an advisory role.

2.3 Employees

As of the end of 2013, Tencent had almost 27,000 employees (Google finance 2014). According to the company, more than 50 % of these employees are R&D staff (Tencent 2014b). Most of Tencent's employees work in China, but Tencent also has offices in South Korea and in the USA. Both of these foreign offices are relatively small though. The South Korean office now employs a little over 20 people, and the office in the USA is "small and nimble" according to Tencent (Tencent Careers 2014). Not much else is disclosed by the company, but their official website offers some insight in the corporate culture of the company. Since Tencent is a leading internet company with a huge R&D department, it would seem reasonable that its employees are mostly highly educated with backgrounds in fields such as computer science.

In recent years, Tencent tried to achieve a more positive and open image. Their vision is to be "the most respected internet company" and one of the ways to achieve this is to "earn the respect of employees by continuously improving our corporate reputation so that Tencent is a company employees are proud to work for". At the same time, Tencent stresses the importance of integrity (going as far as having a separate page for "whistleblowers" on their official site) and innovation (Tencent 2014c). It seems that most of these points are responses to several controversies that have hurt the company's image. We will discuss these controversies further on in this analysis.

2.4 Product Range

Tencent has a very wide product range (Fig. 2). After the launch of the QQ instant messenger, Tencent started mobile and telecommunication value-added services, internet value-added services, the mini casual games portal QQ game, the webportal qq.com, several (casual) games, the multimedia networking service QZone, the C2C (consumer-to-consumer) platform paipai.com, the online payment platform Tenpay, the mobile instant messenger Weixin, the video portal v.qq.com, the e-commerce platform buy.qq.com, and mobile game centers. It developed a search engine (SoSo) and several video games in-house (both casual games and massively multiplayer online games), but also outsources some of the development work. Most of these development companies are South Korean, but Tencent also invested in the American game developers Riot Games and Epic Games. Tencent also offers e-commerce services. The products were traditionally aimed at the PC

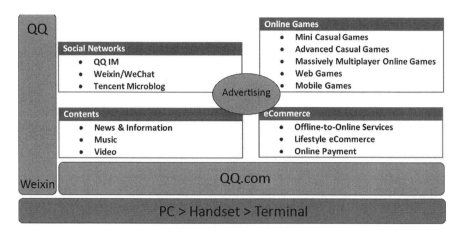

Fig. 2 Tencent's product range (Based on Tencent 2014d)

market, but nowadays Tencent is also very active on the mobile market. Aside from offering the mentioned products, Tencent has invested in many companies and products, including internet companies active on the Chinese, Russian, and Thai markets (Tencent 2014d).

According to the investor factsheet, Tencent "uses technology to enrich the lives of internet users". Apparently, Tencent has been very successful in this ambition, since its products are very popular on the Chinese market. By March 2010, the QQ instant messenger service had reached the milestone of having 100 million user accounts online simultaneously. The Weixin/WeChat messenger had over 300 million registered users in January 2013 and qq.com has been one of the most popular web portals in China since 2006 (Tencent 2014a). As of April 2014, qq.com is the second most visited website in China, according to Alexa. Globally, it ranks seventh (Alexa 2014).

2.5 Revenues

The revenue of Tencent can be broken down into four categories: e-commerce transactions, online advertising, online games, and social networks. Over the past two years, revenue on all these categories has increased, but there has also been a remarkable change in its composition. The revenue from online games is still the biggest, but revenue from e-commerce transactions has increased from 8 % of the total in Q1 of 2012 to 20 % of the total by Q4 2013. In the same period, the percentage of social networks decreased from 29 % to 20 % and that of online games from 57 % to 50 %. The fourth category, online advertising, slightly increased from 6 % to 9 %.

The low percentage of online advertising in Tencent's revenue breakdown is remarkable. Most internet companies rely on advertising for the vast majority of

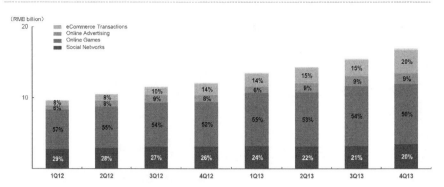

Fig. 3 Tencent's revenue breakdown (Tencent 2014a)

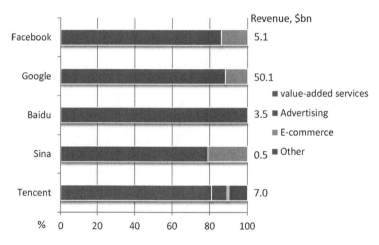

Fig. 4 Internet firms' revenue by source, 2012, % of total (Based on Economist 2013)

their revenue (see Fig. 4). Tencent makes most of its money by value-added services, such as micro transactions in their computer games and social networks. The value-added services revenue is the total of the online games and social networks categories of Fig. 3. The value-added services strategy has been instrumental in Tencent's rise. While Tencent is active overseas (such as with the popular American online game League of Legends), most of its revenue still comes from the home market in China. As can be seen in Fig. 4, Tencent's revenue is higher than that of Facebook. The company's shareholder total return was even the highest of any large firm from 2008 to 2012 (Economist 2013).

2.6 Business (Success) Strategies

The business strategy of Tencent has been highly controversial. Originally the company seemed to mostly copy proven products from competitors and optimize them for the Chinese market. The QQ messenger, the development of which lead to the founding of Tencent, used to be called OICQ and was a copy of the (at that time) popular ICQ messenger. Other companies criticized Tencent for its practices, including Sohu.com's Charles Zhang: "Tencent is a copycat. It's a company that doesn't create anything." Tencent itself calls it "micro-innovation", adding small details to a product and localizing it (Businessweek 2011).

In 2011, Tencent started their "open platform strategy" as a response to criticism of their restricted platforms. It should allow easier access to Tencent platforms for third parties. This, together with the "corporate culture" pointers, are examples of how Tencent tries to improve its public image.

The other part of Tencent's strategy is focusing on making revenue from value-added services instead of from advertising. The company offers its products, such as games or messenger software for free, but for a small fee users can buy extras to improve their experience. In the case of games, this can be clothing or weapons, and in their messenger software or social networks, it could be customized avatars and other cosmetic features. Most of Tencent's competitors also offer their products to users for free, but try to monetize them with advertisements. So far, Tencent's business model has worked very well for the company and there are no signs of change, even though the share of e-commerce related revenue is increasing.

While Tencent has invested in many foreign markets, the company has trouble getting footholds. This is an effect of Tencent's overall business strategy: localizing proven concepts for the Chinese market. The company understands the Chinese market well, but doesn't manage to provide competitive products for the international market. The international investments are also not always meant to enter those markets. For example, the main objective of the investment in US developer Riot Games was to localize their online game League of Legends for the Chinese market, not to get a foothold in the US market (Businessweek 2011). Tencent does not want to give up on the international market just yet though. According to the outlook and strategies for 2014 of the Tencent 2013 annual results, the company states that it will "continue investing heavily in certain long-term projects we deem strategic, including, [...] marketing and popularizing our WeChat service in selected international markets" (Tencent 2014e).

2.7 Quality and Innovation of Product Range

As mentioned before, Tencent is not known for innovation, despite its huge R&D facilities. But because Tencent runs with what works, its products are of high quality, as is evidenced by their popularity in China. The company also continues to invest in other companies and has started strategic partnerships with various parties in order to improve products. An example would be the strategic partnership with Sogou, a company that specializes in search engines. Tencent wants to merge their own search engine SoSo with this company (Economist 2013). Basically, Tencent either buys or copies quality. But the company also has the ambition to keep developing products by themselves. In their annual report for 2013, Tencent mentioned an interest in developing O2O (Online-to-Offline) services, a relatively new business model that seeks to combine online shopping with front line transactions (ChinaAbout 2013). Whether this development will be done through innovation or "micro-innovation" remains to be seen.

3 The Rise of the Company

3.1 Growth Development

Tencent, both as a company and in the amount of users of its products, has grown tremendously since its founding. The company was unprofitable until 2000 but has seen a steady increase in assets, revenue, and net profit since then (Tencent 2010) (Fig. 5).

The financial crisis of 2008 had no visible impact on Tencent's development, which has been growing steadily, probably because of its focus on the Chinese internet market. The total assets and total revenue show an exponential growth, while the net profit rises more evenly.

During the first 11 years of its existence, Tencent mostly launched new products and services, but since 2010 the company has increased its amount of investments in other companies, both in China and abroad. This shows how the company has not only grown financially, but also in its strategies. In November 2013, Moody's changed Tencent's outlook from stable to positive, stating the progress of the

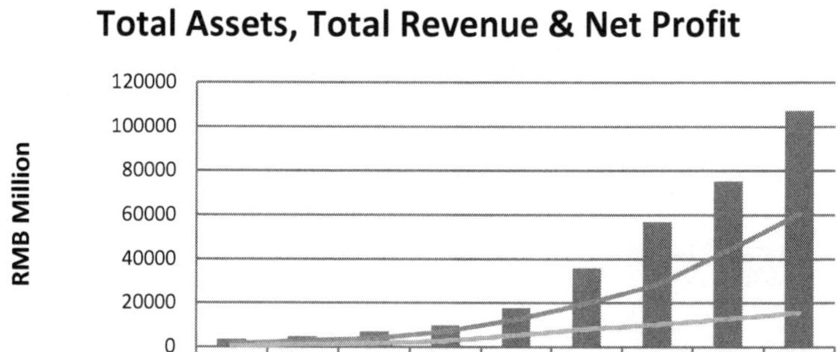

Total Assets, Total Revenue & Net Profit

RMB Million	2005	2006	2007	2008	2009	2010	2011	2012	2013
Total Assets	3427	4651	6925	9856	17506	35830	56804	75256	107235
Total revenue	1426	2800	3821	7155	12440	19646	28496	43893	60437
Net profit	485	1064	1568	2816	5222	8115	10225	12785	15563

Fig. 5 Tencent total assets, total revenue and net profit 2005–2013 in RMB million (Tencent 2014f)

"Open Platform" strategy as one of the reasons. The rating bureau praises Tencent for its ability to keep a healthy balance sheet, despite the expansion of its business scope (Moody's 2013). In June of the same year, Standard & Poor's upgraded the long-term corporate credit rating from BBB+ to A– "to reflect the company's stronger competitive position and improved financial strength. A strong growth in business scale, an expanding user base, and improving service diversity underpin the improvement in Tencent's competitive position" (S&P 2013).

In conclusion, it can be observed that Tencent's growth is based on an ever-expanding business and diversification of services in a growing market. Originally, this was achieved with products developed by Tencent itself. In later years, the company started investing in other companies to expand its business, and allowed access to its platforms to third parties. This has resulted in a steady growth of the company and financial stability.

3.2 Becoming a Brand?

While the name Tencent is well known in China, the company's strongest brand is without a doubt QQ. QQ has grown to become much more than just an instant message service. Most of Tencent's PC-based services are built around qq.com, the company's web portal. For instance, Tencent's video portal can be accessed through v.qq.com, while the open e-commerce platform is accessed via buy.qq.com. The company considers QQ to be its flagship service and has been working to change it from a PC-centered service to a primary smartphone experience, showing how important the brand still is for Tencent (Tencent 2014e).

Internationally, Tencent chooses a different approach. QQ can hardly be called an international brand, and apparently Tencent does not try to make it one. A successful international product of Tencent is WeChat, the international version of its mobile instant messenger Weixin. Tencent is trying to push WeChat as a brand with a big marketing campaign. In 2013, the company started a world-wide ad campaign featuring the famous football player Lionel Messi. It also partnered with other brands by offering relationships. According to VALUE2020, the app has been mostly successful in Asia, but there is a growing user base on basically all continents. The local marketing is only aimed at Asia for the moment, but the app also increased its user base on the other continents (VALUE2020 2013). Still, WeChat is far from an international house-hold brand. There remains work to be done in this field for Tencent. The company realizes this and states that WeChat international expansion is one of their key objectives in order to expand their position on the mobile market (Tencent 2014e).

With QQ at home and WeChat abroad, Tencent has potentially two strong brands. Where QQ was built up slowly, by integrating more services under the same name, Tencent seems to choose a more aggressive approach , with the intention of creating a multi-functional platform out of the brand, with WeChat. So far, however, WeChat is only one product and the name of Tencent is not necessarily associated with it. It remains to be seen how far WeChat, both as a product and a brand, will grow.

3.3 Position in the Home Market

Because Tencent's services and products are so diverse, it is hard to compare the company to others in terms of overall market share. Therefore, we will concentrate on what Tencent itself identifies as its three main streams of revenue: online advertising, e-commerce transactions, and value-added services.

Online advertisement has traditionally been the most important way to monetize in the internet industry. As we have seen before, Tencent chooses a different approach (see Fig. 4). It still considers online advertising as one of its main revenue streams though, and is the fourth largest in this field in China with a market share of 5.2 % in Q3 2013. The top three at that moment were Baidu (30.8 %), Alibaba (15.9 %) and Google China (5.5 %) (China Internet Watch 2013). While a share of 5.2 % is not much compared to the two leading companies in this field, it is still quite high considering the limited importance of the market for Tencent's total revenue. Compare this to Google China's 5.5 % as a company for which online advertising is very important. In this sense, Tencent performs quite well.

The e-commerce market can be divided in B2C (business-to-consumer) and C2C (consumer-to-consumer). Tencent is active in both segments. In the B2C segment, Tencent had a third place of 5.6 % after Alibaba's Tmall (50.6 %) and JD.com (17.1 %) in Q2 2013 (iResearch 2013) (Fig. 6). It should be noted that in March 2014, Tencent started a strategic partnership with JD.com in this field. JD.com will take on several of Tencents e-commerce activities (Reuters 2014a). In the C2C market, the field looks quite different. As of Q3 2012, this market is completely dominated by Alibaba owned Taobao (94.53 %). Tencent's paipai has a share of only 5.46 %. This share has, however, been growing (iResearch 2012).

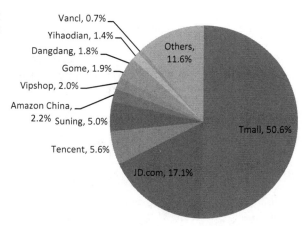

Fig. 6 Share of Chinese B2C websites by GMV in Q2 2013 (iResearch 2013)

In the market of value-added services, still the most important one for Tencent, the company is strong. Because of the growing importance of the mobile market, Tencent wants to concentrate in this area. It wants to achieve this by migrating the QQ service to mobile platforms and by enhancing the Weixin/WeChat app, which it claims is market leading (Tencent 2014e). To give an example of Tencents dominance in this field, in 2010, 73 % of all daily active social network services users in China were using Tencent products (Focke 2011).

Tencent is trying to strengthen its position in the domestic market by starting strategic partnerships with key companies who are active in diverse markets. By teaming up with these companies, Tencent hopes to increase its share. Examples are Sogou (search engine) and the aforementioned JD.com.

3.4 Position in the Global Market

Tencent has almost exclusively focused on the domestic market. After all, its expertise is optimizing products for the Chinese market. However, the company has increasingly tried to get a foothold in international markets. The company launched its QQ instant messenger for the international market on its English language portal imqq.com. It is marketed as being "the most popular personal communications app in history: over 1,000,000,000 registered users across 80+ countries" and cites its built-in translator as one of its main features. It is also connected to the social network QZone, although the international version can only be accessed through QQ and does not have all the features of the Chinese version. The amount of international user accounts should also be taken with a grain of salt, since the vast majority of these accounts are Chinese. In a 2011 interview, Tencent's CEO Ma remarks that the Japanese and American versions of QQ "weren't competitive and those markets were already dominated by big US companies" (Businessweek 2011). It seems that Tencent has met with more success in markets that are not as saturated. The Weixin/WeChat app has already been mentioned, which is very popular in Asia.

In online gaming, Tencent has also gone global. The American Tencent office developed social network games for Facebook under the name of Ice Break Games (but that name does not seem to be in use anymore). It acquired a majority share in US developer Riot Games in 2011 and a 40 % share in Epic Games, also from the USA, in 2012. According to Tencent, Riot Games' League of Legends increased the income from international markets and was important in sustaining growth in the company's online gaming activities during 2013 (Tencent 2014e). League of Legends is a good fit for Tencent, since it is a free to play game that is monetized by micro transactions, the same business model Tencent has used for its own online games. Still, when looking at the official annual results and outlooks of the past years, the company remains focused mainly on the Chinese market. There is word of "continue[ing] to explore opportunities in international markets" in the 2012 overview, but in 2013 the outlook for the next year only mentioned the internationalization of Weixin/WeChat.

When compared to other internet companies, Tencent is one of the biggest firms globally. According to Statista, Tencent ranked fourth world wide in 2013 in terms of market value, behind Ebay, Amazon, and Google, but in front of the likes of Facebook and Chinese competitor Baidu (Statista 2014). The other Chinese juggernaut, Alibaba, is missing in this list, because it is not a publicly listed company. Tencent is a huge company with a diverse portfolio of products that certainly have international potential. The company also wants to expand abroad, but does not seem sure yet with what long term strategy.

3.5 Triple Helix

Many Chinese companies have benefited from the triple helix system of government, business, and education. The Chinese internet industry as a whole has certainly benefited from the educational system and the government. The first internet users in China were mostly academics, and the first Chinese web pages were developed by a Chinese professor. The pioneers of commercial activities in this field were also mostly highly-educated academics, some of whom had experience in the USA (Zhang 2008). Does Tencent fit into this? Obviously Tencent's founders and most of its employees have been educated in China, and the Chinese government created a barrier of restrictions for foreign companies that is often complained about. However, Tencent's main strength is its knowledge of the Chinese market which is focused more on entertainment and mobile phones than most foreign companies realize (NY Times 2007).

In fact, Tencent has actually had a few incidents with the Chinese government. At the end of 2010, Tencent and Qihoo, a developer of security software, had a dispute that escalated enough that the Chinese minister of information technology called both companies immoral and irresponsible (Businessweek 2011). The strong regulation of the Chinese government might benefit Chinese companies in favor of foreign firms, but it can also work against a business. In March 2014, the People's Bank of China demanded that both Tencent and Alibaba halt their new virtual credit cards, which would allow users to make payments by scanning QR codes. While this is a temporary halt so that the People's Bank of China can examine the product and make sure it is safe, some say it is the result of growing tensions between traditional banking institutions and the new internet companies which are developing more e-commerce products (Reuters 2014b).

4 Future Developments

4.1 Future Challenges and Problems at Home

The main challenge for Tencent in the domestic market is that the amount of internet users in China is leveling off. Since Tencent's founding in 1998, the amount of Chinese internet users has grown exponentially, but in more recent years this growth is decreasing.

While the internet penetration rate is still only 46 % (in June 2013), the exponential growth seems to have stopped. This is mainly due to the large regional differences in China. The rural areas of China are still lagging behind in penetration rate compared to the urban areas. In June 2013, 72.1 % of the Chinese internet users were urban, while only 27.9 % were rural (CNNIC 2013). However, even with this stabilization, there is still a healthy growth in new internet users.

Another challenge, which Tencent is already addressing, is the shift of internet users from PC to mobile. As can be seen in Fig. 7, the amount of mobile internet users has grown very fast. The majority of Chinese internet users, 78.5 %, now access the internet using a mobile phone (CNNIC 2013). For the traditionally PC centered Tencent, this meant an important shift. The aforementioned migration of QQ from PC to mobile fits in this trend, as does the expansion surrounding the Weixin/WeChat app. In 2013, Tencent launched a game center for the mobile version of QQ, building on their strength and knowledge in the online gaming market to achieve better results in the mobile segment. However, in the 2013 annual report, the company remarks that "The weakness in our VAS subscription services continued in 2013. This was primarily due to rapid adoption of smart phones by users, whereas our paid subscription services are traditionally focused on PC or feature phones. [...] To better align our VAS subscription services with the mobile internet opportunities, we unified the product teams and product experiences between PC and smart phones, and introduced smart phone-oriented subscription

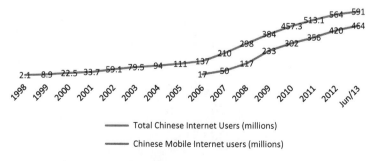

Fig. 7 Amount of Internet users in China 1998–2013 (June) (*Source*: author, data from NMG 2012; CIW 2013; CNNIC 2013)

services, such as Super VIP" (Tencent 2014e). Throughout the entire report it is clear that the company realizes the importance of the mobile market. One of the key points for the 2014 strategy is to "build a prosperous ecosystem for O2O and mobile eCommerce activities", showing the growing importance of both the mobile market and e-commerce for Tencent.

Because of Tencent's realization of and the shift to the mobile market and their strategic partnerships with key players in important Chinese market segments, the future of the company in the domestic market seems bright. It is well underway to solving the problems and challenges it faces at this moment and has managed to stay one of the biggest players in a still expanding market. The partnerships in segments such as search engines (Sogou) and e-commerce (JD.com) will allow the company to keep expanding in these markets, while also concentrating on its own core strength of VAS and online gaming.

4.2 Future Challenges and Problems Abroad

In the international market, Tencent seems to concentrate itself on the Asian market. This is wise for several reasons. In amount of users, for instance, the Asian internet market is by far the largest worldwide.

Almost half of all internet users are from Asia (see Fig. 8). Perhaps even more importantly, the penetration rate of some key Asian countries is still low and likely to grow. India, for instance, is already the third largest internet market (in terms of users) at this moment with 7 % (Fig. 9). The Indian penetration rate however, is only 16 % (Internet Live Stats 2014). With the growing prosperity of the country, there is a huge potential in this market. Of course, India itself also houses a lot of high tech companies, so a good knowledge of the market will be necessary to become successful. Already in 2008, Tencent launched a joint venture with its important share holder MIH to invest in Ibibo, an Indian online travel company.

While the European and (North) American internet markets are also very large and house a lot of wealthy customers, they are already quite saturated and therefore it is hard for companies that are new to these markets to get a foothold. Tencent's

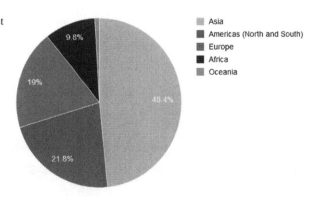

Fig. 8 Percentage of internet users per continent (June 2013) (Internet Live Stats 2014)

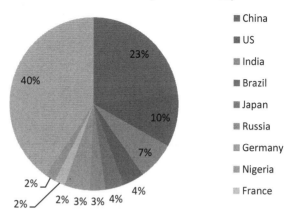

Fig. 9 Percentage of internet users per country (June 2013) (Internet Live Stats 2014)

launch of a US version of QQ was already mentioned. Tencent's main strength in its domestic market (the knowledge of that specific market), seems to have been a weak point in the US market, where the product was not competitive enough. The investment in US developer Riot Games seems to have been a good one, though, with the continuing popularity of its online League of Legends game, both in China and internationally. Perhaps the company should keep investing in these free online games with value-added services, since they remain popular worldwide. As the Riot Games investment, as well as those in various South Korean developers, show, the best course of action for Tencent here is to keep developing in-house for the Chinese markets, while also licensing internationally popular titles. The VAS segment is one that Tencent knows like no other, and which has had proven success in the international market.

Tencent is also expanding its Weixin/WeChat app internationally. This expansion is mostly concentrated on the Asian market, as we have seen before. In 2014 and beyond, the company wants to keep following this strategy (Tencent 2014e). Together with the broadening of WeChat into a brand that houses a lot of different services, this is a good way of entering the international (Asian) market in various segments which Tencent has already demonstrated domestic success. The partnerships with local companies do not only help Tencent with brand building, but can also yield valuable advice on the local markets in order to prevent the US QQ scenario. The first priority for Tencent, however, seems to lie on simply popularizing WeChat.

4.3 Competition

Since Tencent is active in so many segments of the internet market, they face competition from a wide variety of companies. There are, however, two main

Fig. 10 China's search engine market share in 2012 (China Internet Watch 2014a)

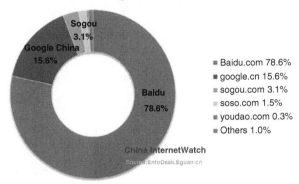

competitors on the Chinese market: Baidu and Alibaba. Both of these companies are big internet firms that offer a variety of services, often in direct competition with products and services of Tencent. In terms of market value, Tencent (74 billion US$) is bigger than Baidu (46 billion US$) (Statista 2014). Alibaba is a privately held company, but its worth is estimated between 55 billion US$ and 120 billion US$ (Economist 2014). So depending on the actual worth of Alibaba, Tencent would rank first or second. Baidu's main activity is its search engine. In 2012, it held a market share of 78.6 % in this field. During the same year, Tencent's SoSo had a share of 1.5 % while Sogou (who became a strategic partner of Tencent in September 2013) had 3.1 % (China Internet Watch 2014a) (Fig. 10). It will be hard for any single company to compete against such figures. Since the strategic partnership of Tencent and Sogou is very recent, it remains to be seen how it will impact the Chinese search engine market. However, we can see that Tencent's recent strategy to strengthen its weaker services is to team up with another competitor of the market leader. Baidu's other products include news services and one of the biggest Chinese online encyclopedias. It is also active in another core market of Tencent: e-commerce. Baidu's own e-commerce platform is called Youa, but it has been unable to compete with Alibaba's and Tencent's services. Therefore, it first bought a majority share of RenRen's Nuomi and then bought the site completely in early 2014 (Tech in Asia 2014). This move was most likely made in the hopes of catching up with Alibaba and Tencent in the important e-commerce market.

The other big Tencent competitor, Alibaba, is mainly active in the e-commerce business. We already analyzed how Alibaba's B2C service Tmall had a share of 50.6 %, while its C2C service Taobao had an enormous 94.53 % share. But the company is also a major player in B2B (business-to-business) e-commerce. In 2013, Alibaba had a share of 46.4 %, miles ahead of number two, Global Sources, with 8.2 % (China Internet Watch 2014b). Tencent bundled its powers with JD.com in March 2014 in order to compete more successfully against Alibaba in the B2C segment. In theory, in both this case and the Tencent-Sogou strategic partnership, this will allow the specialized JD.com to work with the support of the enormous Tencent. Again, because the partnerships are very recent, it will be hard to predict in what way it will allow Tencent to become more competitive compared to Baidu and Alibaba. But the potential is certainly there. Sogou and JD.com have the knowledge, and Tencent has many resources.

In the international market, Tencent faces competition from the big US internet companies such as Google and Facebook. Tencent has trouble reaching the Western market and Western companies have trouble reaching the Chinese market. Both are also trying to expand in the wider Asian market. This can mean both competition and also opportunities should Tencent choose to enter partnerships as it has done on the home market. It has already some experience with these sort of international relationships due to their majority share in Riot Games and minor share in Epic Games, both US companies.

5 Conclusions

5.1 Why Did This Company Become So Successful?

In its founding days, Tencent profited from the young and quickly growing Chinese internet market. It introduced new products made specifically for the Chinese market that would quickly become popular. Said products were not made through Tencent's own innovation, but by taking a proven idea from a (often Western) competitor and adjusting it so that it would be able to compete on the Chinese market. The company calls this "micro-innovation". Judging by the fact that the majority of Tencent's employees work in the R&D department, this is still an important strategy. This does not mean that Tencent is a shady company that can only copy competitors. The products of the company could not have been as successful as they were if this was the case. Tencent knows very well what (Chinese) users want and has built a very successful business model around this knowledge. The quick boom of mobile internet in China lead to some initial problems. By now, however, the company is well underway in its mobile services and has migrated many of its products from PC to smartphones.

Tencent also quickly started diversifying its products and services, while keeping them centered around the central hub of QQ. This allowed for a spillover of users and a brand name that could be used for a variety of products. Most of Tencent's software products are free to use, but allow users to buy small cosmetic upgrades. For Tencent, these value-added services are the main source of income. This differentiates the company from most of its competitors, who still rely mostly on online advertisements to monetize users of free services.

More recently, Tencent has started strategic partnerships with some of its competitors. These partnerships follow a similar pattern: in a certain market segment, the Tencent product has been unable to become the market leader. A partnership is made with another smaller competitor. This smaller competitor can now concentrate on this segment with the huge financial backings of Tencent. In this way, Tencent tries to create a bigger market share in segments such as search engines or e-commerce. Similar to this strategy is the strategy of select investments in other companies. For example, since Tencent makes a lot of its revenue from free to play online video games, it invested in some South Korean developers of said games, as well as in a US game developer.

5.2 Is It Likely This Company Will Become a World Brand?

In China, QQ is certainly a strong brand. While there is also an international version of QQ, Tencent has had trouble getting a share in foreign markets. It is a longstanding ambition of Tencent to also become a big player on the international market. Initially it tried to enter the highly saturated US and Japanese markets with localized versions of the QQ instant messenger. However, its products were simply unable to compete. The company has been more successful in the international market for online games. The Facebook games made by the US Tencent office under the name of Ice Break Games did well, and US developer Riot Games (who are now owned almost completely by Tencent) has a worldwide hit with their free to play game League of Legends. However, in both these cases, the name Tencent is not used, and in the case of Riot Games, the company is mostly allowed to do its own thing, without too much interference from Tencent. So, while these international investments seem to be profitable, they will not lead to building a worldwide brand out of the Tencent name.

After the initial failures in the US and Japanese markets, Tencent has chosen a different approach to its international expansion. The company now tries to expand through the international version of its Weixin smartphone instant messenger, WeChat. It started an international ad campaign featuring famous football player Lionel Messi and has a more specific strategy for some key national Asian markets. In these select markets, Tencent starts partnerships with local companies in order to build up their brand. These partners often have well-known brands themselves and in this way Tencent tries to build the WeChat brand by association.

If Tencent wants to build a truly international brand out of WeChat, it should learn from its own past. Regional preferences are vastly different on the internet market. Therefore, it will be necessary to build up partnerships with regional partners who know their home markets. In this way, Tencent can build products specifically for certain markets, just like it did in its own home market. While WeChat faces heavy competition from similar products like WhatsApp, there is certainly potential, especially if Tencent tries to turn WeChat into a sort of hub with diversified services, like it did with QQ. Again, cooperation with regional partners will be crucial for this.

References

Alexa. (2014). *QQ.com*. Retrieved April 4, 2014, from http://www.alexa.com/siteinfo/QQ.com.

Businessweek. (2011). Bruce Einhorn and Brad Stone, 'March of the pinguins'. *Bloomberg Businessweek* August 8, 2011. pp. 68–73.

China Internet Watch. (2013). *China online advertising platforms market update in Q3 2013*. Retrieved Oktober 25, 2013, from http://www.chinainternetwatch.com/4387/china-advertising-operators-market-update-q3-2013/ statistics originally from EnfoDesk.

China Internet Watch. (2014a). *Chinese search engine market: stats, trends and insights*. Retrieved April 16, 2014, from http://www.chinainternetwatch.com/category/search-engine/.

China Internet Watch. (2014b). *China B2B market overview for 2013*. Retrieved March 21, 2014, from http://www.chinainternetwatch.com/6769/china-b2b-market-overview-2013/.

ChinaAbout. (2013). *What is O2O stand for? What are the differences between O2O, B2C and C2C?* Retrieved April 4, 2014, from http://www.chinaabout.net/o2o-stand-for-differences-o2o-b2c-c2c/.

CIW. (2013). *China internet watch, 'China internet statistics whitepaper 2013'*. Retrieved April 13, 2014, from http://www.chinainternetwatch.com/whitepaper/china-internet-statistics/.

CNNIC. (2013). *China internet network information center, 'statistic report on internet development in China'*. Retrieved April 5, 2014, from http://www1.cnnic.cn/IDR/ReportDownloads/201310/P020131029430558704972.pdf.

Economist. (2013). 'Tencent's worth', *The Economist*, September 21, 2013. pp. 56–57.

Economist. (2014). *The Alibaba phenomenon*. Retrieved March 23, 2014, from http://www.economist.com/news/leaders/21573981-chinas-e-commerce-giant-could-generate-enormous-wealthprovided-countrys-rulers-leave-it.

Focke, A. (2011). *The amazing growth of Tencent*. Retrieved March 18, 2011, from http://blog.thegmic.com/2011/03/18/the-amazing-growth-of-tencent-2/51.

Forbes. (2014a). *China rich list*. Retrieved April 3, 2014, from http://www.forbes.com/china-billionaires/list/.

Forbes. (2014b). *Low-profile China internet billionaire Zhang Zhidong leaves Tencent's Board, CTO Job*. Retrieved April 3, 2014, from http://www.forbes.com/sites/russellflannery/2014/03/19/low-profile-china-internet-billionaire-zhang-zhidong-leaves-tencents-board-cto-job/.

Google finance. (2014). *Tencent profile*. Retrieved April 3, 2014 from, https://www.google.com/finance?cid=695431.

Internet Live Stats. (2014). *Number of internet users by region*. Retrieved April 13, 2014, from http://www.internetlivestats.com/internet-users/#byregion.

iResearch. (2012). *China online shopping GMV hits 284.22 Billion Yuan in Q3 2012 with decelerated growth*. Retrieved November 9, 2012, from http://www.iresearchchina.com/views/4534.html.

iResearch. (2013). *China online shopping grows 2.8-fold over RSCG in Q2 201*. Retrieved August 27, 2013, from http://www.iresearchchina.com/views/5123.html.

Moody's. (2013). *Rating action: Moody's changes outlook for Tencent to positive*. Retrieved November 6, 2013, from https://www.moodys.com/research/Moodys-changes-outlook-for-Tencent-to-positive--PR_286097#.

NMG. (2012). *Nanjing Marketing Group, 'Pretty Graphs on Chinese Internet User Demographics'*. Retrieved January 18, 2012, from http://www.nanjingmarketinggroup.com/blog/chinese-internet-users/pretty-graphs-chinese-internet-user-demographics-january-2012.

NY Times. (2007). *New York Times*, 'Internet Boom in China Is Built on Virtual Fun', February 5, 2007.

Reuters. (2014a). *Tencent-JD.com partnership goes straight for Alibaba's throat*. Retrieved March 10, 2014, from http://www.reuters.com/article/2014/03/10/us-jd-tencent-hldg-idUSBREA2902T20140310.

Reuters. (2014b). *China's central bank halts Tencent, Alibaba mobile payment process*. Retrieved March 14, 2014, from http://www.reuters.com/article/2014/03/14/china-centralbank-tencent-alibaba-paymen-idUSL3N0MB1D220140314.

S&P. (2013). *Standard & Poor's, 'Tencent Holdings upgraded to 'A-' and 'cnAA' on improved competitive position and financial strength*. Retrieved June 24, 2013, from http://www.standardandpoors.com/prot/ratings/articles/en/ap/?articleType=HTML&assetID=1245353601777.

Statista. (2014). *Market value of the largest internet companies worldwide as of May 2013 (in billion U.S. dollars)*. Retrieved April 9, 2014, from http://www.statista.com/statistics/277483/market-value-of-the-largest-internet-companies-worldwide/, 15:25.

Sun, S. L., & Quan, M. J. (2009). 'Ma, Huateng', from Wenxian Zhang and Ilan Alon, *Bibliographical Dictionary of New Chinese Entrepreneurs and Business Leaders* Edwar Elgar Publishing:Cheltenham and Northampton, pp. 111–112.

Tech in Asia. (2014). *Baidu acquires remaining stake in Renren's daily deals site*. Retrieved January 24, 2014, from http://www.techinasia.com/baidu-buys-remaining-nuomi-stake-from-renren/.

Tencent. (2010). *Tencent roadmap*. Retrieved April 7, 2014, from http://www.tencent.com/en-us/at/roadmap.shtml.

Tencent. (2014a). *Tencent investor fact sheet*. Retrieved March 31, 2014, from http://www.tencent.com/en-us/content/ir/fs/attachments/investorintro.pdf.

Tencent. (2014b). *About Tencent*. Retrieved March 31, 2014, from http://www.tencent.com/en-us/at/abouttencent.shtml.

Tencent. (2014c). *Corporate culture*. Retrieved April 4, 2014, from http://www.tencent.com/en-us/cc/culture.shtml.

Tencent. (2014d). *Tencent investor presentation*. Retrieved April 4, 2014, from http://www.tencent.com/en-us/content/ir/fs/attachments/InvestorPresentation.pdf.

Tencent. (2014e). *Tencent announces 2013 fourth quarter and annual results*. Retrieved April 2, 2014, from http://www.tencent.com/en-us/content/ir/news/2014/attachments/20140319.pdf.

Tencent. (2014f). *Tencent annual results 2005–2013*. Retrieved April 2, 2014, from http://www.tencent.com/en-us/ir/news/2014.shtml.

Tencent Careers. (2014). *Careers at Tencent Worldwide*. Retrieved April 4, 2014, from http://careers.tencent.com/global/.

VALUE2020. (2013). *First world map of WeChat userbase*. Retrieved January 10, 2013, from http://value2020.wordpress.com/2013/01/10/first-world-map-of-wechat-user-base/.

Zhang, J. (2008). China's dynamic industrial sector: The internet industry. *Eurasian Geography and Economics, 49*(5), 549–568.

Part II
India

Dr. Reddy's: A Case Study on Conquering the World with Affordable Medicine for the Masses

Maximilian Egender and Irina Rotari

Abstract

Dr. Reddy's Ltd. has become a global player within the American, Asian and European pharmaceutical markets over the last 30 years, having started as a small pharmaceutical ingredients supplier in 1984. This success was due to three key factors: a strong corporate governance, long term thinking and innovativeness, and control of the entire value chain. The advantage gained through R&D will be the main driving factor for the company to increase its market share within the next few years and to develop new long-term strategies. Company acquisitions and local production in key markets such as Europe, Russia, and emerging markets enhance the supply chain by being continuously able to strengthen and expand to new pharmaceutical markets in a growing number of countries. Good relations with governments, the willingness and understanding to open up foreign manufacturing plants, and not only importing products but strengthening different countries' economies, make Dr. Reddy's a reputable company which will show much more of its potential within the next years.

1 Introduction

Dr. Reddy's Laboratories Ltd. is a pharmaceutical company based in Hyderabad, Andhra Pradesh, India. The company was founded by Anji Reddy. Dr. Reddy's manufactures and markets a wide range of pharmaceuticals in India and overseas. The products of the company include over 190 medications, 60 APIs (active pharmaceutical ingredients) for drug manufacture, diagnostic kits, and critical care and biotechnology products.

M. Egender (✉) • I. Rotari
The Honor's Program of the International Business School, Hanze University OAS, Groningen, The Netherlands
e-mail: m.g.egender@st.hanze.nl

Dr. Reddy's is not just a generic company, but an API company with a much broader activity. It is the only Indian company to have significant R&D activities being undertaken overseas. Dr. Reddy's has enormous capabilities in chemistry, formulation development, manufacturing, environmental management, and in research. Having this depth of capabilities as well as a history of continuous progress, a size of more than 12,000 employees, and a global orientation, Dr. Reddy's represents a company with great potential to become a brand in Western (US and European) markets (Drreddys 2013).

2 Company Profile

2.1 History

1984–1990: Taking the first steps. In 1984, Dr. Reddy's originally launched the production of active pharmaceutical ingredients. In 1986, Reddy's started operations on branded formulations. Within a year, Reddy's had launched Norilet, the company's first recognized brand in India. Soon, Dr. Reddy's obtained another success with Omez, and Reddy's became the first Indian company to export the active ingredients for pharmaceuticals to Europe. Reddy's started to transform itself from a supplier of pharmaceutical ingredients to other manufacturers into a manufacturer of pharmaceutical products in 1987.

1991–1999: Expanding and Innovating. The company's first international move in 1992 took it to Russia, where Dr. Reddy's formed a joint venture with Biomed. Dr. Reddy's Research Foundation was established in order to do research in the area of new drug discovery. The focus has since changed to innovative R&D, hiring new scientists, especially Indian students studying abroad in doctoral and post-doctoral courses. In 1994, Reddy's started targeting the US generic market and in 1997, it was ready for the next major step. From being an API and bulk drug supplier to regulated markets like the USA and the UK, and a branded formulations supplier in unregulated markets like India and Russia, Reddy's made the transition into generics by filing an Abbreviated New Drug Application (ANDA) in the USA. In the same year, Reddy's out-licensed a molecule for clinical trials to Novo Nordisk, a Danish pharmaceutical company. Reddy's strengthened its Indian manufacturing operations in 1999 by acquiring American Remedies Ltd.

2000–2009: Growing Globally. In 2000, Dr. Reddy's Research Foundation set up an American laboratory in Atlanta which was dedicated to discovery and design of novel therapeutics. The laboratory is called Reddy US Therapeutics Inc and its main aim is the discovery of next-generation drugs. Reddy's research thrust focused on large niche areas in Western markets: anti-cancer, anti-diabetes, cardiovascular and anti-infection drugs. In the year 2001, it became the first non-Japanese pharmaceutical company from the Asia-Pacific region to obtain a New York Stock Exchange listing, a ground-breaking achievement for the Indian pharmaceutical industry.

Reddy's started its European operations in 2002 by acquiring two pharmaceutical firms in the United Kingdom. The acquisition of BMS Laboratories and its wholly owned subsidiary, Meridian UK, allowed Reddy's to expand geographically into the European market.

The American launch of Reddy's house-branded ibuprofen tablets in 400, 600 and 800 mg strengthened in 2003. Direct marketing under the Reddy's brand name represented a significant step in the company's efforts to build a strong and sustainable US generic business. It was the first step in building Reddy's fully-fledged distribution network in the US market.

In 2005, Dr. Reddy's entered into a marketing agreement with Eurodrug Laboratories, a pharmaceutical company based in the Netherlands, to improve its product portfolio for respiratory diseases. Dr. Reddy's acquired Betapharm Arzneimittel GmbH from 3i for 480 million € in March of 2006. This is one of the largest-ever foreign acquisitions by an Indian pharmaceutical company. Betapharm is Germany's fourth-largest generics pharmaceutical company.

In 2008, Reddy's also acquired Dowpharma's small molecule business in the UK. Dr. Reddy's announced in 2009 that it entered into a strategic partnership with GlaxoSmithKline plc (GSK) to develop and market select products across emerging markets outside India (Dr. Reddy's History 2013).

2.2 The Founders

"I always wanted to start something where others had felt there was a barrier to tackle" (Dr. Reddy's 2013b). When Dr. K. Anji Reddy said this, he was expressing the driving vision that led him to create Dr. Reddy's Laboratories. In setting up the company, Dr. Reddy overcame a challenge that others had not undertaken: making methyldopa when the state-owned Indian Drugs & Pharmaceuticals (IDPL) stopped producing it. Later, he acquired and revived the ailing Cheminor Drugs in the face of prevailing skepticism, which put the expansion of the company on an ever-rising trajectory.

Born in Tadepalli, Guntur district, Andhra Pradesh, India, Dr. Reddy found his life's passion in science. He graduated from the University of Bombay with a specialization in Pharmaceutical Science and Fine Chemicals and went on to get a PhD in Chemical Engineering from the National Chemical Laboratory, Pune. After a stint at the state-owned IDPL and partnerships at two other firms, he founded Dr. Reddy's Laboratories in 1984. New drug discovery was the next frontier to be breached. Dr. Reddy's Research Foundation (DRF) was established, making Dr. Reddy's the first company to start drug discovery programs in India. DRF was recognized as a scientific and industrial research organization by the Department of Scientific and Industrial Research, Ministry of Science and Technology, Government of India. Dr. Reddy's mission to provide innovative new medicines for healthier lives, at a price the common man can afford, was now being achieved in full measure.

Dr. Reddy received several national and international awards and Lifetime Achievement Awards. In April 2011, the Government of India honored him with the Padma Bhushan award, the third highest civilian award in the country, for his contributions to the Indian pharmaceutical industry.

2.3 Employees

Dr. Reddy's Board of Directors consists of the following experts in diverse fields including medicine, chemistry and medical research, human resource development, business strategy, finance, and economics. They review all significant business decisions and committees appointed by the board to focus on specific areas.

- Mr. GV Prasad - Chairman & Chief Executive
- Mr. Satish Reddy - Vice Chairman and Managing Director
- Mr. Ravi Bhoothalingam - Independent Director
- Mr. Anupam Puri - Independent Director
- Dr. Omkar Goswami - Independent Director
- Dr. J.P. Moreau - Independent Director
- Ms. Kalpana Morparia - Independent Director
- Dr. Bruce LA Carter - Independent Director
- Dr. Ashok Ganguly - Independent Director
- Mr. Sridar Iyengar - Independent Director

Committees appointed by the Board focus on specific areas and make informed decisions within the framework of delegated authority. They make specific recommendations to the Board on matters within their areas or purview. All decisions and recommendations of the committees are placed before the Board for its information or approval. The Management Council is at the top of the organizational structure. Dr. Reddy's management develops and implements policies, procedures and practices that realize our company's purpose and values. The management also identifies, measures, monitors and controls risks in the business and ensures safe, sound and efficient operations. The Management Council meets every quarter under the chairmanship of the CEO (Dr. Reddy's Management 2013a).

2.4 Product Range

Having started in 1984 as an API manufacturer, Dr. Reddy's Laboratories are currently offering over 150 patented medications and more than 60 API, while having more than 500 DFM fillings, and assuring safety and quality of the medicinal product. The main business of Dr. Reddy's Laboratories, however, is the production and distribution of generic drugs: drugs that can be legally reproduced after the branded drug goes off-patent, which is usually after a time period between ranging from 20 to 25 years, as well as biologically-similar alternatives, new chemical entities, and differentiated formulations.

In other words, Dr. Reddy's is mostly involved in cheap and efficient reproduction of medications, which are no longer protected by patents. Thus, they can be sold under the brand-name price since expensive steps, such as research and innovation of the drug, have already taken place. Dr. Reddy's Laboratories offers more than 200 generic drugs which are distributed to countries in the West and to Asia. The production of generic drugs is more cost efficient since the drugs have already been developed and tested. Therefore, based on the original price of the off-patent drug, generic drugs are substantially cheaper to purchase, in agreement with Dr. Reddy's Laboratories' philosophy of making crucial pharmaceuticals available for everyone. These generic drugs are mostly offered in the major therapeutic areas of cardiological diseases, pain management, anti-infection drugs, as well as those used in dermatology and oncology. Generic and biologically-similar pharmaceuticals are sold under brand names, also known as branded generics, in order to supply people, who are willing to pay a small premium in order to get an efficient and recognizable product, with high quality yet affordable drugs.

Well known generic brands by Dr. Reddy's include Omez, Ciprolet, and Nise, which are holding leadership positions in various key markets, especially in India, Russia, and Commonwealth of Independent States countries. In developed markets such as the USA, Germany, UK, and Australia, however, the drugs are not sold under branded names but their generic names, also called pure generics, in order to keep costs low in the production stage and lower the healthcare costs for the patients.

Furthermore, Dr. Reddy's Laboratories' product range does not only contain copycat or generic drugs but also includes APIs and is the second largest provider of APIs since it distributes to more than 75 countries in the world. Being a world leader in generic APIs has again multiple advantages, such as keeping prices low and making it available for patients in the shortest amount of time.

2.5 Revenues

As can be derived from Table 1, Dr. Reddy's Laboratories has performed very well during the past two years. Revenues of more than 96,737,323.00 Indian Rupees (1.3 billion €) have been made during the fiscal year 2012 with a gross profit of more than 55 %. The year 2013 followed with a remarkable growth of 20 % in revenues, which demonstrates the quick growth the company is experiencing due to their successful business strategies mentioned above. Because Dr. Reddy's LTD is listed on NASDAQ, the past years were very beneficial for the stockholders due to a strong increase in earnings per share as well as dividend payout. The company's stock is currently strongly bullish and share prices have been rising significantly when compared to other indexes within the last 5 years which makes Dr. Reddy's a stable and efficient investment opportunity.

Table 1 Financial performance Dr. Reddy's FY2012 and FY2013 (Dr. Reddy's 2013a)

Consolidated financial performance according to IFRS In ₹ million					
	FY2013		FY2012		Growth
Particulars	₹ (Rs.)	%	₹ (Rs.)	%	%
Revenue	**116,266**	**100**	**96,737**	**100**	**20**
Cost of revenues	55,687	48	43,432	45	28
Gross profit	**60,579**	**52**	**53,305**	**55**	**14**
Operating expenses					
Selling, general & administrative expenses	33,584	29	28,867	30	16
Research and development expenses	7,674	7	5,911	6	30
Impairment loss on other intangible assets	507	0	1,040	1	(51)
Impairment loss on goodwill	181	0	0	0	0
Other operating (income)/expenses, net	(2,479)	(2)	(765)	(1)	224
Results from operating activities	**21,112**	**18**	**18,252**	**19**	**16**
Finance income/(expense), net	460	0	160	0	187
Share of profit of equity accounted investees, net of income tax	104	0	54	0	93
Profit before income tax	21,676	19	18,466	19	17
Income tax expense	(4,900)	(4)	(4,204)	(4)	17
Profit for the period	**16,776**	**14**	**14,262**	**15**	**18**
Diluted EPS (₹ per share)	**98.44**		**83.81**		**17**

2.6 Business (Success) Strategy

"If one analyzes why we have been so successful, the single most important fact is our strength in the R&D and our ability to commercialize technologies developed in a quick and efficient manner" (Drreddys 2013).

This quote by the Chairman and CEO of Dr. Reddy's, G.V. Prasad, states why the company was able to become a world pharmaceutical company in less than 30 years: the fact that high priority was put on the R&D sector. There are multiple daughter companies wholly owned by Dr. Reddy's, such as Promius Pharma, which focus solely on innovation and new product development in order to be in the position to not only produce generic drugs but also to research new and affordable alternatives.

Another important fact, which greatly contributed and still contributes to the company's success, is the patient-friendliness of the company. Dr Reddy's is different from other pharmaceutical companies because it does not exploit the end-consumer by exaggerating medicinal product, but puts effort into making medicine affordable for everyone. This fact almost instantly provided the company with a good reputation. Furthermore, Dr. Reddy's was the first pharmaceutical company in India that approached the end-consumer directly, providing in depth customer services and using it as a tool to keep patients both satisfied and updated on upcoming products. Another major point contributing to the success of the company is the very diverse manufacturing and distribution of medicinal products in emerging and developed markets. In emerging markets, generic drugs by Dr. Reddy's Laboratories are sold under branded names, whereas the opposite approach is taken when acting in developed markets: that is, distributing the product solely under the generic name to make it more competitive in Western markets in particular.

Hence, a focus on R&D, the right marketing efforts, and the company's philosophy that healthcare has to be affordable, made Dr. Reddy's a world leading pharmaceutical company in less than 30 years.

2.7 Quality and Innovation of Product Range

Through multiple R&D laboratories all over the world, Dr. Reddy's Laboratories assures high quality standards for all their products. Targeting Western specialty generics in order to establish a foundation for drug production constituted the first step for the company towards its own innovation and research. The company has multiple research and development institutes in India and North America which are pioneering next generation pharmaceuticals using genomics and proteomics. The laboratory Reddy US Therapeutics Inc., found in Atlanta, is only doing research on next-generation drugs, and focuses on Western niche markets such as anti-cancer, anti-diabetes, and anti-infection drugs. Additionally more and more new medical products are developed on a biologically-similar basis, focusing more on the conversion of natural ingredients rather than just on synthetic ones. Dr. Reddy's Laboratories are also strongly engaging in novel molecule innovations which are crucial in developing new treatments for therapeutic use.

3 The Rise of the Company

3.1 Growth Development

"HYDERABAD Feb 2014: Dr Reddy's Laboratories capitalized on the regulatory troubles of Indian rivals to post its highest ever quarterly income and operating profit during October-December 2013. India's largest pharmaceutical company by sales said on Tuesday that net profit in the third quarter swelled by 70 % to 618 crore compared to the year-ago period. Revenue grew by 23 % to 3,534 crore." (Economic Times 2014)

Based on this citation, written by The Economic Times in February 2014, it becomes clear what a huge growth potential and thus growth development Dr. Reddy's Laboratories is displaying in the past year especially, but also in general, since founded in 1984. The biggest growth in market size and capitalization has been made primarily on the US market. Displaying their biggest revenues rising by more than 76 % over the last year, including a rise of 22.5 % in the North American market are the results of some several crucial factors. The business benefited the most from the launch of new products in the generic business and the expansion of key products with limited competition due to patenting and complex development. Additionally, Dr. Reddy's Laboratories was able to increase its market share in the US because competing pharmaceutical companies, such as Wockhardt and Ranbaxy, had been dealing with legal issues concerning the safety of a new plant and so production was unable to meet the market demand (Economic Times 2014).

Whereas the generic business has been very lucrative, especially in the USA, other sectors of the business, such as the PSAI sector (pharmaceutical service and active ingredients), have been sluggish in the home market. Nevertheless, the company has grown by more than 23 % over the past year and, even though the PSAI sector has been declining during the fiscal year of 2013, a recovery of the business is expected in the home market. This recovery is expected due to a rapid stabilization of the home market after being disrupted by new drug pricing policies introduced in India, which regulates the prices of drugs. The new drug pricing is not based on manufacturing costs but on the simple average market price of the product with over 1 % market turnover in allover market in the Indian market (Economic Times 2014).

3.2 Becoming a Brand

Dr. Reddy's, as already mentioned, has a long history of being guided by principle. The strong belief that they can make medicine of higher quality and lower price compared to the Western companies was a driving factor for the company to enter the overseas market as an API supplier in 1986. At that time, Dr. Reddy's Laboratories was one of the first suppliers in the overseas market. It gained more and more attention when it became the biggest supplier of methyldopa to the German pharmaceutical giant Merck. By delivering high quality for low prices and by getting US FDA (Food and Drug Administration) approval for their plants, Dr. Reddy's Laboratories was able to supply ibuprofen to the US market shortly thereafter. Hence, within a short time, Dr. Reddy's made a name in the European and North American markets. This reputation began to grow as the company also launched several products for which they had gained 180- marketing exclusivity rights: that is, being able to make extra revenues of more than 200 million US$ just by having exclusive selling rights due to patenting and FTF regulations (Mahalingam 2013).

Not only has Dr. Reddy's Laboratories been successful in expanding into the European and US market, but it also has been reaching out to the emerging markets. It has become a trustworthy partner with Russia, which is currently the biggest growing market of the pharmaceutical company.

Through the company's willingness to strive to its best potential and to take on new challenges by entering into such difficult markets as the US, it inspired other smaller Indian companies and became a benchmark for success.

3.3 Position at the Global Market

Dr. Reddy's Laboratories has a strong position in the global market. While playing a minor role in the domestic market, it established itself in the global market with its generic business and over-the-counter drugs in North America, West Europe, and in Russia, its fastest growing market.

The pharma market accounts currently for more than 65 % of Dr. Reddy's Laboratories total revenues. The main business of the company in the North American market is the development and production of global generics, whereas a pipeline with more than 200 generic drugs are on file in order to instantly replace products which are going off-patent within the next few years. In addition to those generics, which have yet to be launched, other key products with limited competition have been constantly introduced to the market over the previous years and are expected to continue to build high market share with little price erosion. Being able to use technology more effective in creating generics and biologically-similar drugs, Dr. Reddy's will surely continue to grow within the North American pharma sector (Livemint 2014).

The strongest growing market for Dr. Reddy's Laboratories, however, is the Russian market, which is currently experiencing a strong restructuring of their pharmaceutical sectors as it is trying to reach a level of 50 % in domestic production of pharmaceuticals. The huge increase in demand is mainly in the middle to low cost generics produced by Dr. Reddy's Laboratories as well as over-the-counter drugs. Since the company already has strong business connections with Russia since 1988, it was able to increase its revenues significantly (20 % on average) during the past years (Mahalingam 2013).

Even if Russia passes a specific law, which requires generic and innovative companies to have a manufacturing presence when selling its products, Dr. Reddy's Laboratories has already stated that they are willing to locate production facilities in Russia, and the only thing to evaluate is whether to acquire existing facilities or build new ones (Ponomarevar 2011).

3.4 Position in the Home Market

Despite the generally strong growth of Dr. Reddy's Laboratories in the USA, Russia, and the emerging markets, Dr. Reddy's Laboratories is not one of the biggest players in the domestic market; it does not even rank in the top 10 in the domestic pharma market although it is ranked as the second largest pharmaceutical company in India. The strong focus on profitable foreign markets is surely to some extent a reason for the lack of performance in the domestic market. The Indian pharmaceutical market is flooded with several new products from companies such as Sun Pharma and Cipla, whereas Dr. Reddy's Laboratories had been focusing on a few selected brands which limits the company's portfolio to a much greater extent and thus makes it difficult to acquire additional market share (Mahalingam 2013).

Therefore, in the past four years, the company invested heavily in boosting the sales force by 50 % and marketing efforts have been expanded into rural areas, as they are seen as an emerging market in India itself. Furthermore, through the development of new product lines and the extension of existing key brands in the area of gastrointestinal or cardiovascular, which account for more than 50 % of its revenues, the company will have new possibilities to gain a bigger market share. However, as Dr. Reddy's has been showing so little effort in the domestic market as compared to foreign markets, it will be very challenging for the company to gain acceptance within the Indian medical community and therefore increase sales since time has shown that the Indian pharma community is hesitant when it comes to new portfolios, unlike the North American community. Furthermore, Dr. Reddy's may also be influenced by the new Drug Pricing Controls, as already mentioned, which will increase the prices for some of its essential products perhaps causing a decent loss in profits in the home market (Economic Times 2014).

Since the medical portfolio of the company is relatively small compared to its competitors, another way of gaining market share more quickly is by acquisition of other medical businesses, individual brands, or entire portfolios. However, Dr. Reddy's Laboratories has far more possibilities than only acquiring other businesses or expanding their existing portfolio, including making use of the huge R&D facilities which are developing biologically similar products. These products have little competition in the domestic market and are expected to increase from 2 billion US$ to 4–6 billion US$ through 2016. Since the amount of market entries are much smaller due to complexity of the product and production process in this new emerging pharmaceutical sector, Dr. Reddy's will use this in its favor in order to establish a growing market share. Additionally, by entering into a partnership with Merck Sereno, a division of the pharmaceutical company Merck, Dr. Reddy's will lower the risk by having development costs split, which are estimated to be at more than 200 million US$. The fact that the company is already heavily engaged in the development of biologically-similar products, and that developed countries are still far from launching biologically-similar products to such an extent, gives Dr. Reddy's a crucial advantage in its home market among its Indian competitors. High entry barriers and the difficulty of domestic companies to increase their capabilities also work in Dr. Reddy's favor. Thus, the key driver for the company to gain market share with little competition within its domestic market is its high expenditure in R&D (Mahalingam 2013).

3.5 Benefits from the Government, Businesses and the Educational System

From the previous sections, we can conclude that Dr. Reddy's has already become a global player in the pharmaceutical industry where it is strengthening its domestic market or taking advantage of its generics business to rapidly gain revenues in its oversea markets. However, it is questionable how favorable governments and the business and educational systems were for Dr. Reddy's Laboratories.

Dr. Reddy's Laboratories is a multinational pharma company, which provides high amounts of tax yearly to the governments from producing, importing or exporting products.

The new regulations in the Indian Drug Pricing Policy will most likely lead to higher prices and to shrinking profit margins, and also to having to pay more taxes, which is a clear disadvantage for the company as well as for the whole pharma sector in India. Furthermore, Russia passed a law which would force pharmaceutical suppliers to build domestic plants in order to be able to distribute their products to the Russian market. This would lead to higher taxation as well in the Russian market, although the good, general relationship between Russia and Dr. Reddy's Laboratories would suggest that both parties would be in favor or such an idea since having production facilities in Russia opens new supply channels towards Eastern European countries. A special-purpose program will support the restructuring of the Russian pharmaceutical industry, which might provide beneficial incentives for companies such as Dr. Reddy's to produce in this market in the near future (Ponomarevar 2011).

Nevertheless, the general advantages and benefits, which Dr. Reddy's inherits and will expand over the next years, are therefore primarily their own success in technology, long term thinking, and a high degree of innovativeness.

4 Future Developments

4.1 What Are the Future Challenges/Problems to Be Overcome at Home and Abroad?

As one of the largest pharmaceutical companies in India, Dr. Reddy's Laboratories averages 200 orders a day alone for its US generic pharmaceutical and over-the-counter products. A triple-digit percentage revenue increase in the past year demonstrates the agility of the company's move into the generic marketplace. Getting to market first following US FDA approval is a key with generics.

Dr. Reddy's needed a streamlined supply chain and the flexibility to position its new products against the large number of prescription drugs due to come off patent protection. Since it manufactures in India, Dr. Reddy's must plan for additional lead times to get product to the USA.

When drugs move from branded to generic, pharmaceutical companies face a host of regulatory and supply chain challenges to get products to clinicians and retail pharmacies. Since the FDA approves the sale of branded drugs as generic as late as the day of patent expiration, acting quickly and efficiently means being first out of the gate, sometimes even getting products to the drug wholesalers or store distribution centers the next day. That drives critical planning for the right warehousing and distribution solutions linked with transportation. Further complicating the process, the FDA also may require label and packaging changes to some medicines prior to approval for generic sales.

With its previous solution, Dr. Reddy's lacked such a reliable rapid dispatch of its dosage-form generics. The company also was expanding from generic prescription drugs to over-the-counter products with formulas packaged under private labels for chain drugstores and mass merchandisers. With a promising pipeline of drug applications on file, there was no shortage of new product launch plans along with ongoing order fulfillment and service. Time delay following FDA approval for generic sales could mean lost opportunity and positioning (Healthcare Case 2014).

4.2 Customer Challenge

Since Dr. Reddy's Laboratories' company mission is to make "affordable medicine for everybody" the challenge is going to be to sustain in the low pricing class in order to build and keep their customer base. New imposed regulations, as mentioned in the report are therefore obstacles which have to be overcome by the company through even more technological advantages too still make profit by keeping costs throughout the production process low.

Also in sight of the expansion in the Russian market, Dr. Reddy's has to show initiative and strong cooperation with the new healthcare project in order to gain a favorable position in the pharmaceutical industry.

As Dr. Reddy's plays more of a minor role in their domestic drug market due to the very high competition, a different approach, such as the publication of highly technological medicine, rather than lower costing has to be found in order to take a leading position in the Indian market.

4.3 Which Companies Are Its Competitors Now and in the Future?

Teva Pharmaceutical Industries is the biggest name in the no-name world of generic pharmaceuticals. The company makes hundreds of generic versions of brand-name antibiotics, heart drugs, heartburn medications, and more.

Ranbaxy Laboratories is quite the rainmaker in India's pharmaceutical business. The company is one of India's largest drug manufacturers and a top global generics producer. Anti-infectives amoxycillin (not to be confused with the common antibiotic, amoxicillin) and ciprofloxacin, and cardio drug simvastatin are among Ranbaxy's top sellers; all come in several administration forms.

Sun Pharmaceutical Industries is one of India's brightest stars in the pharmaceutical industry. The company develops, makes, and markets generic pharmaceuticals in a variety of dosage forms (oral tablets and capsules, injectables, creams, and nasal sprays). Its products target chronic therapeutic areas including cardiology, gastroenterology, neurology, psychiatry, and orthopedics. Sun Pharma also manufactures APIs for other drug makers. The company markets its products around the globe and has 20 manufacturing plants in the Americas, Asia, and Europe (Hoovers 2014).

4.4 Dr. Reddy's and the Netherlands

"Dr Reddy's Laboratories (DRL), which is in the process of acquiring the Netherlands-based specialty pharmaceutical company OctoPlus NV for about 27.4 million euro, has so far managed to get nearly 93 % of the firm in its favor" (Economic Times 2013).

"HYDERABAD, OCT 22: Dr Reddy's Laboratories Ltd together with its subsidiaries today announced its intent to buy OctoPlus, Amsterdam for an offer price of 27.39 million€.

The Hyderabad-based pharma company disclosed the intended public offer to acquire the issued and outstanding shares of OctoPlus N.V. (Euronext Amsterdam: OCTO).

OctoPlus is a service-based specialty pharmaceutical company. Dr Reddy's offer price of 27.39 million € (cum-dividend) in cash represents 100 % of the issued and outstanding ordinary shares. The offer price represents a premium of 30 % over the closing price of OctoPlus as of October 19.

Dr. Reddy's currently holds an irrevocable commitment from shareholders representing over 50 % of OctoPlus's issued and outstanding shares. Furthermore, the Executive Board and the Supervisory Board of OctoPlus have unanimously recommended the offer to the remaining shareholders.

This deal will help expand the expertise and scientific capabilities of Dr. Reddy's. G.V. Prasad, Vice-Chairman and CEO of Dr. Reddy's, said, "As we globalize our R&D efforts, we are looking forward to build a research base in Leiden (Netherlands). The acquisition will help us ramp up our technology capabilities in drug delivery" (Somasekhar 2012)."

5 Conclusions

Dr. Reddy's Ltd. has become a global player within the American, Asian and European pharmaceutical markets over the last 30 years, having started as a small pharmaceutical ingredients supplier in 1984. The remarkable and continuous growth and sustainability within the drug industry was due to three key factors: a strong corporate governance, long term thinking & innovativeness, and control of the entire value chain.

The overall company philosophy, which is to produce and supply affordable medication in the generic and biologically-similar section and achieve a company profit, shows a strong ethical business practice. Having recognized the need to be transparent in terms of accounting policies and by the early implementation of an independent board, Dr. Reddy's was the first Asian Pacific company to be listed on the New York Stock Exchange.

Through the high corporate governance, a long-lasting and trustworthy relationship with the shareholder was built over years, which greatly contributed to a steady rise in share prices and gave great possibilities to expand the business year by year, always with regard to long term thinking rather than to quick profit generation.

Hence, the mutual trust by shareholders acquired over decades made it possible for the company to expand its most crucial sector, the R&D sector. This sector is the key to upcoming product launches with little or no competition due to complicated formulations and innovative medication processes in the generic and biologically-similar field. The advantage gained through research will be the main driving factor for the company to increase their market share within the next few years and to develop new long-term strategies in order to make Dr. Reddy's medication a monopolistic supplier of several new drug discoveries before other pharmaceutical companies.

Adding to the strong corporate governance and the innovativeness and long-term thinking is the fact that Dr. Reddy's is in control of its entire supply chain. The supply network built over the past decades assures that the quality standards are met most of the time and gradually reduces the dependency on other suppliers. Company acquisitions and local production in key markets such as Europe, Russia, and emerging markets enhance the supply chain by being continuously able to strengthen and expand to new pharmaceutical markets in a growing number of countries.

These factors can be seen as the key reasons why Dr. Reddy's was able to expand so remarkably over the last 30 years and why the company is expected to grow its overall global market share in the pharmaceutical sectors. Good relations with governments, the willingness and understanding to open up foreign manufacturing plants, and not only importing products but strengthening different countries' economies, makes Dr. Reddy's a reputable company which will show more of its potential within the next years.

If Dr Reddy's Laboratories should indeed acquire the Netherlands-based specialty pharmaceutical company OctoPlus NV, it will have the possibility to enlarge its investments in Netherlands. Through further collaborations offered by Dutch local pharmaceutical companies, Dr. Reddy's can have a bright future in the Netherlands. By keeping its international orientation and offering profitable business strategies in terms of logistics, promotion and legislation, the Netherlands remains an attractive market for pharmaceutical companies such as Dr. Reddy's.

References

Dr. Reddy's. (2013a). *Dr. Reddy's FY2012 and FY2013 Investors/Financials*. Retrieved March 28, 2014, from http://www.drreddys.com/investors/financials.html.

Dr. Reddy's. (2013b). *About us, our founder*. Retrieved February 2, 2014, from http://www.drreddys.com/aboutus/our-founder.html.

Dr. Reddy's History. (2013). *Our Journey since 1984*. Retrieved February 2, 2014, http://www.drreddys.com/25yearsofhealth/milestones_growing_2009.shtml.

Dr. Reddy's Management. (2013a). *About us, board and management*. Retrieved February 2, 2014, from http://www.drreddys.com/aboutus/board-of-directors.html.

Drreddys. (2013). *Dr. Reddy's memory book*. Retrieved February 2, 2014, from http://digital.drreddys.com/memorybook/Index.aspx.cited.

Economic Times. (2013). *Dr Reddy's Laboratories acquires 93 % shares of OctoPlus*. Retrieved March 28, 2014, from http://articles.economictimes.indiatimes.com/2013-02-12/news/37058880_1_octoplus-nv-drl-g-v-prasad.

Economic Times. (2014). *Dr Reddy's Laboratories expects 8–10 pc growth in India generics business this fiscal*. Retrieved March 30, 2014, fromhttp://articles.economictimes.indiatimes.com/2014-01-10/news/46066424_1_dr-reddy-laboratories-new-drug-pricing-policy.

Healthcare Case. (2014). *Dr. Reddy's Stays Ready with flexible supply chain*. Retrieved March 28, 2014, from http://www.ups.com/content/us/en/bussol/browse/industries/healthcare/dr-reddys-laboratories.html.

Hoovers. (2014). *Pharma industry*. Retrieved March 28, 2014, from http://www.hoovers.com/company-information/cs/company-profile.Sun_Pharmaceutical_Industries_Limited.13a9963460c7243f.html.

Livemint. (2014). *Dr. Reddy's Laboratories expects 8–10 pc growth in India generics business this fiscal*. Retrieved from http://www.livemint.com/Money/NnVqbxIch6N9Zcfhcd1WQP/Dr-Reddys-US-business-drives-growth.html.

Mahalingam. (2013). *Business Outlook, 'Inside Dr. Reddy's'*. Retrieved March 27, 2014, from http://business.outlookindia.com/article_v3.aspx?artid=287250.

Ponomarevar. (2011). *Russia and India Report. 'Dr. Reddy's considers factory acquisition*. Retrieved March 26, 2014, from http://in.rbth.com/articles/2011/09/21/dr_reddys_considers_factory_acquisition_13027.html.

Somasekhar. (2012). *Dr Reddy's to buy Dutch firm OctoPlus*. Retrieved October 22, 2012, from http://www.thehindubusinessline.com/companies/dr-reddys-to-buy-dutch-firm-octoplus/article4021502.ece.

Infosys: A Case Study on Becoming a Global Brand in Consulting Technology and Outsourcing Solutions

Mariusz Soltanifar

Abstract

Infosys is a global leader in consulting, technology, and outsourcing solutions. This chapter examines the national and international context of the company, and its services and global presence. The strategy at Infosys is to strengthen the value of all its employees and constantly invest in developing their competencies. Infosys, being a global brand, might be interested in the knowledge and experience in a region such as the Northern Netherlands, but it would require several actions to be undertaken at the same time in the framework of the triple helix, by the government, industry and academia.

1 Introduction

Trade between India and Europe is expanding rapidly. The Indian economy is amongst the fastest growing in the world. Being present in the emerging market, Indian companies seek several opportunities in Europe which is India's most important trading partner. This deepening relationship presents numerous opportunities for companies, such as Infosys, which are eager to expand overseas. The necessity of discovering potential markets and new economic challenges requires Infosys, as well as other companies, to engage in cross-border business to stay competitive. In this chapter, Infosys's global expansion is analyzed with respect to the Northern Netherlands region and its investment opportunities. By providing business consulting, technology, engineering, and outsourcing services, Infosys might be potentially interested in developing new centers in this region.

M. Soltanifar (✉)
International Business School, Hanze University OAS, Groningen, The Netherlands
e-mail: m.soltanifar@pl.hanze.nl

Currently, Infosys enables clients in more than 30 countries to stay a step ahead of emerging business trends and remain competitive by helping them to transform and to thrive in a changing world through co-creating advanced solutions which combine strategic insights and execution excellence. With 7.4 billion US$ in annual revenues and more than 160,000 employees, Infosys delivers a broad diversity of products and services to enterprises.

The following chapter analyzes the secret of success at Infosys and covers Infosys's history from 1981 onwards. It also considers recent developments and strategic choices to be made. It examines the national and international context of the company, and its services and global presence, including the Netherlands. Desk research making use of secondary sources sketches an overview of the opportunities and threats for Infosys for developing a successful strategy. Finally, several conclusions are drawn which could be translated into practical recommendations related to the business opportunities in the area of the Northern Netherlands.

2 Company Profile

Infosys is a global leader in consulting, technology, and outsourcing solutions. The company enables clients in more than 30 countries to outperform the competition and stay ahead of the innovation curve. Helping companies to manage their business and powering their transformation to a smarter organization, Infosys allows them to focus on their core business priorities. Infosys's expertise spans many industries. From helping to build lighter and stronger passenger jets or creating more fuel efficient smart cars, to enabling banks to provide financial inclusion to the most remote corners of the globe or empowering technology executives with solutions to maximize global agility, Infosys delivers powerful innovations (Infosys 2014a). Strategic insights support enterprises to transform and to thrive in a changing world through strategic consulting and the co-creation of breakthrough solutions, including those in mobility, sustainability, big data, and cloud computing. Currently, "Infosys has 93 global development centers of which 34 are in India and 59 are outside India, and 71 sales offices around the world of which two are in India and 69 are outside India" (Infosys 2014a). The number of clients in the period of 2010 through 2014 is presented below (Fig. 1).

Infosys acts together with Infosys BPO—the Business Process Outsourcing subsidiary (BPO Ltd), which was set up in April 2002. Infosys BPO focuses on integrated end-to-end outsourcing and delivers transformational benefits to the clients through reduced costs, ongoing productivity improvements, and process reengineering. Infosys BPO operates in Australia, Brazil, China, Costa Rica, the Czech Republic, India, Japan, Mexico, the Netherlands, the Philippines, Poland, South Africa, and the United States. It closed Financial Year (FY) 2012–2013 with revenues of 583.1 million USD (Infosys 2014a).

Fig. 1 Number of clients at Infosys (2010–2014) (Infosys 2014b)

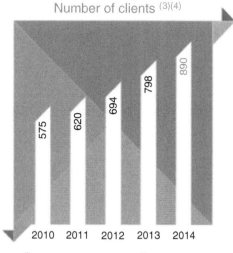

(3) At the end of fiscal year, (4) Consolidated

2.1 History

Infosys was established in 1981. From a capital of 250 US$, the company has grown to become an 8.095 billion US$ company with a market capitalization of approximately 33 billion US$ (Infosys 2014a). Infosys was co-founded in 1981 by N. R. Narayana Murthy, Nandan Nilekani, N. S. Raghavan, S. Gopalakrishnan, S. D. Shibulal, K. Dinesh, and Ashok Arora after they resigned from Patni Computer Systems. N.R. Narayana Murthy and six of his friends met at an apartment 1 day in January 1981 to talk about starting a company that wrote software codes. Six months later, with a loan of 250 US$ (reportedly from Narayana Murthy's wife), they had started Infosys, landed their first project with US-based Data Basics Corporation, and moved to Bangalore (Interbrand 2013).

From the beginning, the company was founded on the principle of building and implementing great ideas that drive progress for clients and enhance lives through enterprise solutions (Infosys 2014a). Infosys was incorporated in 1981 as Infosys Consultants Private Limited, a private limited company under the Indian Companies Act, 1956. It changed its name to Infosys Technologies Private Limited in April 1992, to Infosys Technologies Limited in June 1992, when it became a public limited company, and to Infosys Limited in June 2011. Infosys completed its initial public offering of equity shares in India in 1993 and its initial public offering of ADSs (American Depositary Shares) in the United States in 1999. In July 2003, June 2005, and November 2006, it completed sponsored secondary offerings of ADSs in the United States on behalf of its shareholders' (Infosys 2014a).

On June 1st 2013, Narayana Murthy, one of the founding members of Infosys and its long time CEO, returned from his retirement to assume office in Infosys as its Executive Chairman (Hindustan Times 2013).

"Infosys made an initial public offer (IPO) in February 1993 with an offer price of Rs. 98 per share against book value of Rs. 10 per share. The Infosys IPO was under subscribed but it was 'bailed out' by US investment bank Morgan Stanley which picked up 13 % of equity at the offer price" (In.com 2012). In December 2012, Infosys transferred the listing of its American Depositary Shares (ADS) from the NASDAQ to the NYSE (NYSE 2013). On 31 March 2013, "Infosys had 798 clients across 30 countries. It earns 62 % of its revenue from North America, 23 % from Europe, 2 % from India and remaining 13 % from rest of the world" (Infosys 2012b).

Shortly after Infosys was founded in 1981, its managers faced a major turning point when they made a decision to operate without giving in to the petty corruption rife in the Indian economy. Within just a few years, that decision had truly defined the company. Over the next 25 years, Infosys managers went to extraordinary lengths to avoid even the most modest of practices that they considered inappropriate (Harvard Business Review 2006).

Summing up, for the past 30 years, Infosys has catalyzed some of the major changes that have led to India's emergence as the global destination for software services talent. Infosys has pioneered the Global Delivery Model and became the first IT company from India to be listed on NASDAQ Stock Exchange. The headquarters of Infosys is located in Bangalore, Karnataka where is has been located since 1983 (Infosys 2014a).

2.2 Employees

Infosys and its subsidiaries had 158,404 employees as of December 31, 2013 (Infosys 2014a). Now, Infosys has a growing global presence in 73 offices and 94 development centers located in the United States, India, China, Australia, Japan, the Middle East, and Europe (Infosys 2014a). Additionally, Infosys is the second largest employer of H-1B visa professionals in the USA, as of 2012 (United States Department of Labor 2012). In recent years, Infosys has begun shifting operations to the USA and other countries. In 2012, Infosys announced a new office in Milwaukee, Wisconsin, to service Harley-Davidson, and this was the 18th international office in the USA (The Economist 2013). Infosys hired 1,200 US employees in 2011, and expanded the workforce by an additional 2,000 employees in 2012 (Infosys 2012a). The number of employees at Infosys is presented in the graph below (Fig. 2).

Enabling and empowering of a global workforce ensures talent capability across Infosys. The Education, Training and Assessment department (formerly known as Education and Research) is one of the company's key business-enabling "competency development" units. Infosys has developed an enterprise-wide environment for knowledge acquisition, dissemination, and management to cater to the continuous learning requirements of its employees and make them ready for the

Fig. 2 Number of employees at Infosys (2010–2014) (Infosys 2014b)

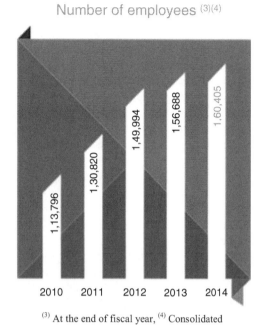

(3) At the end of fiscal year, (4) Consolidated

Fig. 3 Learning offerings and interventions offered for employees at Infosys (Infosys 2014b)

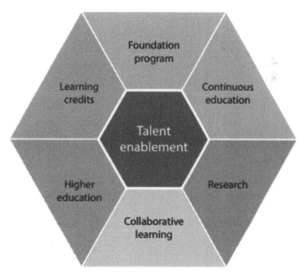

dynamic business requirements across the company (Infosys 2014b). The key significant learning avenues created for Infosys's employees are illustrated below (Fig. 3).

2.3 Service

Infosys is a NYSE listed global consulting and IT services company offering a broad range of services. Its end- to-end business solutions include: Consulting and Systems Integration comprising consulting, enterprise solutions, systems integration and advanced technologies; Business Information Technology (IT) services consisting of application development and maintenance, independent validation services, infrastructure management, engineering services comprising product engineering and life cycle solutions and business process management; Products, Platforms and Solutions, and more. A service that desires more attention is called Finacle, which is a banking product offering core banking, mobile banking, and e-banking needs of retail, corporate and universal banks globally. Infosys is also active in several other areas, such as cloud computing, enterprise mobility, and sustainability (Reuters 2014). The range of Infosys's services is presented in Table 1.

The company offers business process management services through Infosys BPO. Infosys BPO enables clients to outsource several operations, which relate to specific industry vertical processes and functional horizontal processes. Infosys BPO's service offerings include banking and financial services; telecommunications; insurance, healthcare and life sciences; manufacturing; media and entertainment; retail and CPG (consumer packaged goods); and energy, utilities and services. For its clients in the banking and financial services industry, it offers services in credit card operations, collections, banking operations, mortgage and loan account servicing, payments processing, trade clearing and settlement services, registrar and transfer agency services, fund administration and reporting, reference data management, hedge fund servicing and platform solutions. For its clients in the telecommunications industry, it offers services in order fulfillment, service assurance, billing and revenue assurance, data cleansing and validation services, telecom-specific analytic offerings and technology-led point solutions. For the company's clients in the insurance, healthcare and life sciences industries, it offers services in new business fulfillment, pensions and annuities, policy maintenance, claims administration, reinsurance finance and accounting, underwriting, statutory reporting services. For its clients in the manufacturing industry, it offers services in customer operations, master data management, material planning, mid-office support, product data management, quoting and demand fulfillment, supply chain and logistics support. For its clients in the media and entertainment industry, it offers services in advertisement analytics, content development, content management and desktop publishing. For its clients in the CPG industry, it offers services in master data management, trade promotions management, store solutions, supply chain solutions, reporting and analytics. For its clients in the energy, utilities and services industries, it offers services in master data management, supplier performance management and analytics, engineering documentation, metering infrastructure support, data validation, new product/feature support and meter data analytics (Reuters 2014).

Table 1 The range of Infosys's services (Reuters 2014)

Service	Description
Consulting & Systems Integration Services (C&SI)	Focus on delivering end-to-end business transformation which includes providing front-end business strategy consulting services, business requirements definition, business process re-engineering, business and technology solution design, package evaluation and implementation, complex program management, organizational design and change management, systems integration services and upgrades and maintenance. These solutions relate to product suites from SAP and Oracle and also extend to product suites from IBM Corporation, Microsoft Corporation, Pegasystems Inc., SalesForce.com Inc., Software AG and TIBCO Software Inc. Services to clients in areas, such as customer relationship management, supply chain management, human capital management, corporate performance management, business analytics, business process management, enterprise application integration and system integration.
Business IT Services	Customized software solutions. New applications or enhancement of the functionalities of its clients' existing software applications. System design and software coding and running pilots at its global development centers, while activities relating to the defining of requirements, transition planning, user training, user acceptance testing and deployment are performed at the client's site. Maintenance and production support services. Application management platform (IAM) adopting a range of tools to aid in the acquisition, collating and use of organizational knowledge and incident diagnosis in production support. End-to-end validation solutions, including test consulting, quality assurance organization transformation, testing for business transformation and testing for package implementations, upgrades and rollouts. Testing solutions comprising of technology based solutions for test life cycle automation and non-functional testing and vertical specific solutions through alliances with test tool vendors, such as HP, IBM, Microsoft, iTKO Lisa, Green Hat, Micro Focus, resulting in transformation of its clients' IT infrastructure.
Products, Platforms & Solutions Services	Licensable systems, which deliver functionalities. They can be used as standalone, customized or as building blocks in an enterprise application. Health Benefit Exchange providing an insurance hub, for individuals and small businesses to buy qualified plans. Infosys Trading Platform helping companies to differentiate their brokerage services by providing superior trading experience to customers. Infosys Omni-Channel Personalization Engine helping retailers foster consumer relationship by presenting personalized content across channels. Its Supply Chain Performance Management Suite provides insight into the supply-demand service chain performance.

The function-specific service offerings of Infosys BPO include customer service, finance and accounting, HR (human resource) outsourcing, legal process outsourcing, sales and fulfillment operations, and sourcing and procurement. Its customer services include customer engagement solutions, including sales, ongoing service and recoveries situations, and customer relationship management through various service channels. Its finance and accounting services include accounts payable, accounts receivable, billing and invoicing, collections and credit management, general ledger operations, financial planning and control and compliance related services. Its HR outsourcing services include payroll processing, benefits administration, learning and development, HR helpdesk, recruitment and staffing services, workforce administration. Its legal process outsourcing services include contract management services and solutions, legal process outsourcing, document review services. Its sales and fulfillment operations services include sales support operations, customer data management, account planning, order administration, customer advocacy, returns management, warranty management, demand forecasting, material and inventory management and reverse logistics. Its sourcing and procurement services include sourcing, category management, transactional procurement, performance and compliance management, e-Business solutions and spend, demand and supply market analytics (Reuters 2014).

The company's business platforms, which it refers to as InfosysEdge, are built around specific themes. Infosys SocialEdge is its social media marketing and employee engagement platform. Infosys BrandEdge is its digital marketing platform, built using Infosys BLUE framework, addresses the marketing needs of organizations, from building digital assets and launching marketing campaigns to listening to customers, as well as analyzing and acting on customer insights. Infosys CommerceEdge is its e-commerce and social commerce platform. Infosys TalentEdge is its talent management platform. Infosys ProcureEdge is its end-to-end Source-to-Pay platform. Infosys WalletEdge is its mobile commerce and payments platform. Infosys TradeEdge is its trader partner platform. Infosys BPO's platforms include McCamish Systems' VPAS and PMACS platforms which provide solutions to the insurance and financial services industries; solutions in strategic sourcing, category management and managed procurement services provided by Portland Group; and integrated technology and BPO offerings on a cloud model for human resources and sourcing and procurement services using the TalentEdge and Infosys ProcureEdge platforms (Reuters 2014).

To summarize, Infosys provides a broad variety of engineering solutions to support its clients across the product lifecycle of its clients' offerings, ranging from product ideation to realization. Its solutions offerings include the execution of product and software development programs; the management of products and commodity management where it combines its engineering, supply chain and business process outsourcing capabilities; the participation to product co-innovation where it works with its clients to take their offerings to market and invest along the way; the development, implementation and implementation of business platforms; and the operation of cross-industry services as shared services where it provides specialized engineering capabilities. Its solution offerings caters to a cross-section of industries, including aerospace, automotive, banking and financial services, business services, chemicals, consumer products, energy, high technology, industrial products and equipment, media and entertainment, medical devices, metals and mining, pharmaceuticals, retail, telecommunications and utilities.

2.4 Products

Infosys products focus on providing innovation-led business growth for clients. Infosys experts cater to market needs driven by global mega-trends, including digital consumers, emerging economies, new commerce, and healthcare. The offerings are built around the latest technologies in cloud computing, mobility, big data, rich media, and social media to provide guaranteed business outcomes. The current Infosys product categories are: banking suite, cloud and big data, customer services, digital commerce, digital marketing, distribution, sourcing and procurement, and talent management. Infosys is also active in the areas of assist, big data, branding, commerce, digitizing, procurement, smart grid, talent, trade, and wallet edge. In the financial area, the company is active in core banking, customer relationship management, digital commerce, consumer e-banking, corporate e-banking, inclusion solutions, Islamic banking, mobile banking, payments, treasure and wealth management (Infosys 2014a). Infosys delivers several types of services helping organizations to stay stronger and become more competitive in the global business landscape by leveraging the company's domain and business expertise through: application management, application outsourcing, business applications, business process outsourcing, cloud, engineering, infrastructure management, infrastructure outsourcing, management consulting, enterprise mobility, sustainability and testing (Infosys 2014a).

In the endeavor to future-proof the businesses of Infosys's clients, the company has identified seven key areas that are rapidly increasing in influence, and present great scope for IT-led innovations. These are presented in the Table 2.

From all of the listed products and services, one requires a special attention—Finacle, which is an example of an outstanding innovation in retail banking. It partners with banks to transform product, process and customer experience. Finacle is a flexible and fully web-enabled solution, which addresses the core, e-banking, mobile, customer relationship management, wealth management, treasury, and Islamic banking requirements of universal, retail and corporate banks globally. Other offerings include the Finacle core banking solution for regional rural banks: Finacle digital commerce solution, which enables next generation digital payments; Finacle alerts solution, which alerts end-users of events recorded by diverse business systems; Finacle Advizor, which combines human intervention with banking self-service channels through the interplay of video, audio and data communication; and Finacle WatchWiz, a monitoring solution, which allows banks to monitor, diagnose and resolve issues.

Table 2 Seven key areas shaping IT-led innovations identified by Infosys (Infosys 2014a)

No.	Key area	Description
	Digital consumers	Personalized solutions usher in on-demand solutions, accelerate innovation and access new demographic segments. These solutions maximize customer value across the lifecycle. Digital media is redefining consumer mindsets, patterns of purchase, and decision-making. Digitally active consumers have embraced the internet, telecom, media, and social space, changing the way consumers communicate, transact and make purchase decisions. These consumers rely on internet research, friends, and online peer reviews as opposed to "sponsored" communication. This new breed of active, informed, and assertive members stand out for their independence, uniqueness and participation.
	Emerging Economies	Access to "local" knowledge is critical as emerging economies transform the global marketplace. An ecosystem that harnesses collaboration helps realize "reverse innovation" across industries. Products and services must be re-engineered, not re-created, to address the specific needs of micro-segments.
	Healthcare Economy	IT minimizes healthcare costs by eliminating wastage, avoiding redundant processes and helping to incorporate best practices in treatment. Intelligent medical devices and evidence-based medicine ensure patient self-care. In addition, peer-to-peer collaboration through social media develops a preventive healthcare lifestyle.
	New Commerce	The ubiquity of the internet and mobile devices should be harnessed to meet micro-requirements of customers. Next-generation mobility solutions co-create value by redefining stakeholder engagement. They also address differences within and across markets, and drive sustainable growth.
	Pervasive Computing	Enterprises must analyze real-time data from multiple embedded devices to design products and services that better address customer requirements. Computing and storage infrastructure plays a significant role in cost-efficiency, quality of service and agility. Artificial intelligence, cloud-based solutions and sensor networks are a business imperative today.
	Smarter Organizations	Smart decision-making demands simple processes. Operational excellence and accelerated innovation help companies deliver higher value to customers. It, however, requires balancing the challenges of a globally connected marketplace with the demands of localization. Tomorrow's companies should facilitate collaboration among different stakeholders to adapt to change.
	Sustainable Tomorrow	A smart enterprise can grow sustainably through equitable social contracts, effective resource utilization and green innovation. Smart solutions and analytical insights help companies take on the challenges of sustainable growth.

Its professional services complement the solutions portfolio and include consulting, package implementation, independent validation, migration, application development and maintenance, system integration, software performance engineering and support. As of March 31, 2012, Finacle is used by 160 banks across

78 countries, powers operations across 48,500 branches, and enables its customer banks to serve 423 million accounts and 347 million consumers globally.

Infosys competes with Accenture Limited, Atos Origin S.A., Cap Gemini S.A., Deloitte Consulting LLP, Hewlett-Packard Company, IBM Corporation, Computer Sciences Corporation, Dell Perot Systems, Cognizant Technology Solutions Corporation, Tata Consultancy Services Limited, Wipro Technologies Limited, Oracle Corporation and SAP A.G., Genpact Limited and WNS Global Services (Reuters 2014).

Several IT and engineering solutions and services delivered by Infosys help to accelerate innovation, increase productivity, reduce costs, and optimize asset utilization. They are offered in a broad scope of the industries, including Aerospace and Defense, Airlines, Automotive, Communication Services, Consumer Packaged Goods, Education, Ebergy, Financial Services, Health care, High-Tech, Hospitality and Leisure, Industrial Manufacturing, Insurance, Logistics and Distribution, Media and Entertainment, Medical Devices, Pharmaceuticals and Biotech, Public Sector, Publishing, Resources, Industries Retail, and Utilities (Infosys 2014a).

With such a variety of products and services, Infosys is growing fast and generates revenue which is discussed in the next subchapter.

2.5 Revenue

The revenue of Infosys is primarily derived from software development and related services and from the licensing of software products. Arrangements with customers for software products are either on a fixed-price, fixed-time frame, or on a time-and-material basis. According to Bloomberg, "Infosys Ltd. (INFO) forecast full-year sales growth that beat analyst estimates as India's second-largest software-services exporter cut costs and won more outsourcing contracts. The shares rose. Revenue in the 12 months started April 1 will climb 7 % to 9 % in US$ terms. That compares with revenue growth of 6–8.3 %, according to the average of six analyst estimates compiled by Bloomberg. The company also posted a 25 % jump in fourth-quarter earnings. Billionaire co-founder N.R. Narayana Murthy, who returned as chairman in June to help revive revenue growth, has reshuffled top management and boosted margins by trimming costs. Infosys won orders from Volvo Cars and US pharmacy benefit manager Prime Therapeutics LLC helping the company based in Bengaluru, earlier known as Bangalore, increase sales" (Bloomberg 2014).

Shares of Infosys rose 0.8 % to the highest level since April 7th in Mumbai trading. The net income of Infosys rose to 29.9 billion rupees (496 million US$) in the 3 months ending in March 31st, 2014. That exceeded the 28 billion-rupee median of 40 analysts' estimates compiled by Bloomberg. Sales for the fourth quarter rose 23 %. Additionally, worldwide information technology services spending are expected to increase 3.7 % to 671 billion US$ in 2014, accelerating from 2.8 % growth last year (Bloomberg 2014). On 31 April 2014, its market capitalization was 30.69 billion US$ (Infosys 2014c). Table 3 shows the revenue and profit for the recently concluded quarter and for the last 12 months.

Table 3 The revenue and profit of Infosys for the recently concluded quarter (April 2014) and for the last 12 months (Infosys 2014a)

	As per IFRS (Rs cr)	As per IFRS ($ m)
Q4 14 revenues	12,875	2,092
Q4 14 net profits	2,992	487
FY14 revenues	50,133	8,249
FY14 net profits	10,648	1,751

Table 4 The 5-year revenue and profit CAGR of Infosys (Infosys 2014a)

	As per IFRS (Rs cr) (%)	As per IFRS ($ m) (%)
Revenue	18	12
Net profit	12	6

Table 4 depictures the 5-year revenue and profit of Infosys.

3 The Rise of the Company

Infosys, along with its majority owned and controlled subsidiaries, is a leading global Consulting and IT services firm. The company provides end-to-end business solutions that leverage technology. The company offers solutions that span the entire software life cycle encompassing consulting, design, development, software re-engineering, maintenance, systems integration, package evaluation and implementation and infrastructure management services. In addition, the company offers software products for the banking industry and business process management services' (Infosys 2014a).

3.1 Business Strategy

Infosys is at the moment a very successful and dynamically-growing company, offering a high quality of provided services and products offered. "Known for its out-of-the-box approach to innovation, Infosys has a stated aim of making the business of its clients future proof using seven drivers—digital consumers, emerging economies, sustainable tomorrow, smarter organizations, new commerce, pervasive computing and healthcare economy" (The India Times 2013).

Infosys's strategy is based on the vision articulated in the Infosys 3.0 strategy and strengthens focus on its core competence area of Business IT Services. The company continues to explore and invest in the products and platform space. Given the very different R&D environment demanded by products and platforms, and the objective of delinking revenues from person-month effort, the Board approved the transfer of its existing Products, Platforms and Solutions business (excluding Finacle) to a wholly-owned subsidiary of Infosys Limited (Infosys 2014b). The company also undertakes several activities leading to cost optimization, enhancing sales productivity, and improving delivery effectiveness.

In the years that followed, Infosys quickly grew to the third largest India-based IT company (2012 revenues) and was one of the first truly global Indian companies. Innovation has always been at the heart of the company and it had a number of firsts to its name. Significantly, it was the first Indian company to offer employees stock options and along with it, untold prosperity to one and all (stories of "Infosys millionaires" that included chauffeurs, secretaries and office assistants are legendary). Similarly, Infosys was also the first Indian company to be listed on NASDAQ. Little wonder then that Forbes ranked Infosys 19th amongst the world's 100 most-innovative companies, in 2012. The Wall Street Journal Asia has also named Infosys as India's most-admired company almost every year since 2000. Infosys's values strongly resonate with those of its founder, N.R. Narayana Murthy. Whether, it is the (equitable) distribution of wealth, fair remuneration, or even philanthropy, the founder's values permeates the personality and the very fabric of the company (Interbrand 2013). The overview below presents the best India brands in 2013 by Interbrand. Infosys occupies the 5th position as mentioned earlier.

In addition, IT giant Infosys leads five Indian clean-energy projects that have been shortlisted for the annual Ashden Awards, referred to as the Green Oscars. The awards recognize worldwide contributions towards green energy initiatives and a move away from fossil fuels. Infosys has been nominated in the "Ashden Award for Sustainable Buildings" category for the Bangalore-based company's cutting edge design of new buildings which helps keep offices cooler and maximizes natural light. "Since 2008, global IT giant Infosys has cut more than 80 million US$ from its energy bills and reduced electricity consumption per staff member by 44 %. Its success lies in seizing every opportunity to reduce energy consumption in its existing buildings—from reducing the size of chiller plants for air conditioning, to painting roofs white so they reflect the heat", reads the award nomination statement. Winners will receive up to 40,000 pounds and global recognition as one of 2014s green energy leaders (The India Times 2014) (Table 5).

Infosys competes with Accenture Limited, Atos Origin S.A., Cap Gemini S.A., Deloitte Consulting LLP, Hewlett—Packard Company, IBM Corporation,

Table 5 Best Indian brands in 2013 by Interbrand (based on Interbrand 2013)

Rank	Brand	Sector	Brand value ($m)
1	TATA	Diversified	10,907
2	Reliance	Diversified	6,247
3	Airtel	Telecommunications	6,220
4	State Bank of India	Financial Services	3,838
5	Infosys	Technology	3,797
6	HDFC	Financial Services	3,277
7	Mahindra	Diversified	2,576
8	Icici	Financial Services	2,571
9	Godrej	Diversified	2,456
10	Larsen & Toubro	Diversified	2,320

Computer Sciences Corporation, Dell Perot Systems, Cognizant Technology Solutions Corporation, Tata Consultancy Services Limited, Wipro Technologies Limited, Oracle Corporation and SAP A.G., Genpact Limited and WNS Global Services (Reuters 2014).

A positive image of a growing company is strongly supported by The Infosys Foundation, established in 1996. It is a not-for-profit organization which supports the company's social initiatives devoted to the cause of the destitute, the rural poor, the mentally challenged and the economically disadvantaged sections of society, in addition to helping in the promotion of arts and culture. Additionally, Infosys cooperates with the government, other businesses and educational organizations in several ways. Infosys has formed Global Academic Relations with academic and partner institutions. It explores co-creation opportunities between Infosys and academia through case studies, student trips, and speaking engagements. They also collaborate on technology, emerging economies, globalization, and research. Some initiatives include research collaborations, publications, conferences and speaking sessions, campus visits and campus hiring (Infosys 2014b).

3.2 Company Growth

According to the report published by Gartner, the world's leading information technology research and advisory company, "Infosys is the third-largest India-based IT services company by 2012 revenues" (Gartner 2013). The other players and position of Infosys in the market is depictured below (Table 6).

The top five Indian service providers have continuously chipped away market share from the large multinational corporation providers. In the past 5 years, they have been winning large outsourcing deals (those with a total contract value of more than 100 million US$). Their target customer segment still remains the Fortune 1000 companies. Most of these firms have a large-deal pursuit sales team that goes after deals of more than 35 million US$ in contract value and there is a strong focus on, and investments in, cloud, analytics, mobility, infrastructure and

Table 6 Infosys positioned in the top 5 India-based IT Services Providers by worldwide revenue, 2012, in millions of dollars (Gartner 2013)

Company	Global ranking 2011	Global ranking 2012	2011 revenue	2012 revenue	2012-2011 growth (%)	2011 market share (%)	2012 market share (%)
TCS	16	16	9,451	10,888	15.2	1.1	1.2
Cognizant	28	23	5,875	7,053	20.1	0.7	0.8
Infosys	27	26	6,279	6,691	6.6	0.7	0.7
Wipro	31	31	5,334	5,737	7.6	0.6	0.6
HCL technologies	47	41	3,316	3,916	18.1	0.4	0.4
Total			30,255	34,285	13.3	3.5	3.7

knowledge processes. "India-based providers have become much more aggressive in infrastructure management because it offers them the potential to grow bottom-up within accounts" (Gartner 2013).

"Revenue contribution from project-based and staff augmentation deals have continued to decline for the top five Indian-based providers, and the outsourcing service line component has steadily increased. They have also made significant strides in developing industry—specific BPO services through acquisitions and/or organic growth. There is an increasing focus on "integrated services play". Indian providers use an integrated approach of applications, infrastructure and BPO, thereby allowing them to get a better handle on their clients' IT-business process leveraging, through which they can deliver greater cost savings and drive business value. This allows them to expand their margins as well. All these providers also have a strong focus on infrastructure services, particularly remote infrastructure management services, which account for 65 % to 70 % of their infrastructure services revenue, Gartner reports. Gartner views Indian players as providers that predominantly have an India-based delivery model and management that is largely India-based. Most are headquartered in India, but there are some exceptions, such as Genpact, Cognizant, Syntel and iGate, which are headquartered in the U.S. However, the delivery, management, operating style and behavior of these companies are like those of other Indian providers" (Gartner 2013).

Infosys regularly acquires several companies. On January 4, 2012, Infosys BPO Limited (Infosys BPO) acquired Portland Group Pty Ltd., a provider of strategic sourcing and category management services based in Australia. In October 2012, the company acquired Lodestone Holding AG (Reuters 2014). In December 2003, Infosys had acquired Australia-based IT service provider Expert Information Services for 23 million US$ (The Hindu Business Line 2003). In January 2012, Infosys BPO acquired Australia-based Portland Group, provider of strategic sourcing and category management services, for about 37 million AU$. In September 2012, Infosys acquired Switzerland-based Lodestone Management Consultants for about 345 million US$ (Forbes 2012).

In 2010, Infosys signed an agreement with Microsoft to manage key parts of worldwide internal IT operations. The agreement calls for Infosys to take over responsibility for managing Microsoft's IT help desk and desk-side services operations, as well as servicing the company's applications, devices and databases in more than 100 countries (Computer World 2010).

Cloud-platform solutions, mobile, and analytics are likely to drive growth, even as the industry contends with cuts in US federal government IT spending and offshore scrutiny of IT vendors (Bloomberg 2014). This creates a window of opportunities for Infosys as well.

All of the details that are especially important to relations with investors "are forward-looking statements, which involve a number of risks and uncertainties that could cause actual results to differ materially from those in such forward-looking statements. The risks and uncertainties relating to these statements include, but are not limited to, risks and uncertainties regarding fluctuations in earnings, fluctuations in foreign exchange rates, ability to manage growth, intense competition in IT services including those factors which may affect cost advantage, wage increases in India, ability to attract and retain highly skilled professionals, time and cost overruns on fixed-price, fixed-time frame contracts, client concentration, restrictions on immigration, industry segment concentration, ability to manage international operations, reduced demand for technology in key focus areas, disruptions in telecommunication networks or system failures, ability to successfully complete and integrate potential acquisitions, liability for damages on Infosys's service contracts, the success of the companies in which Infosys has made strategic investments, withdrawal or expiration of governmental fiscal incentives, political instability and regional conflicts, legal restrictions on raising capital or acquiring companies outside India, and unauthorized use of intellectual property and general economic conditions affecting industry. The company does not undertake to update any forward-looking statements that may be made from time to time by or on behalf of the company unless it is required by law" (Infosys 2014a).

4   Future Developments

According to Segers and Stam, Asian FDI in the Netherlands has increased significantly over the years, and according to their prognosis, Asian companies will continue to increase their presence in the Netherlands (Segers and Stam 2013). This statement could also apply to Infosys as well. Infosys has successfully expanded and is expanding global presence with new centers in several countries worldwide. It continues also to support enterprises.

In December of last year, Infosys unveiled a new product platform that helps global brands in the fast-moving consumer goods (FMCG) segment to drive profitable growth in emerging markets. Named "TradeEdge", the software platform delivers insights for brands to predict and meet consumer demand and improve sales and operational performance. According to the global consulting firm McKinsey, retail consumption in emerging markets will be about 30 trillion US$ by 2025, accounting for half the global demand and presents a huge growth opportunity to global brands like Proctor & Gamble in light of slowing consumption in developed markets. Highlighting the innovative features of TradeEdge platform, Infosys emphasizes that the next billion consumers would be in the emerging markets, and global brands will have to know the market better, reach customers faster, and do so at lower costs. The platform allows FMCG firms and their distributors to exchange information on sales, inventory, and products in weeks through a cloud-based enterprise resource planning system and adopt best practices in hours. The platform improves product placement and maximizes return on promotions through visual merchandising by providing insights into share of shelf at a fraction of audit costs. The platform also helps reduce waste of perishable products with a solution that monitors their temperature and location of cooling units. TradeEdge can be used to serve retailers which can order and pay for products cost-effectively using basic mobile phones and reduce ordering costs up to 80 % with suggested orders based on previous data and forecasts (India TV 2013).

Within a decade, revenue from Europe has increased nearly tenfold to two billion US$, far higher than for the rest of Infosys, highlighting its ability to drive growth in key markets and industry verticals. In 2004, the company crossed the one billion US$ revenue milestone. "Very few companies have created that kind of growth story in Europe" (The Economic Times 2013). This success in Europe might play an important role in attracting Infosys to invest in the Northern Netherlands region.

4.1 Opening New Centers Worldwide

One of the ways to grow Infosys users is to expand the company's local presence. This also applies to non-English-speaking European markets, especially the Nordic countries and the Benelux (Belgium, Netherlands and Luxembourg) region, where Infosys plans to appoint a regional head and local sales team over the next 6 months (The Economic Times 2013). The current activities of the company in the Netherlands are discussed in the next subchapter.

4.2 Infosys in the Netherlands

Infosys in the Netherlands operates in the Amsterdam metropolitan area, Utrecht and Eindhoven. In November 2013, the company announced that Infosys BPO would open a new delivery center in Eindhoven, the Netherlands (Reuters 2014). The 120-seat center strengthens Infosys BPO's global footprint and reinforces its position in Europe.

Infosys sees Europe "as a major growth opportunity. In order to ensure close contact with the clients, Infosys needs to be in close proximity to its current and future clients" (Netherlands Foreign Investment Agency 2013). With respect to that expansion, Infosys leverages the new center to deliver critical business processes such as finance and accounting and other high value services for its global clients, and provides end-to-end outsourcing services in Dutch, English, French and German. The company chose to set up the back office in Eindhoven due to availability of a talented workforce and a positive environment fostered by the Dutch government (Business Today 2013). This opening enables Infosys BPO to respond quickly and efficiently to client needs for accelerated solutions across the EMEA (Europe, Middle East and Africa) region. Altogether, it makes Eindhoven an ideal location for Infosys BPO's new delivery center: the favorable business environment created by the NFIA (Netherlands Foreign Investment Agency), the Brabant Development Agency and Brainport Development, coupled with the availability of a highly competent and skilled workforce with multi-linguistic capabilities (Infosys 2013a).

The Eindhoven center strengthens Infosys BPO's global footprint, reinforces its position in Europe, and serves as "a regional hub for Infosys BPO. It strengthens the company's ability to cater to client needs across functions, languages, and time zones quickly and with greater flexibility. The team in Eindhoven plays a key role to accelerate innovation and transformation for Infosys's clients across industries" (Brabant Development Agency 2013).

The south of the Netherlands is an attractive region for Infosys. The cooperation with the Brabant Development Agency, based in Tilburg, which has a staff of 60, delivers additional doubts as to the willingness by Infosys to invest in the Northern Netherlands. With regards to the proximity of several other centers, it is worthy to note that Infosys has expanded its operations in Central Europe, also. A 400-seat facility in Brno was opened in 2007 (Infosys 2007) which provides both IT services to BPO's clients in Europe and a growing BPO Center in Poland. This center won the "Most Dynamically Developing BPO Center in Poland" award from Forbes Magazine. Infosys was recognized for high quality work and execution speed involved in transitioning Lodz DC from a transactional Business Process Outsourcing center to a high-end Knowledge Process Outsourcing (KPO) center (Infosys 2012b).

According to Forbes, major ICT companies have a presence in the Netherlands and more than 60 % of all Forbes 2000 ICT companies have established their presence in the Amsterdam area, including Microsoft, Google, Cisco, Tata, IBM, Oracle, Capgemini, Zarafa, and Infosys (Nuffic 2013). With regards to this statement, Infosys puts effort in getting new contracts. At the beginning of this year, Infosys bagged an approximately 100 million US$ multi-year outsourcing contract from Netherlands-based courier delivery service TNT (The Times of India 2014). TNT Express, which focuses on Europe and connecting Europe with the rest of the world, has set a target to achieve 220 million in savings by 2015 through consolidating services, optimizing infrastructure, increasing productivity and reducing indirect costs. TNT Express is investing 200 million in infrastructure and IT until the end of 2015 to optimize and automate depots and hubs and in business supporting and customer IT, the company's website says. For instance, TNT Express is launching new online booking and payment tools to improve its customer interface technology. Logistics companies like UPS, DHL and FedEx have had outsourcing engagements with Indian IT vendors for some time now. Wipro has serviced FedEx and Cognizant and Infosys have provided IT services to DHL (The Times of India 2014).

Last year, Infosys has announced a major 4-year strategic partnership with COMMIT, a public-private research community in the Netherlands, to help create healthier societies across the World (Bloomberg 2013). COMMIT is a Netherlands use-inspired fundamental ICT research program based on a public-private partnership paradigm uniting academic research and (non-) profit organizations. Funded by the Government of Netherlands with 50 million € and with total revenues of 110 million €, COMMIT is the leading public-private ICT research community focusing on solving grand challenges in information and communication science for tomorrow's society. Ten universities, five technological institutes, and over sixty small and large businesses participate in sixteen public-private multi-party projects. In the frame of the project, Infosys will bring its widely acknowledged technology leadership and financial investments to COMMIT's Sensor-based Engagement for Improved Health (SENSEI) project as part of a wider consortium of partners. COMMIT's SENSEI project aims to promote a healthier society globally through the use of an engaging smart phone application that enables users to exercise more efficiently. In the frame of the project, Infosys will draw on its proven technical expertise in sensor networks, complex event processing, security, and velocity data management to enhance SENSEI's smart phone application and ensure that it is as effective as using a personal trainer. The application delivers personalized coaching guidelines on a user's smart phone based on factors such as current vital statistics, exercise regime, long and short-term medical history, location, diet habits, and weather conditions. Infosys and COMMIT will collaborate to enable the application to access a wide variety of data sources beyond traditional exercise parameters such as mood recognition, speech analysis, and also social content analysis from the user's Facebook and Twitter accounts. These insights will be used to design a more accurate and effective fitness regime. The partners will work with specialist sports schools and experts from diverse fields such as human movement and media interaction professors, fitness coaches, and sports and nutrition professors in continuing to develop the solution. Infosys will also provide systems integration and overall program management for the project (Bloomberg 2013).

To conclude, as stated by consulting company Pricewaterhouse Coopers, Belgium is also seen as a gateway for Indian companies looking to invest in Europe. Belgium is at the heart of the wealthiest, most populous area of Europe. Its neighbors are France, Germany, Luxembourg, and the Netherlands and, across the Channel, the UK. Belgium has a large pool of highly skilled, multilingual workforce talent in which Infosys invests. Brussels, the capital of Belgium and administrative center of the European Union, is one of the most cost-efficient cities in northern Europe. Belgium offers attractive tax investment regulations and has a positive track record as an investment destination. Belgium has excellent infrastructure, including Europe's second-largest port in Antwerp, and it boasts of one of the densest networks of road and rail. Belgium is particularly successful in the logistics, automotive, pharma, engineering and chemicals sectors (Pricewaterhouse Coopers 2012).

5 Conclusions

The possibility that Infosys will establish itself in the Northern Netherlands or will enlarge its operations here are relatively low. Having a well-established center in Eindhoven significantly decreases this chance. The availability of a talented workforce and a positive environment fostered by the government makes the south of the Netherlands an attractive destination for Infosys. The location of Infosys in the Netherlands is highly connected with talented workforce, and it is located in

Brabant, one of the most innovative regions in the world. The strategy at Infosys is to strengthen the value of all of the employees and constantly invest in developing their competencies. Infosys, being a global brand, might be potentially interested in the knowledge and experience in the Northern Netherlands region, but it would require several actions to be undertaken at the same time in the framework of the triple helix, by the government, industry and academia.

Appendix: Financial Snapshot

Revenue

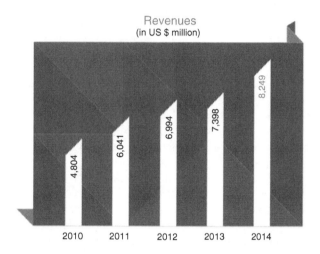

(Infosys 2014b)

Net profit

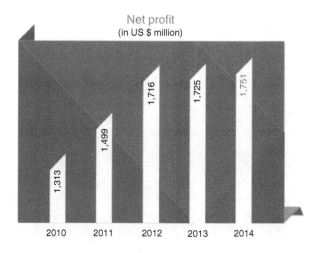

(Infosys 2014b)

References

Bloomberg. (2013). *Infosys partners with Netherlands' COMMIT to help create healthier societies*. Retrieved November 18, 2013, from http://www.bloomberg.com.
Bloomberg. (2014). *Infosys forecast beats estimates on outsourcing contracts (3)*. Retrieved April 15, 2014, from http://www.bloomberg.com.
Brabant Development Agency. (2013). *Infosys BPO Expands Global Presence with New Centre in the Netherlands*. Retrieved November 8, 2013, from http://www.foreigninvestments.eu.
Business Today. (2013). *Infosys opens office in Netherlands*. Retrieved November 9, 2013, from http://www.businesstoday.in.
Computer World. (2010). *Microsoft signs outsourcing pact with Indian giant Infosys*. Retrieved May 20, 2014, from http://www.computerworld.com.
Forbes. (2012). *News analysis: Infosys buys lodestone for $350M*. Retrieved October 9, 2012, from http://www.forbes.com.
Gartner. (2013). *Top 5 India-based IT services providers' worldwide revenue*. Retrieved May 20, 2014, from http://www.gartner.com.
Harvard Business Review. (2006). *Infosys in India: Building a software giant in a corrupt environment*. Retrieved December 1, 2006, from http://www.hbr.org cited May 10th, 2014.
Hindustan Times. (2013). *Murthy returns to save struggling Infosys*. Retrieved June 1, 2013, from http://www.hindustantimes.com.
In.com. (2012). *Companies. Infosys Technologies Bio*. Retrieved April 13, 2014, from http://www.in.com.
India TV. (2013). *Infosys builds retail platform for global consumer brands*. Retrieved December 10, 2013, from http://www.indiatvnews.com.
Infosys. (2007). *Expands operations in central Europe*. Retrieved April 24, 2007, from http://www.infosys.com.
Infosys. (2012a). *Infosys to expand its U.S. operations with a new Delivery Center in Wisconsin*. Retrieved July 23, 2012, from http://www.infosys.com.
Infosys. (2012b). *Infosys BPO wins the "Most dynamically developing BPO center in Poland" award from Forbes Magazine*. Retrieved February 12, 2014, from http://www.infosys.com.
Infosys. (2013a). *Infosys BPO expands global presence with new center in the Netherlands, Bangalore, India; Eindhoven, Netherlands*. Retrieved November 8, 2013, from http://www.infosys.com.
Infosys. (2014a). *Company information*. Retrieved May 20, 2014, from http://www.infosys.com.
Infosys. (2014b). *Annual report 2013–2014, evolving in changing times*. Reports and filings. Retrieved May 10, 2014, from http://www.infosys.com/investors/reports-filings/annual-report/annual/Documents/Infosys-AR-14.pdf.
Infosys. (2014c). *Market cap, INFY*. Retrieved March 20, 2014, from http://www.infosys.com.
Interbrand. (2013). *Best Indian brands, 2013*. Retrieved April 10, 2014, from http://www.interbrand.com.
Netherlands Foreign Investment Agency. (2013). *Indian outsourcing major Infosys BPO's delivery center in Eindhoven*. Retrieved May 9, 2014, from http://www.nfia.nl.
Nuffic. (2013). *Major ICT companies have a presence in the Netherlands*. Retrieved March 25, 2013, from http://www.nesoindia.org April 16th, 2014.
NYSE. (2013). *Infosys celebrates cross-listing on NYSE Euronext London and NYSE Euronext Paris and highlights recent transfer to NYSE*. Retrieved February 19, 2013, from http://www.nyse.com.
Pricewaterhouse Coopers. (2012). *Belgium: The European gateway for Indian companies*. Retrieved May 9, 2014, from http://www.pwc.be.
Reuters. (2014). *Infosys Ltd (INFY.K)*. Retrieved March 10, 2014, from http://www.reuters.com.
Segers, R. T., & Stam, T. (2013). *Asia reshaping the global economic landscape*. Maastricht: Shaker Media.

The Economist. (2013). *Services: The next big thing*. Retrieved January 19, 2013, from http://www.economist.com.
The Economic Times. (2013). *Infosys may eye acquisitions in Nordic countries, says president BG Srinivas*, May 5, 2014. Retrieved from http://articles.economictimes.indiatimes.com/2014-05-05/news/49634177_1_bg-srinivas-sd-shibulal-lodestone
The Hindu Business Line. (2003). *Infosys to buy Australian firm expert for $22.9m*. Retrieved March 16, 2014, from http://www.thehindubusinessline.in.
The India Times. (2013). *Best Indian Brands 2013: Who made it to the list of top 10*. Retrieved July 31, 2013, from http://www.indiatimes.com.
The India Times. (2014). *Infosys leads 5 Indian projects shortlisted for Green Oscars*. Retrieved April 9, 2014, from http://www.indiatimes.com.
The Times of India. (2014). *Infosys bags $100-million deal from Netherlands-based TNT Express*. Retrieved January 28, 2014.
United States Department of Labor. (2012). *US, Top 10 employers, H-1B temporary visa program—selected statistics*. Retrieved May 10, 2014, from http://www.foreignlaborcert.doleta.gov.

Part III

Japan

Panasonic: A Case Study on Constant Change and Reinvention of a World Brand

Uli Mathies

Abstract
Panasonic's nearly one hunderd-year history can be divided into several phases. The constant factor in Panasonic's history was—and is—change. And this may also contain the simple answer to the question about Panasonic's secret of success: the ability to transform as required by an ever-changing environment, the willingness to keep developing, and the openness to learn and take risks have been engrained in the company's collective memory. Giving up is not an option, and the only way out is the way forward. Therefore it can be boldly concluded that Panasonic as a corporation will still exist 50 years from now, and maybe even a 100 years from now. The company may look differently, produce different products or services, and market them in a completely different way, but chances are high that Panasonic will still be a major player in the domestic and global markets.

1 Introduction

Contrary to the other companies featured in this book, Japanese electronic product manufacturer Panasonic can look back on a long and colorful history. Founded in the early twentieth century as 'Matsushita Electric Housewares Manufacturing Works', Panasonic grew from a modest dirt-floor workshop to a gigantic global corporation with a vast scope of markets and a product range including appliances, TVs and monitors, phones and computers, car audio and satellite navigation systems, and even entire building systems and home interiors. In its almost 100 years of existence, Panasonic has undergone as many changes and ups and downs as the national and international environment it has operated in. One could

U. Mathies (✉)
International Business School, Hanze University OAS, Groningen, The Netherlands
e-mail: u.d.s.mathies@pl.hanze.nl

almost say the one constant factor in Panasonic's history is change. Nevertheless, in March 2013 Panasonic was voted among the top ten of "Japanese companies expected to still be around in 50 years" in an industry survey conducted by Risk Monster, a credit management outsourcing service that calculates bankruptcy risk (Japan Today 2013). The analysis concluded that the ability "to survive fierce global competition and still exist 50 years later" depended on possessing the right technical capability, but "companies will also need to be able to effectively leverage that capability." Other significant factors named were product quality, market share, originality, management philosophy/approach, and trustworthiness—all variables also determined by Segers and Stam (2013) as being crucial in the fast-growing competitiveness of Asian firms.

What, one therefore wants to ask, is Panasonic's secret of success? Which elements in their company strategy, their products and technology, and their approach to human resources have secured the company a competitive advantage that has lasted almost a 100 years and is deemed strong enough to make it at least another 50? What has helped the dated company through times of economic turmoil and persistent recession to time and again beat the competition in the global business arena?

In order to answer these questions, we will conduct a thorough case study covering Panasonic's rich history from 1918 onwards, consider recent developments and strategic choices, and examine the national and international context of the company. Conclusions will be drawn and translated into practical recommendations, the latter specifically with the interests and opportunities of the Northern Netherlands in mind.

2 The History and Rise of the Company

2.1 Foundation and Early Years (1918–1950)

2.1.1 Foundation

Panasonic was founded in 1918 as 'Matsushita Electric Housewares Manufacturing Works' in Osaka in Japan by 23 year old Konosuke Matsushita (1894–1989). Initially a tiny three-man workshop producing self-designed electric light sockets and insulator plates, the company quickly earned a reputation for high quality at low prices (Panasonic Company website 2014). The young founder Matsushita, who due to life circumstances was thrown into poverty and lacked any formal education, combined technical inventiveness with clever entrepreneurship, a commitment to lifelong learning, and great determination. Thanks to his perception for market potential, his innovative marketing practices, and most of all his outstanding visionary leadership, the company turned into a textbook example for the post-WWII Japanese economic miracle. John Kotter (1997) dedicated an entire biography to Matsushita, celebrating him as the most inspirational leader, author, educator, philanthropist, and management innovator of his time. It was Matsushita's accomplishment that from its modest beginnings in Japan the company gradually and continuously grew into one of the largest and most affluent global electronic corporations.

2.1.2 1920s

By the early twenties, Matsushita was launching new items every month, all of them said to be better and less expensive than the ones from his competitors; in addition, he paid special attention to customer needs and after-sales services (Kotter 1997). In 1923, he came up with a bullet-shaped battery-powered bicycle lamp that would operate reliably much longer than all previous models and which he boldly sold directly to bike stores by circumventing wholesalers. The second generation of battery-powered bicycle lamps, with a square-shaped design, was the first one to carry the 'National' brand name in 1927.

Matsushita felt a strong obligation to society and made it his mission to make electrical products that were considered luxury goods available to a wide clientele. With the National "Super-Iron" in 1929, the company started on mass production and formulated the 'Basic Management Objective and Company Creed', which stated the company's goal of "contributing to the development of society and the improvement of people's lives" (Panasonic Company website 2014). More invention followed, including among others an electric space heater, an electrically-heated table, a new type of thermostat, and later electric motors and electric fans. Matsushita's inexpensive three-vacuum-tube radio won first prize in a broadcasting contest in 1931.

2.1.3 1930s

In the early thirties, the company was manufacturing around 200 products, had grown to more than 100 office staff, and employed more than 1,000 factory workers (Dayao 2000). Matsushita took action to formalize the company's mission and structure: At the first commemoration of the company's foundation in 1932, he announced that "the mission of a manufacturer is to overcome poverty by producing an abundant supply of goods" (Panasonic Company website 2014). He divided the company into three autonomously managed divisions each with its own administration, product development and manufacturing facilities. In addition, he set up a trade department to explore overseas sales opportunities. Following Matsushita's belief that "business is people", the 'Employee Training Institute' was opened in 1934 at the new Kadoma factory and head office; it offered primary school graduates a 3-year study that combined engineering and business. And in December 1935, setting the step towards international business, Matsushita incorporated the company, renaming it 'Matsushita Electric Industrial Co. Ltd.' (MEI). As during the Great Depression of the thirties, the firm's sales dropped dramatically, but Matsushita's endurance and foresight prevented bankruptcy: by moving employees around instead of laying them off, cutting work hours and production schedules instead of shutting down facilities, and asking workers to help sell merchandise, the company survived where others failed (Kotter 1997).

2.1.4 WWII

Like Japan's economy at large, MEI was hit hard by WWII. While military contracts led to the establishment of 'Matsushita Shipbuilding Company' and 'Matsushita Airplane Company', by the end of the war the company had lost most factories and offices. To make things worse, as a former supplier to the Japanese army, MEI was burdened with severe restrictions by the Allied powers (Kotter 1997). Many years were spent struggling to regain control of the company's operations. Eventually, Matsushita, with the massive help of his workers, succeeded in convincing the military government that his company should be allowed to restart production of peacetime goods. Declaring it their duty to "address the task of rebuilding the nation and enriching people's lives", Matsushita gradually resumed the production of consumer wares (Panasonic Company website 2014). In 1947, Sanyo was established as a subcontractor for components (Sanyo later turned into a competitor and was acquired by Panasonic in 2009). After many years of hardship and financial crisis, the company started over from scratch in 1950, soon to be back in business and thriving.

2.2 Rebuilding of the Company (1950–1989)

2.2.1 Post-war period

During the Japanese post-war boom (Segers and Stam 2013), Matsushita Electric continued their expansion course, founding and acquiring other companies on the way. In 1949 and 1951, the company's shares were listed at the Tokyo Stock Exchange, the Osaka Securities Exchange, and the Nagoya Stock Exchange, respectively. Realizing that his company needed more specialized knowledge of electronics and Western technologies before entering the international stage, Matsushita set up a technical cooperation agreement with Philips of the Netherlands, creating 'Matsushita Electronics Corporation' as a joint venture in 1952. Six years later, he received the honor of being decorated Commander in the Order of Orange Nassau by Her Majesty Queen Juliana of the Netherlands for his contributions to economic cooperation and to promoting friendship between the two nations. Subsequently, he initiated the establishment, and became first chairman, of the Japan-Netherlands Society in Kansai which was independent from that in Tokyo (still active as the Netherlands Society in West-Japan).

In 1959, Matsushita founded Matsushita 'Electric Corporation of America' in New York as the first post-war overseas sales company. During this period, many products were introduced by MEI: an agitator-type washing machine (1951), the company's first black and white television sets (1952), their first electric refrigerator (1953), a portable radio (1954), the electric rice cooker (1956), the first tape recorder, and an air conditioner (both 1958). The company's first color television set was marketed in 1960 (Panasonic Company website 2014). New local companies were 'Kyushu Matsushita Electric Company', the 'Osaka Precision Machinery Company' (later renamed 'Matsushita Seiko'), and the 'Matsushita Communication Industrial Group' (which manufactured the first tape recorder).

Rapid growth led to the opening of manufacturing plants around the world, starting with 'National Thai', the first overseas factory, in 1961 and 'Matsushita Electric' (Taiwan) in 1962; plants in Mexico, Puerto Rico, Costa Rica, Peru, Tanzania, the former Malays, the Philippines and Australia followed.

2.2.2 1960s

At the beginning of this new phase of globalization, at the age of 65, Matsushita announced his resignation as president and that he would "support the company from behind the scenes as chairman" (Panasonic Company website 2014). With his son-in law, Masaharu Matsushita, as president, the company entered into a period of seemingly unlimited growth. The implementation of a groundbreaking sales and distribution system and the development of new hit products further accelerated MEI's rapid expansion. Popular products included console stereos and speakers, a fully automatic washing machine, and a console TV (all 1965), which were marketed under various brand-names, among which National, Panasonic, and Technics.

To demonstrate the astonishing advances of the company and to solicit customer reactions and input, the company held their first major technological exhibition in 1969 in Tokyo. Only 17 years after the technical cooperation agreement with Philips, MEI was capable of presenting cutting edge technology that mesmerized more than 15,000 visitors, including academics, researchers, and industry insiders.

Believing that MEI should contribute to worldwide prosperity, Matsushita advised that the company take a global perspective. Over the years, MEI built up their international capabilities, expanded support operations for overseas business, and trained staff to act internationally. In 1971, the company entered the community of international enterprises by registering for trading of its shares on the New York Stock Exchange (Panasonic Company website 2014).

2.2.3 1970s

Economic turbulences in the wake of the oil crisis of the seventies also affected MEI. In order to deal with the constantly changing domestic and international situations and to regain profitability, the company renewed its top management in 1977. The new president Toshihiko Yamashita returned to the foundations of the corporate division system and implement a policy of personnel exchange, which would activate the company's organizational structure (Panansonic Company website, 2014).

2.2.4 1980s

In 1986, triggered by a dooming financial crisis in Japan, vice-president Akio Tanii took over and restructured the company, guided by a Management Innovation Plan. Four product groups were given priority (information and communications equipment, computerized manufacturing equipment, semiconductor devices, AV equipment), and the company's marketing focus was changed. Under the motto "Human Electronics", a campaign for better product design was launched, combining sensitivity to human needs with advanced technologies (Panasonic Company website 2014).

2.2.5 The founder

Konosuke Matsushita himself retired in 1973 from active service, but remained executive adviser until his death in 1989. During these later years, as MEI's success started to spread abroad, Matsushita started to be recognized as one of the world's great entrepreneurs. He was featured on the covers of Time (1962) and Life (1964) magazine; he welcomed foreign statesmen and VIPs on his premises; and his management methods were studied as role models for executives (Kotter 1997). He wrote numerous books on management philosophy, leadership, and ethics; studied human nature with a group of researchers; acted as a philanthropist; founded an independent graduate school of government to reform Japan's politics (1980); and created a Japanese version of the Nobel Prize (1985). By the time of his death at age 94, MEI produced more than 14,000 products. Few organizations had more customers; the company employed 120,000 people worldwide and had estimated revenues of above 49 billion US$; and Matsushita's personal wealth was estimated at three billion US$ (Kotter 1997). In his home country, he was canonized as "God of management" and considered a national saint (Katayama 1989).

2.3 Stagnation and First Restructuring (1989–2006)

2.3.1 1990s

In the early nineties, after a record-setting period of economic expansion, the Japanese economic bubble burst. Both real estate and stock market indices crashed, and in the aftermath of a credit crunch in the financial markets, the Japanese economy was thrown into a serious prolonged recession (Segers and Stam 2013). MEI registered a steep drop in sales, as a consequence of which Tanii stepped down in 1993. The new president Yoichi Morishita announced a four-point strategy to rebuild the company, which reinforced the company's corporate mission and responsibilities to society and their tradition of autonomous management. In addition, management innovation was to be based on a new concept of "creativity and daring" (Panasonic Company website 2014).

2.3.2 The new century

Despite of all efforts, MEI increasingly suffered from stagnation. At this point, the company was worth 72 billion US$ in sales, employing 293,000 people around the world, and ranked as the tenth largest industrial company not in oil or autos. McInerney's (2007) analysis of Panasonic's problems and account of the subsequent 11-year restructuring (1995–2006) poignantly dissects the factors that had contributed to the situation:

> "Like other Japanese industrial giants, Matsushita had thrived by investing in dedicated engineering staffs and relentlessly entering electronics markets with high-quality, lower-cost products. That worked well in the decades after World War II, when the corporation's fine execution gave it a solid position in Japan and elsewhere. But ... success led to complacency and ossification, as problems were hidden by the large, semi-protected

domestic market. The company characteristically reacted to stagnation in the late 1980s with a huge investment in R&D, but that only eroded margins faster. ... [The company] was isolated from customers, with factories determining output levels and its understaffed sales offices lacking in rudimentary account management skills." (Landry 2007)

The, by McInerney's (2007) account, "largest corporate restructuring in history" was accomplished without importing an outside CEO by following the template drafted by McInerney and his partner, two New York-based Japan specialists, investors and business advisors. Company-wide changes took off with the appointment of Kunio Nakamura, formerly head of the American subsidiary, to MEI president in 2000. As part of the company's first 3-year mid-term plan, Value Creation 21 and its follow-up Leap Ahead 21 (see notes), he aggressively restructured the company to enable adaptation to competitive forces in the environment and increase market responsiveness (Kosuga 2009). Bureaucratic complexities were removed and structures flattened, management information flow and decision making mechanisms (re-) instated, branding and marketing revamped, and the sales and distribution system reformed (Reorganization 2004). Full ownership of a number of subdivisions of the Matsushita Group had to be acquired before the whole company was restructured into 14 independent business domains in 2003. This was a huge break with MEI's tradition of virtually autonomous business units organized along product lines, each functioning like a self-sufficient corporate kingdom. Now, efficiencies could be gained by eliminating overlapping redundancies, centralizing investments into research and development, and integrating functions of manufacturing, marketing, and sales (Tanikawa 2004). Another one of Matsushita's most sacred corporate principles was discarded: for the first time in history, workers were laid off. Cultural changes included the establishment of a "customer first" attitude and a corporate culture that fostered diversity and competitiveness.

Also in 2003, the global brand was unified as 'Panasonic' and accompanied by the establishment of the global brand slogan "Panasonic ideas for life." Still, the name National was kept as a region-specific brand for Japan only, and the name Technics as product-specific brand in tandem with Panasonic. In a bold move in 2005, the company decided to cease the domestic production of money-losing tube TV sets and to entirely focus on the—then high-margin—flat-screen plasma display panel (PDP) technology. A year later the scale of PDP production reached a combined monthly output of 460,000 units at four plants, and the company captured half the global market, again proving the company's "long-nurtured traditions of engineering excellence, which empowered managers and employees to commit to the intense work involved in developing a world-class product" (Landry 2007). This example also shows how easily technological change can turn fate, as in the fall of 2013 Panasonic announced their immediate stop of all plasma research and development due to price pressure from more affordable LCD TVs (Reuters 2013). As this last fact indicates, even Nakamura's "largest corporate restructuring in history" was only temporarily blessed with success (see Fig. 1). Rapid and drastic changes to the business environment, markets, and technology kept challenging the company.

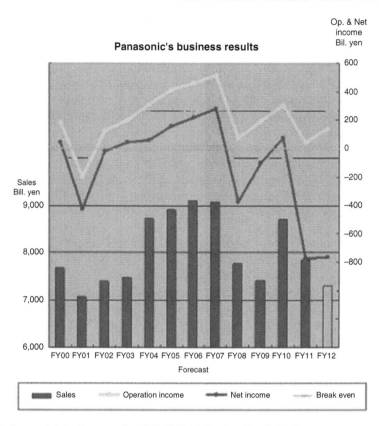

Fig. 1 Panasonic's business results FY2000-2012 (SemiconPortal 2012)

2.4 Continuing Reforms (2006–2012)

In 2006, president Fumio Ohtsubo took over from Nakamura, while continuing reforms with his 3-year mid-term business plans GP3 and Green Transformation 12 (see notes). During his tenure, Matsushita Electric Industrial Co. Ltd. officially became Panasonic Corporation Worldwide on the 90th anniversary of the company in 2008. This final step in a multiyear effort to eliminate the multitude of brand names reflected the company's unified brand positioning and its new digital network product strategy. Ohtsubo explained: "Now we have one brand. Under one brand we can propose a total solution for our daily lives" (Tarr 2008). At the same time, he announced that Panasonic would venture into the development of wholesome integrated solutions consisting of AV electronics, appliances, and energy generation components. With reference to company founder Matsushita's ideals of serving society, the company made a commitment to environmental management in the "Eco Ideas Declaration" (Laposky 2008). This comprehensive company-wide effort included three approaches relating to (1) manufacturing/production (reduction of CO_2 emissions; proper management and disposal of chemical substances; saving resources through enhanced productivity), (2) product design (increasing the energy-efficiency of products, recycling initiatives), and (3) outreach (ecological activities with employees and their families, inclusion of local community, initiatives beyond national borders). In order to illustrate the earth-friendly ambitions, an "Eco & Ud House" was built at the Ariake facility in Tokyo, "a prototype residence that incorporates cutting-edge technologies that help deliver on the ecological principles, as well as follow a design philosophy that is user-friendly and supportive of the needs of all people to be healthy and happy" (Laposky 2008). The Eco Ideas strategy found continuation in the 2010 announcement that Panasonic aimed to become the "No. 1 Green Innovation Company in the Electronics Industry" by its 100th anniversary in 2018. Its declared aim is "integrating contributing to the environment and attaining business growth" by making green targets, such as for CO_2 reduction and recycling, part of the corporate vision (Miyai 2011).

Panasonic's new concepts and intermittent improvements notwithstanding, the company kept writing losses, and over a period of 6 years their shares dropped by two thirds, double the decline on the benchmark Nikkei average over the same period (Kelly 2012). The 2009 acquisition of rival Sanyo Electric—producer of among others solar panels and lithium batteries and seen as needed for Panasonic's repositioning as green technology company—in combination with the exuberant restructuring expenditures, contributed to the company spreading itself even further (Kelly 2012). Aggravating external factors were the 2011 Fukushima earthquake, which damaged the supply chain; a strong yen which kept prices high; stern foreign competition led by Samsung; and production halts caused by floods in Thailand in 2012 (Cooper 2012; Yasu 2012). A massive restructuring plan was implemented between January and March 2012 (Panasonic Announcement 2011). The number of employees was reduced by roughly 17,000–350,000, and the 2010 organizational structure of six business segments based on technology platform (digital AVC networks, home appliances, Panasonic Electric Works and Panahome, components and devices, Sanyo, and Other) was converted to one of three business sectors based on business model ("B2C" consumer business sector, "B2B" components and devices business sector, and "B2B" solutions sector, comprising nine business domain companies and one marketing sector). Still, in their 2012 quarterly report for the fiscal year ending in March (FY 2012), Panasonic announced a record net loss of 780 billion yen (9.7 billion US$), and the Big Three credit rating agencies—Standard & Poor's, Moody's, and Fitch Group—downgraded Panasonic amid concerns over weak demand for many of its products; even worse: "Its overall lackluster performance adds up to a lost decade for the electronics pioneer—with a 10-year cumulative loss of close to 454 billion yen" (Kelly 2012). The key financial figures are summarized in Fig. 1 and the notes.

2.5 The Turn-Around (2012 to Present)

Reacting to the disastrous financial reports, Panasonic decided to remove president Ohtsubo in a Japanese corporate coup d'état-like manner and to install the younger Kazuhiro Tsuga as new CEO (Harner 2013). When Tsuga came into office in June 2012, he described the company as "chaotic" (Harner 2013) and no longer a "normal" company capable of delivering solid returns to shareholders (Wakabayashi 2013). Although a new massive restructuring plan, devised under Tsuga's predecessor, had just cut the number of employees, Panasonic still had about three times the workforce of competitor Samsung and double that of Sony's. Of the vast range of Panasonic's product groups, only appliances managed to attain remotely healthy operating margins (Kelly 2012), and Panasonic's financial standing continued to deteriorate during the first year of his tenure. Tsuga immediately got into action by reducing the company's headcount by another 20,000 jobs or about 6 % and by reforming the Head Office (Wakabayashi 2013). He indicated that—contrary to his predecessors—his business model was to reinvest business earnings instead of making big capital equipment investments, and to compete in the business-to-business market instead of only focusing on mass consumers (Harner 2013).

In March 2013, Tsuga revealed a new 3-year business plan, Cross-Value 2015, as his first major initiative to reshape the company. The plan contained two main objectives:

1. Eliminate unprofitable businesses;
2. Develop strategies for future growth in a group formation through its business division system to revitalize each business.

To this end, four action points were described:

- Restructure all unprofitable businesses by the fiscal year ending in March 2016 (FY 2016): In order to generate operating profit, the structure of the money-losing TV, semiconductor, mobile phone, circuit board, and optical product businesses had to be changed. Panasonic took the first steps by deciding to cease the production of plasma display panels (PDP) and to focus entirely on the LED technology segment, and in this way moving its TV business more towards the major market. Similarly, affiliated companies in, among others, the mobile phone and digital camera businesses were sold off, transferred or merged.
- Expand business and improve efficiency by shifting from in-house approach: Examples can be found in the logistics business, where the decision had been made to sell off the majority 66.7 % stake to Nippon Express Co., Ltd.; and in the medical business, where external capital is supposed to be injected into Panasonic Healthcare Co., Ltd.
- Improve financial position: The company set the ambitious target of generating a free cash flow of 600 billion yen over a 3-year period by narrowing down capital expenditures, disposing of assets, and reducing working capital, in addition to improving profitability of business itself.

- Follow a growth strategy from the customer's viewpoint: This included pursuing a "better life" for customers and strengthening the relationships with industrial partners.

A major change in the organizational structure, namely the establishment of a business division system supported by four companies, was considered pivotal to the actions and objectives named above. Panasonic consolidated 88 business units into 49 business divisions, each of which is responsible for everything related to the division from product planning to production and sales. The business divisions were grouped under four companies: Appliance Company, Eco Solutions Company, AVC Networks Company, and Automotive & Industrial Systems Company. The companies combine the forces of their divisions by centralizing resources for managing business development, creating new business, and strengthening key devices.

3 Current Company Profile

3.1 Company Structure

In March 2014, the Panasonic Group consists of the parent Panasonic Corporation and 522 consolidated subsidiaries in and outside of Japan. The company employs almost 286,000 people worldwide, and generates net sales of ca. 7,400 billion yen. More than half of the company's sales are generated on the domestic market.

Based on the 2013 restructuring plan, Panasonic's wide spectrum of products and services is grouped into four comprehensive companies, which supply electronics for all areas of their customers' lives (Appliances Company, Eco Solutions Company, AVC Networks Company and Automotive & Industrial Systems Company). The companies are designed to support the underlying business divisions and to help facilitate partnerships with the industry. Ambitious financial targets have been set for each company. In order to get a more complete picture of the current standing of Panasonic as a corporation, we will discuss each divisional company separately: their set-up and purpose, declared objectives, and devised strategies as laid out in the annual reports (FY2013 and FY2014) and on the company website (Table 1).

Table 1 Financial targets FY2013-16 (based on Panasonic Corporation 2013)

	Appliances company	Eco solutions company	AVC networks company	Automotive and industrial systems company
Net sales	1,650 billion yen[a]	1,770 billion yen	1,980 billion yen[a]	2,700 billion yen
Operating profit ratio	Over 5.5 %[a]	4.9 %	Over 5.0 %[a]	5.0 %
Cumulative free cash flows	108 billion yen	120 billion yen	Over 50 billion yen	265 billion yen

[a]Production and sales consolidated

3.2 Appliance Company (AP)

- Overview: AP has approximately 42,000 employees worldwide distributed over 56 production sites, of which nine are in Japan, 41 in the rest of Asia, five in the Americas, and one in Europe. The company comprises nine main business divisions (major products in parenthesis), namely: Cooking (including refrigerators, microwave ovens, rice cookers); House-keeping (including dishwashers, washer-dryers); Health & Beauty (including water purifier, health care appliances, beauty care appliances); Air Conditioning; Energy; Heating; Water Heating; Cold Chain (including food service/store/kitchen equipment, beverage vending machines); Devices (including compressors, motors).
- Objectives: AP wants to contribute to the realization of "comfortable living" and a "comfortable society". The company's designated goal is to become the "Global No. 1 Appliance Company" by 2018. Opportunity for growth is seen in both B2C and B2B businesses by (1) expanding market share, especially oversees; and (2) by capturing the increasing demand for high-value-added products in emerging countries.

Strategy: Specific initiatives include (1) establishing stable profitability in the B2C segment as a pillar business with the key markets China, Asia, Europe and Brazil; (2) establishing a foundation of highly profitable businesses for the medium- and long-term in the B2B facilities segment, especially in China and Asia; and (3) improving profitability in the B2B devices segment by transforming business strategies. For FY2015, an integration of consumer electronics under AP and AVC is planned.

3.3 AVC Networks Company (AVC)

- Overview: Panasonic's new AVC Networks Company, employer of ca. 47,000 people, integrates the audio-visual technology of the former AVC Networks Company with the wireless-communications technology of the former Systems & Communications Company. It is made up of four divisions: Digital AV Business (digital TV, DVD, audio, display devices); Imaging Business (including digital cameras and camcorders); System Network Business (in-flight AV equipment for airplanes, projectors, PC, security cameras, fixed-line telephones); Mobile Communication Business (mobile and smart phones).
- Objectives: AVC wants to create cross-value by fusing strong AV and ICT technologies backed by patents in both areas. The main strategic goals are to rigorously restructure underperforming B2C businesses while driving growth by strengthening B2B businesses, focussing the latter on Japan, Asia, and the USA. New opportunities are seen in the cooperation with IT companies for the research and development of cloud-connected products.

Strategy: Specific initiatives include the above-mentioned elimination of unprofitable businesses, especially in the areas of flat-panel TVs, digital cameras, and mobile phones. Changes are ongoing as reflected by the quarterly reports of FY 2013 and 2014.

3.4 Automotive and Industrial Systems Company (AIS)

- Overview: The AIS Company has ca. 111,000 employees and comprises 152 group companies in Japan and oversees. It develops, manufactures, sells and services products related to the automotive industry (multimedia- and eco-car related equipment, electrical components), industrial (electronic components and materials, semiconductors, optical devices, primary/secondary batteries, chargers, battery appliances and components), and manufacturing businesses (electronic component mounting systems, welding and robot systems), and bicycle-related products.
- Objectives: Due to its large share of sales (2,510 billion yen in FY2013) and with its broad range of B2B possibilities, AIS is positioned as a new "growth engine" for the Panasonic Group. It is designated to take a lead role in realizing ecological and smart solutions and in creating "Cross-Value Innovation" that transcends business division boundaries. In collaboration with their customers, AIS wants to contribute to "creating a better world" in the fields of automotive, industry and ICT.

Strategy: Profit improvement plans focus on four unprofitable businesses (portable rechargeable batteries, optical, printed circuit boards, and semiconductors); they include reducing fixed costs, streamlining production, and shifting to new business areas. In order to create new businesses, a globally operating Business Development Division of 400 people from different professional backgrounds has been established. The latest strategic ideas for AIS relate to "computerization and electrification" and to shifting focus from ICT to industrial areas.

3.5 Eco Solutions Company (ES)

- Overview: ES employs 55,000 people worldwide and consists of four divisions: Lighting Business Division, Energy Systems Business Division (active and passive products to save energy), Housing Systems Business Division (home remodeling), Panasonic Ecology Systems Co. (technologies to purify air, water and soil), in addition to the Marketing Division (Japan) and Global Marketing Division.
- Objectives: In continuation of Panasonic's 2008 "Eco Ideas Declaration" and its objective to become the "No. 1 Green Innovation Company in the Electronics Industry" by 2018, ES's idealistic goal is to "offer solutions for creating comfortable environments for homes" and non-residential buildings, "while reducing

environmental burden" and thus contributing to "the development of a sustainable society" (F. Ohtsubo 2013). This "synergy between comfort and eco-friendliness" aims at taking environmental concerns into consideration throughout the whole life-cycle of a product and in all managerial operations.

Strategy: With ES, Panasonic introduces a novel concept that only at second sight reveals its radical newness (see discussion in Paragraph 4 "Future Developments" below). ES sells products of the other Panasonic companies (AP, AVC, AIS) in addition to the specific products and services of ES itself. The basic idea is to "shift focus from selling individual products to providing added value, including in design, construction, maintenance, monitoring, and services." (F. Ohtsubo 2013). By building a high-profit business structure, ES wants to become a driving force for the growth of the whole Panasonic Group. Domestic and international expansion plans are set for FY2015.

3.6 Current Market Position

Panasonic's market position varies depending on the industry and divisional company.

3.6.1 Appliance Company (AP)

As can be seen in Table 2, both B2B and B2C businesses show considerable room to expand their global market share. The percentage of the main B2C products—washing machines, refrigerators, and air conditioners—is in the single digits and that of the B2B products—cold chains and compressors—is in the low double digits. Panasonic, aware of the fact that with these numbers they are more a regional appliance company, set plans to become the "Global No. 1" by 2018. Main growth opportunities are seen in B2B facilities and devices, the sales and operating profits of which are supposed to expand to 50–60 % of AP's overall sales and profits (currently ca. 40 %).

3.6.2 AVC Networks Company (AVC)

The AVC Networks Company shows mixed results as regards to market share. For consumer electronics, Panasonic, amongst other Japanese consumer electronic producers, has been surpassed and marginalized by Apple and, most importantly, by Samsung (Harlan 2012). Looking at B2B and industrial products, however, a different picture emerges. In the Finance and Retail industry, Panasonic is the market leader in Japan when it comes to IC (card) readers and writers. Furthermore, in the Public Services domain, Panasonic is the market leader in North America for B2B PC's (such as the Toughbook) and smartphones. In the Event, Company and Education segment, Panasonic is even the global market leader in projectors that produce more than 10,000 lm.

Table 2 AP company global market share (FY2013) (Based on Panasonic Corporation 2013)

	Air-conditioners	Refrigerators	Cold chains	Washing machines	Large-scale air-conditioners	Compressors for air-conditioners
Total units (millions)	71	97	2.7	82	4.5	129
Panasonic units (millions)	6.6	3.5	0.4	4.9	0.18	14
Share	9.3 %	3.6 %	14.5 %	6.0 %	4.1 %	11.1 %

Note: Air-conditioners refer to room air-conditioners. Drying machines are excluded from washing machines

3.6.3 Automotive & Industrial Systems Company (AIS)

The automotive segment of AIS is one of the world's largest original equipment manufacturers of factory-installed mobile audio equipment such as head units, speakers and navigation modules. AIS is or has been subcontractor to the most well-renowned automobile manufacturers, such as Europe's largest automaker Volkswagen, Daimler, Audi, largest US automaker General Motors, Ford, Toyota, and Nissan. The 2012 market share numbers testify to Panasonic's success in this industry (Panasonic IR Day 2012). For example, for display audio (audio-visual interface used in navigation systems and on-board computers) in Japan, Panasonic has increased its market share from 27 % in 2011 to 42 % in 2012 and a predicted 45 % in 2013; in the global multimedia business, large-screen information displays accounted for a market share of over 70 % in 2012; and the car-navigation system Gorilla scored 60 % in the aftermarket. With regards to the ICT field, several main products, such as conductive polymer capacitors and mobile connectors, have a number one global market share ranging from 35 % to over 50 % (Panasonic IR Day 2013).

3.6.4 Eco Solutions (ES)

For ES, it is exceptionally difficult to retrieve concrete and reliable figures on market share or performance relative to competitors. Company information only indicates that both Lighting Business Division and Energy Systems Business Division have the number one market share in Japan, and that Panasonic Ecology Systems holds the number one global market position for ventilation fans (Panasonic IR Day 2012). An independent market study of Li-ion automotive batteries conducted by Roland Berger Strategy Consultants (2012) predicted that Panasonic, with a global share of 13 %, will be one of five forerunners to control 70 % of the world market by 2015. With regards to solar cell technology, Panasonic was listed among the top 20 global photovoltaics (PV) module suppliers in 2013, indicating that—despite an increase in shipment volumes compared to 2012—the mainly Asian competition was still significantly ahead of ES (Osborne 2014). Altogether, as of 2013, 89 % of all ES Company sales took place in Japan (F. Ohtsubo 2013).

3.7 Brand Development

Over the years, Panasonic has marketed their products under a multitude of brand names, including National, Technics, JVC, Quasar, and Panasonic. In May 2003, the company announced that their most popular brand Panasonic was chosen as a unified global brand, accompanied by the global brand slogan "Panasonic ideas for life." Initially, the name National was kept as regional brand in Japan, but eventually was phased out by March 2010. From September 2013 onwards, the new brand slogan "A Better Life, A Better World" was introduced in anticipation of the company's 100th anniversary of its founding in 1918. The slogan is based on Matsushita's "Basic Management Objective" and expresses Panasonic's corporate vision and attitude of "striving to achieve". "A Better Life" refers to the company's focus on B2C products in the segments home, society, business, travel and automobiles. "A Better World" signifies their ambition to contribute globally through B2B marketing in the area of environmental protection (Masumizu 2014). In February 2014, Panasonic presented a new catch phrase, "Wonders! by Panasonic" to visualize overcoming stagnation and the positive changes in the company; matching New Wonders! products were launched in April. The "Wonders!" campaign was first focused on the domestic market where Panasonic makes more than half of its sales.

3.8 HR Approach and Employees

Following Konosuke Matsushita's belief that "business lies in people", Panasonic's HR approach is exceptionally focused on training and development. The company's "Code of Conduct" (Chap. 3, Employee Relations) puts forth the principle "The basis of management is people", and describes personnel development as a manager's most important responsibility (Panasonic Company website 2014). In Panasonics "Human Resources Development Policy", it is specified that managers must "develop people before making products". To this end, concrete guidelines clarify that managers should "show clear leadership based on strong beliefs; create an organization and culture which allows employees to fulfill their potential; encourage others to develop themselves; provide opportunities to take on new challenges and to achieve their goals; create workplaces where diversity is valued and respected; appreciate staff members for their efforts; develop healthy management/employee relations". Employees, in turn, are downright required to show a "challenging spirit", to keep thinking and acting innovatively, and to continuously strive for further development (Panasonic Company website 2014). The employee policy is about building win-win relationships between the company and employees. This is accomplished by a variety of initiatives founded on the principles of the participative management, performance-based evaluations, and respect for employees. Panasonic goes beyond Japanese or even international standards in that next to on-the-job training (which is similar to its competitors), it has a complete employee training institute, the Human Resources Development Company (HRDC), which gives employees the chance to get an education next to their job. For many Japanese companies, the traditional practices of life-long employment and senior-based compensation and advancement have led to a lack of intrinsic motivation in employees and thus to reduced productivity (Tapp 2002). Meanwhile, attempts to adjust to the economic challenges of the contemporary market place by re-engineering the HRM system along the lines of strict performance orientation Western style have suffered functional failure (Kishita 2006). Panasonic's policy to consequently invest in the education and (self-)development of their employees is a golden path in the middle and gives the company a competitive advantage over both domestic and global competitors.

3.9 Company Philosophy

Matsushita's "Basic Management Objective and Company Creed", as formulated in 1929, still constitutes the declared mission of Panasonic Corporation in 2014: "Our business is something entrusted to us by society. Therefore, we are duty-bound to manage and develop the company in an upstanding manner, contributing to the development of society and the improvement of people's lives" (Panasonic Company website 2014). Many aspects of Panasonic's business life—such as their brand promise, their dedication to customer services, their environmental targets, or their human resource approach—are rooted in Matsushita's business and management philosophy, which Katayama (1989) labeled "a curious mix of capitalism and religion". In his autobiography "Quest for Prosperity" (1988), when recalling the events leading up to the company's first mission statement in 1932, Matsushita talks about eliminating poverty as a "sacred task" and names business in general "a holy mission" (Dayao 2000). His life-long fervent belief was that the ultimate aim of a manufacturer was to overcome poverty and to generate wealth for the benefit of everyone (Kotter 1997). Matsushita's "Seven Principles" of 1932 still guide the company today: (1) Contribution to Society, (2) Fairness and Honesty, (3) Cooperation and Team Spirit, (4) Untiring Effort for Improvement, (5) Courtesy and Humility, (6) Adaptability, and (7) Gratitude (Dayao 2000). Panasonic's website explains in detail how the core values described in the Basic Management Objective and Company Creed and the Seven Principles are translated into a modern-day code of conduct and actual business practices (Panasonic Company website 2014).

4 Future Developments

4.1 General Company Success Strategies: Matsushita's Heritage

For Panasonic, as for Japanese companies in general, performance in the past can be seen as the best predictor for future potential. Based on Panasonic's corporate philosophy, a number of factors stand out as being uniquely related to the company's success—even beyond Matsushita's lifetime:

4.1.1 Clever entrepreneurship

Matsushita, by trial and error, developed a range of entrepreneurial strategies and practices that secured the early success of MEI. Remarkably, a similar set of techniques was later researched and praised by the proponents of the culture-excellence school of management such as by Peters and Waterman in 1982 (Kotter 1997). Among others, Matsushita felt strongly for a clear customer orientation with focus on after-sales service; constantly improving productivity; high quality at low price, mass production; improving products invented by others, while leaving product invention and basic R&D to others; speedy product development; innovative marketing; and a specialized retail distribution system. All of these elements are still highly relevant for Panasonic's strategy and functioning today.

4.1.2 Paternalistic management and empowerment

Matsushita is said to have pioneered the Japanese paternalistic management tradition, in which employees are viewed as members of the wider company "family" and are secured by lifetime employment and senior-based compensation (Kotter 1997). In this system, Japanese firms provide far-reaching welfare-style benefits independent from performance, which can include housing subsidies, scholarships for children, recreation facilities, or support for family events; in return, workers devote themselves to the job and the company, which among others is measured by their willingness to endure uncompensated overtime and to sacrifice vacation days (Tapp 2002). For his part in the reciprocal bond, Matsushita made a point in treating his employees with exceptional care—at a time when in the West, in the wake of Taylor's scientific management, workers still were considered to be "human machines" and subjected to control and demeaning treatment at work. Matsushita offered, by all comparisons, outstanding working conditions, health-promoting activities, institutions for training and development, and—as the first company in Japan—the 5-day work-week. In order to promote loyalty and a feeling of community, he introduced a daily-recited company song (Kotter 1997). While the paternalistic system can lead to a decreased motivation to excel, especially in younger (i.e. lower paid) and higher-educated employees (Tapp 2002), Matsushita knew to trigger intrinsic motivation by empowering his employees and practice a naturally inspiring leadership style. He systematically involved people in the management of the divisionalized company, entrusted them with highly demanding tasks, and had the faith that they would grow into their roles (Kotter 1997). This is unusual for Japanese company culture, where typically group-ism serves to maintain harmony; consensual decision-making, or "ringi", discourages any individual from taking responsibility for performance; and individual achievement is not recognized (Tapp 2002). Panasonic's "business lies in people" and "respect for the employee" approaches are very much in line with Matsushita's management philosophy and still constitute a major competitive advantage for Panasonic.

4.1.3 A commitment to life-long learning and the learning organization

If one thing was characteristic for Matsushita, it was his desire to learn and his drive for continuous improvement. These ambitions included both his company, for which he was in constant search for superior methods, and his own person. Up to an old age, he tirelessly worked on educating himself and others, studying human nature, pushing for higher and higher goals, and propagating an optimistic set of beliefs in his own philosophy of "Peace and Happiness through Prosperity" (Kotter 1997). He also invested significantly in the training and life-long learning of his employees. Matsushita's motivating aspirations grew with actual accomplishments and formed his leadership style. His willingness to remain open-minded for learning from others and to reflect humbly on lessons learned contributed significantly to the adaptability and flexibility of his company in an ever-changing environment. The ability to remain a learning organization, to keep an open mind, and to continuously make an effort to break down the boundaries between industries and departments, ranks and stakeholders, will be crucial for Panasonic's future.

4.2 Specific Success Strategy: The Integrated Systems Approach of Eco Solutions

At first sight, Eco Solutions Company (ES) is just another one of Panasonic's new four divisional companies. It focuses on the development, manufacture, and sales of products and services relating to the segments photovoltaics (HIT solar cells), lighting (fixtures, control systems, LED bulb, fluorescent lamps), air conditioning and purification (ventilation fan systems, humidifier, purifier), electrical construction materials (light switches/outlets, panel boards, electric tools, wiring), and home building (kitchen and bathroom systems, self-cleaning toilets, heat pump systems); in addition, ES company offers elderly and nursing care equipment and services. Only when digging deeper does it becomes obvious that Panasonic is indeed doing something rather unique with this company. ES is driven by a novel business and marketing concept that transcends organizational boundaries and that makes it the most spectacular and pioneering part of the whole Panasonic Group.

4.2.1 Integrated systems philosophy

ES Company has the declared purpose to promote and provide "optimized solutions based on full utilization of the Panasonic Group's product lineup and various services", thus contributing to the development of a sustainable society (Panasonic corporation 2013). While competitors like Apple and Samsung (and Google on a software scale) have already pioneered an integrated systems approach with their audio-visual and communication hardware (Michael 2011), Panasonic goes one step further. They aim not only at integrating phones, TVs, stereos and computers; they want to integrate virtually *everything*. ES not only produces their own company-related products, but also sells products of the other parts of Panasonic Corporation while offering comprehensive integrative solutions that allow these products to work together. Simultaneously, they want to make both the production processes and the use of their products or services more sustainable, ecological, and environmentally friendly. Taking all this information together, one could say that "Eco Solutions" is not only one of Panasonic's divisional companies, but is also the name of an overarching concept that pulls together everything done by Panasonic.

4.2.2 Model smart town Fujisawa

The epitome of Panasonic's sustainability ambitions and the practical application of Eco Solutions as an umbrella organization is the eco-conscious smart city project Fujisawa Sustainable Smart Town (SST). Conceived even before the massive Japanese earthquakes of March 2011 and first announced in May of that year, Fujisawa SST was promoted as one of the most advanced eco cities in the world:

Panasonic will apply its "comprehensive solutions for the entire house, entire building and entire town" to Fujisawa SST, combining its energy saving technologies in energy creation, storage and management with a safe and secure environment. Specifically, the company plans to preinstall its solar power generation systems and household storage battery systems across the town, including homes, various facilities and public zones, which would be the first of its kind in the world. Panasonic intends to replicate Fujisawa SST as a business model in other parts of Japan and overseas. (Panasonic Announcement 2011)

A business collaboration of initially nine partner companies and one city, Fujisawa SST is taking shape on a cleared 19-hectare site of a former Panasonic factory in Fujisawa City, about 50 km west of Tokyo. The neighborhood, with a planned population of 3,000, will comprise 1,000 technologically advanced green homes, as well as stores, healthcare facilities, a nursery school, elderly housing, a nursing home, and public green spaces and parks. Each home will be equipped with the means to generate most of the electricity for its inhabitants, either with a standard photovoltaic setup or with an optional fuel cell cogeneration system for when the sun is not shining. The overall goal for the community is to reduce CO_2 emissions by 70 %, cut household water usage by 30 %, and allow for a 3-day lifeline maintenance in case of emergency. The concept of Fujisawa SST, however, goes beyond energy; it also takes into account aspects such as security, mobility, and healthcare, and its mission is "to structure a smart town based on people's lifestyles, designed for the way people live" (Panasonic Company website 2014). In continuation of the 2008 "Eco Ideas", houses will be equipped with energy-saving appliances, such as air conditioners, washing machines, LED lights, and AV equipment. Linked with each other by an integrated Home Energy Mangement System (HEMS), these intelligent household machines communicate with one another for optimal energy savings.

In Panasonic's vision, this goes as far as fridges remembering a family's eating habits or heating systems recognizing and targeting people entering a room (Yoneda 2013). Construction of the first single-family homes has started in September 2013, and the town is scheduled to open in spring 2014 (Panasonic Company website 2014). Haruyuki Ishio, Director of Panasonic's Corporate Division for Promoting Energy Solutions, indicated in a recent interview that Panasonic was proud of Fujisawa SST as it showcases the company's home energy solutions including the home itself and serves as a worldwide model for the realization of an eco-friendly city in action (Yoneda 2013). Therefore, the concepts and processes behind Fujisawa SST are being translated into other projects for Japan and—under consideration of regional characteristics—around the world.

4.3 Eco Solutions Company Focus and Development Strategy

More than the other three divisional companies, and with 89 % of all sales in 2013, ES still has its core business in Japan (F. Ohtsubo 2013). Panasonic's basic strategy is to strengthen its domestic core businesses to support growth; this entails turning mainstay products into flagship products, creating housing space networks (residential) as well as "eco-conscious and smart business solutions" (non-residential), and marketing via showrooms and new distribution channels (F. Ohtsubo 2013). International expansion, however, is slowly but steadily developing. While in 2012 overseas business was limited to the energy sector (Panasonic IR Day 2012), ES' international plans for 2013, as presented in Panasonic's annual report (FY2013), also included home remodeling and engineering. The geographic focus rested on growing markets in Asia (China, India, and other Asian countries), with some reference to exploring and/or expanding in Middle Eastern and African markets, while Europe or the United States were not mentioned. Explanations for this seemingly single-minded Japan-/Asia-focus can be found in the geographic and market advantage ES has in that region. Here the company could profit from existing networks and subsidiaries, and is not confronted with the bigger players in the Western economy, where market saturation and fierce cost-competition would make it difficult for ES to effectively position itself. In addition, the Japanese market for photovoltaics (PV) has experienced a domestic consumer demand surge, which for ES has led to a 10 % increase in sales in the FY2014 third quarter in comparison to the same period a year ago (Panasonic Financial Announcement 2014). ES' strategy to accomplish growth by strengthening domestic and regional core business, thus, seems to be paying off. Meanwhile, as a new development in 2013, Panasonic announced "a full-scale expansion of its interior LED lighting business" into Asia and Europe, "as part of the company's drive to increase overseas sales of such products" (Panasonic Company website 2014). The unique properties of LED technology have opened the possibility to overcome country-specific limitations and to promote lighting fixtures globally. There are more signals that ES is about to gain share in the Western market: In January 2014 Panasonic launched two upgraded, conversion efficient HIT photovoltaic modules in Europe, targeting the residential rooftop markets and taking it up against dominating tier one Chinese solar cell producers (Osborne 2014).

4.4 The Future of Panasonic

Taking all information into account, Panasonic as a whole appears to be in transition from a classic electronics provider to a leading innovative green cooperation offering products and services through their B2C and B2B businesses. Eco Solution, both as one of the divisional companies and as an overarching vision, builds the center stone in this development by integrating its eco-friendly concepts and technology with the technology and products of Panasonic's other divisions, namely the Appliance Company (AP), AVC Networks Company, and Automotive & Industrial Systems Company (AIS). While in 2013 ES and their energy-related B2B businesses were pushing into the growing markets of Asia, AP and AIS constituted the healthy, sustainable, financial base of the Panasonic Group. The accelerating frequency of news about Panasonic entering the Western markets with their eco- and energy technology leads to the bold assumption that the company aims to (re-)establish a key position amongst leading European manufacturers in that segment. Especially with their 100-year anniversary in 2018 in mind, Panasonic is pushing heavily to regain a competitive global position and to realize their vision of becoming the "No. 1 Green Innovation Company in the Electronics Industry".

Both recent financial figures (F. Ohtsubo 2014) and a number of sustainability and innovation awards (Panasonic Company website 2014) confirm that the tides have changed for Panasonic. It has paid off to restructure or eliminate unprofitable businesses, to reduce reliance on consumer electronics where Panasonic has lagged behind the competition, and to invest into new ventures (Einhorn et al. 2014). The FY2014 third quarter results show a 10 % increase in consolidated group sales, which exceeds original expectations; similarly, the full-year forecast predicts high two-digit increases in operating profit for Eco Solutions and AIS in comparison to the previous year (F. Ohtsubo 2014). All signals indicate that Panasonic is "back" and ready to roll out their integrated systems approach in the Western world, heading towards a "New Panasonic" in FY2019.

5 Conclusions and Recommendations

5.1 Conclusions

Panasonic's nearly 100-year history splits into several phases. The first 30 years, until the end of WWII, were a period of rapid growth and expansion; out of nothing, Matsushita established a flourishing manufacturer of a vast variety of consumer electronics with excellent domestic standing. WWII was a big incision and almost entirely wiped out the company. After survival was secured, the company took off on a 40-year triumphal quest for globalization; from clever entrepreneurship, Matsushita moved on to inspirational leadership, supplying his company with a solid foundation of moral and spiritual values. Realizing that his products lacked technical sophistication in comparison to the West, he made sure that all knowledge necessary to catch up was acquired. Until his death, his company was the epitome of the "Japanese miracle". Due mainly to external circumstances, Panasonic was thrown into stagnation and crisis from the 1990s onwards; now it became painfully clear that the company's organizational structure and business processes had not evolved in the same pace as the company's expansion. A period of continuous restructurings and adjustments began, which now has gone into its third decade and the end of which is still not in sight. Through all of this, one can comfortably say that the constant factor in Panasonic's history was—and is—change.

And this, right here, may also be the simple answer to the question about Panasonic's secret of success: the ability to transform as required by an ever-changing environment, the willingness to keep developing, and the openness to learn and take risks have been engrained in the company's collective memory. Giving up is not an option, and the only way out is the way forward. Therefore it can be boldly concluded, in sync with the colleagues mentioned in the introduction, that Panasonic as a corporation will still exist 50 years from now, and maybe even a

100 years from now. The company may look differently, produce different products or services, and market them in a completely different way, but chances are high that they will still be major players on the domestic and global markets.

Going a bit deeper in the analysis, the following elements have been detected as contributing to the enormous success of the company:

- Company philosophy: Tradition is highly valued at Panasonic. Matsushita's core principles and beliefs are still as present at Panasonic today as during its founder's lifetime. The company's 2014 mission, vision and core values are direct quotes from Matsushita; other elements, such as brand promise, environmental targets, dedication to establishing a relationship with the customer, and personnel management, are firmly rooted in Matsushita's philosophy. In addition, the company is taking a long-term perspective and shows the ability to wait for the right moment. With Eco Solutions, Panasonic started powerfully in Japan and Asia, leaving out any mentioning of Western markets in their communication. While generating a steady income in other, less high-ranking segments, the company took—and keeps taking—the time to prepare everything to become a top player in the specific field of energy and remodeling; in the meantime, almost sneakily, facts are created by intermittently making major moves into Europe.
- Products and technology: Under Matsushita, Panasonic was known for good quality at a low price. This was made possible by sophisticated mass production and by an imitation strategy with regards to the company's technology. Panasonic's innovative power lies in clever entrepreneurship, in recognition and anticipation of trends, and in astute marketing and sales strategies, which again is proven by the Eco Solutions concepts and by Panasonics declared ambition to transform into a green company.
- Approach to human resources: As mentioned above, Matsushita's vision on leadership still shapes Panasonic's human resource management approach. An attitude of respect and care towards the employee, and above-average investments in training and development lead to high loyalty of management and staff towards the organization. In addition, traditionally-neglected areas, such as gender diversity, work-life balance, and healthy ageing have recently received increasing attention.

As a result of all of these factors, Panasonic manages time and time again to reinvent itself in an ever-changing environment. It maintains the ability to survive challenging external (crisis in industry, domestic market, or world economics) and internal (financial, marketing, structure) situations, and to come out of them thriving. Panasonic may not become the most profitable company, but chances are that it will continue to be an important player in its major fields (appliances, AVC, automotive/industrial systems). The green innovation concept and the integrated systems approach, in turn, will open new markets and lead to new cooperations, thus revitalizing the company as it is about to enter into its second century of existence.

5.2 Recommendations

When looking at the possibilities to win Panasonic as a collaborating partner with companies or other institutions in the Netherlands, the obvious point of connection is energy. The Northern provinces of Drenthe, Friesland, Groningen and Noord-Holland play a key role in the Dutch energy economy. Since 2003, they are the driving forces behind the network organization Energy Valley, a joint venture of governments, the business sector, and knowledge institutes that has the purpose to encourage employment and to support national objectives related to renewable energy (Energy Valley website 2014). The Dutch government has declared energy one of nine so-called top sectors, in which the Netherlands excels globally and which receive high government priority. In the top sectors, industry and science cooperatively develop innovations with the ambition that their products and technologies contribute to finding solutions to societal issues (Top Sector Energy website 2014). Targets for the Dutch Energy sector between now and 2020 include the transition to more sustainable, low-carbon energy, while structurally increasing the earnings potential. The Energy Valley region is a key factor in this process and has a wealth of initiatives to show for in the fields of biogas, solar, and heating networks (numbers from Energy Valley website 2014): 97 % of the entire Dutch gas production on land takes place in the Energy Valley area (to put this into perspective, in Europe only Russia and Norway produce more gas). In addition, 20 % of the Dutch conventional and 22 % of the renewable electricity production are located in the North, as well as 42 % of the country's wind energy, 44 % of the green gas, and 31 % of the biogas production. Currently, there are approximately 4,200 companies and 32,375 full-time positions in the Northern energy cluster. The energy investments exceed 27 billion € in the coming decade. The region is strategically positioned within the EU energy infrastructure and directly borders the North Sea with its outstanding harbor facilities. The Energy Valley cluster works closely together with the energy cluster in North Western Germany, joining forces on pan-European energy issues and, since 2012, collaborating with Scotland and Norway in the European North Sea Energy Alliance (ENSEA). Funded by the European Union, the ENSEA project "aims to accelerate the implementation of a resource-efficient Europe by strengthening the research and innovation potential of European regions" (ENSEA website 2014). On a more local level, Energy Valley, in cooperation with knowledge institutes and the Energy sector, founded the Energy Academy Europe (EAE), an exclusive institute bundling research, education and innovation regarding energy. Among others, the Hanze University of Applied Sciences and the University of Groningen are offering a wide variety of educational programs to train the next generation of energy experts; at the same time, research on energy-related subjects is conducted in close contact with the market.

Another initiative of the Energy Valley network deserves special mentioning, since it is reminiscent of Panasonic's Fujisawa SST project, namely PowerMatching City, a living lab demonstration of the future energy system in the neighborhood of Hoogkerk in Groningen:

PowerMatching City is, first and foremost, the European field trial to connect supply and demand of electricity and heat in an intelligent way (smart grids). Purpose of the ongoing project is to fully profit of characteristics of both centralised and renewable energy systems. ... During the first phase 25 households participated. At the end of 2011 the second phase took off. Nowadays 42 households are taking part in Power Matching City, more clustered together than before. Examples speak volumes: do households want to turn on the washing machine when there's a lot of wind and electricity from wind turbines is plentiful and therefore much cheaper than average? Then the system will automatically choose the optimal moment, in order to wash at the lowest possible tariffs. (PowerMatching City website 2014).

In conclusion, the Netherlands has an agenda that fits perfectly with Panasonic's Eco Solutions and green innovation concepts. Considering the fact that approximately 60 years ago Panasonic's founder Matsushita collaborated with Philips on technical knowledge transfer and that he personally received the highest honors from the Queen of the Netherlands, it seems appropriate to suggest a renewed partnership between the Japanese corporation and governmental entities, knowledge institutes, and businesses located in the Northern Netherlands.

6 Notes

6.1 Key Financial Figures

The following overviews of Panasonic's balance and income statement as well as the key financial ratios are summarizations based on the data provided by Panasonic. All figures are in millions of Yen, for fiscal years ending March 31, for the Panasonic Corporation and its subsidiaries.

Balance Sheet

Year	2009	2010	2011	2012	2013
Long Term Debt	651,310	1,028,928	1,162,287	941,768	663,091
Total Assets	6,403,316	8,358,057	7,822,870	6,601,055	5,397,812
Panasonic Corp. Shareholders Equity	2,783,980	2,792,488	2,558,992	1,929,786	1,264,032
Total Equity	3,212,581	3,679,773	2,946,335	1,988,566	1,304,273
Shares issued (1000s)	2,453,053	2,453,053	2,452,053	2,453,053	2,453,053
No. of shareholders	277,710	364,618	364,618	557,102	577,756
No. consolidated comp.	540	680	634	579	538

Income Statement

Year	2009	2010	2011	2012	2013
Net Sales	7,765,507	7,417,980	8,692,672	7,846,216	7,303,045
Operating Profit	72,873	190,453	305,254	43,725	160,936
Income (loss) before income taxes	382,634-	29,315-	178,807	812,844-	398,386-

(continued)

Year	2009	2010	2011	2012	2013
Net income (loss) Panasonic Corp.	378,961-	103,465-	74,017	772,172-	754,250-
Capital Investment	494,368	385,489	403,778	333,695	310,866
Depreciation	325,835	251,839	284,244	295,808	277,582
R&D Expenditures	517,913	476,903	527,798	520,217	502,233
Free Cash Flow	352,830-	198,674	266,250	339,893-	355,156

Ratios

Year	2009	2010	2011	2012	2013
Operating Profit/Sales	0.9	2.6	3.5	0.6	2.2
Income (loss) before taxes/Sales	4.9-	0.4-	2.1	10.4-	5.5-
Net income (loss)/Sales	4.9-	1.4-	0.9	9.8-	10.3-
Return on Equity	11.8-	3.7-	2.8	34.4-	47.2-
Shareholders Equity/Total Assets	43.5	33.4	32.7	29.2	23.4
Payout Ratio	-	-	28.0	-	-

(Panasonic Corporation 2013)

6.2 Mid-Term Management Plans

Since 2000, Panasonic (then MEI) has released five mid-term business plans: in 2001, 2004, 2007, 2010, and 2013. So far, the target figures were achieved only once with the plan "Leap Ahead 21".

Year	President	Name	Main objectives	Target figures (2-year period)
2001	Nakamura	Value Creation 21	"Deconstruct & Create": implementation of structural reform (14 business domains) and growth strategy "Super Manufacturing Company" Lean and agile Panasonic	Sales: 9 trillion yen OPM: 5 %
2004	Nakamura	Leap Ahead 21	Accelerating growth business Reinforcing management structures	Sales: 8.2 trillion yen OP: 410 billion yen OPM: > 5 %
2007	Ohtsubo	GP3 = Global Progress, Global Profit, Global Panasonic	Double-digit growth in overseas sales (emerging markets) Four strategic businesses Continuous selection and concentration (plasma TV)	Sales: 10 trillion yen RoE: 10 %

(continued)

Year	President	Name	Main objectives	Target figures (2-year period)
2010	Ohtsubo	GT12 = Green Transformation 12	Accelerate growth with Six Key Businesses Expand overseas businesses in emerging countries Strengthen solutions & systems businesses Promote/implement collaboration with SANYO Environmental targets	Sales: 10 trillion yen OPM: > 5 % RoE: 10 % FCF: > 800 billion yen (3-year period)
2013	Tsuga	CV2015	Business division system supported by four companies	OP: > 350 billion yen OPM: > 5 %
		= Cross-Value Innovation 2015	Eliminate unprofitable businesses Shifting from in-house approach Improve financial position Growth strategy from customer viewpoint	FCF: > 600 billion yen (3-year period)

(Koitabashi et al. 2013; Kosuga 2009; F. Ohtsubo/F. Ohtsubo 2010)

References

Cooper, D. (2012). *Panasonic 2012 Q3: $9 billion loss, Sanyo writedowns, restructuring.* Retrieved February 3, 2012, from http://www.engadget.com/2012/02/03/panasonic-q3-2012/.

Dayao, D. L. C. (2000). *Asian business wisdom. Lessons from the region's best and brightest business leaders.* Singapore: John Wiley & Sons.

Einhorn, B., Yasu, M., & Amano, T. (2014). *Panasonic Revives as Other Japanese Tech Giants Falter.* Retrieved February 13, 2014, from http://www.businessweek.com/articles/2014-02-13/panasonic-revives-as-nintendo-sony-falter.

Energy Valley website. (2014). Retrieved April 6, 2014, from http://www.energyvalley.nl.

ENSEA website. (2014). Retrieved April 6, 2014, from http://www.ensea.biz/.

Harlan, C. (2012). *As Apple and Samsung dominate, Japan's tech giants are in free fall.* Retrieved September 29, 2012, from http://www.washingtonpost.com/world/as-apple-and-samsung-dominate-japans-tech-giants-are-in-a-free-fall/2012/09/28/04c6eb36-0944-11e2-afff-d6c7f20a83bf_story.html.

Harner, S. (2013). *Japan's Samurai CEOs (1) Panasonic's Tsuga Kazuhiro.* Retrieved April 13, 2013, from http://www.forbes.com/sites/stephenharner/2013/04/13/japans-samurai-ceos-1-panasonics-tsuga-kazuhiro/.

Japan Today. (2013). *Japanese companies expected to still be around in 50 years.* Retrieved March 3, 2014, from http://www.japantoday.com/category/lifestyle/view/japanese-companies-expected-to-still-be-around-in-50-years. Original source (in Japanese): Mynavi. Available via World Wide Web: http://news.mynavi.jp/news/2013/03/13/101/ cited March 3rd, 2014.

Katayama, F. H. (1989). *God of management.* Retrieved May 22, 1989, from http://money.cnn.com/magazines/fortune/fortune_archive/1989/05/22/72020/index.htm.

Kelly, T. (2012). *UPDATE 4-New Panasonic chief to chase TV profit, not volume*. Retrieved February 28, 2012, from http://www.reuters.com/article/2012/02/28/panasonic-idUSL4E8DS42E20120228.

Kishita, T. (2006). The HRM of Japanese firms in the days to come of global competition. *Research and Practice in Human Resource Management, 14*(1), 29–48. http://rphrm.curtin.edu.au/2006/issue1/japanese.html.

Koitabashi,T., Shiraishi, T., & Itoh, M. (2013). *Panasonic aims to become top-tier manufacturer of auto parts*. Retrieved April 8, 2013, from http://business.nikkeibp.co.jp/article/eng/20130408/246326/?ST=print_e.

Kosuga, M. (2009). Business process innovations in Panasonic corporation: A case study. In G. Lee (Ed.), *Business process management of Japanese and Korean companies* (pp. 63–77). Singapore: World Scientific.

Kotter, J. P. (1997). *Matsushita leadership: Lessons from the 20th Century's most remarkable entrepreneur*. New York: The Free Press.

Landry, J. T. (2007). Panasonic: The Largest Corporate Restructuring in History [Book review]. *Harvard Business Review*, Retrieved July-August 2007, p. 27. http://hbr.org/2007/07/reviews/ar/1.

Laposky, J. (2008). Panasonic's Redoubles green efforts. *TWICE This Week in Consumer Electronics, 23*(16), 16.

Masumizu, H. (2014). *Panasonic announces new catchphrase 'Wonders! by Panasonic'*. Retrieved February 20, 2014, from http://www.japantoday.com/category/business/view/panasonic-announces-new-catchphrase-wonders-by-panasonic.

Matsushita, K. (1988). *Quest for prosperity*. Kyoto: PHP Institute.

McInerney, F. (2007). *Panasonic: The largest corporate restructuring in history*. New York: Truman Talley Books.

Michael, H. (2011). *The shifting sands of integrated systems*. Retrieved November 1, 2011 http://www.phonearena.com/news/The-shifting-sands-of-integrated-systems_id23397.

Miyai, M. (2011). Panasonic's environmental vision and its practices'. In M. Matsumoto, Y. Umeda, K. Masui, & S. Fukushige (Eds.), *Design for innovative value towards a sustainable society*. Heidelberg: Springer. Chapter 1.

Osborne, M. (2014). *Panasonic's interest in European market returns after launch of new HIT PV module*. Retrieved January 9, 2014, from http://www.pv-tech.org/news/panasonics_interests_in_european_market_returns_after_launch_of_new_hit_pv.

Panasonic Corporation (2014). 'FY 2015 Business Policy', March 27th, 2014.

Panasonic Announcement. (2011). Retrieved October 31, 2011, from http://news.panasonic.net/archives/2011/1031_7234.html.

Panasonic Announcement of Financial Results. (2014). Retrieved April 1, 2014, from http://panasonic.net/ir/release/.

Panasonic Company website. (2014). Retrieved March 3, 2014, from http://panasonic.net/.

Panasonic Corporation. (2013). Annual Report for the year ended March 31st, 2013.

Panasonic Corporation/F. Ohtsubo. (2010). Panasonic Group, 'New Midterm Management Plan', March 7th, 2010.

Panasonic IR Day. (2012). *Panasonic corporation, automotive systems company/M. Shibata, 'Automotive Systems Company Business Strategy*. Retrieved May 23, 2012, from http://panasonic.net/ir/presentation/irday/.

Panasonic IR Day. (2013). Panasonic Corporation, Automotive & Industrial Systems Company /Y. Tamada, 'Automotive & Industrial Systems Company Midterm Strategy', May 30th, 2013.

PowerMatching City website. (2014). Retrieved April 6, 2014, from http://www.powermatchingcity.nl.

Reorganization. (2004). *Business wire, reorganization of new Matsushita Group; New organizational structure towards business growth of Matsushita Electric Industrial and Matsushita Electric Works*. Retrieved September 28, 2004, from http://www.thefreelibrary.com/Reorganization+of+New+Matsushita+Group%3B+New+organizational+structure...-a0122726903.

Reuters. (2013). *Panasonic to exit Plasma TV panel business by end-March 2014*. Retrieved October 8, 2013, from http://www.reuters.com/article/2013/10/09/us-panasonic-plasmatv-idUSBRE99801720131009.

Roland Berger Strategy Consultants. (2012). *Update to the Roland Berger study on automotive Li-ion batteries: Five frontrunners share most of the market. Market consolidation driven by pressure on prices*. Retrieved April 19, 2012, from http://www.rolandberger.com/press_releases/512-press_archive2012_sc_content/Update_to_study_on_Li_ion_battery_market.html.

Segers, R. T., & Stam, T. (2013). *Asia: Reshaping the global economic landscape*. Shaker: Maastricht.

SemiconPortal. (2012). *Panasonic abnormal according to its president*. Retrieved November 6, 2012, from https://www.semiconportal.com/en/archive/news/main-news/121106-panasonic-biz-restructuring.html.

Tanikawa, M. (2004). *Work in progress/Matsushita changes gears: A pillar of Japan Inc. finally turns around*. Retrieved August 28, 2004, from http://www.nytimes.com/2004/08/28/your-money/28iht-mmatsu_ed3_.html?src=pm&pagewanted=1.

Tapp, S. H. P. (2002). A comparison of job attitudes of Japanese employees working in Japanese firms and Gaishikei (Foreign-Affiliated) firms. *Japanese Journal of Administrative Science, 16*(2), 45–62.

Tarr, G. (2008). Panasonic sees strength in unified brand. *TWICE: This Week in Consumer Electronics, 23*(21), 1, 42.

Top Sector Energy website. (2014). Retrieved April 6, 2014, from http://topsectoren.nl.

Wakabayashi, D. (2013). *Panasonic to Pare Unprofitable Units*. Retrieved March 28, 2013, from http://online.wsj.com/news/articles/SB10001424127887324685104578387963550254482.

Yasu, M. (2012). *Panasonic names Tsuga president after predicting record loss*. Retrieved February 28, 2012, from http://www.bloomberg.com/news/2012-02-28/panasonic-names-kazuhiro-tsuga-new-president-replacing-fumio-ohtsubo.html.

Yoneda, Y. (2013). *Interview: Panasonic's Haruyuki Ishio gives us the inside scoop about Fujisawa sustainable smart town*. Retrieved July 22, 2013, from http://inhabitat.com/interview-panasonics-haruyuki-ishio-gives-us-the-inside-scoop-about-fujisawa-sustainable-smart-town.

Rakuten: A Case Study on Entering New Markets Through an Innovative Business-to-Business-to-Consumer Strategy

Thomas S. Willenborg

Abstract In its home country of Japan, Rakuten found a great domestic market situation to start off an e-commerce company in 1997. With its online shopping mall Rakuten Ichiba, the company was able to undercut prices and systematically cut out the middlemen. But Rakuten's success was not only characterized by external factors. The company aimed for an online marketplace where buyers and sellers meet to conduct trade. Its platform combined technology with human expertise in order to empower people such as local retailers to sell their products online without worrying about technological and logistical aspects. The company levered the Japanese hospitality to build a reliable corporate culture and shaped an outstanding service that focuses on encouraging long-term relationships between merchants and customers. Strategic acquisitions have shaped an ecosystem that is currently seen as the most diverse and encounters people in many everyday life situations. A constant focus on global expansion and untapped business and niche segments contributes to its overall success.

1 Introduction

Rakuten, Inc., headquartered in Tokyo, is a global internet services company offering a great variety of consumer and business-focused services. According to a recent global e-commerce study, Rakuten is, besides Amazon, today's most diversified e-commerce company worldwide with businesses ranging from marketplaces, to accompanied internet services, online advertising, media content, in-house media devices, shipping and logistics, and payment and financing services (Schiliro 2013). Since the 1990s, Rakuten has been one of the most successful

T.S. Willenborg (✉)
Datatrans AG, Zurich, Switzerland
e-mail: t.s.willenborg@aggiemail.usu.edu

venture start-ups in Japan. In 1997, Rakuten started with its core business, an online shopping mall called Rakuten Ichiba, selling everything from consumer electronics and computers to fashion, home furnishings, sporting goods, etc. In Japan alone, more than 60 % of its population uses the marketplace accounting for an almost 30 % share of the overall 28.2 billion € e-commerce market in Japan (Rakuten, Inc. 2012). Just the Japanese market makes Rakuten one of the world's largest online marketplaces.

With a different approach than its competitors, Rakuten Ichiba banks on a new strategy that uses a business-to-business-to-customer (B2B2C) model. The B2B2C model is a shop-based marketing place, focusing on the exchange between buyers and sellers rather than on being a shop or a collection of shops. In a recent article about Rakuten's global ambitions, Bernhard Luthi, Chief Operating Officer at Rakuten US, mentioned that its "concept is based on making connections between people based on areas of interest, which means that individuals as well as merchants can become curators, influential to other interested parties" (Thau 2014). It is an attempt to go beyond an ordinary online shopping mall and become a true bazaar or shopping arcade with a focus on entertaining "discovery" shopping. Rakuten tries to merge humanity with algorithms using a hybrid approach by empowering merchants and encouraging them to interact with their customers through their website.

Basically, merchants are charged a monthly fee to set up a store on Rakuten, allowing them to customize their web presence and interact directly with their customers. This approach adds a social component to an online shopping experience that is usually only based on convenience and efficiency. Mr. Hiroshi Mikitani, the founder of Rakuten, gave a great example of how this empowerment was used. In an article in Harvard Business Review about humanizing e-commerce, he told the story about the "chick diary". In the early beginnings of Rakuten, a farmer approached Mr. Mikitani, wanting to sell fresh eggs online. Even though Mikitani thought in the beginning that this would be a terrible idea, as eggs can be bought conveniently in the supermarket next door, the farmer was confident mentioning that eggs in a supermarket are at least 1 or 2 weeks old and that his eggs would be fresher since they could be shipped overnight. Furthermore, he added that his eggs are organic as he feeds his chickens with a special diet to make them really rich. So, he opened a store on Rakuten. In order to make the very most of the online channel, the farmer started to interact with his customers by starting a daily chick diary. "He posted photos of quality tests he had devised to let customers know how the chickens were doing... He told stories that made people interested in trying his eggs, and once they bought from him they kept buying—at a premium" (Mikitani 2013b). Developing a story around his products helped him to build his own brand and maintain a strong customer relationship.

Applying this model, backed with strategic acquisitions of leading online shopping malls worldwide, Rakuten ensured that it now represents more than 40,000 merchants just in Japan.

2 Company Profile

2.1 History

Initially, Rakuten was founded as MDM, Inc. by Hiroshi Mikitani in February 1997 and was renamed into Rakuten, Inc. 2 years later in 1999. Between these 2 years, their online shopping mall "Rakuten Ichiba" began its service with only 13 merchants and "Rakuten Super Auction" was launched a year later in 1998. Mikitani started operations with only six employees, all talented IT engineers with a deep knowledge of the internet. He had the package that was needed to attract young talent and convince them of his idea to create a "bazaar-like shopping experience". He brought an international mindset from his experience in the USA, his several years of work experience in investment banking, and was well educated since he held an MBA from Harvard Business School.

This experience came in handy as, "usually, online shopping malls require relatively large initial investments to exploit economies of scale, with a small incremental cost for each new store" (Walter and Zhang 2012). Mikitani was able to generate enough internal funds due to abundant cash flow coming from the monthly charge that merchants had to pay in order to use the platform. Furthermore, he avoided extensive system development costs in the beginning by employing young, yet skilled, university students. This made Rakuten not reliant upon any external funding from venture capital and ensured a smooth development of the system.

In order to prosper with the new system at hand, Rakuten had to attract as many new stores to join the platform as possible, focusing aggressively on small locally-based shops across Japan during that time. As part of the internet boom in the 1990s, many brick-and-mortar stores considered the option of selling their products online but did not have the know-how and funds to start their own online business.

Rakuten leveraged this demand and promoted its platform. They built their sales force by employing relatively inexperienced workers that were trained to become sales representatives. As a result, Rakuten shaped a business model of revenue generation and was able to grow healthily by avoiding extensive spending on ordinary recruitment channels and reliance on external funding.

2.2 The Founder: Hiroshi Mikitani

Hiroshi Mikitani, who founded Rakuten in 1997 (Fig. 1), was born on March 11, 1963, in Kobe, Japan. In his early life he had already great exposure to entrepreneurship because his father was an economist and professor at Kobe University and worked as a visiting professor at Yale. He was able to establish an international mindset while he lived in the USA during the time his father worked there. In the USA, he experienced a society that highly respects people that start their own business or work for smaller venture companies. He learned that it does not matter how big your employer is as long as you can create value for yourself.

Fig. 1 Hiroshi Mikitani

This is a big difference to his home country Japan, where "entrepreneurship is not the norm for someone with a good university education" (Mikitani 2013b).

He started off his career path as an investment banker at the Industrial Bank of Japan after he graduated from Hitotsubashi University in 1988. After a few years, he was transferred to work in the United States where he later decided to study at Harvard University, earning an MBA in 1993.

He always felt that Japan needed some new high growth industry but the big turning point came when he lost some of his friends and relatives as a consequence of the strong earthquake that hit Kobe, Japan on January 17th in 1995. He knew he wanted to start something new and left his job in banking to start doing business consulting in 1997. His family was shocked when he left the traditional Japanese path and was not working his way up through the ladder of the bank over a lifetime. However, his consulting company led him ultimately to his foray into e-commerce.

At that point in time, "everyone was talking about internet business but nobody believed internet shopping would work and people would start buying things from the internet. That was conventional wisdom" (Geron 2012). In contrast, Mikitani saw a great importance in internet business as "Japanese people like to communicate with each other, and it's much easier to do that on the Net" (Betz 2001). He thought that e-commerce was becoming the center of internet business and came up with several business ideas such as selling educational services or financial advice. After perusing different ventures with little economies of scale, he came up with the idea of building an electronic marketplace and founded Rakuten.

He got the idea from a famous historical event in medieval Japan which happened around the 1600s. "A warlord named Nobunaga Oda changed marketplaces in Japan by taking away control of the market from feudal trade associations and opening trade to all merchants for a small fee" (Betz 2001). The policy that made Oda's city a prevailing commercial center was called "Rakuichi Torakuza" and means, literally translated, "free markets and free guilds".

The marketplace was Mikitani's contribution towards developing a new high growth industry for Japan and to be more open and act more globally. He mentioned that Japan is famous for its manufacturing excellence but never really complied with global standards. He criticized the Japanese business establishment intensively for these shortcomings and used his company to create new demand through the internet.

His success resulted mainly from his personal beliefs and social motivation to provide the system and expertise to small Japanese shop owners and society in general, and it made a huge social impact on Japan. He believed that it is important to have a broader social mission or responsibility in order to succeed and to fend off people questioning what you are doing.

2.3 Employees

Rakuten's business model is different from its competitors. They are looking to empower their merchants in order to let them build relationships with their customers. To achieve this, they provide three things: the system, the traffic, and the expertise. Selling things online can be a tough endeavor if merchants do not know how to attract customers, create appealing and vivid online stores, and turn first-time buyers into lifelong customers. This is why employees play a vital role in Rakuten's business model of empowerment. Merchants need practice and advice from skilled people. That makes Rakuten's platform not a pure technology play but a combination of technology and people (Geron 2012).

Japan provided ideal conditions for this combination, as it is famous for its high level of hospitality and customer service. As a part of Japan's heritage, Rakuten was able to focus not only on convenience and speed, as is usually favored by Western countries, but also on delivering a personalized approach. The people factor is one of the critical success factors that are now being exported.

However, Rakuten was facing a big issue due to its expansion as the consultants that advised the merchants were mostly Japanese natives and hardly spoke English. In order to cope with this issue and to give the company a more global focus, Rakuten announced its "Englishnization" program in 2010, changing the company language to English. This conversion created frustration amongst the employees for whom it was not just a language issue but rather a cultural shock. Rakuten quickly intervened and supported them to keep their motivation and regain their former strength.

Today, Rakuten employs more than 10,000 people worldwide bringing hands-on experience to merchants on how to excel using the online channel. They built specific Rakuten Universities and hold "Rakuten Expos" all around the world to teach their merchants.

As part of their global expansion course, Rakuten banks on its double-track human resource policy. Besides intensive headhunting for top talents, they are also employing a great amount of new graduates every year and, thereby, keep the spirit of the early days. For instance, more than 600 fresh graduates started different career paths at Rakuten in 2010 (Walter and Zhang 2012). In addition, Rakuten found acquisitions to be a very effective recruitment tool as they could recruit highly talented people from investment banks and consulting firms and assign them to top management positions (Walter and Zhang 2012).

2.4 Product Range

In its more than 16 years of existence, Rakuten has built a one-stop resource for competitive hosting services. Its services range from internet-related e-commerce and financial services to operating services and professional sports business (Fig. 2).

The first and oldest business activity Rakuten ever engaged in was its internet shopping mall, Rakuten Ichiba, which is an online marketplace where merchants and customers meet in order to carry on commerce. The business models of Rakuten Ichiba has been adopted by several other countries including country-specific stores for the USA, Brazil, UK, Germany, France, Austria, Singapore, Taiwan, Thailand, Indonesia, and Malaysia, and an overall global market (Rakuten, Inc. 2014b). Due to its promise of empowerment, it is supported by an e-commerce consulting service for their merchants to help them boost their online channel.

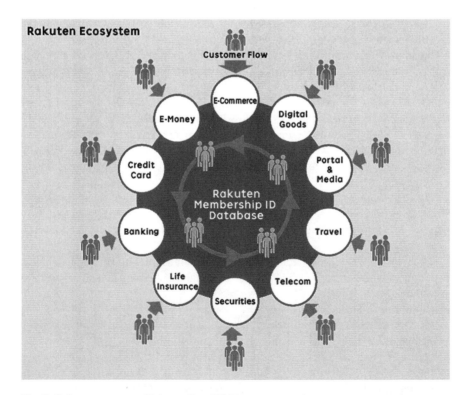

Fig. 2 Rakuten ecosystem (Rakuten, Inc. 2014b)

Over the years, Rakuten grew extensively into other business areas and constantly enhanced its incredible range of products. In regards to their e-commerce efforts, customers are offered an online auction service (Rakuten Auction), online golf course reservations (Rakuten GORA), online travel reservations (Rakuten Travel), online marketing service including affiliate marketing (LinkShare), third-party logistics for their internet shopping mall merchants (Rakuten Logistics), digital contents provision services (Rakuten Download), and online book and CD/DVD purchase services (Rakuten Books).

The financial services industry is also greatly covered with its credit card (Rakuten Card) and banking business (Rakuten Bank), offering credit cards and business financing as well as the full range of internet banking services including consumer card loans. Rakuten Edy, for example, is electronic money in the form of prepaid rechargeable contactless smart cards providing customers in Japan with the opportunity to pay with their mobile phones in stores such as 7Eleven, McDonalds and even online at its competitor Amazon. In order to top off the financial services, an online brokerage service, which reduces brokerage fees by cutting out the middleman, is provided by Rakuten Securities. Furthermore, Rakuten Insurance and Life Insurance offer comprehensive online and face-to-face insurance services to Japan's inhabitants.

With its different portal sites and operating services, Rakuten provides a gateway to the internet by acting in different areas as an internet connecting service (Rakuten Broadband), a corporate mobile phone service (Rakuten Mobile), or a search engine (Rakuten Infoseek). Furthermore, its portfolio comprises integrated internet marketing services (Rakuten Research), students recruiting community service (Minnano-Shushoku), and B2B business matching services (Rakuten Business).

Finally, Rakuten engages in professional sports business and has managed a professional baseball team (Tohoku Rakuten Golden Eagles) since its foundation in 2004. A big part of the engagement is the planning and selling of related merchandise.

2.5 Revenues

With a growing business diversification in mind, the company still generates most of its revenues through its internet services segment. More than 60 % of their revenues are generated from its internet services comprised of its e-commerce platforms, web portals, online travel reservations, search engines, and e-reading services. The internet finance segment was another growth driver in the past years, amounting to almost one third (31 %) of overall revenues in 2012. As a result, the company recorded an all time high for consolidated net revenues of over 3.9 billion € and a net income of 174 million € in 2012 (Fig. 3). Thereby, they strengthened their role as a growth driver of the world economy (Rakuten, Inc. 2012).

Main drivers for Rakuten's enormous cash flow are the monthly fees collected from merchants for setting up a virtual store on Rakuten's marketplace and the commissions received from payments. However, after 2 years of rapidly decreasing

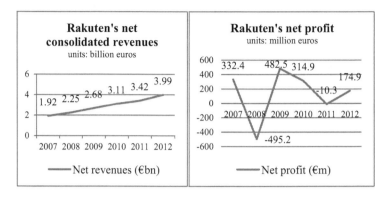

Fig. 3 Rakuten's net consolidated revenues and profit (Rakuten, Inc. 2012)

capital expenditures in 2008 and 2009, the company recovered again from 2010 onwards. In 2012, Rakuten's net cash admittedly decreased by 75 million € as a result of capital investments to accelerate growth but capital expenditures increased again to 217 million € to drive capex ratio up to 5.4 %.

In their annual report for fiscal 2012, Rakuten stated that the increase in revenues of 16.7 % on a year on year basis was achieved due to three reasons:

1. The gain of an "overwhelming advantage in the Japanese e-commerce market" that was driven by a growing gross merchandise volume (GMV) resulting in over 10 billion € in 2012.
2. The start of reaping "the benefits of introducing the Rakuten business model in other countries".
3. The "solid earnings trends in the internet finance business" resulting from a change of Rakuten's card business in 2011. Rakuten registered a 36 % increase in card shopping transactions in 2012. This led to 1118 million € in revenues and 198 million € of operating income for their internet finance business.

(Rakuten, Inc. 2012)

Even though Rakuten's revenues still appear to be significantly lower than its competitors, they managed to maintain a constant growth rate average 14 % per year between 2006 and 2012 (Schiliro 2013).

2.6 Business (Success) Strategies

Rakuten's secret of success lies within the unique understanding of an online marketplace. Rakuten Ichiba is "based on the concept of not having internet-savvy people run the business, but creating a platform that enables ordinary people skilled in retail to open their own online shop" (Rakuten, Inc. 2012). This highly profitable business model focuses on a shop-centric rather than product-centric approach, satisfying both consumers and merchants equally. It tries to introduce "discovery shopping" amongst customers by creating "an environment where merchants and consumers can interact in the same way they might in a real-world marketplace, where transactions can be engaging, exiting, informative, and personal" (Rakuten, Inc. 2012). In order to achieve this goal, Rakuten constantly enhances its e-commerce ecosystem by providing a full range of products and services to increase the user's experience and foster the relationship between shop owners and their customers.

Excelling in an area without expertise is almost impossible. In particular, selling things online can be a very tough endeavor even if the right technology is in place. In order to cope with that, Rakuten keeps a close relationship with its merchants, advising them on how to make the most out of their online channel and empowering them to interact with their customers. Rakuten's skilled e-commerce consultants follow-up with their merchants on a regular basis to discuss further product promotions and shop improvements.

This concept is called "omotenashi" or empowerment and follows the philosophy of supporting its merchants towards a great online presence. In comparison with its competitors, Rakuten does not maintain its own inventory. Thus, merchants do not need to fear to end up in a competing battle with the marketplace. Yet merchants are leveraged in a status of a full partnership.

Its service engagement of "empowering merchants" is embedded in their corporate culture. Corporate culture is a system of beliefs and goals that is "reflected in the attitudes and values, the management style, and the problem-solving behavior of its people" (Schwartz and Davis 1981). At Rakuten, everyone follows Rakuten's corporate culture through "Rakuten Shugi", which means the Rakuten way. It is a system of five principles representing the core themes they pursue, no matter where the employees are or what projects they undertake.

Five principles of success:
1. **Always improve, always advance**. The famous concept of continuous improvement stems from Toyota as part of Kaizen. At Toyota, they used the approach to focus on always improving the cars while Rakuten applies this concept to people. In this way, they are contributing to society by giving additional motivation to its employees.
2. **Be passionately professional**. It is an important component, as they understand that only passionate employees will do the utmost to strive for the best results. Mr. Mikitani once mentioned in an article about corporate culture that only "people who find joy and challenge in their jobs will go far" (Mikitani 2013a).
3. **Hypothesize/Practice/Validate/"Shikumika"** (**Systemize**). Passion needs a clear concept in order to avoid chaos and help the best ideas come out on top.
4. **Maximize customer satisfaction**. It is an important understanding to take good care of all customers in an ecosystem and focus not solely on the end user. This includes venders, merchants, and consumers.
5. **Speed, Speed, Speed**! A major downside a lot of companies face as they grow is losing flexibility and speed in getting things done. Small companies can make

use of their agility. Embedded in their corporate culture, they want to keep the speed and do not accept slowness.

These five principles helped to shape the corporate culture Rakuten possesses today. According to Mikitani, there is nothing more important to their success. It is no wonder that even in an acquisition process of a prospective company that the cultural fit will be discussed at an early stage to ensure a successful collaboration in the long run. The corporate culture reflects the service the company offers and is the key to making a difference in global e-commerce, where most companies focus solely on efficiency and convenience. The unique combination of technology and people underpins this strategy. It enables merchants to excel in the online channel and helps to increase the monetization of their services. The hybrid approach of humans and algorithms lets retailers focus on their core business rather than on the logistics and technology behind the scenes.

2.7 What About Quality and Innovation of the Product Range?

In e-commerce business, trust is still one of the main concerns online merchants and marketplaces are facing. It is no secret that high-quality standards contribute to building trust so it is no wonder that Rakuten also puts enormous efforts into maintaining and improving their quality standards. In particular, decentralized marketplaces may entail quality or service issues. In order to avoid these issues, Rakuten employs a tight screening process and monitors transactions. Integrated survey programs give customers the opportunity to provide Rakuten with feedback on transactions. Merchants with negative feedback are examined carefully and if necessary banned from the platform. Additionally, they offer refunds to customers if goods do not arrive. These measures raise the quality of services and ultimately create trust.

However, as stated in their five principles of success, Rakuten focuses on all of its customers and is also working towards generating trust amongst affiliated merchants. A close relationship is maintained by the e-commerce consultants in order to keep merchants updated about new platform features and technical abilities.

To fuel the platform constantly with new features and extend its knowledge base, Rakuten introduced dedicated research organizations in Tokyo, New York, and Paris. The Rakuten Institute of Technology "encourages its R&D members to cultivate their curiosity, develop their interests and face challenging problems to create opportunities in combining emerging technologies with innovative services" (Rakuten, Inc. 2014a).

The innovation process is not only limited to the Rakuten Institute of Technology but also receives great input from strategic acquisitions. For example, "Shop Together", is a social shopping tool that was introduced in 2011. Initially, it had been developed for Buy.com, a US company that joined Rakuten in 2010. It enables customers to chat with other people that are viewing the same product.

Furthermore, it integrates with social networks to exhaust the full range of social interaction to contribute towards the overall goal of socially-enhanced discovery shopping.

Another strategic investment was made when Rakuten bought into Pinterest in order to become the basis for buying products off the site. Thereby, the company incorporates the "discovery shopping" approach again and merges different business segments in order to create new innovative shopping concepts.

3 The Rise of the Company

3.1 Growth Development

The business model of Rakuten's online marketplace turned out to be profitable right from the beginning, earning its first one million US$ only 2 years after they launched their business. At that time, a profit margin of nearly 17 % in e-commerce was remarkable and assured fast growth. In the beginning, Rakuten cooperated with different Japanese start-ups such as Culture Convenience Club and SoftBank. The IPO on JASDAQ in 2000 was a key milestone to diversification of businesses and services as they entered M&A activities to acquire promising ventures. During the following 10 years, they started a shopping spree with more than 20 strategic acquisitions and investments. Decisive factors that initially enabled the M&A activities were, on the one hand, the great market capitalization that almost doubled from 2004 to 2010 to 7.3 billion €, and on the other hand, the cash-rich nature of its core business (Walter and Zhang 2012).

The M&A activities were accompanied with providing corporate venture capital to new acquired companies. That was different from typical corporate venture capital models as they provided resources only to their own group or acquired companies. These resources were not only limited to financial aid but also included intangible resources such as business know-how, networks, and brand name. This can be seen as a hybrid model between a Silicon Valley business cluster and a Japanese "keiretsu" system (Walter and Zhang 2012). The development of an own hybrid conglomerate incubator model at Rakuten was initiated for different reasons. First, they tried to avoid inhospitable fundraising and recruitment in Japan. As a result, new companies became part of Rakuten Group instead of employing investment and exit strategies. Second, they needed M&A activities in order to keep the constant growth once the Japanese market was saturated. Finally, Rakuten wanted to allocate only a small quantity of stock options to its employees and keep a relatively low liquidity in order to prevent employees from monetizing their stock options and starting new businesses. With this model, they built a "financial and managerial employment ecosystem" (Walter and Zhang 2012) and strengthened the whole group development.

Taking these efforts into account, the company managed an outstanding growth development over the past decade and is now operating in ten countries globally and aspires to expand this number to over 27 countries in the coming years. By the end of 2013, the group held more than 50 companies diversified over seven different business segments (Walter and Zhang 2012).

3.2 Becoming a Brand?

Its aggressive M&A strategy subsequently shaped the Rakuten ecosystem and strengthened its brand awareness throughout different business segments and countries. In 2003, when they initially started the expansion into new business areas, they boosted its outreach through different mergers and acquisitions. In order to develop the Rakuten brand, acquired ventures were renamed shortly after their acquisitions. By 2004, Rakuten's website was ranked as the second most visited website as measured by unique audience in Japan (MarketLine 2012). In the same year, they entered into the professional sports business and founded "Tohoku Rakuten Golden Eagles", a Japanese baseball team (Fig. 4). This stroke also contributed greatly to an overall brand awareness, "putting the Rakuten brand in newspapers across the country on a daily basis" (Rakuten, Inc. 2014b).

According to their mission, Rakuten believes "that the only way for a business to grow over the long term is to contribute to the world so significantly that people can't imagine life without it" (Rakuten, Inc. 2014c). This ongoing process will be fulfilled through empowering people and building a fair society. From 2005 until 2010, active expansion continued so that the Rakuten ecosystem finally took a shape. In 2010, the company started to expand heavily overseas and entered the next stage of being a genuine global business. All these efforts worked towards the goal of shaping an ecosystem that is hard to live without and eventually raised brand awareness to strengthen its global presence.

3.3 Position in the Home Market

In 2001, when Rakuten announced its ambitious goal to reach about 1 trillion yen of gross transaction volume, the company was still in the beginning phase of shaping its position in the home market. At that time they had nearly 36 billion yen of gross transaction volume and started to expand into new business segments. In the same year, they launched a hotel reservation service and an online bookshop. In order to deter customers from switching to another platform, they also introduced its loyalty program "Rakuten Super Points" only a year later in 2002. In the digital world, network effects as used in loyalty programs are more powerful than ever. These

Fig. 4 Rakuten Eagles baseball logo

opt-in strategies made customers keen to buy on Rakuten's website and strengthened its position on the domestic market as people could redeem points for discounts at any other merchant or business within Rakuten Group. In order to enhance synergy for Rakuten group and its customers, the company acquired myTrip.net to take the lead in the online travel market and entered investment banking business with its newly acquired venture DLJdirect SFG Securities. With the foundation of a professional baseball team in 2004, Rakuten even managed to jump-start the professional sports business and leveraged its position with daily news about Rakuten's sports team. A few years later, they officially announced its vision for a "Rakuten ecosystem" and connected its online and offline services across the group. This was fueled with later investments in the financial services industry, including eBANK Corp. and Bit Wallet, Inc., to offer banking and e-money services to its customers. Over the years, Rakuten became the one-stop resource for a majority of online services in Japan, including e-commerce, digital goods, portal and media, travel, telecom, securities, life insurance, banking, credit cards, and e-money. According to a report from MarketLine, Rakuten holds leadership positions in each of its core businesses in Japan and therefore dominates its domestic market in online services (MarketLine 2012).

3.4 Position in the Global Market

With its mission to become the world's largest internet service company, Rakuten follows its strategy to target high-potential e-commerce markets. Even though foreign markets currently only account for about 10 % of its consolidated revenues, they are trying to expand and build their international awareness with cross-border sales between various domestic markets (Schiliro 2013). This strategy is supported by acquisition of local e-commerce businesses that adopt the Rakuten Ichiba concept. At a later stage, established e-commerce businesses will expand into other business segments such as travel, finance, etc. Besides acquisitions, they form tight partnerships with other online malls in the regional markets to differentiate from competitors. In 2012, over 2.4 billion internet users were counted globally. Almost 45 % thereof were located in Asia, 21 % in Europe, and 11 % in North America (MarketLine 2012). Rakuten is banking on information such as internet-user statistics and e-commerce penetration rates to align its international expansion.

As a result, they started their internationalization process in selected Asia-Pacific markets. "Taiwan Rakuten Ichiba" was the first adoption of its successful online shopping mall outside Japan in 2008. In the following years, they entered strategic business and capital partnerships with TARAD.com, Thailand's largest e-commerce website, and Baidu, Inc., the world's largest Chinese search engine, to develop them into promising B2B2C e-commerce sites. Due to a joint venture with a big Indonesian conglomerate, they also launched a new online shopping mall in Indonesia in 2011.

Besides the Asia-Pacific activities, they aggressively expanded in Europe and America due to a string of mergers and acquisitions. In 2005, they fully acquired LinkShare Corp., a vast U.S. affiliate marketing network with expert consulting services and patented technology. In order to position Rakuten's shopping mall concept in American markets, they bought the leading US e-commerce website Buy.com in 2010 and purchased a 75 % stake in Brazil's leading e-commerce platform provider Ikeda.

In the same years, they also started to develop a footprint in Europe and acquired the most important e-commerce sites in Germany, France, and the United Kingdom. For example, France's PriceMinister is accessed by more than 11 million users a month and also operates in Spain and the UK. The Germany-based Tradoria GmbH handles over 8 million products from 4,400 member stores and Play.com is the UK's biggest e-retailer with over 14 million registered users. In Europe in particular, the expansion was accompanied by friendly relations with luxury-goods producers to fight counterfeit products on Rakuten's auction sites. For instance, an alliance with Louis Vuitton was announced in 2010 to work "proactively" against sales of fake goods. Similar deals are expected to follow with other major brand owners (MarketLine 2012).

As a consequence of their strategic alignment to target high growth markets, they entered into the e-book business on a full scale with the acquisition of KOBO, Inc. in Canada in 2012. This was in response to Amazon who had been in the e-reading business for a few years already.

3.5 To What Extent Was the Triple Helix of Governmental, Business and Educational System Beneficial to the Rise of This Company?

Japan's retail industry offered Rakuten an optimal breeding ground to start off an e-commerce business such as an online shopping mall. In the 1990s, Japan had only a few large-scale retailers and many small-scale retailers, called "mom and pop stores". "The dominance of the small-scale firms in Japan implies that the distribution system is decentralized and not highly integrated vertically" (Krugman 1991). This is a big disadvantage because a decentralized distribution system has many layers of wholesalers, resulting in high prices that inflate with each markup. This circumstance proved advantageous for Rakuten, as they were able to cut out the middlemen and thus pull down prices for goods tremendously. Mr. Mikitani gave a powerful demonstration of this in a New York Times article: "Buy a share of Rakuten through a traditional Japanese stockbroker, and pay commissions equal to 3 % of the share's value, which is about 1,065,000 yen at current prices, or 10,000 US$. Buy it online from Monex, a securities broker here, and pay a 10 US$ commission" (Strom 2000). The trigger for the excessiveness of small-scale shops goes back to the 1950s where the government passed the so-called "large scale retail store law". The law notifies small retailers of plans to build a large store in their neighborhood and lets them comment on the new store. Between 1970 and

1990, the law was even stricter, preventing almost any new store over 500 square meters from being established. However, the landscape that was shaped out of those many small-scale retailers paved the way for Rakuten Ichiba as a platform that joins forces of small retailers and turns them into one large virtual store without losing too much control.

Another characteristic of the Japanese market faded away as a consequence of the strengthening of the yen in the 1980s and the Japanese people began to travel abroad. This contributed towards a waning tolerance for high prices as they learned how expensive Japan is. People were used to paying high prices but also expected many things of retailers such as most repairs and other services in return. The great service mentality lies within Japan's heritage. Rakuten utilized the extremely high level of hospitality and customer service to create added value and embed it as part of their business strategy in terms of its "empowerment" concept.

4   Future Developments

4.1   What Are the Future Challenges/Problems to Be Overcome at Home and Abroad?

Rakuten operates in several different businesses around the world and is, therefore, exposed to a number of business risks and faces challenges from different areas. These are all related to their business environment, and its general business expansion and development at home and abroad.

As the company is mainly operating in the internet sector, they are heavily dependent on industry development. "External factors, such as regulatory systems that limit the internet use, the growing awareness of information security issues, especially in relation to personal information" (Rakuten, Inc. 2012), and also the economic trends of the internet services market are their main concerns. For example, the internet advertising market, which is heavily dependent on economic trends, is likely to affect Rakuten's financial performance as it holds a particular share on the overall group performance.

The internet itself also constitutes a big challenge for Rakuten as competition begins to mount. Customers possess strong bargaining power due to low switching costs among online retailers and marketplaces. As a result, Rakuten may be forced to step into fierce competition on prices and services if competitors with revolutionary services and powerful system-development capabilities emerge (Rakuten, Inc. 2012).

The internet is built upon technology that brings constant changes to new products and services. In order to cope with rapid changes, Rakuten needs to respond swiftly to avoid offering obsolete products and services.

Due to Rakuten's active expansion, they may also face issues related to their business development. Changing names of acquired ventures to "Rakuten" and integrating old memberships may lead to a loss of loyalty among members of the original company and may ultimately cause a decrease in memberships.

In general, their M&A activities may harm the overall group performance if, for example, due diligence is not performed to a certain extent due to time restrictions, etc. Furthermore, changes in business environment may cause a deviation from an anticipated development of a newly-acquired venture.

However, taking a closer look at Rakuten's domestic market in Japan, one has to consider influencing factors such as the rapidly-shrinking birthrate and aging population which all contributes to market saturation. Taking all these factors into account, Rakuten has to expand overseas as the domestic market is likely to stagnate in the long run.

Certainly, expanding overseas brings new challenges along because launching a new business in another country may lead to potential risks such as "differences in languages, geographical factors, legal and taxation systems, economic and political instability, and differing commercial practices" (Rakuten, Inc. 2012).

4.2 Which Companies Are Its Competitors Now and in the Future?

Competition is a big challenge for e-commerce companies and needs to be well observed. In the e-commerce industry, it can be classified into four categories:

1. **Diversified online competitors**, such as search engines, social networks, web portals, and other internet companies.
2. **Diversified physical competitors**, such as traditional brick- and mortar retailers
3. **Specialized online competitors**, such as businesses' own online retail platform
4. **Specialized physical competitors**, such as businesses' store networks

(Schiliro 2013)

Most companies entering e-commerce are attracted by the fast market growth and its future potential. Due to the constantly growing IT services industry, it is possible to enter the market with simple and low-cost solutions. Additionally, low switching costs for customers and merchants confront Rakuten with a great variety of competitors and substitutes, ranging from regional-specific companies to big multinationals. In recent years, Rakuten chose Amazon as its biggest competitor and is constantly challenging it. In Japan, Yahoo is another strong rival as both Amazon and Yahoo benefit from well-established brand names and can make use of their economies of scale to compete more efficiently (MarketLine 2012).

In addition to its current competitors, Rakuten faces a growing threat from larger internet companies such as Google and Apple. In fact, these conglomerates leverage their existing infrastructure to build their own online shopping platforms. Due to a significant user base resulting from other service areas, it is highly expected that they will gain widespread acceptance within no time.

5 Conclusions

5.1 Why Did This Company Become So Successful?

In its home country of Japan, Rakuten found a great domestic market situation to start off an e-commerce company in 1997. Japan's retail situation at that time was very untransparent and a wealth of distribution layers ultimately caused high prices for goods. With its online shopping mall Rakuten Ichiba, the company was able to undercut prices and systematically cut out the middlemen. In general, the 1990s were predestinated to enter the e-commerce business as the internet boom had only just begun.

Of course, Rakuten's success was not only characterized by external factors. Their permanent belief in providing a huge social value with its online shopping mall contributed greatly to constantly raising motivation. The company aimed for an online marketplace where buyers and sellers meet to conduct trade. Its platform combined technology with human expertise in order to empower people such as local retailers to sell their products online without worrying about technological and logistical aspects. The company levered the Japanese hospitality to build a reliable corporate culture and shaped an outstanding service that focuses on encouraging long-term relationships between merchants and customers.

Strategic acquisitions have shaped an ecosystem that is currently seen as the most diverse and encounters people in many everyday life situations. A constant focus on global expansion and untapped business and niche segments contributes to its overall success.

5.2 Is It Likely that This Company Will Become a World Brand?

Rakuten has already shown its global ambitions to become the world's biggest internet service company. They are constantly developing its business all around the globe and foster their ecosystem not only in Japan. In only 17 years of existence, the company managed to expand into ten different countries and continues the global presence with strategic mergers and acquisitions on a constant basis. The connection between different countries becomes more and more important and has already begun to yield fruit. The company is pooling their forces to take on global leadership. Rakuten's chief marketing and operating officer Bernhard Luthi is convinced that they can take on their competitors "by uniting and empowering independent retailers into one strong force" (Thau 2014).

References

Betz, F. (2001). *Executive strategy: Strategic management and information technology*. New York: Wiley.

Geron, T. (2012). *Rakuten CEO Hiroshi Mikitani on Amazon, Pinterest and fixing Japanese Business*. Retrieved September 6, 2012, from http://www.forbes.com/sites/tomiogeron/2012/09/06/rakuten-ceo-hiroshi-mikitani-on-amazon-pinterest-and-fixing-japanese-business/

Krugman, P. (1991). *Trade with Japan: Has the door opened wider?* Chicago: University of Chicago Press.

MarketLine. (2012). *Rakuten: Global e-retail expansion strategy*. London: Datamonitor Plc.

Mikitani, A. (2013a). Corporate culture: It's the secret to our success. *Leadership Excellence, 30*(3), 6.

Mikitani, A. (2013b). *Rakuten's CEO on humanizing e-commerce*. Harvard Business Review. Retrieved May 17, 2014, from http://hbr.org/2013/11/rakutens-ceo-on-humanizing-e-commerce/ar/1

Rakuten, Inc. (2012). *Annual reports for FY 2012*. Retrieved May 17, 2014, from http://global.rakuten.com/corp/investors/documents/annual.html

Rakuten, Inc. (2014a). *Rakuten Institute of Technology—R.I.T.* Retrieved May 17, 2014, from http://rit.rakuten.co.jp/index.html

Rakuten, Inc. (2014b). *About us: Our history*. Retrieved May 17, 2014, from http://global.rakuten.com/corp/about/history.html

Rakuten, Inc. (2014c). *About us: Brand concepts*. Retrieved May 17, 2014, from http://global.rakuten.com/corp/about/philosophy/brand.html

Schiliro, A. (2013). *E-Commerce companies—World—2013–2018 Trends—Corporate strategies*. Paris: Xerfi Global.

Schwartz, H., & Davis, S. M. (1981). Matching corporate culture and business strategy. *Organizational Dynamics, 10*, 30.

Strom, S. (2000). Online overseas; Taking a Warlord's advice to shake up the marketplace. *New York Times*, 32.

Thau, B. (2014). *Rakuten's global ambitions: Japan's biggest e-commerce player uses third-party marketplace model to expand*. Retrieved January 7, 2014, from http://chainstoreage.com/article/rakuten%E2%80%99s-global-ambitions

Walter, A., & Zhang, X. (2012). *East Asian capitalism: Diversity, continuity, and change*. Oxford: Oxford University Press.

Uniqlo: A Case Study on Creating Market Share with Affordable and Timeless Designs

Frederike Schulz-Müllensiefen and Aenne Stöckmann

Abstract

The Japanese designer, manufacturer, and retailer, Uniqlo, is known for casual, high-quality clothing for very affordable prices. During the Japanese recession, the company was valued especially for its low prices. They soon expanded their business throughout Japan. Step-by-step, they expanded internationally and were then competing successfully with the major fashion retailers. Today, it is the fourth largest fashion retailer worldwide. Uniqlo made it possible to successfully educate countries worldwide, within less than 25 years, in its unique product strategy and it is still continuing to enlarge its business operations. By 2020, the company is aiming to become the world's biggest specialty retailer of private label apparel with a continuous growth rate of 20 %. The company's success can be explained by its initial success during the Japanese crisis. The consumer's demand for affordable but high quality clothing was high during this time of recession, as consumers had to cut back on expenditures. After this sudden success, Uniqlo's founder Tadashi Yanai managed to expand brand awareness and achieved success globally.

1 Introduction

The Japanese designer, manufacturer, and retailer, Uniqlo, is known for casual, high-quality clothing for very affordable prices. During the Japanese recession, the company was valued especially for their low prices. They managed to communicate this unique selling position and soon expanded their business throughout Japan. Shortly thereafter, the company was listed on the Tokyo Stock Exchange and

F. Schulz-Müllensiefen (✉) • A. Stöckmann
The Honor's Program of the International Business School, Hanze University OAS, Groningen, The Netherlands
e-mail: f.schulz-mullensiefen@st.hanze.nl; aenne.stoeckmann@icloud.com

became a wholly-owned subsidiary of Fast Retailing Co., Ltd. Soon, step-by-step, they expanded internationally and were then competing successfully with the major fashion retailers. Today, Fast Retailing is the fourth largest fashion retailer worldwide.

Uniqlo made it possible to successfully educate countries worldwide, within less than 25 years, in their unique product strategy and they are still continuing to enlarge their business operations.

By 2020, the company is aiming to become the world's biggest specialty retailer of private label apparel with a continuous growth rate of 20 %.

2 Company Profile

2.1 History

In June 1984, the Yamaguchi-based company, Ogori Shoji, opened the first "Unique Clothing Warehouse" store in Hiroshima City that was specialized in men's wear (Uniqlo 2014a). Soon, the original brand "Unique Clothing Warehouse" got renamed to "Uniqlo". They changed their product line into casual clothes for both men and women, and since Uniqlo's product are comparably cheap, but still high quality, they had a major competitive advantage during the Japanese "Great Recession" in the 1990s by tailoring to citizens who were reducing their spending (Business Insider 2014). They soon gained popularity in the Japanese market.

The first Uniqlo roadside store opened only 1 year later, in 1985, and it enjoyed immediate success (Uniqlo 2014a). In 1991, Ogori Shoji Co., Ltd. changed their name to the by now well-known name Fast Retailing Co., Ltd. (Fast Retailing 2014b). Only 3 years later, Fast Retailing Co., Ltd already listed shares on the Hiroshima Stock Exchange. Three years after that, the first shares were listed on the Tokyo stock exchange.

Only 10 years after the first Uniqlo store had opened, 100 stores already existed successfully (Business Insider 2014). In 1998, the brand offered the "1900-yen fleece campaign", which made the brand even more popular in Japan. Nevertheless, the brand experienced a periodic falling of sales and profits (Fast Retailing 2014j). As a result, the company started concentrating on expanding their line of women's wear (Fast Retailing 2014j). Furthermore, it began changing their store strategy to large-format stores with gracious floor space located in urban areas, instead of emphasizing roadside stores in suburbs (Fast Retailing 2014m). With this in mind, they opened their first urban Uniqlo store in Tokyo. The headquarters also shifted to Tokyo in order to promote merchandising and marketing (Fast Retailing 2014b).

With this new strategy, Uniqlo started expanding outside Japan. In 2001, the first four overseas stores opened in London, and only 1 year later, in 2002, two Uniqlo stores were opened in Shanghai (Uniqlo 2014a). Moreover, the Uniqlo Design Studio was established as an independent organization with over 50 designers. In 2003, the newly-launched cashmere campaign, which is still a popular product of

Uniqlo, gained high consumer interest and popularity (Uniqlo 2014f). Next to establishing the Uniqlo Design Studio subsidiary in New York, Uniqlo opened 21 stores in the UK. Unfortunately, only eight of them remained open, because they failed to establish a brand identity first (Business Insider 2014).

To enhance their new strategy, they opened the first large-format Uniqlo store in Osaka in 2004 which had 1600 square meters of floor space. Later in the same year, Uniqlo entered a joint venture with Lotte Shopping Co., Ltd. (South Korea) in order to expand their brand to the South Korean area (Fast Retailing 2014c). Only 9 months later, in 2005, the first Uniqlo store in Seoul, South Korea, was opened. In the same year, new stores in New Jersey, Hong Kong, and Tokyo were opened. Moreover, Uniqlo expanded their product line to "Uniqlo Kids" and "Body by Uniqlo", which is focusing on women's underwear (Fast Retailing 2014d). Most importantly, Uniqlo adopted a holding company structure in order to develop new business opportunities (Fast Retailing 2014d). In addition, they formed a new strategic business partnership with Toray Industries, Inc. in 2006. In the same year, the first global flagship store was opened in New York (Fast Retailing 2014d).

In 2007, the brand opened another specialty store: the T-Shire store in Harajuku. Moreover, one of the largest Uniqlo stores was opened in eastern Japan. Additionally, another global flagship store opened in London in the same year. Furthermore, the expansion in South Korea was continuing and Uniqlo opened the first large-format store in South Korea. At the end of the year, Uniqlo managed to open a store in Paris, which was their first shop in France (Fast Retailing 2014d). Next to this, they developed the new "Uniqlo Heattech" clothing line, which lead to a rise in sales and even more in popularity (Fast Retailing 2014e).

In 2008, Uniqlo established a joint venture with Wing Tai Retail Pte. Ltd. in order to be able to expand into Singapore. At the end of 2008, subsidiaries G.U. Co., Ltd., Viewcompany Co., Ltd., and Onezone Corp. merged and formed Gov. retailing Co., Ltd., which is a footwear business that operated under the name Uniqlo Co. Ltd in 2010.

In 2009, Jil Sander, who is a well known worldwide designer, signed a design contract with Uniqlo and launched their new line "J+" at the end of the year (Fast Retailing 2014d). Moreover, Uniqlo started signing affiliation contracts with celebrities, such as, for example, Shingo Kuneida, a professional wheelchair tennis player. In the same year, Uniqlo opened their third flagship store in France.

The year 2010 was another very successful year for the company. At the beginning of the year, they expanded to Russia and the first store opened in Moscow. Furthermore, two global flagship stores were opened. One was opened in China and another one in Japan. Additionally, Uniqlo expanded to Taipei and Kuala Lumpur. Later in 2010, Uniqlo established a joint venture with Grameen Bank in order to pursue a business initiative in Bangladesh (Fast Retailing 2014f).

In addition to contributing to several social activities, they opened new flagship stores in Taiwan, South Korea, and New York in 2011. They expanded to Bangkok, Thailand, and reopened the store in Tokyo to make it become the largest store with 3300 square meters of floor space. Additionally, Uniqlo launched a global partnership agreement with the United Nations High Commissioner for Refugees (UNHCR) to further pursue ongoing company initiatives (Fast Retailing 2014g).

By 2012, Uniqlo was named the fourth largest retail apparel company and owned 1163 stores (Forbes 2012a). In this year, they expanded to the USA and the Philippines as well as opened a new flagship store in Tokyo. Moreover, they launched the new product line "Uniqlo X undercover" in cooperation with the "Undercover Fashion Label" (Fast Retailing 2014h).

In 2013, Uniqlo opened several new stores in Jakarta, Bangladesh, Hong Kong and in Shanghai (Fast Retailing 2014h).

Uniqlo became a popular and, most importantly, a steadily growing and expanding internationally operating company. According to their press release in January 2014, they launched a "pop-up store road" in Berlin, Germany, in order to connect with local communities and to introduce the brand to the new market. In April, they are going to open a new flagship store in Berlin. Next to France and the UK, Germany is already the third country in Europe where Uniqlo clothing is offered (Fast Retailing 2014l). Furthermore, they are planning on expanding their brand presence throughout the USA (Fast Retailing 2014l). Currently, Uniqlo ranks as one of the ten most valuable brands in Japan, according to the consultancy Interbrand (The Economist 2010).

2.2 The Founder

The founder of Uniqlo is Tadashi Yanai.

Yanai was born on the 7th of February, 1949, in Ube, Yamaguchi Prefecture, Japan. Yanai grew up living above the clothing store of his parents in Yamaguchi Prefecture in the southwest of Japan (Urstadt 2010).

Studying politics and economics, Yanai graduated from Waseda University in Tokyo with a Bachelor's degree in political science in 1971 (4 Traders 2014). After graduation, he began working at a well-known shopping center, called JUSCO, but decided to resign 10 months later. In 1972, Yanai started to work at Ogori Shoji, which is a men's clothing shop chain opened by his father (Tadashi 2003).

In 1984, he finally opened the first Uniqlo store in Hiroshima City and became the president of the company. After changing the name from Ogori Shoji to Fast Retailing, Yanai expanded the presence of the company to Harajuku in 1998. Since 2002, Yanai has been the CEO and Chairman of Fast Retailing (Tadashi 2003).

Today he is the wealthiest person in Japan with a net worth of 9.0 billion US$ (Urstadt 2010). Yanai is married and has two children (Business Insider 2013).

2.3 Employees

Currently, Fast Retailing employs 59,617 employees in 21 countries and regions (Fast Retailing 2013a).

Uniqlo has severe regulations regarding their responsibility towards employees as well as employee behavior and training. It is their goal "to foster both corporate and personal growth by establishing environments that cultivate people into becoming capable of performing innovative work from a global perspective" (Fast Retailing 2010), as stated by the company Fast Retailing. They developed a training program in order to develop new strategies, give business insights, and help employees to understand their ideal of "Changing clothes. Changing conventional wisdom. Change the world". Uniqlo expects every employee to share the same vision and work together, professionally as a team. In addition to this, it supports their view that every employee, regardless of their position, is able to acquire the way of thinking of an international manager, and hence supports the company with the same effort and motivation (Fast Retailing 2013a). Furthermore, Uniqlo's employee franchising program gives store managers the possibility to become independent franchise owners. This is also an advantage for the company, since chances are greater for store managers to identify problems and issues concerning the whole Uniqlo organization more quickly. Standards can be set accordingly and will improve the overall performance for all of the firms' stores (Fast Retailing 2013b).

The company describes itself as respecting the employee and interested in employee satisfaction. Uniqlo supports their employees with childcare and nursing care programs to enable them to remain even longer with their company (Fast Retailing 2010). Furthermore, they designed a rule which states that 4 days a week are "no overtime days".

Moreover, they promote employee diversity. In 2001, Uniqlo started focusing on offering job positions for people with disabilities in Japan. In 2007, Fast Retailing, and accordingly Uniqlo, was awarded with the "Award of Merit for Supporting Second Challenges" for their efforts of hiring disabled people (Fast Retailing 2013c).

Uniqlo offers a universal wage system for shop managers and higher-ranked employees, which means that employees will be working under the same conditions in different countries and will hence earn the same amount of money (RocketNews24 2013).

Uniqlo puts distinct efforts into presenting their professionalism to the customer. Every employee, no matter in what position, has to go through several trainings offered by the company to ensure professional work behavior. Every employee working in a Uniqlo store has to go through a training every single day to remind them of their behavior and of the ways they were taught to interact with customers (New York Magazine 2010). Every advisor, which is how Uniqlo calls their employees who help customers in the stores, has to have a notebook with them to make notes on everything a manager tells them or on improvements suggested by the customer (New York Magazine 2010). To assure their professionalism, all employees are expected to additionally train their behavior and skills independently. To ensure this, every employee gets tested on a regular basis (New York Magazine 2010).

This professionalism is also expected from the upper positions. For example, a poster in every manager's office says "Always follow company directions. Do not work in your own way" (New York Magazine 2010). This emphasizes Uniqlo's shared vision and professionalism.

2.4 Product Range

In contrast to their main competitors, Uniqlo has a very distinctive business model. Instead of offering the newest fashion trends, they limit their product line to around 1000 basic items but offer them in various colors (The Economist 2010). By offering the same product line for a long time, they can strike far cheaper. higher-volume deals with their suppliers compared to other stores (The Economist 2010), and can therefore provide affordable high-quality clothing. Moreover, by offering casual clothes in different designs instead of frequently changing trend-inspired product lines, they hope to attract a larger target group. Uniqlo has already been proven successful with their basic lines and, since 2009, are trying to even extend their product line, such as with their J+ collection, to attract even more customers (The Economist 2010).

In general, Uniqlo is striving for a contemporary look, matching their slogan "Made For All". They target men, women and children. The product range can be divided into outerwear, knitwear, tops, bottoms, accessories, and underwear.

In the outerwear product line, they offer casual jackets, Blazers, jeans and their special product line Ultra Light Down. Looking at the design, it is certain that all designs are simple, without any special highlights and in plain colors. Ultra Light Down is a product line in the form of vests, jackets, and parkas, containing 90 % down and 10 % feathers to aim for a light but yet warm jacket.

The knitwear product line contains the well-known cashmere line, extra fine merino, cotton clothes and cardigans. The knitwear again is shaped by simplicity and versatility. The cashmere product line became popular due to the comparably affordable price in combination with high quality. It is available in different styles, colors, and cuts (Uniqlo 2014d). Extra fine merino, includes cardigans and sweaters in simple styles made from ultra fine fibers (Uniqlo 2014d).

The tops product lines contain all kinds of modest tops, including fleece and UT2014 product lines. The fleece product line includes printed as well as plain fleece T-Shirts and jackets. The UK 2014 product line appears less contemporary, with different tops with graphics based on famous comic-inspired characters (Uniqlo 2014b).

The bottom product line contains jeans, skirts, shorts, and leggings, all made from jeans or cotton in simple designs. The jeans vary from different formats such as ultra stretch, skinny, slim, regular, and relaxed.

The underwear product line varies from their Heattech product line, to regular underwear, socks, body shapers, and loungewear. Heattech combines innovative materials which "absorbs the moisture generated by the human body before converting it into heat" (Uniqlo 2014e), which makes it an innovative attempt to develop advanced apparel.

In addition, Uniqlo also offers accessories which are marketed by practicability. This product line contains head accessories, scarves, stoles, ties, gloves, and belts. They are mostly produced in simple colors and with high-quality fabrics.

Additionally, Uniqlo offers a free App for the iPhone and Android containing exclusive app offers, a barcode scanner, and online shop access. Moreover, the customer has the opportunity to connect to the "uniqlommunity" which is a community that keeps the customer updated on recent events and product offers. The customer is also able to use a camera with different effects, gets updated on the weather forecast, and is able to use the "uniqlock" which is an alarm with integrated weather announcement and positive melodies to wake up to (Uniqlo 2014c).

2.5 Revenues

According to the 5-year financial summary published by Fast Retailing, Uniqlo had a net income of 90 billion yen in 2013. This is the highest net income for Uniqlo, regarding the years 2009–2013 (Fast Retailing 2014p).

In 2009, Uniqlo possessed a net income of 49 billion yen (Fast Retailing 2014p). The net income experienced a rise to 61 billion yen in 2010, but then decreased to a net income of 54 billion yen in 2011 (Fast Retailing 2014p). However, there was an increase of almost 20 billion yen net income in 2012 (71 billion yen). Finally, the net income of Uniqlo had an increase of almost 20 billion yen again (90 billion yen) (Fast Retailing 2014p).

2.6 Business Success Strategies

Uniqlo's business strategy is composed of four main points: developing products of exceptionally high quality, becoming Japan's top brand by expanding urban market share, a rapid international expansion, and Heattech (Fast Retailing 2014m).

2.6.1 Developing Products of Exceptionally High Quality

In order to ensure that the products are of exceptional quality, Uniqlo refined its SPA business model, the specialty store retailer of private label apparel, making it possible to control the whole business process (Fast Retailing 2014m).

The company bases its product development on customer feedback. This means that when the Uniqlo customer center receives comments, such as asking for another fabric, the company takes this into account and tries to implement the customer's wishes (Fast Retailing 2014m). Moreover, Uniqlo's Material Development Team can provide high-quality material at a low cost due to the direct negotiations with global manufacturers and economies of scale (Fast Retailing 2014m).

Furthermore, Uniqlo stresses the importance of implementing quality control in factory production technology and also in management (Fast Retailing 2014m). Consequently, a team of technical experts (Takumi Team) is sent to all partner factories in China in order to provide technical instructions. Additionally, supervisors from the Production Department, which is based in the Shanghai office, visit the partner factories weekly to check the quality as well as the progress of production (Fast Retailing 2014m).

2.6.2 Becoming Japan's Top Brand by Expanding Urban Market Share

Due to the fact that Uniqlo's brand image and appeal to the customer has improved, the company has become more and more attractive for developers of department stores and commercial buildings. Beginning in 2009, high-street and department store outlets were opened by Uniqlo (Fast Retailing 2014m). The biggest store in Japan was opened in September 2011 in the Ikebukuro's Tobu Department Store in Tokyo. These urban stores generate great sales and are of great popularity with customers, which is why it should expand the customer base and increase the brand value (Fast Retailing 2014m).

Although Uniqlo has been underrepresented in the urban centers of Japan with only few stores in relation to the population of major cities, including Tokyo, Osaka, Nagoya, and Fukuoka, the goal is to expand the urban market share by anticipating the opening of outlets and high-street stores in department stores and malls (Fast Retailing 2014m).

Moreover, from the overall market in Japan, Uniqlo had a 5.5 % share, comprising a 3.9 % share of the women's wear market in respect to an 8.9 % share of men's wear (Fast Retailing 2014m). Sales by product type compared to the Japanese apperal market can be found in Fig. 1.

Furthermore, Uniqlo began developing large-scale stores with the goal to extend the total sales floor-space in Japan (Fast Retailing 2014m). This represents a shift from standard stores with around 800 square meters to large-scale stores with 1600 square meters or more. Although sales and profitability per square meter tend to decrease when sales floor area increases in the apparel industry, Uniqlo has a

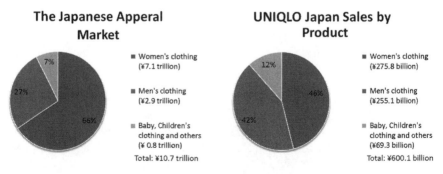

Fig. 1 The Japanese apparel market and Uniqlo sales by product category (Based on Fast Retailing 2014m)

business model that achieves sales and profit per square meter comparable to those of a standard store (Fast Retailing 2014m).

2.6.3 Rapid International Expansion

The forecast for Uniqlo's overseas business is the achievement of net sales of 216 billion yen and an operating income of 16 billion yen for the fiscal year, which ends in August 2013. The sales generated from overseas operations account for more than 20 % of the overall sales from Uniqlo (Fast Retailing 2014m). Sales and profitability are continuously increasing in Asia, accounting for more than 80 % of all overseas sales. One store after another has opened in China, Hong Kong and South Korea. The store network has expanded at a fast pace across the region: the opening in Singapore took place in 2009, Taiwan and Malaysia in 2010, Thailand in 2011, and the Philippines in 2012 (Fast Retailing 2014m).

The plan is to open 144 stores in Asia in the fiscal year (Fast Retailing 2014m). On top of that, Uniqlo seeks to build its brand through global flagship stores in the major cities around the world in order to build an international store network. These have been established in New York, London, Paris, Shanghai, Shinsaibashi, Taipei, Seoul, and Ginza (Fast Retailing 2014m) (Fig. 2).

2.6.4 Heattech, Inc.

Heattech is a unique highly-functional line of comfort innerwear. It resulted from the collaboration between Uniqlo and Toray Industries and launched in 2004. It has gained great popularity from the customers and in the 2007 fall/winter season, the production was almost outpaced by demand (Fast Retailing 2014m).

2.7 What About Quality and Innovation of the Product Range?

Uniqlo is well known for their affordable prices, but Uniqlo cannot be compared to a discounter. Their main focus is high-quality products, characterized by top-quality fabrics and fashioning. Uniqlo occupies 16 textile masters, each with at least 20 years of experience, in order to ensure high-qualitative dyeing, sewing, and the right selection of materials (New York Magazine 2010).

Rather than chasing trends, Uniqlo focuses on its basic product lines and modifies them in different ways, to follow their slogan "Made For All". Basic garments are modified and continuously improved in terms of cuts, colors, shapes, and fabrics.

Furthermore, Uniqlo is trying to improve their basic product lines with the help of the popular German fashion designer Jil Sander. Although her designs look more upscale, her designs remained faithful to the company's business philosophy. Her first collections can be identified by being slightly more stylish, but apart from this characteristic, they were still plain, easy to combine, and affordable (New York Magazine 2010).

Moreover, Uniqlo launched the "Uniqlo Innovation Project" (UIP) in order to "create a completely new category of superior functional clothing that is neither

Fig. 2 Flagships (Fast Retailing 2014m)

sportswear nor fashion" (Fast Retailing 2011). With this campaign, the company is trying to extend their "Made For All" philosophy. Uniqlo expected this campaign to enrich their success in global markets.

3 The Rise of the Company

3.1 Growth Development

After the first opening of Uniqlo in Hiroshima, Japan in 1984, "The Great Recession" in Japan in the early 1990s led to a downturn in economy. This lasted for an entire decade, but led to great popularity for Uniqlo, as the citizens were able to cut back spending while buying cheap clothes. Consequently, by 1994, there were 100 Uniqlo stores in operation. However, the largest part of the growth was centered in the suburbs of Japan with roadside stores (Business Insider 2013).

Furthermore, the company experienced an increase in popularity in 1998 after launching a fleece apparel campaign. Nevertheless, the company went through a decline in profits and sales soon after. Uniqlo's response to this was to reorganize and grow the women line, which led to a recovery. Moreover, the company began to concentrate on larger stores (Business Insider 2013).

While first expanding globally, Uniqlo opened too many stores too quickly. As a result, it had to close many of these stores again. By 2002, Uniqlo had 21 stores in the UK, but only eight of these stores continued to be open in 2006 (Business Insider 2013).

Today, Uniqlo has more than 800 stores worldwide, including a large number of stores in urban centers. Although most of Uniqlo's stores are still located in Japan, there are also stores in the USA, France, Singapore, Malaysia, the Philippines, China, Taiwan, and the UK. It is the biggest apparel chain in Asia and in 2012, Uniqlo was the fourth-largest retailer, following GAP, H&M, and Inditex (Business Insider 2013).

3.2   Becoming a Brand?

According to the dictionary, a brand is defined by "the process involved in creating a unique name and image for a product in the consumers" mind, mainly through advertising campaigns with a consistent theme. Branding aims to establish a significant and differentiated presence in the market that attracts and retains loyal customers (Business Dictionary 2014).

Using this definition as a definition for an established brand, one can say that Uniqlo is now a successful brand which is valued by their customers. However, the company noticed that they should find a preeminent name which would be remembered by its uniqueness. Hence, they changed their name from "Unique Clothing Warehouse" to "Uniqlo". After only selling men's wear, they also decided to expand their product range and developed a new product line with the philosophy "Made For All", which is still the guiding principal. Over time, this principle, in combination with affordable prices, is what differentiates the brand Uniqlo from its competitors. They positioned this image successfully and over time it became associated with high-quality and satisfaction in the consumer's minds. As is visible in the company's revenues, the number of sales increased over time and the company developed a loyal customer base successfully.

3.3   Position in the Home Market

In Japan, clothing retailers are divided into three groups with regards to the value chain. First, there are clothing retailers who specialize in the retail business (e.g. department stores, boutiques, etc.). Second, there are clothing retailers who plan, but outsource, the production. Third, there are clothing retailers who use a vertical integration system controlling all processes, including planning, manufacturing, and sales (Porter Prize 2009).

Uniqlo belongs to the third group. However, it approaches the system in a unique way, as it procures material and initiates joint fabric developments, but does not have its own factories. Uniqlo is among the top ten of Japan's most valuable brands (Economist 2010). Furthermore, Uniqlo is Japan's largest apparel retail chain. It has a 5.5 % share of the 10.7 trillion yen apparel market. At the end of August 2013, the company had a network of 853 stores, which annually generate net sales of more than 683.3 billion yen (Fast Retailing 2014j).

3.4 Position in the Global Market

Next to positioning itself successfully in the home market, Uniqlo also became a well-established brand in the global market and is still expanding. Currently, Uniqlo records more than 1100 stores in the UK, France, Germany, China, Hong Kong, Indonesia, Japan, South Korea, Malaysia, Taiwan, Thailand, Singapore, Philippines, USA, and Russia. In August 2013, Fast Retailing was ranked at third place, after Inditex and Hennes & Mauritz, for their market capitalization in worldwide apparel specialty stores (Fast Retailing 2014i). In 2013, the company recorded an international increase in both sales and income. Furthermore, they emphasized their success in China, Hong Kong, Taiwan, South Korea, USA, Australia, and Russia (Fast Retailing 2014k). The main occurrence of Uniqlo stores is still in Asia, which is the reason that Asia accounts for approximately 80 % of Uniqlo's international sales (Fast Retailing 2013d). The company predicts their international performance will increase with a rise in net sales of 39.9 % and an expansion in operating income of 52.6 % up until August 31, 2014 (Fast Retailing 2014i).

4 Future Developments

4.1 What Are the Future Challenges/Problems to Be Overcome at Home and Abroad?

Over the years, Uniqlo established itself well in their home market. Accordingly, future challenges in the home market are less likely to occur than in their current brand establishment abroad. Since Uniqlo became popular in Japan during the time of the big recession, the expected income of the country could be an indicator for future challenges in the home market. According to the Organization for Economic Co-operation and Development (OECD), the average household net-adjusted disposable income is 24,147 US$ a year, which is higher the OECD average of 23,047 US$ (OECD 2014). Nevertheless, this does not necessarily predict a challenge for Uniqlo in the future, since on the one hand, there is a considerable gap between the richest and poorest Japanese inhabitants. According to the OECD statistics, the top

20 % of the population earn more than six times as much as the bottom 20 %. This means that the bottom 20 % are still dependent on the possibility of buying cheaper clothes. On the other hand, Uniqlo is already well established, and it is reasonable to conjecture that the brand is well valued for their quality-price relationship, even in times of economic growth.

Uniqlo is currently trying to expand their business in Europe. This is itself a challenge for the Japanese retailer. Geographically, Uniqlo faced a challenge, since it is geographically removed from its headquarters and suppliers. Furthermore, they had to overcome differences in doing business between Western countries and Japan.

Apart from geographical und cultural challenges, the company has to educate their new customers on the unique selling point of the business. Most of the people would probably describe fashion as the ability to chase trends, which is the opposite of what Uniqlo does. They rather "identify styles within product categories that won't quickly go out of fashion" (Forbes 2012b). Accordingly, they have to educate their new customers on this strategy, in order to set up a loyal customer base abroad.

Furthermore, Western style is distinctively different compared to Asian style. Therefore, the company chose to connect in America with "theory", an American management team for the US-sector in order to tailor clothes slightly to the American taste and demand (Nikkei 2014).

In Europe, Uniqlo managed to establish 18 stores in France, the UK, and Russia. Here again the focus has been on Europeanization.

Next to cultural and geographical challenges, Uniqlo has to be flexible to respond to the subtle difference in tastes among non-Asian countries and educate new customers on the advantages of their product.

4.2 Which Companies Are Its Competitors Now and in the Future?

According to industry ranking of the global specialty retailers of private label apparel (SPA), the four largest and most successful clothing retailers are Inditex (which is the parent company of Zara), H&M, Gap, and then, finally, Fast Retailing (Uniqlo) (Fast Retailing 2014a).

With revenues of 21.71 billion US$ Inditex (Zara) has the largest sales. Following Zara, H&M has the second largest sales with revenues of 19.66 billion US$. With revenues of 15.65 billion US$, Gap is the third most successful clothing retailer. Finally, Fast Retailing is at fourth place with revenues of 11.16 billion US$ (Fast Retailing 2014a).

Uniqlo's strategy has already been mentioned. In short, the company's strategy is to provide products of high quality and high value. Therefore, they choose long-term appeal over trends (Petro 2012a).

Spanish company Zara, on the other hand, focuses on responding to consumer trends. Therefore, they believe in reacting to the fast-changing tastes of the customers. Consequently, their success follows on their highly-responsive supply chain, which makes sure that new fashion can be delivered as soon as it emerges. Twice a week, new products are delivered to the 1670 stores around the entire world, adding up to more than 10,000 new designs every year (Petro 2012b).

The Swedish fashion retailer H&M, however, emphasizes merging a commitment to durability while remaining responsive to fashion trends. The reason that H&M can respond quickly to new trends is that the network of 20–30 production offices is placed nearby the suppliers. This company launches two main collections every year, one offered in spring and the other one in fall, but within each season, there are various sub-collections allowing H&M to keep their inventory fresh. The main collections in spring and fall are traditionally long-lead items, which mean that the design and fabrication take the longest, whereas the sub-collections are usually trendier short-lead items. Furthermore, H&M proves to have an excellent IT infrastructure, as every store is connected to corporate logistics and procurement systems and the central H&M warehouse (Petro 2012c).

Company Gap, which was already famous in the 1970s, had a serious setback in the past years, and it seemed as if their time had gone. However, the company was able to recover with their last collection. Moreover, Gap focuses on embracing the digital age by allying with influential fashion bloggers (Thau 2013).

Facing these strong competitors, where each has a different success strategy, Uniqlo's founder and CEO Tadashi Yanai still has the ambitious plan to surpass leader Inditex (Urstadt 2010). Nevertheless, Inditex' managing director, Manel Jadraque, speaks about planning to grow 20–25 % a year for the next 3 years. Inditex wants Zara to double every 4 years (Donaldson 2014). Therefore, it is not possible to say whether Yanai will reach his goal to be world market leader. Uniqlo's competitors are strong and each has a unique strategy.

5 Conclusion

The company's success can be explained by its initial success during the Japanese crisis. The consumer's demand for affordable but high quality clothing was high during this time of recession, as consumers had to cut back on expenditures. After this sudden success, Uniqlo's founder Tadashi Yanai managed to expand brand awareness and achieved success globally. Now, Uniqlo is the fourth largest clothing retailer worldwide, which makes Uniqlo a well-established world brand.

References

4 Traders. (2014). *Business leaders*. Retrieved January 31, 2014, from http://www.4-traders.com/business-leaders/Tadashi-Yanai-213/biography/

Business Dictionary. (2014). *What is branding? Definition and meaning*. Retrieved February 12, 2014, from http://www.businessdictionary.com/definition/branding.html

Business Insider. (2013). *How clothing chain Uniqlo is taking over the world*. Retrieved February 12, 2014, from http://www.businessinsider.com/the-story-of-uniqlo-2013-4?op=1

Business Insider. (2014). *The story of Uniqlo.* Retrieved February 12, 2014, from http://www.businessinsider.com/the-story-of-uniqlo-2013-4#by-1994-ten-years-after-the-first-store-opened-100-uniqlos-were-in-operation-4

Donaldson, T. (2014). *Desigual looks to expand, compete with Zara.* Retrieved March 31, 2014, from https://www.sourcingjournalonline.com/desigual-looks-expand-compete-zara/

Fast Retailing Co., Ltd. (2010). *Our responsibility to our employees.* Retrieved February 12, 2014, from http://www.fastretailing.com/eng/csr/report/pdf/csr2011_e_12.pdf

Fast Retailing Co., Ltd. (2011). *Towards a focus on global UNIQLO growths.* Retrieved February 12, 2014, from http://www.fastretailing.com/eng/ir/library/pdf/ar2011_en_06_n.pdf

Fast Retailing Co., Ltd. (2013a). *Human resources.* Retrieved February 12, 2014, from http://www.fastretailing.com/eng/csr/employee/humanresources.html

Fast Retailing Co., Ltd. (2013b). *Personnel development.* Retrieved February 12, 2014, from http://www.fastretailing.com/eng/csr/employee/career.html

Fast Retailing Co., Ltd. (2013c). *Promoting diversity.* Retrieved February 12, 2014, from http://www.fastretailing.com/eng/csr/employee/diversity.html

Fast Retailing Co., Ltd. (2013d). *Overview of business segments.* Retrieved February 12, 2014, from http://www.fastretailing.com/eng/about/business/segment.html

Fast Retailing Co., Ltd. (2014a). *Industry ranking.* Retrieved March 11, 2014, from http://www.fastretailing.com/eng/ir/direction/position.html

Fast Retailing Co., Ltd. (2014b). *1949–2003.* Retrieved February 12, 2014, from http://www.fastretailing.com/eng/about/history/

Fast Retailing Co., Ltd. (2014c). *2004.* Retrieved February 12, 2014, from http://www.fastretailing.com/eng/about/history/2004.html

Fast Retailing Co., Ltd. (2014d). *2005.* Retrieved February 12, 2014, from http://www.fastretailing.com/eng/about/history/2005.html

Fast Retailing Co., Ltd. (2014e). *2007.* Retrieved February 12, 2014, from http://www.fastretailing.com/eng/about/history/2007.html

Fast Retailing Co., Ltd. (2014f). *2010.* Retrieved February 12, 2014, from http://www.fastretailing.com/eng/about/history/2010.html

Fast Retailing Co., Ltd. (2014g). *2011.* Retrieved February 12, 2014, from http://www.fastretailing.com/eng/about/history/2011.html

Fast Retailing Co., Ltd. (2014h). *2012.* Retrieved February 12, 2014, from http://www.fastretailing.com/eng/about/history/2012.html

Fast Retailing Co., Ltd. (2014i). *Industry ranking.* Retrieved February 12, 2014, from http://www.fastretailing.com/eng/ir/direction/position.html

Fast Retailing Co., Ltd. (2014j). *Japan.* Retrieved February 12, 2014, from http://www.fastretailing.com/eng/group/strategy/japan.html

Fast Retailing Co., Ltd. (2014k). *Results summary.* Retrieved February 12, 2014, from http://www.fastretailing.com/eng/ir/financial/summary.html

Fast Retailing Co., Ltd. (2014l). *UNIQLO announces plans to open five new stores this spring/summer in the U.S.* Retrieved February 12, 2014, from http://www.fastretailing.com/eng/group/news/1401081000.html

Fast Retailing Co., Ltd. (2014m). *UNIQLO business strategy.* Retrieved February 12, 2014, from http://www.fastretailing.com/eng/group/strategy/tactics.html

Fast Retailing Co., Ltd. (2014p). *5 years Financial summary/Fast Retailing Co., Ltd.* Retrieved February 12, 2014, from http://www.fastretailing.com/eng/ir/financial/statement.html

Forbes. (2012a). *Uniqlo: How Japanese billionaire Tadashi Yanai plans to clothe America.* Retrieved February 12, 2014, from http://www.forbes.com/sites/kerryadolan/2012/10/05/uniqlo-how-japanese-billionaire-tadashi-yanai-plans-to-clothe-america/

Forbes. (2012b). *The future of fashion retailing: Part 1—Uniqlo.* Retrieved March 31, 2014, from http://www.forbes.com/sites/gregpetro/2012/10/23/the-future-of-fashion-retailing-part-1-uniqlo/

New York Magazine. (2010). *How did Uniqlo become the hottest retailer in New York?*. Retrieved February 12, 2014, from http://nymag.com/fashion/features/65898/index5.html

Nikkei. (2014). *Uniqlo forced to outgrow one-design-fits-all model*. Retrieved March 31, 2014, from http://asia.nikkei.com/print/article/13226

OECD. (2014). *OECD better life index*. Retrieved March 31, 2014, from http://www.oecdbetterlifeindex.org/countries/japan/

Petro, G. (2012a). *The future of fashion retail: Part 1—Uniqlo*. Retrieved March 11, 2014, from http://www.forbes.com/sites/gregpetro/2012/10/23/the-future-of-fashion-retailing-part-1-uniqlo/

Petro, G. (2012b). *The future of fashion retail: The Zara approach (Part 2 of 3)*. Retrieved March 11, 2014, from http://www.forbes.com/sites/gregpetro/2012/10/25/the-future-of-fashion-retailing-the-zara-approach-part-2-of-3/

Petro, G. (2012c). *The future of fashion retailing—The H&M approach (Part 3 of 3)*. Retrieved March 23, 2014, from http://www.forbes.com/sites/gregpetro/2012/11/05/the-future-of-fashion-retailing-the-hm-approach-part-3-of-3/

Porter Prize. (2009). *Fast Retailing Co., Ltd. UNIQLO*. Retrieved February 9, 2014, from http://www.porterprize.org/english/pastwinner/2009/12/03114807.html

RocketNews24. (2013). *Japanese fashion chain UNIQLO introduces worldwide equal pay system across its stores*. Retrieved February 12, 2014, from http://en.rocketnews24.com/2013/04/25/japanese-fashion-chain-uniqlo-introduces-worldwide-equal-pay-system-across-its-stores/

Thau, B. (2013). *The gap: Anatomy of a brand comeback*. Retrieved March 23, 2014, from http://www.forbes.com/sites/barbarathau/2013/08/16/the-gap-anatomy-of-a-brand-comeback/

The Economist. (2010). *Uniqlo: Uniquely positioned*. Retrieved February 12, 2014, from http://www.economist.com/node/16436304

UNIQLO. (2014a). *About us*. Retrieved January 29, 2014, from http://uniqlo.archive.tha.jp/us/company/

UNIQLO. (2014b). *Clothing*. Retrieved February 12, 2014, from http://www.uniqlo.com/uk/store/clothing/uq/ut/women/

UNIQLO. (2014c). *The UNIQLO App - Download the world of UNIQLO into the palm of your hand*. Retrieved February 12, 2014, from http://www.uniqlo.com/uk/store/feature/uq/uniqlo/app/

UNIQLO. (2014d). *Women's Cashmere/Crew & V-Neck Sweaters & Cardigans*. Retrieved February 12, 2014, from http://www.uniqlo.com/uk/store/list/basic/women/knitwear/cashmere

UNIQLO. (2014e). *Women's HEATTECH/T-Shirts, Leggings, Socks & Accessories*. Retrieved February 12, 2014, from http://www.uniqlo.com/uk/store/clothing/uq/heattech/women/

UNIQLO. (2014f). *Women's Merino/Crew, Polo & V-Neck Merino Sweaters*. Retrieved February 12, 2014, from http://www.uniqlo.com/uk/store/list/basic/women/knitwear/extrafinemerino

Urstadt, B. (2010). *Uniqlones*. Retrieved March 23, 2014, from http://nymag.com/fashion/features/65898/

Part IV

South Korea

Lotte: A Case Study on Market Entries Through Acquisition

Manuel Schlothauer and Denise Wilhaus

Abstract

The Lotte Group operates in 19 foreign countries and entered also the European market with acquisitions. The company owns a strong market position in South Korea and is also known as the "leading retailing company in South Korea" with a 10 % value share in South Korean retailing in 2012. Furthermore, the company owns a fast food chain with the biggest value share, and even outperforms Hyatt Hotels Corp., Wyndham Worldwide Corp. (Ramada), and Starwood Hotels and Resorts Worldwide (Sheraton) with its hotel chain Hotel Lotte Co., Ltd., and thus is the leading company in South Korea's travel and tourism industry. Lotte Group's unrelated diversification, mainly through acquisition, drives the basis of past, present and prospective success and is enforced through triple-helix support. If the conglomerate continues its expansion in Europe, branded divisions would only be found within hospitality or, less probably, in retail. The conglomerate grew through acquisition and it is most unlikely that it will attempt to convey its brand success to Western countries. Win-win growth through acquisition is more to be expected in Europe.

1 Introduction

Starting as a confectionary manufacturer in 1948 in Japan, Lotte Group developed into one of South Korea's biggest conglomerates, also described as chaebol. The company founded by Kyuk Ho Shin employs about 69,000 employees from 78 businesses (Lotte 2014), expanded into various sub-businesses, and is now engaged in food, retail, tourism, finance, petrochemicals as well as construction.

M. Schlothauer (✉) • D. Wilhaus
The Honor's Program of the International Business School, Hanze University OAS, Groningen, The Netherlands
e-mail: manuel.schlothauer@gmail.com; denise_wilhaus@hotmail.de

With its headquarters in Seoul and in Tokyo, the Lotte Group operates in 19 foreign countries and entered even the European market with acquisitions of, for instance, Cadbury's E Wedel branded confectionary from Kraft Foods in Poland, through which the company became the second largest confectionary business in Poland. The company owns a strong market position in South Korea and is also known as the "leading retailing company in South Korea" (Euromonitor International Ltd. 2013a) with a 10 % value share in South Korean retailing in 2012. Furthermore, the company owns a fast food chain with the biggest value share (46 %), and even outperforms Hyatt Hotels Corp., Wyndham Worldwide Corp. (Ramada), and Starwood Hotels and Resorts Worldwide (Sheraton) with its hotel chain Hotel Lotte Co., Ltd., and thus is the leading company in South Korea's travel and tourism industry.

To explain the success and the enormous expansion of the Lotte Group, this case study displays the current situation of the company by establishing a company profile, and analyzes the rise of the company with its growth development, business success strategies and its position in the home and the global market. Furthermore, potential future developments of the Lotte Group are discussed.

2 Company Profile

2.1 History

The Lotte Group was founded by Kyuk Ho Shin in 1948 in Japan, as a general confectionery manufacturer, and launched "Lotte Confectionery" in 1967 as its first facility in South Korea. Since then, Lotte developed into one of South Korea's largest food manufacturer with the establishment of subsidiaries within the food segment.

In the 1970s, the company expanded outside of the food business and launched companies within the tourism, retail, and petrochemical/construction/manufacturing segments.

In the 1980s, the Lotte Group succeeded in becoming one of the leading businesses in South Korea while it expanded into the high-tech industry with further subsidiaries and acquisitions.

After extending into various industries in the 1970s and 1980s, the Lotte group expanded within the 1990s to foreign markets such as Japan, China, other East Asian countries and the USA.

Further expansions within the six different segments, food, retail, tourism, petrochemical/construction/manufacturing, finance, and service/study/foundation, followed in the 2000s, as well as the entry into the European confectionery market with the acquisition of the Belgian chocolate manufacturer Guylian in 2008.

An additional acquisition in the European market was made in 2010 with the purchase of Cadbury's E. Wedel-branded confectionery from Kraft Foods in Poland.

The Lotte Group is generating a new in-country attraction with building of the 555 m high Lotte World Premium Tower in Central Seoul, which is to become the country's and OECD's tallest building and rank amongst the highest worldwide. Designed by the US-American Kohn Pedersen Fox, the tower will include various entertainment facilities as well as a hotel and office space in its 123 floors above street level (Post 2011; CTBUH 2014).

2.2 The Founders

Kyuk-Ho Shin, also known under his Japanese name Shigemitsu Takeo, was born on Oct. 4, 1922 in Ulsan, Korea, as the eldest of five children. After graduating from the Waseda University in Japan in 1946, Shin founded in 1948 the Lotte Co. Ltd in Japan, and established the Lotte Confectionary in South Korea in 1967. Since the Lotte Group is one of South Korea's business conglomerates, also called chaebol, all the subsidiaries of the Lotte Group are under the control of a single family. "Chaebol" literally means a group or party of wealth. Chaebol are associated with a certain management style that is based on Confucian values, and influenced by family relations, alumni, region, and the government (Chang 1988).

2.3 Employees

The Chairman-In-Chief and the Chief Executive Officer is the founder of the Lotte Group, Kyuk-Ho Shin. His son, Dong-bin Shin, functions as the Chairman of the Company (Fig. 1). The Lotte Group employs about 69,000 employees from 78 businesses (Lotte 2014) and further key employees are the Chief Executive Officers of each subsidiary of the Lotte Group. The recruiting process of future employees is influenced by the applicants' attended university and the regional origins. Management trainees within chaebol groups are usually recruited from prestigious universities and even applicants from certain regional origins, mainly the regional origin of the founders, are preferred due to similar personality traits and shared values (Chang 1988).

The various subsidiaries are divided into six different fields: food, retail, tourism, petrochemical/construction/manufacturing, finance, and service/study/foundation. The subsidiaries in detail can be seen in the product range.

2.4 Product Range

Starting within the food industry, Lotte Group subsequently expanded into various industries and developed into a conglomerate company that is engaged in retail, tourism, finance, petrochemicals, and construction. Figure 2 shows the various subsidiaries with their major businesses.

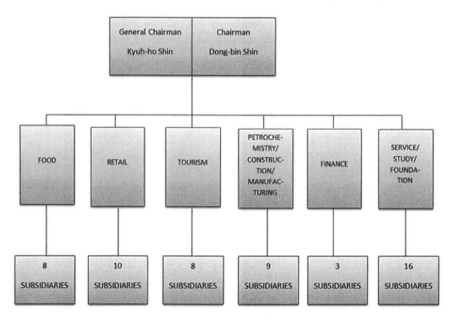

Fig. 1 Organizational chart of the Lotte Group (Lotte 2014)

2.5 Revenues

Figure 3 presents the distribution of the sales of the Lotte Group from the years 2010 to 2013. The retail sector achieved the highest sales with 37–41 % of all sales, followed by the petrochemical/construction/manufacturing sector with a range from 28 to 32 % of sales. The total sales improved yearly by at least 10 %.

Table 1 reveals the sales attributed to the Japanese Lotte Group and the South Korean Lotte Group, as well as the total sales.

2.6 Business (Success) Strategies

By examining the conglomerate's historic development, a clear direction towards diversification mostly through acquisition becomes apparent (Ansoff 1988). The drivers for this strategic preference are economies of scope, dominant logics, exploitation of superior internal processes and the prospective growth of market power as per Johnson and colleagues (2011), and these ideally result in positive conglomerate synergy which is dealt with in Sect. 3.1.

With Lotte Chilsung Beverage, Lotteria, Lotte Ham and Milk, and Lotte Samkang, the group maneuvered its way to become one of South Korea's biggest food manufacturers already in the 1970s. Only a couple of years later, Lotte Shopping was established and draws up one example of the conglomerate's successful vertical integration: downstream being its own supplier and upstream being

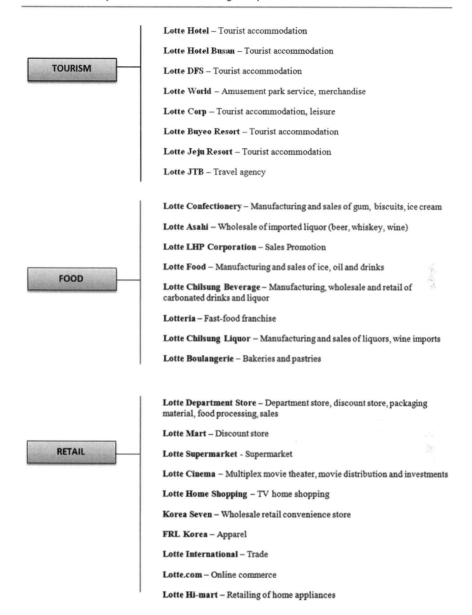

Fig. 2 (continued)

its own customer (Informa plc. 2013). Nevertheless, the results of the Lotte Group's horizontal integration led to the so-called unrelated diversification which has been found to be the riskiest type of diversification, yet with possibly the most favorable outcomes for the stakeholders involved in the long run (Johnson et al. 2011).

PETROCHEMISTRY/ CONSTRUCTION/ MANUFACTURING

Lotte Chemical – Petrochemical processing

KP Chemtech – Synthetic resin, synthetic fiber, by-products

Daesan MMA – MMA, PMMA

Lotte E&C – Civil engineering, construction etc.

CM business headquarters of Lotte E&C – Construction Project Management

Canon Korea Business Solutions – Manufacturing, sales and services in all-in-one digital equipment, copiers, printers, and other office machines

Korea Fujifilm – Manufacturing and sales of digital cameras, digital printers, and photographic materials

Lotte Aluminum – Aluminum processing, packaging materials, beverage cans, PET bottle manufacturing and sales

Lotte Engineering & Machinery MFG – Cooling and heating devices, parking facilities, air ducts/air conditioning and heating installations, equipment service

SERVICE/STUDY/ FOUNDATION

Lotte Data Communications Company – Software development, computer equipment

Hyundai Information Technology – Various public institutions system and information technology-related businesses

Lotte Giants – Professional baseball team

Lotte Skyhill C.C. – Construction and management of golf course

Daehong Communications – Advertising agency

Lotte Asset Development – Real estate development and financial consulting, development and management of shopping centers

Lotte Logistics – Logistics management, consulting

Lotte PS Net – Electronic financial services

MYbi – Electronic finance, service

eB Card – Offline/ online integration e-payment service

Lotte R&D Center – Future food, genetic engineering, bio-engineering

Lotte Academy – Training and consulting

Lotte Strategy & Insight Center – Strategy analysis on economy and industry

Lotte Scholarship Foundation – Scholarship foundation

Lotte Welfare Foundation – Social welfare foundation

Lotte Samdong Foundation – Non-profit social welfare foundation

FINANCE

Lotte Card – Credit business, travel agency, insurance agency, telemarketing

Lotte Insurance – Insurance agency

Lotte Capital – Lease, personal loans, corporate loans, installment financing

Fig. 2 Subsidiaries and businesses of Lotte Group (Lotte 2014)

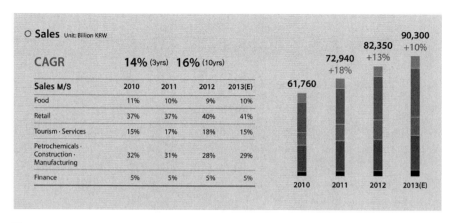

Fig. 3 Sales in percentages (Lotte profile 2013)

Table 1 Financial results of the Japanese and South Korean Lotte Group (Lotte 2014)

FY2012 Japan-South Korea Lotte Group financial results				
Sales				
Business classification		Japan group (Unit: million yen)	S. Korea group (Unit: million won)	Total (1 won = 0.0708 yen) (Unit: million yen)
Foods	Confectioneries	160,416	1,002,659	231,404
	Frozen desserts	67,384	407,370	96,226
	Beverage	–	1,916,297	135,674
	Restaurant, etc.	63,504	1,879,214	196,552
	Total	291,304	5,205,540	659,856
Retail		–	22,238,430	1,574,481
Tourism, service		270,481	4,295,925	574,632
Chemical, construction		–	15,239,958	1,078,989
Finance, investment		3146	4,190,204	299,812
Total		564,932	51,170,058	4,187,772

McKinsey & Co. examined Lotte Group and similar chaebol regarding their strategic motivation and found that 49 % of acquisitions were so called "step-out moves, [thus] completely unrelated to the parent companies' existing activities" and the second slightly greater half "were about equally split between [...] category expansions into adjacent businesses and value-chain expansions that positioned the parent company up- or downstream from its existing business" (Fig. 4) (Hirt et al. 2013). Under the premise of experiences being colored by expectations, behavioral economist Ariely (2009) explains behavior of the organizational development of Lotte Group as "predictably irrational". The conglomerate's objective is to be affecting all parts of its customer's lives. Such growth by unrelated diversification through acquisition might seem irrational, daunting and high risk in the first

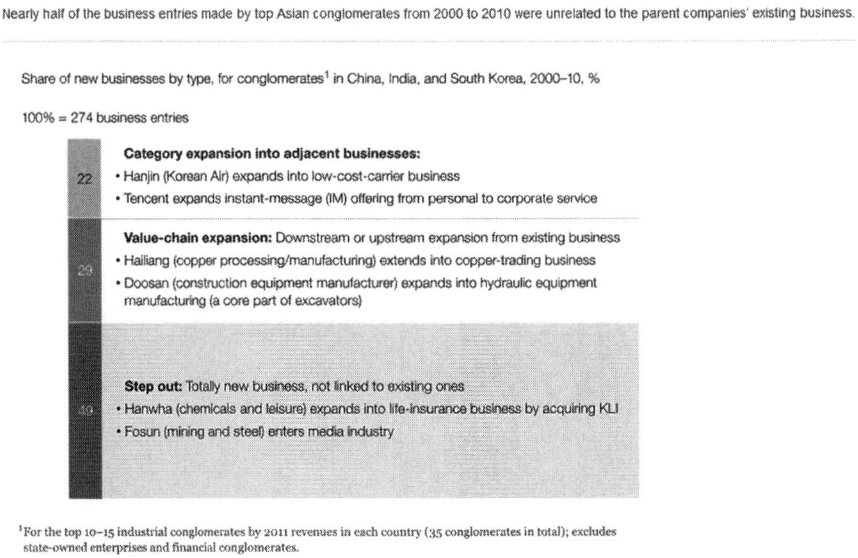

Nearly half of the business entries made by top Asian conglomerates from 2000 to 2010 were unrelated to the parent companies' existing business.

Share of new businesses by type, for conglomerates[1] in China, India, and South Korea, 2000–10, %

100% = 274 business entries

Category expansion into adjacent businesses:
- Hanjin (Korean Air) expands into low-cost-carrier business
- Tencent expands instant-message (IM) offering from personal to corporate service

22

Value-chain expansion: Downstream or upstream expansion from existing business
- Hailiang (copper processing/manufacturing) extends into copper-trading business
- Doosan (construction equipment manufacturer) expands into hydraulic equipment manufacturing (a core part of excavators)

29

Step out: Totally new business, not linked to existing ones
- Hanwha (chemicals and leisure) expands into life-insurance business by acquiring KLI
- Fosun (mining and steel) enters media industry

49

[1] For the top 10–15 industrial conglomerates by 2011 revenues in each country (35 conglomerates in total); excludes state-owned enterprises and financial conglomerates.

Fig. 4 Share of new businesses by type, for conglomerates in China, India and South Korea, 2000–2010 (in percentage) (Hirt et al. 2013)

place but, as aptly proven earlier, is to be expected in the future and has successfully paid off for the stakeholders involved thus far.

2.7 Quality and Innovation of the Product Range

> We enrich people's lives by providing superior products and services that our customers love and trust (Lotte 2014).

As a leader in various South Korean industries, such as the food, tourism and retail industry, the Lotte Group strives to supply its customers with high quality products and services. The group has developed into one of South Korea's major business conglomerates that is able to offer premium products and services with the help of strict quality control, and innovative and differentiated services. For instance, Lotte Hotels & Resorts was rated as the best hotel in South Korea for the quality of customer service in 2013 and scored even higher than Hilton Hotels & Resorts and Westin Chosun Hotels (Korea Times 2013). Additionally, Lotte Hotel & Resorts is planning to open South Korea's first six-star hotel in 2014. Another fitting example for innovation and quality is the Lotte World Tower and Mall that will be South Korea's tallest skyscraper once it is completed.

3 The Rise of the Company

3.1 Growth Development

As delineated earlier, the Lotte Group consists of a variety of sub-groups and subsidiaries which easily cause the danger of self-divesting. In order to counteract negative ramifications, in 2010 the conglomerate established its executive office of win-win growth which directs the various strategies within the group to mutual support and growth of individual sales turnover. As one key performance index, win-win growth accounts for almost 15 % in executive assessment. The policy headquarters' criteria are conveyed by the educational framework "Growing Up Together", a curriculum every employee of the conglomerate ought to complete.

Lotte Group's major focus herewith lies on partnerships along the value chain incorporating suppliers and governmental institutions alike. In 2010, the head department for win-win growth outlined five overarching tasks to ensure prospective betterment of cooperation within the conglomerate and coopetition with third parties. By the fiscal year 2014/2015, the organization aims to improve the group-wide cash payment rate, to further expand its win-win growth fund size, to enlarge budgets in training, to maintain supplier satisfaction levels and to remain on an upward growth momentum on-year. In addition, the "strengthening [of] overseas partnership" has been highlighted already as a major goal in 2012/2013 (Lotte Co., Ltd. 2013).

MarketLine identified three outstanding strengths of the conglomerate that empowers the group to effectively grasp future market opportunities. One of Lotte Group's sub-groups is confectionery in which it remains South Korea's number one. With plants across the country and more than 200 categories of confectionery, dairy products and medicine, Lotte Confectionery managed to even launch premium products in dairy and medicine in a country with an average household net-adjusted disposable income of only 12,600 € per year, 68 % of the Dutch average (OECD 2014). The conglomerate's second backbone is its stand in the South Korean retail industry in which it also operates as number one, outperforming strong competitors such as Shinsegae Department Co., Ltd. through services offered in almost 20 department stores, 60 discounters and 140 supermarkets from Seoul to Busan to Jeju-do. As illustrated earlier, the conglomerate's paramount management focus is win-win growth, the outstanding results of which have been confirmed by MarketLine using the example of Lotte Group's petrochemical division. Whereas KP Chemtech provides the main substance needed for the production of PET, Lotte Chemical supplies additional ingredients for a joint inter-group cooperation with competitive pricing and innovative synergy (Informa plc. 2013).

3.2 Becoming a Brand?

Due to the many subsidiaries, such as Lotte Confectionary or Lotte Shopping, is it difficult to analyze whether Lotte itself is recognized as one big brand, or if the subsidiaries are brands their own. Still there are many indications of Lotte becoming a brand, or already being a brand at least within South Korea, as Lotte Department Store was given the title of the best retail brand of 2013 in South Korea from Interbrand, the world's largest brand consultancy (Interbrand 2013). The Lotte Group aspires to become one of Asia's top ten global groups with a brand value that is characterized by three different components: trust, originality, and pleasure.

Trust The Lotte brand is trustworthy of providing products and services of high quality as well as perfect management. Lotte stands for accuracy and honesty and provides safety in the environment, facility, and equipment.

Originality Lotte stands for originality, guaranteeing new and unique experiences with its modern and trendsetting products and services.

Pleasure Lotte, as a brand with various subsidiaries, provides the pleasure of an increased life quality through the purchase and consumption of its products and services.

Another indication of being a brand is the company's brand recognition with its universal logo, or corporate identity that is present on many products and services of the Lotte Group (Fig. 5).

The logo serves as a representative symbol that reminds consumers of the values associated with the company, the brand value. Furthermore, the Lotte Group advertises its products and services with commercials and celebrity endorsement, which additionally enhances brand perception and expectation, the way consumers perceive a brand, and what they expect from it. However, the Lotte logo and its name are mainly used for self-created businesses but not for acquisitions, where the company simply adopts the original brand's name and logo. Therefore, it is most likely that despite the expansion into the European market, the Lotte Group won't be recognized as a brand in Europe, because the company will acquire and adopt already existing brands.

Fig. 5 Lotte Logo (Lotte 2014)

3.3 Position in the Home Market

Due to the conglomerate's complex horizontal and vertical structures and the broad product range, a value share analysis of selected sub-companies has been conducted.

As per Euromonitor International Ltd. (2013a), Lotte Group's retail firm Lotte Shopping Co., Ltd. "remains the leading retailing company in South Korea" and held a 10 % value share in South Korean retailing in 2012. In addition, the conglomerate secured its pole position in department stores with a 39 % value share and in supermarkets with a 20 % value share. Since 2007, Toys "R" Us also contributes to Lotte Group's portfolio with a 36 % value share in 2012. With a 22 % value share in hypermarkets, Lotte Shopping Co., Ltd. ranks third in South Korea, yet its acquisition of the country's largest electronics retailing firm Hi-Mart Co., Ltd. is predicted to accelerate its success over the sub-company's major competitor Shinsegae Co., Ltd.

Only ranked behind Paris Croissant Co., Ltd., the conglomerate's consumer food service sub-firm Lotteria Co., Ltd. achieved a 2 % value share in this industry but remained South Korea's first fast food chain with a 46 % value share in 2012. The main contributions have been made by its franchised sub-brands Natuur, Krispy Kreme, TGI Friday's, Angel-in-us Coffee, and Lotteria. As mentioned earlier, the conglomerate repeatedly strengthens its home market position through horizontal integration as Lotteria's main suppliers are, amongst others, Lotte Chilsung Beverage, Lotte Samkang, and Lotte Boulangerie (Euromonitor International Ltd. 2014a).

Outperforming Hyatt Hotels Corp., Wyndham Worldwide Corp. (Ramada), and Starwood Hotels and Resorts Worldwide (Sheraton), Hotel Lotte Co., Ltd. leads South Korea's travel and tourism industry with an 11.2 % value share. In addition to accommodation, this sub-firm includes Lotte Group's duty-free shops and amusement parks, as well (Euromonitor International Ltd. 2014b).

With a 6 % value share, Lotte Chilsung Beverage Co, Ltd. ranks third in South Korea's market for alcoholic drinks and first in soft drinks with an off-trade value share of 32 %—ranging from 4.8 % up to 61.1 % with the company's energy drink brands (Euromonitor International Ltd. 2013b, c).

3.4 Position in the Global Market

With a value share of 0.3 % in packaged food worldwide, the subsidiary Lotte Confectionary Co., Ltd. only generates 6 % of its global sales outside of the Asia Pacific region. Even though it is the conglomerate's second-largest division, its divestment is predicted to increase cash flow and facilitate ROI on the Lotte Group's acquisition of the earlier mentioned Hi-Mart Co., Ltd. With acquisitions of Guylian and E. Wedel in 2008 and 2010, the conglomerate managed to improve its outlook in the Western European chocolate industry. According to Euromonitor International Ltd. (2010), Lotte Confectionary ranked second with 300 million US$ behind Mars, Inc, which presented value sales of 550 million US$ in Poland in 2010. Whereas the company ranked 23rd worldwide in 2007, its global stand in packaged food worsened to rank 26 in 2012, where it competes with Wilmar International Ltd. and Perfetti Van Melle Group.

Fig. 6 Global sales (Based on Lotte profile 2013)

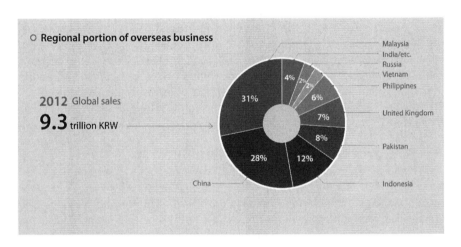

Fig. 7 Regional portion of overseas business (Lotte profile 2013)

With new hotels in Moscow/Russia, Tashkent/Uzbekistan, Hanoi and Ho Chi Minh City/Vietnam, and Tamuning/Guam, Lotte Group's divisions in hospitality report global growth, especially in 2013 and 2014 (Interfax-America Inc. 2010; Lotte City Hotel Co., Ltd. 2013a, b; Lotte Hotel Co., Ltd. 2004, 2013).

Figure 6 presents the global sales distributed over different sections of the Lotte Group, and shows that global sales are rising continuously. The major global sales are made within the retail and the petrochemicals/construction/manufacturing sectors.

Lotte's overseas business mainly operates within Asia, which can be seen in Fig. 7. Almost 60 % of all overseas business takes place either in Malaysia (31 %) or China (28 %).

4 Future Developments

4.1 What Are the Future Challenges/Problems to Overcome at Home and Abroad?

Future challenges can result from private ownership of the company due to its limited financing options. Privately-owned companies face significant disadvantages with regard to financing in comparison to publicly held companies which have more financial flexibility.

Further problems can occur due to the increasing reinforcement of regulations concerning bio-safety as well as drug and food approval processes which can result in increasing prices and might delay product launches. Expanding to a global, or to the European, market forces the Lotte Group to adjust its production processes and product quality to global or European standards. This can again lead to delays and increasing product prices.

The product prices might also be affected by the extreme competition on its current market, as well as its potential future markets. The market segments in which the Lotte Group is cooperating are characterized as highly competitive (Informa plc. 2013) with mainly large multinational companies competing. This can become especially problematic when the Lotte Group decides to brand its products and services outside of the Asian market. In general, it would become very challenging to launch "Lotte" as a brand within the highly competitive Western markets, where the Lotte Group is completely unknown.

4.2 Which Companies Are Its Competitors Now and in the Future?

Due to the many subdivisions of the Lotte group, the company has many current competitors as well as potential competitors. Therefore, other conglomerates such as Hyundai can be seen as competition, as well as other businesses that are active within any of the following sectors: food, retail, tourism, petrochemical/construction/manufacturing, finance, or service/study/foundation. Because of the high number of potential competitors, this section covers solely some current competitors of the segments food, retail, and tourism within South Korea as well as potential competitors within Europe.

Food Current competitors within South Korea of Lotte Confectionery, the parent company of the Lotte Group that is categorized under the Food segment, are Crown Confectionery Co. Ltd as well as Seoul Food Industrial Co. Ltd. Future competitors within the food segment, in case of a market entry in the European market, are multinational food and consumer goods companies such as the Swiss company, Nestle, and the Anglo-Dutch company, Unilever.

Retail For the different subsidiaries of the Lotte Group that are categorized under retail, the Hyundai department store Co. Ltd, as well as other big retail stores such as Homeplus Co. Ltd, for example, are the current local competitors.

Tourism Current competitors, as well as future competitors when expanding abroad, are big international luxury hotel chains such as Park Hyatt or Ritz Carlton, for example.

5 Conclusion

5.1 Why Did This Company Become So Successful?

South Korean conglomerates such as the Lotte Group are widely described as chaebol, "a family-controlled industrial conglomerate" (Merriam-Webster, Inc. 2014) with a great number of affiliated organizations in a great number of industries that highly contribute to the country's economy (Murillo and Sung 2013). Already in 1988, Chang elaborated on the unique success factors of those all-industry conglomerates. First and foremost, Confucian business values underpin an occupational ethic of "hard work; respect on education; and family prestige and heritage" (Chang 1988) in all hierarchical levels. In addition, a favorable policy within the earlier mentioned triple helix context, as well as high extroversion and flexibility of the entrepreneurs involved, supported growth and expansion. Back in the 1990s, the so called K-S mark catapulted students directly into leading positions in South Korean chaebol, meaning a diploma from Kyunggi High School and Seoul National University (SNU). After the millennium, this definition has been expanded to the acronym SKY, which includes Korea University and Yonsei University in addition to the previously stated SNU (Card 2005).

Murillo and Sung (2013) identified the following key virtues of South Korean chaebol within the Lotte Group:

- Clear-cut vision developed by a charismatic leader
- Success in political lobbying
- Economically effective and aggressive entrepreneurship
- Sound management system, balanced between autocracy and group-orientation
- Risk aversion
- Agility of decision-making
- Long-term perspective thanks to family ownership
- Internal capital and labor market

Lotte Group's unrelated diversification, mainly through acquisition, drives the basis of past, present and prospective success and is enforced through triple-helical support which was explored earlier in this chapter.

5.2 Is It Likely that This Company Will Become a World Brand?

The Lotte Group managed to positively infiltrate almost all aspects of South Korea's every day life. "Lotte" is a brand, an organization renowned for deeply rooted Confucian values, such as family and solidarity within East Asian cultural heritage. The analysis of the Lotte Group's international activities thus far indicates that, if the conglomerate continues its expansion in Europe, branded divisions would only be found within hospitality (e.g. Lotte Hotel Co., Ltd.) or, less probably, in retail (e.g. Lotte Shopping Co., Ltd.). The conglomerate grew through acquisition and it is most unlikely that it will attempt to convey its brand success to Western countries. Win-win growth through acquisition is more to be expected in Europe.

References

Ansoff, H. I. (1988). *The new corporate strategy*. New York: John Wiley & Sons.
Ariely, D. (2009). *Predictably irrational, revised and expanded edition: The hidden forces that shape our decisions*. New York: HarperCollins.
Card, J. (2005). *Life and death exams in South Korea*. Retrieved March 28, 2014, from http://www.atimes.com/atimes/Korea/GK30Dg01.html
Chang, C. S. (1988). Chaebol: The South Korean conglomerates. *Business Horizons, 31*(2), 51–57.
CTBUH. (2014). CTBUH Skyscraper Database, 'Lotte World Tower'. Retrieved February 3, 2014, from http://www.skyscrapercenter.com/building.php?building_id=%2088
Euromonitor International Ltd. (2010). *Lotte's European expansion still at a low pace*. London: Passport.
Euromonitor International Ltd. (2013a). *Lotte Shopping Co Ltd in retailing (South Korea): Local company profile*. London: Passport.
Euromonitor International Ltd. (2013b). *Lotte Chilsung Beverage Co Ltd in alcoholic drinks (South Korea): Local company profile*. London: Passport.
Euromonitor International Ltd. (2013c). *Lotte Chilsung Beverage Co Ltd in soft drinks (South Korea): Local company profile*. London: Passport.
Euromonitor International Ltd. (2014a). *Lotteria Co Ltd in consumer foodservice (South Korea): Local company profile*. London: Passport.
Euromonitor International Ltd. (2014b). *Hotel Lotte Co Ltd in travel and tourism (South Korea): Local company profile*. London: Passport.
Hirt, M., Smit, S., & Yoo, W. (2013, February). Understanding Asia's conglomerates. *McKinsey Quarterly*. Retrieved March 28, 2014, from http://www.mckinsey.com/insights/growth/understanding_asias_conglomerates
Informa plc. (2013). *Lotte Group*. London: MarketLine.
Interbrand. (2013). *Interbrand—Best retail brands 2013—Brand view*. Retrieved February 19, 2014, from http://www.interbrand.com/en/BestRetailBrands/2013/Best-Retail-Brands-Brand-View.aspx?country=Korea
Interfax-America Inc. (2010). *S. Korea's Lotte Group opens 1st hotel in Russia*. Retrieved June 15, 2010, from http://www.interfax.com/
Johnson, G., Whittington, R., & Scholes, K. (2011). *Exploring strategy* (9th ed.). Harlow: Pearson Education Ltd.
Lotte. (2014). *Lotte*. Retrieved February 19 2014, from http://www.lotte.co.kr/eng/index.jsp
Lotte City Hotel Co., Ltd. (2013a). *Tashkent Palace: Lotte City Hotel*. Retrieved February 2, 2014, from http://www.lottecityhoteltashkent.com/

Lotte City Hotel Co., Ltd. (2013b). *Lotte Hotel Hanoi: Opening in August 2014*. Retrieved February 2, 2014, from http://www.lottehotelhanoi.com/

Lotte Co., Ltd. (2013). *Win-win growth*. Retrieved February 16, 2014, from https://www.lotte.co.kr/eng/06_withlotte/accompany_organization.jsp

Lotte Hotel Co., Ltd. (2004). *Lotte Legend Hotel Saigon*. Retrieved February 2, 2014, from http://www.legendsaigon.com/

Lotte Hotel Co., Ltd. (2013). *Lotte Hotel Guam: Opening in the end of June 2014*. Retrieved February 2, 2014, from http://www.lottehotelguam.com/

Lotte profile. (2013). *Lotte profile 2013 prepared way*. Retrieved April 27, 2014, from http://www.lottecatalog.com/free/catImage/2137/main_brochure_english.pdf

Merriam-Webster, Inc. (2014). *Chaebol*. Retrieved March 27, 2014, from http://www.merriam-webster.com/dictionary/chaebol

Murillo, D., & Sung, Y. (2013). Understanding Korean capitalism: Chaebols and their Corporate Governance. *ESADEgeo, Center for Global Economy and Geopolitics, 33*. Retrieved March 28, 2014, from http://www.esadegeo.com/download/PR_PositionPapers/43/ficPDF_ENG/201309%20Chaebols_Murillo_Sung_EN.pdf

OECD. (2014). *Korea*. Retrieved February 15, 2014, from http://www.oecdbetterlifeindex.org/countries/korea/

Post, N. (2011). Korea's first supertower is an all-in-the-family affair. *Engineering News Record, 267*(17), 38–39.

Winners & losers. (2013, June 30). *The Korea Times*.

Part V

Vietnam

Vinamilk: A Case Study on Partnering Up to Expand on the World Market

Kim Nguyen

Abstract

Vinamilk has continued to be a pioneer in the food industry because of four reasons. First of all, Vinamilk's product research and technology development have been increasingly improved and updated to ensure food safety in their new products in order to change the domestic consumer behavior that exists in Vietnam, namely the consumer perception that dairy products made in France or the Netherlands would be the best choice. Secondly, Vinamilk has effectively invested in brand building and market expansion. The company pays attention to studies on local markets, and to consumer habits, age, and gender demands to let its retailer network grow and to promote each specific product in different areas of Vietnam. Moreover, Vinamilk also is spreading to overseas markets, including the difficult markets such as the USA, Australia, Cambodia, Laos, New Zealand, and Middle East countries. Thirdly, investing in people is the core of success for Vinamilk. Finally, in order to have sustainable development as well as preserve prestige in the market, respect for business ethics and the actions to bring sustainable values to the society and the community play a very important role.

1 Introduction

Vietnam Dairy Products Joint-Stock Company (Vinamilk) is the largest dairy company in Vietnam, with 39 % of market share, and was recognized as one of the 200 best enterprises in Asia in 2010, was fourth in 2012 VNR 500 ranking, and topped the list of 50 best companies on Vietnam's stock market in 2013

K. Nguyen (✉)
The Honor's Program of the International Business School, Hanze University OAS, Groningen, The Netherlands
e-mail: nguyen.thi.kim.khanh@st.hanze.nl

(Vietnamnet 2013a). Vinamilk is the most popular and pioneer brand name for dairy products, and their portfolio includes powdered milk, liquid milk, yogurt, condensed milk and fruit juices. Vinamilk's products are produced and distributed not only nationwide, but also around the world including New Zealand, Thailand, and the USA. It has 183 distributors and nearly 94,000 sales points covering 64 provinces in Vietnam. Exported products from Vinamilk, including infant formula, nutritional powder, condensed milk, fresh milk, soy milk, and yogurt, are now present in 26 national markets in the world including the USA, Australia, Canada, Russia, Japan, Thailand, South Korea, Sri Lanka, the Philippines, South China, and various Middle East countries (Vinamilk 2014a).

In 2013, Vinamilk established a factory in Poland with a charter capital of 3 million US$. The company's main activity is wholesale of agricultural raw materials: trade in live animals, agricultural raw materials for the production of milk, food, and beverages (Vneconomy 2013). Vinamilk is expected to invest in depth in Europe to become one of the 50 largest dairy businesses in the world, with expected sales of 3 billion US$ in 2017 (Bloomberg 2012).

Since its establishment 37 years ago, Vinamilk has developed a reputable brand in Vietnam and gradually penetrated the world market. The possibility for the company to expand to overseas markets in Europe would be high. In order to find out if this plan is realistic or not, this chapter presents an overview of the company's current position in the world and how it can enter into the competitive market in Europe.

2 Company Profile

2.1 History

Vinamilk was founded in 1976 under the name of Southern Coffee-Dairy Company, a subsidiary of the General Food Directorate, and had six factories in operation in Vietnam. In 1978, the company introduced powdered milk and cereal with milk powder for the first time in Vietnam. In 2004, it acquired Saigon Milk Joint Stock Company and increased its share capital to 430 billion US$ (Vinamilk 2013a). In 2003, the company converted to a joint stock company and changed its name to Vietnam Dairy Products Joint Stock Company (Vinamilk). Ms. Kieu Lien Mai has been General Director of Vinamilk since 1992 and became one of 50 outstanding leaders in Asia in 2012–2013 (Bloomberg 2012). She was born in Paris in 1953, graduated from a prestigious university in Moscow, and joined Vinamilk as an engineer in charge of the production of condensed milk and yogurt in Truong Tho Dairy Factory, Milk Company—South Coffee (forerunner of Vinamilk). In 1983, Mai studied Economics at the University of Leningrad (Russia), and after that, she was appointed as Deputy Director of Vinamilk in 1984. She has held the position of General Director from 1992 to the present (Soha 2014). In 2014, Mai was cited by Forbes Asia magazine in its 2014 list of the most powerful business women in Asian and ranked 23 out of 48 (Vietnambreakingnews 2014).

In 2011, the Miraka Milk Powder factory in New Zealand, which accounted for 19 % of the equity of Vinamilk, came into operation, and this is the first investment abroad for Vinamilk.

In January 2014, Vinamilk invested in building a new factory, located in the Phnom Penh Special Economic Zone, with a total area of 30,000 m^2 in Cambodia, named the Angkor Dairy Products Company Limited Company. This plant was a total investment of 23 million dollars, which was contributed 51 % to Vinamilk (Vneconomy 2014).

Nowadays, Vinamilk is the leading dairy company and is in the top ten of the strongest brands in Vietnam. During more than 30 years, Vinamilk has built eight factories and three plants with a variety of products available from the 200 sterilized, pasteurized, and dairy products sold not only in Vietnam, but also around the world.

2.2 Employee Information

In 2012, the total number of employees in Vinamilk in Vietnam was 4853, almost half of whom ranged in age from 30 to 40, and 50 % of employees possess a bachelor degree. The workforce of Vinamilk is a consolidation of about 5000 people of different occupations, ages and areas of expertise. Together with expansion in production scale and operation areas, Vinamilk is always consistent in the viewpoint of respect for the employees. Each person, no matter what field or level he or she is, is given an equal chance to show his or her own value and contribute to the corporation's success (Tables 1, 2 and 3).

2.3 Products Range

Vinamilk offers over 200 products to satisfy different classes of income. Vinamilk presents extensive product lines under five brand names: Vinamilk (liquid milk, yogurt, and ice cream), Vfresh (fruit juice and soy milk), Dielac (powdered milk), Ridielac (nutrition powder) and condensed milk, all of which aim for higher margin value-added products. Due to health concerns, Vinamilk is now shifting to more products that offer an additional value for the customer. For example, for yogurt products, Vinamilk has introduced new value-added products such as Collagen milk and liquid milk with ADH, and powdered milk with more nutritional

Table 1 Number of employees in 2010–2012 (Vinamilk 2013c)

	2010	2011	2012
Total number of permanent employees	4510	4564	4853

Table 2 Profile of Vinamilk's labor force in 2013 (Vinamilk 2013b)

	Năm	2010	2011	2012
Number of employees		4510	4564	4853
Gender	Male	3282 72.8 %	3354 73.5 %	3605 74.3 %
	Female	1228 27.2 %	1210 26.5 %	1248 25.7 %
Categories	Manufacture-process	1604 35.5 %	1625 35.6 %	1703 35.1 %
	Sales	391 8.7 %	316 6.9 %	307 6.3 %
	Agricultural activities	152 3.4 %	185 4.1 %	235 4.8 %
	The support activities (purchasing, accounting, human resources, administration, IT, ...)	2363 52.4 %	2438 53.4 %	2608 53.7 %
Age	<30	1468 32.5 %	1413 31.0 %	1448 29.8 %
	30–>40	1902 42.2 %	1925 42.2 %	2046 42.2 %
	40–>50	845 18.7 %	923 20.2 %	1009 20.8 %
	>50	295 6.6 %	303 6.6 %	350 7.2 %
Education level	Vocational/work training	2307 51.2 %	2275 49.8 %	2322 47.9 %
	College	339 7.5 %	357 7.8 %	396 8.2 %
	University	1816 40.3 %	1879 41.2 %	2075 42.8 %
	Postgraduate	48 1 %	53 1.2 %	60 1.1 %

ingredients. Also, Vinamilk has products for all income levels, with broad packaging, products size, and flavors. Main business areas:

- Producing and trading milk and dairy products
- Producing and trading beverages
- Breeding dairy cows, producing fresh milk materials (in 100 % capital owned companies)

Main products and brands:
Vinamilk has more than 200 products, divided into five main groups:

- Powdered milk and nutrition powder: Dielac, Ridielac.
- Condensed milk: Ong Tho Milk, Southern star Milk.
- Liquid milk: Vinamilk 100 % Flex, ADH.

Table 3 Subsidiaries and Associates in 2013 (Vinamilk 2013c)

No.	Company name	Business line	Share capital (VND billion)	Vinamilk's ownership rate (%)
Subsidiaries				
1	Vietnam Dairy Cow One Member Co., ltd.	Breeding dairy cows and producing fresh milk material	1550	100
2	Lam Son Dairy One Member Co., ltd.	Producing, trading dairy products	80	100
3	International Real Estate One Member Co., Ltd.	Real estate business	160	100
Associate[a]				
1	Asia Saigon Food Ingredients JSC	Producing cream powder used for foods	120	15
2	Miraka Co., ltd.	Producing and trading dairy products	NZD 55 million	19.3

[a]Based on the presence of Vinamilk's representative in Board of Management of associates

- Yoghurt, ice-cream, cheese: Yoghurt–ice-cream–cheese Vinamilk, Susu, Probi, ProBeauty.
- Soy bean milk and beverages: GoldSoy, Vfresh, Icy.

2.4 Revenues from 2011 to 2015

From Table 4, we can see that revenues have significantly increased from 2011 to 2015. The most remarkable point is that the operating profit in 2015 is expected to triple, from 196.2 million US$ in 2011 to 501.1 million US$ in 2015.

Export sales accounted for 10 % of company revenue. The main export markets of the company are: Middle Eastern countries, Cambodia, the Philippines, and Australia.

2.5 Vinamilk Revenues by Product

Vinamilk dominates the domestic yogurt and condensed milk market, with a market share of 71 % and 88 %, respectively, in 2011 (Vinamilk 2013a). Condensed milk has a low margin (est. gross margin of 13 %), low growth rate (volume growth rate about 2–3 %), and requires significant capital to manufacture. Friesland Campina seems to have given up on this product line and small players do not find it attractive enough to enter. Vinamilk, with its 88 % market share, has been the leader of this market. Yogurt involves heavy investment in coolers and chilled transportation vehicles, which creates a barrier for new entry. With 28 % revenue in 2011, and yogurt factories in the north, south, and central of Vietnam (Vinamilk 2013b), Vinamilk has an advantage for this product which guarantees its dominant market share (Fig. 1).

Table 4 Revenues from 2011 to 2015 (Vietcapital Security 2012)

Growth and valuation					
	11A	12E	13E	14E	15E
Revenues (VND bn)	21,627	26,441	32,101	39,166	47,433
Operating profit (VND bn)	4317	5818	6870	8718	11,025
OP margin (%)	20.00	22.00	21.40	22.30	23.20
Net Profit (VND m)	4218	5202	6047	7409	8877
EPS (VND)	5288	6236	7249	8882	10,641
EPS growth (%)	16	18	16	23	20
DPS (VND)	2000	3000	3000	3000	3000
BPS (VND)	15,641	19,193	26,776	31,658	38,299
PER (x)	24.6	20.8	17.9	14.6	12.2
PBR (x)	8.3	6.8	4.9	4.1	3.4
Dividend yield (%)	2.3	2.3	3.5	3.5	3.5
ROE (%)	33.8	32.5	27.1	28.1	27.8
Debt/(D+E) (%)	0.0	0.0	0.0	0.0 %	0.0
	2011	**2012**	**2013**	**2014**	**2015**
Revenues (Million Dollars)	983.0	1,201.9	1,459.1	1,780.3	2,156.0
Operating profit (Million Dollars)	196.2	264.5	312.3	396.3	501.1
OP margin (%)	20	22	21.40	22.30	23.20
Net Profit (Thousand Dollars)	191.7	236.5	274.9	336.8	403.5
EPS growth (%)	16	18	16	23	20
Dividend yield (%)	2.3	2.3	3.5	3.5	3.5
ROE (%)	33.8	32.5	27.1	28.1	27.8

Note: Exchange rate 1 US$ = 22,000 VND

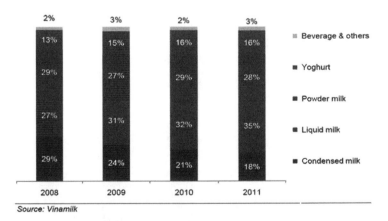

Fig. 1 Revenues by product (Vietcapital Security 2012)

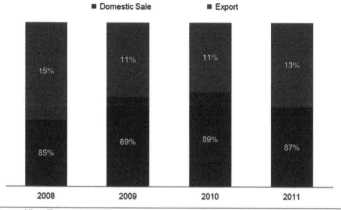

Fig. 2 Revenues by segments (Vietcapital Security 2012)

2.6 Vinamilk Revenues by Segment

Revenues from the domestic market made up almost the entire revenue from 2008 to 2011. However, it decreased slightly in 2011, to 87 %. Apparently, Vinamilk's revenue mainly came from the domestic market; however, its overseas market also increased significantly from 11 to 13 % from 2009 to 2011 (Fig. 2).

3 Vinamilk's Business Strategies

Vinamilk's objective is to maximize shareholder value and pursue strategic business development based on the following principal components. Firstly, the company will develop a comprehensive portfolio of dairy products to target a broader consumer base and expand into higher margin value-added dairy products. Then, development of new product lines to satisfy different consumer preferences would be carried out. Secondly, Vinamilk will develop raw material sources to ensure a reliable and consistent fresh milk supply base. Finally, enhancing supply chain management should be highly considered to help the company reach a broad foreign market.

Furthermore, Vinamilk plans to expand into other overseas markets over the next 5 years, according to Chairwoman and General Director Kieu Lien Mai (Vinamilk 2014a). Vinamilk may export products to the USA and invest in depth to become one of the 50 largest dairy businesses in the world with sales of 3 billion US$ in 2017. To prepare for this strategy, Vinamilk has continued to invest in factories to mass produce high-quality products to meet market demands and focus on expanding the domestic market as well as speeding up exporting to other markets.

3.1 Position in the Home Market

In Vietnam, Vinamilk and Dutch Lady are the largest dairy companies; their combined market share is up to nearly 80 %. Milk imported from companies such as Mead Johnson, Abbott, and Nestle attain about 15 % market share based mainly on milk powder. The remaining 5 % market share is distributed over 20 small-scale milk producers, such as Nutifood, Milk Hanoi, Ba Vi, etc.

Both Vinamilk and Friesland Campina have products in all of the product lines, from UHT (Ultra High Temperature) milk to powdered milk. Others try to penetrate the drinking milk segment, but still their market share is less than 5 % each. Dairy companies locate their factories mostly to be able to supply their large northern and southern markets in Vietnam, and Vinamilk is the only one that has factories located in a central part of the country.

Meanwhile, market leader Vinamilk currently accounts for 80 % of the domestic condensed milk market, 90 % of the yogurt market, 50 % of the processed milk market, and 25 % of the fresh milk market.

3.1.1 Vietnam dairy market share.

Vinamilk and Friesland Campina account for 64 % of the total market share (Fig. 3). The remainder is shared by a number of small players. Vinamilk dominates most markets such as yogurt, condensed milk, and liquid milk. Imported/foreign brands are leading the powdered milk market segment.

Both Vinamilk and Friesland Campina have products in all of the product lines from UHT milk to powdered milk. Dairy companies locate their factories mostly to be able to supply their large northern and southern markets. Vinamilk is the only one that has factories located in a central part of Vietnam (Vietcapital Security 2012).

3.1.2 Liquid milk market share.

With rich and pioneering products, Vinamilk is a market leader in this segment, with almost the half of market share (42 %), followed by Friesland Campina with 27 % (Fig. 4).

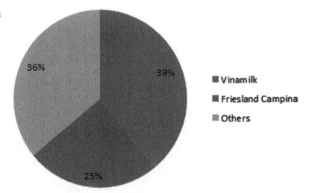

Fig. 3 Dairy market share in Vietnam in 2012 (Vietcapital Security 2012)

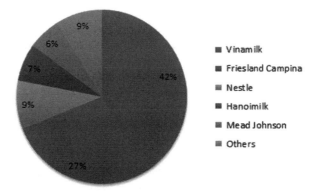

Fig. 4 Liquid milk market share in 2012 (Vietcapital Security 2012)

3.1.3 Powdered milk market share.

The milk powder segment is currently a fiercely competitive market between domestic products and imports. Milk powder and dairy products market accounted for 65 % of the import market share, and Dutch Lady (Friesland Campina) and Vinamilk currently occupies 14 % and 19 % of the market share, respectively. The most profitable product line, powdered milk, is lead by Abbot Vietnam with a market share of 24 % in 2012, followed by Vinamilk with 19 %. Foreign companies still dominate the market, accounting for a 65 % market share. Vietnamese perception on imported/foreign brands is the key reason for the popularity of foreign brands. Vinamilk aims to increase market share by offering a significantly lower price (10–30 % lower compared to international brands) and by gradually educating customers using advertisement, conventions, and events. Vinamilk is expecting to gain its target of 35 % market share (Vinamilk 2013c) but it seems it might take much longer to change customers' view or require a different strategy.

3.2 Position in the World Market

Vinamilk not only dominates the domestic market, but has also affirmed its position in the world market and its products are now present in 26 countries. Export sales in 2012 reached 1687 million US$, which is an increase of threefold from 2008 (over 560 million US$). In 2013, Vinamilk's export revenues were estimated at 230 million US$ (Vietnamnet 2013b).

In 2013, revenue exports of Vinamilk amounted to about 230 million US$, for which Cambodia accounted for 40–50 million US$; this has sufficient market potential for companies who are considering building a plant here. In addition, the company has a stake in a dairy plant in New Zealand, and has invested in UHT milk production lines for the Vietnam market. This demonstrates that they are diversifying and not only producing milk powder serving local markets.

By these achievements, Vinamilk is ranked 17th among its peers in Southeast Asia in terms of market share (Vietcapital Security 2012) (Table 5). Furthermore,

Vinamilk is expected to expand its market not only in Poland, but also in other Europeans countries over the next 10 years.

Despite facing many challenges in crisis times, Vinamilk has been ranked eighth out of the ten leading Vietnamese companies paying the most in income tax in 2013, according to the V1000 Ranking, which is a list of 1000 companies with the highest corporate income tax paid in 2013 (VNeconomy 2013). Also, Vinamilk has been considered as the most efficient domestic company and has a huge impact on business operation of Vietnamese enterprises.

Laying the foundation for business ethics and contributing to the development of education, Vinamilk has supported ten thousands of Vietnam elementary school students during the past 10 years along with the Ministry of Education. Vinamilk has helped bring up the Vietnamese talent generation, motivate Vietnamese young pupils, and improve the outdated educational system. Also, Vinamilk has contributed billions to many charitable organizations and community development programs in Vietnam. For example, the scholarship program "Vinamilk—Nurturing young talent Vietnam" has awarded 1000 scholarships worth 1 billion US$ to elementary pupils who have outstanding achievements. Furthermore, the company has organized "Towering Vietnam Dairy Foundation" and "Fund one million trees for Vietnam", as well as spending 5 billion US$ on providing more than 300,000 children with free milk (Vinamilk 2014b).

4 Future Developments

Vinamilk has faced many challenges in the development and expansion of its products. Firstly, the unavailability or shortage of supply of raw materials affect the ability of on-going operations and increase product costs. Since Vinamilk has mainly used imported raw materials from New Zealand, its products depend on the market price in the world and the company has been faced with fluctuations in prices during the crisis period. Secondly, safety issues regarding dairy quality are one of the factors that will impact the dairy industry in the future. In 2012, the melamine milk scandal made the consumption of milk and milk products decrease dramatically in Vietnam. Therefore, overcoming the widespread negative perception of Vinamilk and the mis-management of printed information and social media will be a challenge for the company in the coming years. Furthermore, Vinamilk needs to find a way to change the consumer perception and buying behavior that only foreign dairy brands can produce quality dairy products at a competitive price. Vinamilk has to prove that the company can totally raise the quality of domestic milk by investing enormous amount of money on modern equipment and by applying the most advanced technology to their new products. Finally, the biggest challenge for Vinamilk is probably maintaining innovation in the domestic market while foreign companies continually expand their market in Vietnam. For example, the biggest competitor for Vinamilk in Vietnam is Friesland Campina, which has 23 % of the market share. For overseas markets, the reputation of the company and its financial strength could become challenges since Vinamilk is originally from a

Table 5 Rankings of peers in Southeast Asia (Vietcapital Security 2012)

Index	Short name	Market cap (USD mn)	Div. yield (%)	P/E	P/B	ROE (%)	ROA (%)
1	UNI-PRESIDENT	8411	1.8	21.2	3.2	15.4	3.5
2	CHAROEN POK FOOD	8323	3.6	11.0	2.6	26.2	9.6
3	THAI BEVERAGE	8214	3.6	15.9	3.9	26.3	10.8
4	LUZHOW LAOJIAO-A	7455	4.2	12.0	5.6	53.1	34.1
5	KUALA LUMPUR KEP	7240	3.1	19.9	3.1	17.1	10.8
6	CHAROEN POK INDO	5445	1.3	18.3	6.7	42.3	29.5
7	SHANXI XINGHUA-A	5147	0.7	24.3	9.2	44.7	27.0
8	INNER MONG YIL-A	5131	1.2	18.1	4.6	27.8	8.9
9	INDOFOOD SUKSES	5103	3.1	14.9	2.4	16.9	6.0
10	CHINA MENGNIU DA	4997	1.1	21.5	2.6	12.9	7.2
11	PPB GROUP BERHAD	4646	1.7	19.0	1.0	5.3	4.9
12	NISSIN FOODS HOL	4585	2.4	24.8	1.2	5.0	3.5
13	INDOFOOD CBP SUK	4417	2.3	20.4	3.9	20.4	13.5
14	UNIVERSAL ROBINA	4198	1.9	20.3	3.4	12.7	7.8
15	YANTAI CHANGYU-B	4188	3.6	12.0	4.0	37.1	25.9
16	CJ CHEIL	3967	0.5	15.1	1.5	11.1	3.5
17	**VIET NAM DAIRY P**	**3438**	**3.1**	**13.8**	**5.1**	**40.8**	**33.2**
18	NIPPON MEAT PACK	3313	1.4	23.6	0.9	3.8	1.8
19	NISSHIN SEIFUN	3211	1.9	19.2	0.9	4.7	3.3
20	ASTRA AGRO LEST	3089	4.9	13.4	3.6	27.9	19.6
21	OLAM INTERNATION	3049	2.6	10.2	1.1	11.7	2.8
22	TOYO SUISAN KAI	2998	1.8	13.1	1.3	10.0	7.1
23	KIKKOMAN CORP	2979	1.3	25.0	1.5	6.0	3.1

(continued)

Table 5 (continued)

Index	Short name	Market cap (USD mn)	Div. yield (%)	P/E	P/B	ROE (%)	ROA (%)
24	CHINA AGRI-INDUS	2852	1.5	14.1	0.8	5.9	1.7
25	FIRST RESOURCES	2656	1.8	10.5	2.5	25.7	15.1
26	THAI UNION FROZE	2626	2.4	13.1	2.2	18.8	6.5
27	YAMAZAKI BAKING	2581	1.7	17.4	0.9	5.2	1.9
28	BEIJING DABEIN-A	2446	0.8	23.8	3.9	17.5	12.9
29	KEWPIE	2262	1.6	14.3	1.1	7.8	4.4
30	FRASER & NEAVE	2191	3.6	24.2	4.3	17.6	10.8
31	GRAINCORP LTD-A	2111	3.9	11.6	1.6	14.1	7.5
32	GENTING PLANTATI	2089	1.2	18.0	1.9	11.2	8.7
33	BEIJING YAN-A	2050	2.1	15.1	1.3	9.0	4.8
34	ANHUI GUJINGD-B	2028	1.4	10.8	2.5	26.1	17.4
35	SMART TBK	2027	2.9	10.4	2.3	24.4	12.5
36	CP POKPHAND CO L	2017	4.1	13.6	2.5	26.5	13.2
37	KAGOME	2007	1.1	23.8	1.7	7.5	4.1
38	HITE JINRO CO	1929	4.3	21.1	1.4	6.8	2.8
39	LOTTE CONFECTION	1918	0.3	21.1	0.8	3.8	2.5
40	BIOSTIME INTERNA	1896	2.0	19.4	6.1	32.9	25.6
41	GUANGDONG HAID-A	1842	0.8	25.5	4.0	16.6	8.8
	Average	3733	2.2	17.4	2.8	18.5	10.7

Source: Bloomberg

poor country with low-skilled employees. However, if Vinamilk wants to turn itself into a leading company in food and beverage, the company will have to expand its product portfolio as the giant group Danone has done in France.

The biggest competitor for Vinamilk in Vietnam is Friesland Campina which products have been available under the Dutch Lady brand for more than 85 years. Friesland Campina's condensed milk has grown to be the best-known consumer brand in the country. Also, the Dutch Lady brand has a range of dairy products for different types of consumers; for instance, Friso is a market leader in infant nutrition product. Its market share is approximately 27 %. In addition, Friesland Campina Vietnam has two production locations in Vietnam (Ha Nam and Binh

Duong) and these dairy farms can produce 60 million liters of fresh milk annually, accounting for around 25 % of the domestic demand for raw material (Vietnamnews 2012). Therefore, in the future, Friesland Campina will become the main competitor for Vinamilk. Also, the domestic market is crowded with domestic competitors such as Bavi, Moc Chau, Dalat, but those companies do not hold a significant percentage of market share.

Since the Netherlands is famous for its dairy products and Friesland Campina, the market leader is established in Leeuwarden in the Netherlands, it would seem unwise for Vinamilk to enter the Dutch market with daily products such as milk and cheese. However, the demands for healthy products such as diet drinks or anti-ageing green tea could increase in the Netherlands due to the fact that the population is ageing rapidly (OECDobsever 2014) and one-third of the population is overweight or obese (Iamexpat 2012). Vinamilk has a valuable chance to reach this potential market with its new generation products such as Lincha tea with honey, which the company says helps improve the health of people.

Furthermore, a significant amount of dairy companies exist in the Netherlands including Simdico Food. Uniekaas Vastgoed have proved that they can operate a dairy business and even make a profit in the Netherlands by producing products that are good and cheaper than domestic ones. Another example is the German brand Crownfield, whose milk can be found in Lidl supermarkets in the Netherlands. Vinamilk, therefore, has an advantage in that the company can produce products using inexpensive labor and raw materials in Vietnam.

5 Conclusions

Vinamilk has continued to be a pioneer in the food industry in general and in the dairy and beverage industry in particular because of the following main reasons. Firstly, Vinamilk's product research and technology development have been increasingly improved and updated. Vinamilk has used the latest technology to ensure food safety in their new products in order to change the domestic consumer behavior that exists in Vietnam, namely the consumer perception that dairy products made in France or the Netherlands would be the best choice. Vinamilk uses the most advanced technology in the world in its dairy factories. All processes in the plant are fully automated, and are controlled by Tetra Pak Group's integrated robots (Vinamilk 2014b). In addition, many experts from Germany and Switzerland are invited to work directly in the factory to analyze the nutritional demand of the Vietnamese and to launch the blended formula for new products which are suitable for each group of customers. Secondly, Vinamilk has effectively invested in brand building and market expansion. This is considered as the most outstanding performance of Vinamilk in Vietnam. The company pays attention to studies on local markets, and to consumer habits, age, and gender demands to grow its retailer network and to promote each specific product in different areas of Vietnam. Moreover, Vinamilk also reaches overseas markets, including the difficult markets such as the USA, Australia, Cambodia, Laos, New Zealand, and Middle East countries. Thirdly, investing in people is the core of success for Vinamilk. The company has tried to create an attractive, dynamic working environment for their employees in order to improve the quality of life and raise skill levels for each member of the company. Vinamilk aims to build a working environment that ensures the following aspects:

- Setting up safe working conditions and healthcare.
- Developing a diversified labour line-up, where personal differences are respected and discrimination is not allowed.
- Setting up labour relationship based on free will and legal compliance.
- Recognizing and rewarding employees' performance.
- Providing training and opportunities for career promotion.
- Promoting a harmonious working culture.

(Vinamilk 2013b).

Finally, in order to have sustainable development as well as preserve prestige in the market, respect for business ethics and the actions to bring sustainable values to the society and the community play a very important role, in addition to implementing proper business operation strategies. For years, Vinamilk has been known as a leading community-oriented enterprise with charitable activities. In 2013, along with the Trade Union, the Communist Youth Union, and all employees of the company, Vinamilk organized a lot of activities to support the community with practical and meaningful activities in a spirit of solidarity. In addition, Vinamilk has coordinated with the Ministry of Education to support primary school children in remote places by providing free drinking milk for 10 years.

By entering a co-operative agreement with three leading European partners at the same time, Vinamilk not only strengthened its position as a leading nutrition company in Vietnam but also has crossed borders to become a world brand of the future. Vinamilk is cooperating with DSM (from Switzerland), Lonza (also from Switzerland) and Chr. Hansen (from Denmark). These all are leading European nutrition groups with over 100 years experience in development and ownership of important scientific nutrition contributions from all over the world. These partners, which have been in close cooperation with Vinamilk during the past years, specialize in researching, developing and applying micro-substance and microbial science for Dielac Alpha, Dielac Mama, and Ridielac. Therefore, Vinamilk products have high quality and meet international standards on nutrition product for infants and children which are accepted in the markets of developed countries such as the USA, New Zealand, and European countries. The growth strategy of Vinamilk is based on the understanding of nutritional demands of Vietnamese children, supplying products which meet specific international standards and nutritional needs, and establishing a prestigious milk brand for Vietnamese consumers. This global co-operation helps to implement the aforesaid strategy and to make Vinamilk a successful global brand.

References

Bloomberg. (2012). *Vinamilk sees revenue doubling in overseas expansion.* Retrieved March 14, 2014, from http://www.bloomberg.com/news/2013-09-30/vinamilk-sees-revenue-doubling-in-overseas-expansion-push.html

Iamexpat. (2012). *Four of ten Dutch are overweight.* Retrieved April 29, 2014, from http://www.iamexpat.nl/read-and-discuss/lifestyle/news/4-out-of-10-dutch-people-are-overweight

OECDobsever. (2014). *Ageing population.* Retrieved April 25, 2014, from http://www.oecdobserver.org/news/archivestory.php/aid/741/Ageing_populations:_How_the_Dutch_cope.html

Soha. (2014). *Mai Kieu Lien vind danh Forbes.* Retrieved March 18, 2014, from http://soha.vn/kinh-doanh/vi-sao-nu-doanh-nhan-mai-kieu-lien-duoc-forbes-vinh-danh-20140302110049957.htm

Vietcapital Security. (2012). *Vinamilk—A safe haven.* Retrieved March 14, 2014, from http://cms.vcsc.com.vn/FileReport/20121219/VNM-20121219-BUY.pdf

Vietnambreakingnews. (2014). *Forbes honour three Vietnamese business women.* Retrieved March 19, 2014, from http://www.vietnambreakingnews.com/tag/southern-milk/

Vietnamnet. (2013a). *Vinamilk tops Forbes Vietnam's list of top 50.* Retrieved March 14, 2014, from http://english.vietnamnet.vn/fms/business/83720/vinamilk-tops-forbes-vietnam-s-list-of-top-50.html

Vietnamnet. (2013b). *Vinamilk invest heavily in dairy farming.* Retrieved April 28, 2014, from http://english.vietnamnet.vn/fms/business/77419/business-in-brief-26-6.html

Vietnamnews. (2012). *Dairies battle for market share.* Retrieved April 29, 2014, from http://vietnamnews.vn/economy/229545/dairies-battle-for-market-share.html

Vinamilk. (2013a). *The wide distribution network.* Retrieved March 14, 2014, from http://www.vinamilk.com.vn/eng/?vnm=market&id=14

Vinamilk. (2013b). *Annual report 2014.* Retrieved April 29, 2014, from http://www.vinamilk.com.vn/eng/?vnm=DownloadFile&m=5

Vinamilk. (2013c). *Annual report 2013.* Retrieved March 17, 2014, from http://www.vinamilk.com.vn/eng/?vnm=DownloadFile&m=5

Vinamilk. (2014a). *Overseas expansion.* Retrieved April 24, 2014, from http://www.vinamilk.com.vn/eng/?vnm=Share_channel&m=1

Vinamilk. (2014b). *Quy sua vuon cao Vinamilk.* Retrieved April 29, 2014, from http://www.vinamilk.com.vn/?vnm=news_detail&id=1383

Vneconomy. (2013). *Vinamilk diem sang dong gop.* Retrieved April 27, 2014, from http://vneconomy.vn/20131111094658496P19C9915/vinamilk-diem-sang-dong-gop-cho-ngan-sach-nha-nuoc.htm

Vneconomy. (2014). *Vinamilk thanh lap cong ty con.* Retrieved March 19, 2014, from http://vneconomy.vn/201402201102178P0C7/vinamilk-gop-3-trieu-usd-lap-cong-ty-con-tai-ba-lan.htm

Part VI
Underlying Strategies and Success Factors of Emerging Asian Multinationals

Corporate Enterpreneurship and Triple Helix

Mariusz Soltanifar

Abstract

Triple Helix (TH) is a concept well known, understood, and applied by many Asian Multinationals (AMNC), and it plays an important role for economic growth and regional development. It seems to be influenced by networks and partnerships and their complexity as well. Corporate entrepreneurship (CE) has been widely acknowledged in international literature and practiced as a vital element of business performance. CE mainly relates to a corporate management style that integrates risk-taking and innovative approaches, as well as reward and motivational techniques that are more traditionally thought of as being the province of entrepreneurship. By encouraging innovation and enriching business performance, CE offers great fundamentals for cooperative development between the government, educational institutes, and businesses. In a constantly demanding environment, the dual forces of technological change and globalisation-heightened competition do have an impact on the way how businesses operate. To cope with this, organizations should fully understand the different meanings of CE, at any level, and try to apply it properly to all decisions made in the framework of TH's cooperation.

1 Introduction

The North of the Netherlands offers an ideal mix of living and working conditions, creating several investment possibilities. Asian business is reforming and its emerging multinationals will change the way we all live, also in this particular

M. Soltanifar (✉)
International Business School, Hanze University OAS, Groningen, The Netherlands
e-mail: m.soltanifar@pl.hanze.nl

region. In order to ensure their presence here, a successful cooperation between the government, industry and academia has to be established.

Several companies looking to stake ground in Dutch as well as global markets face several challenges. They must create and sustain brands that have appeal outside their home markets, navigate a range of regulatory and political frameworks, and drive innovation to create differentiated products or services to potentially attract new customers. Additionally, those companies particularly interested and relying on acquisitions must overcome cultural and other differences to successfully integrate new overseas operations; however they are not the scope of this chapter. The most critical challenges are likely to be centered around talent: how to acquire the leadership and knowledge to compete on a global stage. This is crucial for Asian multinationals who act often in the frame of a knowledge-based economy and a knowledge-based society.

The following chapter reports the study on an interconnection between the Triple Helix (TH) and corporate entrepreneurship (CE) and analyzes the investment possibilities for Asian Multinationals (AMNC). TH is a concept well known, understood, and applied by several AMNC, and it plays an important role for the economic growth and region development. It seems to be influenced by networks and partnerships and their complexity as well. Additionally, the study presents the results of researching TH organizations and pinpoints several actions to be undertaken in order to create a potential for those types of companies which are conquering the world. Two Dutch cases are analyzed which show substantial possibilities for transferring knowledge and experience to the Northern Netherlands region.

Corporate entrepreneurship (CE) has been widely acknowledged in international literature and practiced as a vital element of business performance. It develops new ideas, procedures, or products, and thereby stimulates innovation, which is regarded as inherent to effective management practice. CE mainly relates to a corporate management style that integrates risk-taking and innovative approaches, as well as the reward and motivational techniques that are more traditionally thought of as being the province of entrepreneurship. These decisions might directly apply to the level and scope of cooperation. By encouraging innovation and enriching business performance, CE offers great fundamentals for cooperative development between the government, educational institutes, and businesses located in the Northern Netherlands, the region which is the scope of this study.

In a constantly demanding environment, the dual forces of technological change and globalisation-heightened competition impact the way how businesses operate. To cope with this, organizations should fully understand the different meanings of CE, at any level, and try to apply it properly to all of the decisions made in the framework of TH's cooperation.

2 Triple Helix and Corporate Entrepreneurship

Triple Helix (TH) is a concept which underlines the importance of government, industry and academia relations. In line with Leydesdorff, "the TH model enables us to study the network linkages among them, both in the evolutionary terms of the transition to post-industrialism and in terms of communication-theoretical concepts" (Leydesdorff and Heimeriks 2001). The TH model was introduced in 1995 by Etzkowitz and Leydesdorff and illustrates the importance of those interconnections and the value of the abovementioned network linkages. Since then, it has been widely used, particularly in studies of the knowledge-based economy and innovation, both by AMNC as well as companies or organizations in general.

According to Bressers (2012), "governmental agencies increasingly share power with experts from knowledge institutions and businesses and businesses become societally involved through corporate social responsibility (CSR). Knowledge institutions become commercially active and increasingly operate on the verge of science and consultancy. Public policy and science become blurred, yet also remain individually visible. Organizations maintain their primary characteristics, but connections with each other are growing and the organizations assimilate some of each other's roles" (Bressers 2012). In the recent years, this development, in all of the interconnected and abovementioned areas, has been dubbed the rise of the TH concept.

In conclusion, the concept of the Triple Helix System of innovation was recently introduced as an analytical framework that synthesizes key features of the TH interactions into an "innovation system" format, defined according to the systems theory as a set of components, relationships and functions. The relationships between components are synthesized into five main types: technology transfer, collaboration and conflict moderation, collaborative leadership, substitution, and networking (Ranga and Etzkowitz 2013).

The following subchapters discuss core concepts in the TH organization literature, connecting it with knowledge about complexity and cooperation. Ongoing transformation of TH and the importance of networking, in knowledge-based economies are emphasized. TH is also presented as a key for improving conditions for innovation, and increasing investment possibilities for AMNC at the same time.

2.1 Triple Helix Characteristics

TH theory emphasises the development which occurs collaboratively in a mutual three-party process that involve actors (entities) from industry, government, and academia. The TH theory was originally developed to "analyze innovation at the societal level and as a historical outcome. One historical trend that the theory aims to describe is the increasing role of knowledge for innovation, and in particular the role of the university in an increasingly knowledge-based society. Where academia had earlier been seen primarily as an up-stream activity or as part of a knowledge

Table 1 Triple Helix actors and their role in the innovation process (Etzkowitz 2003)

Triple Helix actors	Role in innovation process
Industry	Locus of production
Government	Source of contractual relations that guarantee stable interactions and exchange
University	Source of new knowledge and technology, the generative principle of knowledge-based economies

context to innovation, the TH positioned the university closer to the actual innovation process. Another trend that the theory aims to describe is the increasing role of a collaborative mode of innovation. The three institutional spheres, so called, helices, interact and communicate at different levels in TH processes that not only drive change but also lead to internal transformations of the respective institutional sphere" (Fogelberg and Thorpenberg 2012).

The TH "denotes a transformation in the relationship among industry, government and academia as well as within each of these spheres" (Etzkowitz 2003). In this transformation process all of the actors (entities) engaged need to fulfil several roles. They are briefly presented in Table 1.

The common objective of the TH model is to realize an innovative environment consisting of university spin-off firms, tri-lateral initiatives for knowledge-based economic development, and strategic alliances among firms, government laboratories, and academic research groups (Etzkowitz and Leydesdorff 2000). By providing "a flexible framework to guide efforts, from different starting points, to achieve the common goal of knowledge-based economic and social development" (Etzkowitz and Klofsten 2005), TH enables proper innovation management and a policy model for innovation as well.

The TH model of industry—government—academia relations depictured in Fig. 1 presents an alternative between bilateral and trilateral coordination mechanisms or—in institutional terms—spheres.

The spheres (helices) remain in transition because each of the partner institutes also develops its own, and often differentiating, mission. Thus, "a trade-off can be generated between integration and differentiation, and new systems in terms of possible synergies can be explored and potentially shaped. As the various bilateral translations function, a TH overlay can also be expected to develop as a system of meaning exchanges among differently coded expectations" (Leydesdorff 2012). This dynamic overlay, responding to a demanding environment, is portrayed below (Fig. 2).

Above-presented dynamic overlay has to be well thought out in order to ensure a proper process of innovation. As mentioned previously, TH is under ongoing a transformation process. It occurs through hybridization between spheres where elements from industry, government and academia are recombined into new forms. The result of this transformative process is that "universities increasingly act as entrepreneurs, businesses increasingly act as knowledge developers, and

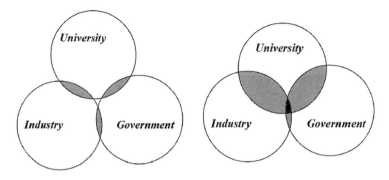

Fig. 1 The origins of the Triple Helix model (Leydesdorff 2012)

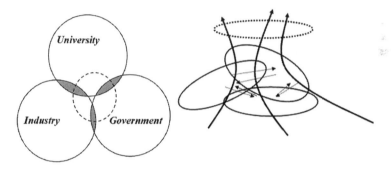

Fig. 2 A differentiated Triple Helix with dynamic overlay (Leydesdorff 2012)

governmental agents maintain their task as the guardian of the rules of the game, but also take available venture capital (VC) to help start new enterprises" (Etzkowitz 2003). The interactivity of the process in which all of the actors (entities) co-evolve towards a notably new structure through communication with each other has to be emphasized at this point.

Bressers (2012) draws our attention to the fact that "by cooperating with many relevant stakeholders actors can attempt to tackle the problem that single actors only have a limited range within which they can steer events. If an actor wishes to influence society in a certain direction it has virtually no chance if it acts alone, only chance and luck will then lead to the desired outcomes. If, however, the actor collaborates with tens, hundreds or thousands of other stakeholders in the same field their combined effort might push the societal change in the envisaged direction. The TH organization, with its internal transformation without reducing the core qualities of the actors, is an important vehicle for such collaborative processes" (Bressers 2012). This collaborative process depends on the way and the intensity with which the aforementioned actors communicate and network. This is discussed in the following subchapter.

2.2 Networking as an Important Triple Helix Component

The connectivity of the government, industry and academia plays a significant role in TH activities. A suitable network among all of the actors (entities) together, representing, respectively, industry, government, and university, presents and creates greater innovation potential and influences the intensity of the connections. The abovementioned actors (entities) might act in different ways as they may possibly understand the communication process differently. The manner in which all of the actors cooperate or acquire new projects or implement new activities undoubtedly depends on their ability to connect with other people, organizations, sectors or ideas. It is notable that the process of engaging all of the actors at the same time becomes more complex. The multitude of these connections increases the complexity of the process from the moment of generating a new idea to successful implementation or commercialization of a particular product or solution. There is really no way to reduce or ignore the complexity of the process, as different situations call for different actions. The complexity of TH should be incorporated into all of the engaged organizations to strengthen and support a better understanding and meaning of all of the available or potential connections. Because of the limited number of pages in this chapter, the complexity is not further discussed, but this does not mean it should be ignored.

According to Etzkowitz (2003), "TH postulates, that this interaction in the tripartite cooperation, is the key to improving conditions for innovation in a knowledge-based society" (Etzkowitz 2003). Thus the interaction between actors is the driving force for change processes, consistent with the discussion of the complexity theory. The networks these actors form are not static: they are in a constant flux (Etzkowitz and Leydesdorff 2000); somehow, these interaction processes between TH participants lead to exchange and alignment (Bressers 2012) and the current technological development facilitates the way these actors communicate.

2.3 Entrepreneurship and Its Importance for Triple Helix Activities

Entrepreneurial activities and a positive attitude toward innovation are a vital part of TH activities. The multidimensionality of the field of entrepreneurship encouraged the development of several forms of entrepreneurship beyond the traditional, neoclassical or Schumpeterian notion of business or economics. In this respect, the new streams in the entrepreneurial concept include several forms and are highlighted in this subchapter. With respect to this, the concept "corporate entrepreneurship" (CE) desires more attention.

The concept of CE is rich with different approaches and assumptions. This phenomenon took different shapes in the history of economic thought (Davidsson 2004; Frederick and Kuratko 2010) and can be expressed in various terms such as intrapreneuring; corporate entrepreneurship (CE); internal corporate entrepreneurship (ICE); corporate venturing (CV); strategic renewal; and internal entrepreneurship and venturing (Sharma and Chrisman; 1999). Several researchers agree that if entrepreneurship occurs within the setting of an established organization, it is labelled with the term intrapreneurship (Pinchot 1985; Pinchot and Pellman 1999) or other synonyms, such as corporate entrepreneurship (Zahra 1991) or corporate venturing (Covin and Miles 1999), that are used to express the same concept.

CE is recognized as a fundamental element of business performance of large, small and medium sized enterprises, and firms in general, irrespective of their size. CE includes new product improvement and new manufacture methods and procedures (Antoncic and Hisrich 2003), and expansion of innovative services, technologies, or production methods. Correspondingly, innovation is seen here as the main driving force of CE.

As mentioned previously, although CE exists in firms in general irrespective of their size, the majority of the research on corporate entrepreneurial attitude has had a primary focus on large American-based companies. This led many countries to follow and adopt uncritically the American models of CE strategies and in addition, smaller companies imitated intrapreneurial strategies of large organizations without considering their diversities. Consequently, the need for further comparative research on CE in economies other than American and in smaller organizations is particularly critical in order to explore the role of CE and its impact on innovation as a crucial outcome of TH activities.

The basic idea that constitutes the concept of CE is the new venture formation (Pinchot 1985) and refers to intrapreneurship. CE and intrapreneurship are the two terms used interchangeably. However, apart from creation of new business ventures, CE also refers to other innovative activities, such as development of new products, services, technologies, strategies, administrative techniques or competitive postures approach. Research on CE, as mentioned before, has been done largely on "formation of new corporate ventures (CV) and on the entrepreneurial orientation (EO), mainly emphasizing characteristics of entrepreneurial organizations and positively referring it to innovation. CE is seen also as a valuable instrument for rejuvenating and revitalising existing companies or organizations and is recognized as a crucial aspect of organizational development and business performance."

From recent research, CE reflects a broad spectrum of activities related to finding and developing new ideas which mainly are positively related to business performance. Many organizations today "rely on CE to develop and differentiate their products and services" (Hayton et al. 2013). CE occurs when organizations strive to "exploit product-market opportunities through innovative and proactive behaviour" (Dess et al. 1999). As such, CE facilitates a firm's efforts to exploit its current competitive advantages as well, such as recognizing and exploiting new opportunities (Ireland et al. 2009) and the competencies required to successfully pursue them (Covin and Miles 1999). Moreover, CE has evolved into a major strategy consideration for organizations today.

The recognized scope of the CE domain has expanded significantly over the past few decades and may also be related to CV and to strategic entrepreneurship. Corbett et al. (2013) explains that "the label CV is used in reference to the same new business phenomena alluded to in prior typologies, while the strategic entrepreneurship category of CE refers to a wide variety of specific phenomena that include, among others, strategic renewal and the Schumpeterian innovation phenomenon to which Sharma and Chrisman (1999) refer" (Corbett et al. 2013). The author also pays attention to the "new insights from a variety of perspectives on the matter of how established organizations might best respond to the entrepreneurial imperatives they face and opportunities confronting them" (Corbett et al. 2013). The author argues that CE is not all good, all the time, and there must be some limits to its adoption and usefulness. The following areas could be developed further: internal processes of how CE evolves, is adopted, and is successful; explanation and prediction of CE adoption; and prediction of high-performing governance choices.

Three related phenomena have paralleled CE's theoretical development for the last decade. These concepts are corporate venturing (CV), entrepreneurial orientation (EO) and strategic entrepreneurship. They are shortly discussed in the following subchapters. Respective to abovementioned thoughts, a proper understanding of all of these concepts might create some extra space for integrating CE into TH activities.

2.4 Triple Helix System

For the past two decades, there has been an increased interest in the field of entrepreneurial attitude. More attention has been given to a new stream of CE, taking into account the different theories regarding entrepreneurship in economic, psychological, and sociological research. In line with Pirich, CE is a process rather than a static phenomenon or a mechanical economic factor (Pirich 2001). Antoncic and Hisrich provide a more comprehensive view on the concept, emphasizing that CE is "a process that goes on inside an existing firm, regardless of its size, and leads not only to new business ventures but also to other innovative activities and orientations such as development of new products, services, technologies, administrative techniques, strategies, and competitive postures". Correspondingly, CE is also perceived as a process of an organizational renewal, defined as "revitalising a company's business through innovation and changing competitive profile" (Zahra 1991). CE can be also expressed in two other forms: new venture creation within existing organizations or "the process of creating new business and the transformation of organizations through strategic renewal".

Since its introduction at the end of the 1980s, EO has changed its definition several times (Belousova and Gailly 2013). In the works written about EO in the 1980s, it is considered as a posture, whereas the 1990s considered the concept in terms of a new entry. "An EO refers to the processes, practices, and decision-making activities that lead to new entry" whereas new entry is understood as "the act of launching a new venture" (Lumpkin and Dess 1996). It can be accomplished by entering new or established markets with new or existing goods or services. In conclusion, EO can be also defined as the strategy-making processes and styles of firms that engage in entrepreneurial activities (Lumpkin and Dess 2001) and can be understood as the engine that drives specific CE activities.

Corporate venturing (CV) approaches have as their commonality the adding of new businesses (or portions of new businesses via equity investments) to the corporation. This can be accomplished through three implementation modes: internal corporate venturing, cooperative corporate venturing, and external corporate venturing (Hornsby et al. 2013).

CV can be seen as a specific kind of CE aiming at starting and developing new ventures inside existing organizations. Respectively, CE can be considered as a process related to proactive initiatives from individual employees. In this process, managers are and should be engaged as representatives of the employer. In contrast, one of the CE's dimensions—innovativeness—refers to product and service innovation with emphasis on development and innovation in technology. CE includes new product development, product improvements, and new production methods and procedures. Covin and Slevin (1991) consider one part of the entrepreneurial posture to be reflected in the extensiveness and frequency of product innovation and the related tendency of technological leadership. In addition to this, Zahra included product innovation and technological entrepreneurship (Zahra 1991) as innovative aspects of manufacturing firms.

Strategic entrepreneurship approaches have as their commonality the exhibition of large-scale or otherwise highly consequential innovations that are adopted in the firm's pursuit of competitive advantage. With strategic entrepreneurship, innovation can be in any of five areas: the firm's strategy, product offerings, served markets, internal organization (i.e., structure, processes, and capabilities), or business model. In either case, the organizational environment becomes a critical area of focus when CE activities are to be launched (Hornsby et al. 2013).

In line with Corbett et al, "the strategic entrepreneurship category of CE refers to a wide variety of specific phenomena that include, among others, strategic renewal and the Schumpeterian (disruptive) innovation phenomenon to which Sharma and Chrisman refer. Additionally, strategic entrepreneurship as part of the CE construct recognises not only the disruptive aspect of Schumpeterian innovation, but also the generative, path creating, new business creation aspect that may be inherent in breakthrough innovation, where firms struggle to understand how to execute opportunities in the face of high levels of uncertainty on multiple dimensions" (Corbett et al. 2013).

2.5 Positioning Entrepreneurship to Facilitate Innovation in the Triple Helix System

CE is broadly recognized as an instrument for facilitating innovation and competitiveness of organizations and businesses, and is bounded by a set of internal and external factors, directly or indirectly shaping innovative activities. The internal factors influencing CE are: the communication process, use of formal control mechanisms, environmental scanning, organizational support, competition-related values, and person-related values. Correspondingly, the external factors influencing CE are: dynamism, technological opportunities, industry growth, demand for new products, favorability of change, and competitive rivalry.

According to Zahra (1991), the other factors influencing CE are environmental factors, such as hostility, dynamism, and heterogeneity (Zahra 1991). Management and the governmental leaders play also a significant role with respect to management style, staffing, and rewarding innovative venture activities or training and trusting individuals within the firm to detect opportunities. All of the activities undertaken should be converted into several visible outcomes. These outcomes can be objective measures, such as profitability, earnings per share, and innovation; and subjective measures, such as employees' satisfaction and commitment to the organization or the organization's learning and memory orientation. Following Hornsby et al. (2013), only by exploring this relationship can "more proficient implementation of CE strategies be enabled." Additionally, management support, work discretion, rewards or reinforcement, time availability, and organizational boundaries need to be deliberated (Hayton et al. 2013).

CE can be studied at the individual, organizational and national level. With regards to TH, the national level might play a significant role in the cooperation between actors (entities), because government might excellently stimulate innovativeness among industry, business and academia, by initiating common projects, for example. Research exploring the antecedents of entrepreneurial-oriented processes and behaviors has been unduly limited (Hornsby et al. 2013). In this context, "the centrality of organizational boundaries as a core dimension of organizational preparedness for corporate entrepreneurship (OPCE), for example, is currently unclear". Although many scholars have theorized the importance of organizational structure as a core aspect of OPCE (Ireland et al. 2009), empirical support for this dimension in practice has been limited and mixed (Hornsby et al. 2002). According to Hornsby et al. (2013), "research into OPCE has been conducted to identify specific organizational antecedents of managers' entrepreneurial behaviour" (Hornsby et al. 2013). In this scholarly vein, several other authors found three factors to be the most important stimulants of managers' entrepreneurial behavior and they are as follows: top management support, organizational structure, and rewards. Hornsby, Kuratko, and Montagno extended this earlier study of OPCE to include work discretion and time availability as two additional factors that serve as determinants of managerial entrepreneurial behavior. This line of research not only made a theoretical contribution but also made a methodological contribution by introducing the instruments that became the precursor of the Corporate Entrepreneurship Assessment Instrument (Hornsby et al. 2013).

Several measurement scales, such as the Corporate Entrepreneurship Assessment Instrument (CEAI) explained by Hornsby et al. (2002) and Kuratko et al. (1990), Entrepreneurial orientation (EO) stressed by Covin and Slevin (1989), and entrepreneurial intensity, are important means of measuring various aspects of CE strategy. The CEAI is an instrument that was developed to measure the key internal organizational factors that influence a firm's entrepreneurial activities and outcomes. Originally developed by Kuratko et al. (1990) and further refined in more recent studies (Hornsby et al. 2002), the CEAI represents a key instrument available to researchers for measuring a firm's OPCE. A recent study by Hornsby results in "a more parsimonious and psychometrically sound set of items for each factor was derived yielding an 18-item instrument based upon the original 48-item measure, analyzing organizational preparedness for CE" (Hornsby et al. 2013). This provides a necessary and critical tool to advance research in the area of organizational antecedents to CE and provide insight into the important consideration of pro-entrepreneurship organizational architecture (Ireland et al. 2009), ensuring that each factor of the CEAI is represented by a parsimonious set of items that are conceptually distinct from each other before examining the instrument's structural or convergent validity. This examination of the psychometric properties of the CEAI provides the field with a more useful and valid empirical tool for conducting research within an important area of CE.

The CE literature has emphasized the need for favorable environmental conditions (Pinchot 1985) for CE, describing and explaining factors inside and outside organizations which influence and condition CE. Several aspects, such as organizational culture, structure, resources and management style, have been studied from many different angles. This might apply to any actors (entities) engaged in TH activities. Without a supportive organizational climate, CE will not reach its full potential. Also, an open communication system, which allows feedback on new ideas to occur quickly (Pinchot 1985), plays a significant role.

There is a large volume of published studies describing a wide diversity of outcomes associated with CE in the literature. However, three outcomes are believed to be the most salient: new businesses; new products, processes or services; and renewal of the existing organization. Sharma and Chrisman have conceptualized it as three relatively distinct aspects: innovation, corporate venturing (CV) and corporate renewal (CR), where innovation can become a basis for both CR and CV (Belousova and Gailly 2013). In this context, innovation stands for creating and introducing new products, production processes, and organizational systems (Zahra and Covin 1995), as well as services and administrative techniques, often with an emphasis on the development of technology (Antoncic and Hisrich 2003).

CE has recently been the center of management studies and attracts many scholars and managers, irrespective of the size of the organization. It can be beneficial and effect the revitalization and performance of firms. It is noteworthy that the terms "CE" and "intrapreneurship" are often used interchangeably, as entrepreneurial activity is connected to carrying out new combinations by introducing new products or processes, identifying new markets or sources of supply, or creating new types of organizations.

Some firms foster an organizational environment that is more entrepreneurially intense than others. Assessing an organization's entrepreneurial environment has been theorized and demonstrated to represent an important element for successfully implementing a CE strategy. With respect to Hornsby, research into organizational change efforts, such as the implementation of a CE strategy, requires an analysis of the current organizational environment or state of "organisational preparedness for CE" (Hayton et al. 2013).

The present research implies that future study of the relationships between organizational preparedness for corporate entrepreneurship (OPCE) and other relevant variables is likely to be a fruitful line of scholarly inquiry, whether in terms of the antecedents to, consequences of, or organizational mechanisms through which OPCE is enacted (Hornsby et al. 2013). Also, the strategic vision of a company or organization is significant. It should be developed and communicated by top managers to ensure innovation. Given the strength of convergence between aspects of the OPCE, such as top management support and EO, Hornsby claims, that "future research should examine the influence of entrepreneurial vision as a driving aspect of OPCE at multiple levels within the firm to better understand when, where, and how this vision is adopted, communicated, and enacted by organizational members given that firms often manifest their entrepreneurial beliefs and behaviors in varied and heterogeneous manners" (Wales et al. 2011).

"In terms of future investigations into potential causally adjacent outcomes of OPCE, as discussed, theory suggests that OPCE should be significantly related to an organization's EO with its analysis of the organization's orientation toward risk-taking, innovative, and proactive firm-level behaviors. This study found positive results for the convergent validity of the CEAI factors with EO; in which EO in turn, leads to a more entrepreneurially supportive organizational environment" (Covin and Slevin 1991). Moreover, future research could provide greater insight into the potential complexities in the interrelationship between organizational preparedness and orientation. Research investigating the path of causality between OPCE and firm performance will be preceded by research investigating relationships between preparedness and orientation and outcomes (i.e., Lumpkin and Dess 1996). These outcomes can be objective measures, such as profitability, earnings per share, innovations; and subjective measures, such as employees' satisfaction and commitment to the organization or the organization's learning and memory orientations. According to Hornsby, only by exploring this relationship will a "more proficient implementation of CE strategies be enabled" (Hayton et al. 2013).

2.6 Triple Helix as a Key to Improving Conditions for Innovation

As mentioned previously, the interaction between tripartite parties directly influences the manner in which the economy innovates. It might have a direct impact on societal change and the environment as well. Both how the government interacts and the visible shift in society from its governmental role to governance requires more attention. There is no single source of power which exists without the government. The idea of governance networks or policy networks strengthens this interaction and is closely related to the TH concept. In line with Börzel (1998), governance networks or policy networks can be defined as "a set of relatively stable relationships which are of non-hierarchical and interdependent nature linking a variety of actors, who share common interests with regard to a policy and who exchange resources to pursue these shared interests acknowledging that co-operation is the best way to achieve common goals" (Börzel 1998). It is notable that any of these actors who belong to any part of the network share common goals or objectives, but they often might have separate interests. A certain degree of trust is needed to cooperate. A reflection on hierarchies is needed also, but it will not be discussed in this chapter.

With respect to Etzkowitz (2013), "innovation is increasingly based upon a 'Triple Helix' of university-industry-government interactions. The increased importance of knowledge and the role of the university in incubation of technology-based firms has given it a more prominent place in the institutional firmament. The entrepreneurial university takes a proactive stance in putting knowledge to use and in broadening the input into the creation of academic knowledge. Thus it operates according to an interactive rather than a linear model of innovation. As firms raise their technological level, they move closer to an academic model, engaging in higher levels of training and in sharing of knowledge. Government acts as a public entrepreneur and venture capitalist in addition to its traditional regulatory role in setting the rules of the game. Moving beyond product development, innovation then becomes an endogenous process of 'taking the role of the other', encouraging hybridization among the institutional spheres" (Ranga and Etzkowitz 2013).

Bressers (2012) points out that "governance networks often include cooperation between government and business, but can also include other parties such as: knowledge actors, citizens, non-governmental organizations and other interest groups. The governance network therefore has the potential to become a Triple Helix organization. Another form of multi-actor cooperation is the public private partnership (PPP). Although quite similar in essence to the idea of the Triple Helix, there are some significant differences" (Bressers 2012). Due to the limited number of pages, they are not discussed here.

2.7 Hanze UAS as a Hub of Theory and Knowledge Integration

Hanze University of Applied Sciences in Groningen (UAS), with its leading strategic themes of energy and healthy ageing and key focus areas on entrepreneurship and excellence, plays an important role in the development of the TH concept. All of the six established Centres of Applied Research and Innovation are engaged currently in several multidisciplinary collaborations between education and business. They are of great value to the innovation capability of the industry in the North of the Netherlands and beyond.

Additionally, more than 30 different professorships in, for example, Allied Health Care and Ageing, Asian Business Strategies, Communication & the Sustainable Society, Demographic Change, Directing entrepreneurial networks,

Energy and many more (Hanze Research Portal 2014), enable a broad spectrum of activities.

By working on innovative and current issues, Hanze UAS is trying to find solutions together with external partners. It underlines a positive attitude of the school towards being engaged in TH activities as well. Both "applied research and innovation are integrated into the various curricula and play an important role in linking education with the working field" (Hanze Research Portal 2014).

It is worthy to mention that "the interaction between the social issues of today and the spatial choices caused by these issues are very much in the focus. Noorderruimte, Centre of Applied Research and Innovation on Area Development, develops and shares expertise about area development in the north of the Netherlands by carrying out applied research based on real-life issues. Some examples of this are integrated solutions for recreation purposes, water storage and nature development, sustainable, energy-efficient renovations in community centres and innovative housing concepts that meet future needs that fit the demands and needs of tomorrow" (Hanze Research Portal 2014).

A close cooperation with Noorderlink, which is a collaboration of several major companies and organizations in the field of HRM (Human Resource Management) and HRD (Human Resource Development), requires more attention as well. "The participating organizations all have their own personnel policy and have a complete P&O department. They also have at least 1000 employees and are located in the North of the Netherlands. Noorderlink strives to maintain a well-balanced mixture between profit and non-profit organizations" (Noorderlink 2014). Its strategic goals are:

- Exchange of knowledge, expertise, and best practices.
- Putting in motion and increasing the employability of staff of the organizations collaborating in Noorderlink.
- Positively profiling the North as an attractive place to work and live.
- To be involved in regional social events (Noorderlink 2014).

Interconnections between academia and industry, through contract research, licensing, start-ups, creating space for companies, government support collaboration (in the form of Research & Development vouchers, academic-industry grants, entrepreneurship programmes, start-up support or building technology-innovation parks), enables the development of talent which is the lifeblood of every organization in Asia. It underlines also the value of talent in the Northern Netherlands. Many AMNC try to acquire highly talented and skilled employees. The latest data written by the Economist Intelligence Unit and published by Heidrick & Struggles, place the Netherlands at the tenth position in The Global Talent Index Report which increases the chance of investment by AMNC in the Netherlands (The Global Talent Index Report: The Outlook to 2015, 2012). With respect to that statement, Noorderlink, together with Hanze UAS, has a great chance to attract potential investors and companies willing to start businesses in this region. It could be seen as a remaining gap to be filled.

In summary, Hanze UAS should start a cooperation with the Asia Triple Helix Society (ATHS) which has been established to initiate and developed research projects that adopt TH and WSI (webometrics, scientometrics, and informetrics) approaches in Asia by engaging researchers, academia, industry, and government. ATHS is an official representative body of the International Triple Helix Association (ITHA) and uses the TH model developed by Etzkowitz and Leydesdorff (2000) which favors the creation and distribution of knowledge through inter-sector collaboration among universities, industry, and the governmental sector (Asia Triple Helix Society 2014).

3 Triple Helix and East Asia: Understanding and Application

The Triple Helix is a concept well known, understood and applied by several AMNC. Perhaps without finding common objectives of TH model and realizing an innovative environment, AMNC would not have such a good position as they currently possess on the global market. Several forecasts say that Asia will soon be carrying more weight in the world than at any time since 1750. Additionally, it is predicted that by 2030 "Asia will have surpassed North America and Europe combined in terms of global power, based upon GDP, population size, military spending and technological investment" (The Economist 2014b). Respectively, TH should be seen as a core concept, influencing the way how Asian businesses operate, helping them to acquire new markets and gain the leading position, as it might apply to any level of cooperation or an economic growth.

In these terms, Asia is more integrated than ever before. "Some 54 % of the continent's trade is within the region, up from about 25 % in 1990. Japan, Taiwan and South Korea are in a tight embrace with poorer China. Dense supply chains link multinational firms with China's factories. Bits of Thailand, Malaysia and Vietnam, too, are becoming part of this giant industrial cluster known as "Factory Asia". India and Indonesia hope to join in. The rise of the renminbi [the official currency of the People's Republic of China – note by author] as a world currency will also help integrate the continent" (The Economist 2014b). The future is bright for AMNC, including several companies analyzed in this chapter. Undeniably, interactions in the tripartite cooperation occurring in a TH framework improves conditions for innovation and enables those companies to occupy top positions among the biggest companies, including Alibaba, Samsung Electronics, PetroChina, Tata Consultancy and Toyota.

The Economist emphasizes, that "Asia now accounts for 27 % of world market capitalization, up from 20 % a decade ago. The biggest Asian firms easily match their global counterparts for size. Big South Korean conglomerates such as LG, Samsung and Hyundai have global scale, and Samsung's profits are not far off Apple's. Toyota and Volkswagen have almost identical sales. PetroChina invests more than Exxon Mobil does. India has produced a clutch of world-class firms in technology and pharmaceuticals, and its crusty conglomerates have been revived. Asia's technology firms make up about 12 % of the listed sector, double the figure in 1994. Property firms have faded. Chinese state-backed, private and collectively-owned firms have created a massive wave of listings. Since 2000, Asia has had 11,000 initial public offerings and now boasts 25,000 listed firms" (The Economist 2014b). All of those actions taken are probably the outcome of adequately integrated TH activities among all of the actors (entities) engaged in economic growth and regional development.

3.1 Accelerating Innovation Through Triple Helix Based on Asian Experience

According to the latest report published by The Economist, "Asian firms are adapting to a demanding environment and becoming stronger. In response to rising wages, production (of clothes, for example) is shifting from China to South-East Asia and Africa, led by Japanese firms which are also worried about a war with the Middle Kingdom. Chinese firms such as Haier, which makes fridges, plan to automate factories and get into cleverer products. And as the Chinese push upmarket, the South Koreans are redoubling efforts to stay ahead. Samsung's spending on R&D rose by 24 % in 2013. If they get their act together, India and Indonesia, Asia's bumbling giants, will attract lots of factory jobs. Their best firms are also getting brainier. Once dismissed as "body shops", India's IT-outsourcing firms are now leaders in big data.

Rising consumer aspirations are helping internet firms disrupt traditional industries. Alibaba, a Chinese internet giant, is expanding into banking, telecoms, and logistics. Analysts think it might be worth $150 billion, more than China's steel industry. China's drive to reform its state-owned firms is meant to make them more responsive to customers. Xi Guohua, the boss of China Mobile, plans to give shares to his staff. Across Asia, demand for health care is likely to create a whole new generation of companies; the industry comprises only 4 % of the region's stockmarket, compared with 12 % in the Western world.

In order to challenge foreign rivals, Asian firms are globalizing, following the example of Samsung and Toyota. Lenovo, a thriving Chinese computer firm, has Western-style governance and many foreign staff. Huawei has overtaken Ericsson in telecom equipment. India's Sun Pharma is now one of the world's largest generic-drug firms. Tencent, China's Facebook, has hired the footballer Lionel Messi to advertise its services abroad. Sprawling business houses are evolving into focused multinationals. Tata Sons is now a superb IT firm and luxury-car maker tied to a ragbag of Indian assets" (The Economist 2014a).

According to Ranga and Etkowitz, "recent decades have seen a shift from an earlier focus on innovation sources confined to a single institutional sphere, whether product development in industry, policy-making in government or the creation and dissemination of knowledge in academia, to the interaction among these three spheres as the source of new innovative organizational designs and social interactions. This shift entails not only various mechanisms of institutional restructuring of the sources and development path of innovation, but also a

Table 2 Triple Helix System and its influence on innovation (Ranga and Etzkowitz 2013)

Triple Helix System	Influences on innovation process

Components	Consisting of the institutional spheres of university, industry and government, each with a wide array of actors, among whom a distinction is made between:
	    individual and institutional innovators
	    R&D and non-R&D innovators
	    "single-sphere" and "multi-sphere" (hybrid) institutions

Relationships between components	Technology transfer, collaboration and conflict moderation, collaborative leadership, substitution, and networking
Functions	In the sense of competencies of system components that determine the system's performance. The main function of a THS is seen in a broader sense, that of generation, diffusion, and utilization of knowledge and innovation. This function is realized not only with the techno-economic competencies described in innovation system theory, but also with entrepreneurial, societal, cultural, and policy competencies that are embedded in what we call the "Triple Helix spaces": the knowledge, innovation, and consensus spaces

rethinking of our main models for conceptualizing innovation, including innovation systems (national, regional, sectoral, technological, etc.) and the TH. Authors introduce TH systems as a novel analytical concept that systematizes the key features of university-industry-government interactions, so far loosely address as a 'metaphor' or a 'framework', into an 'innovation system' format that highlights the key new sources of novelty and the dynamics of their interaction" (Ranga and Etzkowitz 2013). Thus, Triple Helix Systems are defined as a set of components, the relationship between them, and their functions. They are briefly explained in Table 2.

The Triple Helix System (THS) provides a fine-grained view of innovation actors and the relationships between them, in a vision of a dynamic, boundary-spanning and diachronic transition of knowledge flows within the system. The THS accommodates both institutional and individual roles in innovation and explains variations in innovative performance in relation to the development of and articulation between the knowledge, innovation, and consensus spaces. Transcending sectoral or technology boundaries, TH systems emphasize boundary permeability among the institutional spheres as an important source of organizational creativity, allowing individuals to move within and between the spheres and engage in recombination of elements to create new types of organizations. Empirical guidelines for policy makers, universities, and business managers can be derived from this analytical framework in order to strengthen collaboration among TH actors and enhance regional development (Ranga and Etzkowitz 2013). Asian experience and involvement, respectively, in that area should be carefully considered, analyzed, and applied.

3.2 Triple Helix and Its Influence on Business Performance in Asia

As mentioned earlier, any activity integrated into the TH system is essential for business performance, which refers to interactions signed between companies, universities, and academia. Through them, actors (entities) share, produce, and disseminate knowledge, technologies, and innovations. In this context, the TH model predicts that the future economic growth is dependent not only on a new innovation cycle, but of a new innovation structure that links basic and applied research in an increasingly closer manner. In a knowledge-based society, university, industry, and government have equal roles and form a TH to stimulate innovation. According to Etzkowitz, "interaction among university, industry and government is the source of the origination and/or the development of incubator movements, interdisciplinary research centres and venture capital, whether private, public or social. These organizational innovations are as important to the flow of innovation as technological advances" (Etzkowitz et al. 2007). The growing popularity of such interactions across the world, including in the Netherlands, can be explained by the fact that they show a new way of consensus-building, which can enable self-development and secure sustainability of a particular region.

From the analysis of several cases of AMNC, which obtain substantial revenues and profits from international markets, and with reference to numerous Asian milestones and highlights (including those presented in the Appendix of this chapter), it can be concluded that the AMNC's imply strategies to support the quest for growth, offer rare insights about the strategies of outbound investment from companies based in Asia and provide an in-depth perspective on decision-making for companies from both mature and rapid-growth markets. The way these strategies are implied has a great impact on predicted trade flows among individual Asian markets and between Asia and the rest of the world, including the Northern Netherlands region.

4 Triple Helix in the Netherlands: Best Practices

The Netherlands, being a part of the European Union, uses "supra-national level of government which provides an additional coordination mechanism and incentive for organising technological innovation and social transformation. Furthermore, the Netherlands has been a centre of trade and knowledge reproduction for centuries" (Park et al. 2005). Its industrial base is relatively weak in comparison to its European partners.

In 2011, the Dutch government identified nine top sectors which they plan to strengthen with the help of Dutch businesses, education, and research. Approximately 1.5 billion € has been made available to support this. Apart from targeted investments, the government is also focused on identifying and solving bottle-necks impeding the growth of these sectors, such as bothersome rules or lack of qualified personnel. The nine top sectors are: High Tech Material & Systems, Agro-Food,

Water, Energy, Horticulture, Chemicals, Creative Industries, Logistics, and Life Sciences (Volkskrant 2011).

Each sector has its own challenges and opportunities. For example, the port of Rotterdam and Schiphol airport are both working hard to stay ahead of other ports and airports competing in the global logistics sector. Businesses in the creative industry excel in designing and producing art, music, buildings, and games. But, there is unexplored potential in marketing these products. The food and horticulture sectors aim to expand their international positions. The energy sector sees opportunities in the development of renewable energy sources (Government of the Netherlands 2014). Knowledge must be converted into new products and services faster. This can be achieved if businesses, the government, and knowledge institutes step up cooperation by bundling specialist research, for example. For this there are plenty of opportunities. Institutes like the NWO (the Netherlands Organisation for Scientific Research), KNAW (the Royal Netherlands Academy of Arts and Sciences), TNO (Netherlands Organisation for Applied Scientific Research) and the large technology institutes are adjusting their programmes to the top sectors. NWO approves research proposals based on scientific criteria and assigns resources to the various plans in collaboration with the top teams (Government of the Netherlands 2014).

Today, "the Netherlands remains a major player in the global Life Sciences Health industries, one of the core sectors listed above. The Netherlands occupies a strong technological position in molecular imaging, medical informatics, biopharmaceuticals, human and veterinary vaccines, regenerative medicine and biomaterials (biomaterial coatings in medical devices), medical technology, and health infrastructure. The Dutch sector owes this position to collaboration, cooperation, and coalition building between businesses, research institutes, and universities, supported by government, linking research to product and business creation (Holland Trade 2014). With approximately 400 innovative life sciences companies within a 120 mile radius, the Netherlands is the most concentrated region in the world when it comes to creating economic and social value in Life Sciences and Health. Approximately 400 companies are active in R&D activities in the life sciences & health branch, employing 25,000 people. Their turnover is 18 billion € a year. In the wider branch, about 3800 organizations are active, comprising hospitals, production facilities, and wholesalers, together employing a further 98,000 people and generating an annual turnover of 54 billion Euro" (Holland Trade 2014).

In line with Leydesdorff, in various countries the Triple Helix concept has also been used as an operational strategy for regional development and to further the knowledge-based economy. It has also become a "movement" for generating incubators in the university context (Leydesdorff 2012).

Noteworthy, benchmarking of a great practice developed by Utrecht University is advised for Hanze UAS as well. In 2012, Utrecht University, together with the Delft University of Technology, AkzoNobel, and MCKinsey & Company, launched the Netherlands-Asia Honors Summer School. This TH program is funded and organized by a unique public-private partnership between all 13 Dutch research universities, 16 Dutch companies and 4 government ministries. The partners acknowledge Asia's increasing importance and the urgency to introduce the younger Dutch generation to the dynamics of Asia and the opportunities that the continent presents to the Netherlands. The Program offers excellent students from all Dutch research universities the opportunity to attend a summer school in Asia and to experience Asia's society, culture, academia and business (Utrecht University 2014). A profounder look into this experience will allow Hanze UAS to get more connected and strengthen interactivity among actors (entities) engaged. Due to the limited number of pages, this program is not discussed further in this chapter.

In line with abovementioned approaches and definitions, two cases from the Netherlands, which are related both to TH and CE, are presented to demonstrate possible approaches for researching the success of networks of TH organizations. It creates several possibilities for knowledge transfer for some companies, educational institutes, and government in the Northern Netherlands.

4.1 Brainport: An Innovative Global Player

"Brainport Eindhoven Region is a powerful innovative player in a European and global context. It accounts for a third of all Dutch private R&D expenditure, invests 8 % of the GDP on R&D and is one of Europe's top three regions in terms of patent density. The economic success of Brainport Eindhoven Region is the result of a unique cooperation among industry, research, and government. This Triple Helix cooperation generates a very conducive climate for business, for both internationally-renowned companies and innovative small and medium-sized enterprises in the region. These companies cooperate with each other and with knowledge institutes by sharing and multiplying knowledge in an open innovation environment before bringing their products to market.

Brainport Development is the new style development agency of the Brainport foundation. The task of the organization is to drive the region forward and make the economy of the region "future proof". The High Tech Systems & Materials industries are strongly represented in Brainport, with internationally operating top technology companies such as Philips, ASML and FEI Company. The Southeast Netherlands is the third export region of the Netherlands with regard to food production and processing. A large part of the Dutch automotive industry is concentrated in Brainport. It has grown considerably in recent years and now encompasses over 40,000 jobs.

An extensive network of companies in Brainport is active in "lifetec", the collective term for "medical technology and life sciences". The Eindhoven University of Technology invests much research capacity in biomedical and medical technology. This multidisciplinary research is conducted in collaboration with industry and medical institutions in the region.

Design has been in the DNA of the Eindhoven region for decades. Thanks to its industrial and technological background, Eindhoven has developed into a city of innovation and creativity, a fact that is acknowledged by the numerous innovative products invented, developed, and manufactured in Brainport.

TMC is a proud partner of Brainport Eindhoven and active in many of its initiatives. On top of this there are many links among the constituent companies and institutions. And again: TMC is a stimulator and motivator (TMC 2014). Brainport Eindhoven Region is the axis of a network that extends throughout the Southeast Netherlands and beyond the national borders" (Brainport Monitor 2012).

4.2 Transumo: A Successful Program on Sustainable Mobility

Transumo, a TH organization, was a Dutch program on sustainable mobility, which ran from 2004 until 2010. The program was financed for 30 million € (over 40 million USD at October 2011 exchange rates) by the Dutch national government, with money from natural gas revenues. These revenues were dedicated to the improvement of Dutch infrastructure, both the physical infrastructure and the knowledge infrastructure. The latter was the reason for financing Transumo, as the program aimed to develop knowledge and stimulate innovation on sustainable mobility. Transumo was part of a package of 37 programs for knowledge and innovation development (together accounting for 800 million € in governmental subsidies), each on a separate topic. These topics varied from nanotechnology and biotechnology to less technology-oriented matters, such as the abovementioned sustainable mobility, but also innovative water management or sustainable construction and agriculture. Aside from the 30 million € in subsidized financing, the actors who participated in the program together contributed another 30 million € (through a so-called co-financing structure). This created additional pressure on the importance of the Triple helix, as participation was not without liability. Because the national government financed at least half of the program through the subsidy arrangement, it was the core principal of the program. The core mission of Transumo was to accelerate/encourage the transition to sustainable mobility. This will be achieved by initiating, and establishing for the long term, a transition process that leads to the replacement of the current, supply-driven, mono-disciplinary technology and knowledge infrastructure, with a demand-driven, multidisciplinary and trans-disciplinary, participative knowledge infrastructure (Transumo 2009).

In order to do this, Transumo sent out several calls for project acquisition, resulting ultimately in more than 30 projects. Aside from projects, Transumo undertook several program-wide activities, such as seminars, workshops, and knowledge contribution to education programs. The projects and program-wide activities resulted in the participation of more than 150 organizations as consortium partners, mostly stemming directly from the TH. The Transumo case leads to the conclusion that the TH is highly vulnerable to the degree to which the sector around it is accustomed to change and innovation (Bressers 2012).

5   Conclusions and Recommendations

The Triple Helix concept requires more attention and becomes increasingly important for the regional development and economic growth. The Northern Netherlands region can profit from all of the interactions among actors (entities) engaged in TH activities. The TH postulates that interactions within the tripartite cooperation is the key to improving conditions for innovation in a knowledge-based society, and for the creation of investment possibilities for Asian multinationals in this particular region. The significance of exploring the TH framework underlined in this paper influences directly the decision-making process and might contribute directly to the Northern Netherlands region and its development. An appropriate collaboration between all of the actors engaged in TH activities might lead to added value through the adoption and exploitation of ideas which are incorporated in the mutual partnership, creating an additional support base. It can stimulate innovation and improve results, such as producing more innovative products, processes, or solutions.

Finding the match between all of the different interests of stakeholders requires supplementary effort, and now and then might be risky as well. For instance, once business is interested in making money at high rates of return, government might be bound by laws and procedures to avoid high rates of return and the favoring of particular businesses. This is a problem that TH organizations also face: with diverging interests and objectives tensions may arise between the helices (spheres). Only a smooth cooperation of all of the areas will allow the successful integration of the TH and reach the desired level of innovation; realized in an innovative environment which should be simultaneously supported by the local or national government, consisting of tri-lateral initiatives. There is much more involved in those tri-lateral initiatives, not only university spin-off firms, strategic alliances among firms, government laboratories or academic research groups.

Unquestionably, looking at the successful strategies used and applied by AMNC (partially analyzed in this chapter), TH is a starting point for a knowledge-based economy. The Northern Netherlands region, through a proper implementation of interactions between government, industry, and university, can enhance the investment possibility for AMNC willing to establish their business in this region. The region should place more emphasis on the possibility of accommodating them and present prospective talent available in this part of the Netherlands.

A successful cooperation, in a TH framework, is possible not only in the nine core areas identified by the Dutch government, but also in several other directions, including those on which AMNC are focused. The Northern Netherlands region should undertake action to present the power and breadth of the network among government, industry, and academia, which is perceived as an integrated part of TH activities. Hanze UAS and Noorderlink belong to these activities.

An emphasis on dynamics, learning, and interaction should be made. Thus, an investigation of TH interconnections should include its core characteristics and be applied by the participating actors as well. Only in this case can the complex interplay of diverging actors, with many differing interests, perceptions, and beliefs, be created. With the increased importance placed on TH, academia should broaden its interactions with industry and government. Successful and effective inter-linkage between those actors will enable the transition of research discoveries and innovation from the laboratories or class rooms to the marketplace. With greater understanding of corporate entrepreneurship (CE), which mainly relates to a corporate management style that integrates risk-taking and innovation approaches as well as the reward and motivational techniques, enhancement of innovation and the creation of a pro-entrepreneurship organizational architecture is possible. Creating favorable environmental conditions, as has been proven in several Dutch cases, and use of the measurement tools of CE, mentioned in this article, might encourage AMNC to invest in the Northern Netherlands region. Without this, recommendations for the Northern Netherlands development as a part of TH concept lose their relevance.

Appendix

Asia Highlights
- Rapid-growth markets from Asia represent the fastest-growing economic region in the world, with an annual growth forecast at more than 6 % a year.
- The IMF expects advanced economies to grow by just 1.4 % in 2012 and 2 % in 2013. The corresponding figure for East and Southeast Asia in 2013 is 7.9 %.
- Since 2000, Asia has been the fastest-growing source of foreign direct investment (FDI). Its businesses currently produce a quarter of the world's exports (US$3.77 trillion in 2010) and form 87 of the Fortune Global 500 largest firms.
- FDI outflows from East and Southeast Asia recorded a compound annual growth rate of 22.9 % in 2005–2011, jumping from US$70 billion to US$242 billion.
- Investors from East and Southeast Asia are major drivers of growth in global foreign direct investment (FDI) outflows, making up 16 % of the world's total FDI (up from just 7 % in 2005) and driven by increased outflows from mainland China, Hong Kong (SAR), Malaysia, South Korea, Singapore and Taiwan.
- Intra-regional trade is expanding rapidly, reflecting the shift towards higher consumption in Asia. China leads the way in terms of outflows and destination, with growth for Indonesia, South Korea, Thailand and Vietnam close behind.
- Trade flows from Asia to the US and Canada, the Middle East, Latin America and Africa are expected to increase by over 10 % a year up to 2020.
- Cross-border M&A purchases are consuming an ever-larger slice of FDI flows, with purchases from Asia reaching a record US$94 billion in 2010.
- The China-US trade route is forecast to see the biggest increase in the world, predicted to rise by almost US$700 billion by 2020.

(Ernst and Young 2012)

Notes

Case studies, presented as best practices of the Triple Helix System in the Netherlands, have been limited only to a brief description. For more details, please contact the engaged institutions directly.

References

Antoncic, B., & Hisrich, R. D. (2003). Clarifying intrapreneurship concept. *Journal of Small Business and Enterprise Development, 10*(1), 7–24.
Asia Triple Helix Society. (2014). *Vitalising research on university-industry-government relations and WSI in Asian countries*. Retrieved June 18, 2014, from http://www.asia-triplehelix.org.
Belousova, O., & Gailly, B. (2013). Corporate entrepreneurship in a dispersed setting: Actors, behaviors, and process. *International Entrepreneurship and Management Journal, 9*(3), 361–377.
Börzel, T. A. (1998). Organizing Babylon – On the different conceptions of policy networks. *Public Administration, 76*(2), 253–273.
Brainport Monitor. (2012). *Summary, Power the smartest*. Retrieved April 12, 2014, from http://www.brainport.nl.
Bressers, N. (2012). The triple helix organisation in practice: Assessment of the triple helix in a Dutch sustainable mobility program. *Science & Public Policy, 39*(5), 669–679.
Corbett, A., Covin, J. G., O'Connor, G. C., & Tucci, C. L. (2013). Corporate entrepreneurship: State-of-the-art research and a future research agenda. *Journal of Product Innovation Management, 30*(5), 812–820.
Covin, J. G., & Miles, M. P. (1999). Corporate entrepreneurship and the pursuit of competitive advantage. *Entrepreneurship Theory and Practice, 23*(3), 47–65.
Covin, J. G., & Slevin, D. P. (1989). Strategic management of small firms in hostile and benign environments. *Strategic Management Journal, 10*(1), 75–87.
Covin, J. G., & Slevin, D. P. (1991). A conceptual model of entrepreneurship as firm behavior. *Entrepreneurship Theory and Practice, 16*, 7–25.
Davidsson, P. (2004). *Researching entrepreneurship*. New York, NY: Springer.
Dess, G., Lumpkin, G. T., & McGee, J. E. (1999). Linking corporate entrepreneurship to strategy, structure, and process. *Entrepreneurship Theory and Practice, 23*, 85–102.
Ernst & Young. (2012). *Beyond Asia: Strategies to support the quest for growth. South Korea Highlights. Facts on Asia', originally published by UNCTAD, IMF, Oxford Economics*. Retrieved June 23, 2014, from http://www.ey.com.
Etzkowitz, H. (2003). Innovation in innovation: The triple helix of university-industry-government relations. *Social Science Information, 42*, 293–337.
Etzkowitz, H., & Klofsten, M. (2005). The innovating region: Toward a theory of knowledge-based regional development. *R&D Management, 35*(3), 243–255.
Etzkowitz, H., & Leydesdorff, L. (2000). The dynamics of innovation: From national systems and 'Mode 2' to a Triple Helix of university-industry-government relations. *Research Policy, 29*(2), 109–123.
Etzkowitz, H., Ranga, M., Dzisah, J., & Zhou, C. (2007). University-industry-government interaction: the Triple Helix Model of innovation. *Asia Pacific Tech Monitor, 24*(1), 14–23.
Fogelberg, H., & Thorpenberg, S. (2012). Regional innovation policy and public-private partnership: The case of Triple Helix Arenas in Western Sweden. *Science and Public Policy, 39*, 347–356.
Frederick, H., & Kuratko, D. F. (2010). *Entrepreneurship: Theory, process, practice*. South Melbourne, VIC: Cengage Learning Australia.
Government of the Netherlands. (2014). *Investing in top sectors*. Retrieved May 15, 2014, from http://www.government.nl.

Hanze Research Portal. (2014). *Professorships*. Retrieved May 23, 2014, from www.hanze.nl.
Hayton, J., Hornsby, J., & Bloodgood, J. (2013). Part II: The contribution of HRM to corporate entrepreneurship: A review and agenda for future research. *Management, 16*(4), 381–409.
Holland Trade. (2014). *The triple helix in Dutch Life Sciences Health*. Retrieved February 18, 2014, from http://www.hollandtrade.com.
Hornsby, J. S., Kuratko, D. F., Holt, D. T., & Wales, W. Y. (2013). Assessing a measurement of organizational. *Journal of Product Innovation Management, 30*(5), 937–955.
Hornsby, J. S., Kuratko, D. F., & Zahra, S. A. (2002). Middle managers' perception of the internal environment for corporate entrepreneurship: assessing a measurement scale. *Journal of Business Venturing, 17*(3), 253–273.
Ireland, R., Covin, J., & Kuratko, D. (2009). Conceptualizing corporate entrepreneurship strategy. *Entrepreneurship: Theory & Practice, 33*(1), 19–46.
Kuratko, D. F., Montagno, R. V., & Hornsby, J. S. (1990). Developing an entrepreneurial assessment instrument for an effective corporate entrepreneurial environment. *Strategic Management Journal, 11*(Special Issue), 49–58.
Leydesdorff, L. (2012). *The Triple Helix of university-industry-government relations*. Retrieved May 15, 2014, from http://www.leydesdorff.net.
Leydesdorff, L., & Heimeriks, G. (2001). The self-organisation of the European Information Society: The case of 'biotechnology". *Journal of the American Society for Information Science & Technology, 52*(14), 1262–1274.
Lumpkin, G. T., & Dess, G. G. (1996). Clarifying the entrepreneurial orientation construct and linking it to performance. *Academy of Management Review, 21*(1), 135–172.
Lumpkin, G. T., & Dess, G. G. (2001). Linking two dimensions of entrepreneurial orientation to firm performance: The moderating role of environment and industry life cycle. *Journal of Business Venturing, 16*(5), 429–451.
Noorderlink. (2014). *About Noorderlink*. Retrieved May 10, 2014, from http://www.noorderlink.nl.
Park, H. W., Hong, H. D., & Leydesdorff, L. (2005). A comparison of the knowledge-based innovation systems in the economies of South Korea and The Netherlands. Using Triple Helix Indicators. *Scientometrics, 65*(1), 3–27.
Pinchot, G. (1985). *Intrapreneuring. 'Why you don't have to leave corporation to become an entrepreneur*. New York, NY: Harper & Row Publishers.
Pinchot, G., & Pellman, R. (1999). *Intrapreneuring in action. A handbook for business innovation*. San Francisco, CA: Berret-Köhler Publishers, Inc.
Pirich, A. (2001). *An interface between entrepreneurship and innovation: New Zealand SMEs perspective*. Paper prepared for the 2001 DRUID Conference, Aalborg, Denmark.
Ranga, M., & Etzkowitz, H. (2013). Triple helix systems: An analytical framework for innovation policy and practice in the knowledge society. *Industry and Higher Education, 27*(4), 48 p.
Sharma, P., & Chrisman, J. (1999). Toward a reconciliation of the definitional issues in the field of corporate entrepreneurship. *Entrepreneurship: Theory & Practice, 23*(3), 11–27.
The Economist. (2014a). A world to conquer, May 31st, 2014.
The Economist. (2014b). How to keep roaring? May 31st, 2014.
TMC. (2014). *Brainport Eindhoven Region*. Retrieved June 20, 2014, from http://www.tmcporch.com.
Transumo. (2009). *Transumo 2004–9*. Retrieved December 31, 2014, from http://www.transumo.nl.
Utrecht University. (2014). *Research Asia*. Retrieved June 20, 2014, from http://www.uu.nl.
Volkskrant. (2011). Negen kandidaten voor 1,5 mld subsidie, February 5th, 2011.
Wales, W., Monsen, E., & McKelvie, A. (2011). The organizational pervasiveness of entrepreneurial orientation. *Entrepreneurship Theory & Practice, 35*(5), 895–923.
Zahra, S. (1991). Predictors and financial outcomes of corporate entrepreneurship: An exploratory study. *Journal of Business Venturing, 6*, 259–285.
Zahra, S., & Covin, J. G. (1995). Contextual influences on the corporate entrepreneurship-performance relationship: A longitudinal analysis. *Journal of Business Venturing, 10*(1), 43–58.

Asian Human Resource Management and Intercultural Competence

Marcel H. van der Poel

Abstract
While intercultural competence is an emerging topic in international HRM, it is of less importance so far in Asian HRM. Meanwhile, Asian entrepreneurs do seem to act competently in cross-cultural environments. Where Western scholars have claimed that intercultural competence does not come naturally, the current success of Asian businesses non-Asian regions can be partly explained from the interculturally competent behavior of its international professionals. This behavior is related to intrinsic and authentic Asian values aimed at "unity" or "harmony". The Eastern mind-set is focused on relations prior to the tasks, and once a relationship has been established, the opportunities for collaboration will arise. By adhering to the principles of ancient philosophies, Asian entrepreneurs have pragmatically resolved conflicts of interest. This seems to reverse Allport's contact hypothesis that a shared goal and intergroup collaboration is required for improvement of the understanding of the other. What we witness is that once the technological and informational hurdles have been taken, adherence to authentic Asian behavioral guidelines forms a good starting point for effective international business.

1 Introduction

Successful multinational enterprises (MNE's) in the global marketplace—including Asian ones—need to rely increasingly on one of the key products of contemporary international human resource management (IHRM): the global professional. The global professional is unlike the expatriate manager. Where the expat manager transfers knowledge and values (mostly one-dimensional), the global professional

---

M.H. van der Poel (✉)
International Business School, Hanze University OAS, Groningen, The Netherlands
e-mail: m.h.van.der.poel@pl.hanze.nl

creates new knowledge and meaning, carefully balancing local responsiveness with global integration and standardization. The global professional is the one coordinating and integrating the relevant corporate activities and human resources into a worldwide network. The required behavior of the global professional resonates well with the characteristics of Asian business: pragmatic, and constantly aiming at a "best fit". The global professional is capability driven, like a member of quality circles, and is accepting complexity and interdependency, like a responsible member of a collective. The competencies of the global professional further encompass foreign language skills, ease with mobility, and a sound understanding of worldwide business (Adler 2008). Most importantly, the global professional is *interculturally* competent; he/she possesses the capability "to embody and enact intercultural sensitivity, can discriminate cultural differences and navigate these differences in communication across borders" (Bennett 2013). This chapter further explores the concept of intercultural competence and the relevance of it for successful International HRM, particularly in the Asian business expansion context.

2 Intercultural Competence (IC)

The field of intercultural studies knows many frameworks, models, and theories describing intercultural intelligence, intercultural sensitivity, intercultural communication, and intercultural competence—to name the most popular terms. Spitzberg and Changnon (2009) discussed about 20 theories and models, with the concept of intercultural competence largely traced back to the 1970s. The authors did not, however, conclude with a final definition of intercultural competence. They stated instead that the multiple theories and models "display both considerable similarity, [like] motivation, knowledge, skills, context, and outcomes, yet [also] extensive diversity at the level of specific conceptual subcomponents". What the authors found remarkable is the absence of psychological and emotional aspects, as if people only act rationally and cognitively when dealing with cultural differences. The authors further complained that adaptability is predominantly being treated as a personal trait while adaptability is by definition a *process of variability*. This makes it a puzzling "consistent predisposition to behave inconsistently". A final serious concern has been the potential ethnocentricity of the models, which is predominantly a concern regarding their bias toward Western individuality and prioritizing assertiveness skills. According to the authors, some scholars did find it remarkable that most models focus on the individual, and on individual traits, while practically all models assume interaction and would thus need to be relational. Based on contributions from scholars from the Asian region, for example, questions have been raised as to what extent the competencies are located in the interaction itself, rather than in the individual.

The latter resonates well with Bennett's (2013) discussion of a constructivist intercultural perspective when addressing the conceptual focus of various scholars in the field. According to him, the term intercultural refers "to a particular kind of interaction or communication among people, one in which differences in cultures play a role in the *creation of meaning*" (italics added). Hence the interculturality of behavior is a construct and can only be known from the interaction. The German scholar Rathje (2007), however, claimed that such clarity of the concept is "superficial". According to Rathje, proponents of such effectiveness criterion turn IC into an instrument, a means; IC apparently leads to the achievement of a goal (shared meaning, or understanding). Such an approach disregards the difference between competence and performance or "successful interaction", as much as it ignores, says Rathje, the fact that no group or culture can claim coherence. Instead, intercultural competence should be understood "as the ability to bring about normality and therefore cohesion". The existing internal differentiation within groups, or cultures, should lead to a concept of intercultural competence as a human capability to become familiar with the normality of differences rather than adaptation to an assumed coherent set of values and norms. The success of Asian business across borders may largely be based on Rathje's principle: not assuming coherence in values and norms, but solemnly focusing on the required familiarity with differences; hence "glue" rather than a "mould".

While acknowledging all the above, Deardorff's (2009) definition of intercultural competence "as effective and appropriate behavior and communication in intercultural situations" can be seen as relatively popular in the field. In this definition, appropriateness must be understood as the avoidance of violating valued rules, and effectiveness as the achievement of valued objectives. Comparably, Bennett (2008) defined intercultural competence as "a set of cognitive, affective, and behavioral skills and characteristics that support effective and appropriate interaction in a variety of cultural contexts". In both definitions the *combination* of effectiveness and appropriateness is being stressed, since one can be highly effective in a fully inappropriate manner, as well as very appropriate and not achieve anything. In this chapter, we will take behavioral effectiveness and appropriateness in multiple (cultural) contexts as our leading understanding of intercultural competence.

3 The Relevance of Intercultural Competence in International HRM

From the times of the Industrial Revolution, Human Resource Management has evolved from traditional personnel management, via HR practices based on the Human Relations School, into Strategic and International HRM today. Current HRM is rooted in socio-technical approaches (holistic, participatory, self-regulatory, and "TQM"), and is increasingly enriched with so-called complex adaptive systems approaches (dynamic, emergent, open process, self-reflective, self-renewal, and "changing while changing"). The recent developments take place—by definition—in global context: the demand to change while changing is driven by the demands from the outer world (global markets, global stakeholders, and global challenges, like access to rare earth minerals). According to Briscoe et al. (2012) comparative International HRM refers to the investigation of the diverse HRM policies and practices that exist across our countries and regions.

The comparison is mostly based on the *divergence* and *convergence* framework: to what extent do policies and practices need to be different, or can they be similar. For instance, can we use our Performance Management System, developed at our headquarters in the UK, for the assessment of our management in Vietnam? Not surprisingly, the "truth" often lies in the middle, and is sometimes referred to as crossvergence. With the shift to free and open market policies and practices, the Asian Region also needs to find answers to the above strategic questions. Connected to this, others have introduced an additional dimension of *hard* vs. *soft* divergence or convergence, claiming soft convergence as the most likely outcome of HRM transitions in the East (Warner 2000).

Rapid changes over the past decades in areas like education, technology, and communication have also had its impact on typical Asian business issues, including government ownership of enterprises, job security/lifetime employment, leadership and management styles, and labor legislation, to name a few. Typically emerging from this process in the Asian region is a hybrid, or "dual" HRM system. Regulated systems seem to go hand in hand with free market based policies and practices. Employment and promotion based on relationship and seniority is being applied along with merit- and performance-based systems. Dilemmas in Chinese MNC's between embracing international reward practices and maintaining close control over traditional reward practices are being resolved by simply doing both (Kramar and Seyd 2012).

What Asian HR is experiencing relates to what has been acknowledged in literature as a general lack of HR talent around the globe. The globally integrated market, and with that the globally integrated enterprise, is very different from the "regular" MNE. The vast global diversity of HR policies and practices, of labor legislation, of traditions and cultures, of corporate structures and operations, etc., has turned IHRM into a very complex and difficult functional field of expertise. The HR officer who oversees this complexity is very hard to find, leave alone finding one who can deal with it. Current HR expertise by definition is not comprehensive. Take employee relations as an example, who could possibly have an up-to-date overview of all the rights and benefits of workers across 100+ countries? HR managers at MNE's currently try to resolve such issues by contracting specialized expertise from centers of excellence or consultancy firms. Yet the access to information is not the key issue; the design and use of HR systems that can process the information in order to add value is.

The relevance of the *concept* of intercultural competence for International HRM is the focus on the capability of workers to enact appropriately and effectively in a variety of contexts without prior in-depth knowledge of each context. The relevance of the *outcome* of intercultural competence for International HRM is that interculturally competent workers are able to embrace complexity, ambiguity, and uncertainty as perfectly normal conditions for professional relations, and business success (Rathje 2007). In the past decades, IHRM would focus on the adjustment, adaptation, and performance of the expatriate worker. Preparation of expatriate workers would typically be a combination of a culture-specific "do's & don'ts" training, plus a language course. Global professionals, however, know that acquiring in-depth cultural knowledge will be unrealistic for the vast variety of cultures that they will be dealing with, as well as for the relatively superficial nature of most of their cross-cultural contacts. They know they are far better off with cultural (self-)awareness, and a mind-set that will enable them to shift perspectives whenever needed or helpful, irrespective which culture is at stake. In the "my way – your way" framework, global professionals know how and when to let go, when to compromise, and when to seek synergy (win-win). Global professionals know that their intercultural competence is rooted in the conviction that cultures are dynamic, and not a fixed set of norms and values: each interaction is a new opportunity to create new meaning.

Borrowing from language studies, the above move can be described as a change in attention from *emic* (culture-specific) to *etic* (culture-general) descriptions of cultural behaviors (Bennett 2013). The first is helpful in describing unique features, but the latter is indispensable for relevant comparison; global professionals understand the *mechanisms* of culture. Moving toward a more etic understanding of culture has also enabled important shifts in power and dominance. Where the expatriate manager had often been positioned to reconfirm corporate hierarchy and structure (mostly based on cultural dominance), the global professional is aware of the (moral) equality of various cultural approaches, of his or her interdependency, and of the need to make dominance subordinate to effective collaboration. Yet, how would one become a global professional?

4 Developing Intercultural Competence

For Bennett (2013), with reference to cognitive constructivism, the most basic theoretical concept underlying intercultural competence development has been that experience is being constructed, including cross-cultural experience. One can have an intercultural experience without noticing it, which will typically happen when people lack the required categories for constructing it as an intercultural experience. Why do these people in Vietnam not simply learn how our Performance Management System works! In a similar vein, Lou and Weber Bosley (2012), with reference to the constructivist scholars Berger and Luckmann (1966), wrote that if we do not expose ourselves to the new and the different, "the chances of *grasping the dialectics* [of humans being both creator and subject of reality] and how it impacts our thoughts, feelings, choices, behaviors, and so forth are indeed slim". People simply need to learn how perception constructs the reality that we see.

Directly connected is Bennett's (2004) notion of cognitive complexity: "more cognitively complex people can make finer discriminations among phenomena in a particular domain". Bennett makes this clear with the example of the wine connoisseur recognizing, and describing, more different wines than an average person. When our categories for cultural differences become more complex, our perceptions become more culturally sensitive. A greater intercultural sensitivity may result in greater intercultural competence since people are now equipped with an ability to take another perspective when communicating. The chance that it will happen increases when people gain the ability of creating alternative (cultural) experiences as compared to their own (mono-cultural) default experiences, often popularly referred to as an intercultural worldview or global mind-set. People will start doing this when pressure is building to develop greater competence in intercultural matters, for instance in dealing with multicultural teams or workforces that do not deliver. In brief, intercultural competence starts with the ability to construe other worldviews than one's default own, meaning the ability to embrace an increased cognitive complexity. In doing so, people acquire alternative worldviews as part of intercultural sensitivity, which again is an assumed requisite for effective *and* appropriate communication in various contexts.

Other scholars also have highlighted effectiveness and appropriateness as core behavioral components of intercultural interaction. For instance, Offermann and Phan (2002) wrote about cultural intelligence as the ability to function effectively in a diverse context where the assumptions, values, and traditions of one's upbringing are not uniformly shared with those with whom one needs to work. Effective responding will likely require as much understanding of self as of other. The authors see cultural intelligence as a meta-intelligence: as an ability to enact a variety of intelligences *outside the frame of reference in which they were developed*; "cultural intelligence is what allows us to transcend our cultural programming and function effectively in cross-cultural situations".

Still, how do people learn to become interculturally competent? There is serious doubt that being in a multicultural environment automatically will lead to intercultural learning. Rather, there are serious indications that it does not; "intercultural competence is not considered a naturally occurring phenomenon" (Vande Berg and Paige 2009). Bennett (2012) wrote: "increasing evidence shows that simple cross-cultural contact is not particularly valuable in itself". Offermann and Phan (2002) spoke about Pakistanis who, after a lifetime in Britain, still scored on power distance and uncertainty avoidance like Pakistanis in Pakistan.

Meanwhile, many professionals—also in the field of HR—still believe that frequent encounters with people from other cultural backgrounds will automatically lead to an increased intercultural sensitivity and to the desired competence for dealing with cultural diversity. Allport's (1954) contact hypothesis, or Intergroup Contact Theory (ICT), already refuted this popular belief. He postulated that increased exposure *only under certain conditions* would decrease prejudice and stereotypical thinking and improve the understanding of the other. The conditions include equality of group status, commonality in goals, and intergroup cooperation. Pettigrew and Tropp (2006) tested Allport's theory and found that Allport's conditions must be split into essential ones and facilitating ones, and must be seen as interrelated. Status difference, goals, and cooperation must not be observed independently but rather in their interrelatedness.

5 Intercultural Competence and Asian HRM

As can be read from the above, most of the concepts of intercultural competence, and of intercultural competence development, have a Western (Anglo-Saxon) origin. They have predominantly been designed and tested in Western countries and found to be (sufficiently) reliable. But are these concepts also valid outside the Western context? Or does application of these models in a non-Western corporate setting merely result in "corporate rain dancing" or complete ineffectiveness (Trompenaars and Woolliams 2009)? So, what is the relevance of intercultural competence for HR in an Asian context? How much of use is the awareness of the (moral) equality of various cultural approaches in a culture with a supposedly high power distance? How helpful is a conviction that cultures are dynamic in an environment where traditions are highly valued?

Part of the answer lies in acknowledging that the Asian cultures that we refer to are far more diverse and complex than the descriptions we normally find in our Western textbooks. The young, internet-savvy and entrepreneurial generations in many Asian countries are not seeking life-long employment but instead investing heavily in their personal employability by maintaining their personal skills. More in general, because of its reifying effects, it is high time we stop classifying cultures along the cultural dimensions that have been made popular by authors like Hofstede and Trompenaars. Asian cultures are no longer just collectivist.

Another part of the answer may lie in simply acknowledging that many Western descriptions of elements of intercultural competence have been known in other cultures—including many Asian cultures—for decades or even thousands of years, obviously articulated in its own authentic cultural context. Empathy enhancement and sensitivity cultivation are but two human practices (or virtues) that Chinese authors refer to for regulating and fostering human interaction, based on ancient Tai Chi principles (Chen and Starosta 2003). What in Western text is being portrayed as "dialectics" or "constructivist theory" (see above) has for a long time been understood in Chinese context as the dynamics of yin and yang: expressing the intrinsic interdependence and interdetermination of relations. In a similar vein, "Zhong dao" is known as appropriateness, or adjusting one's communication to the situation long before "we" connected cultural (self-) awareness or appropriateness to intercultural competence. Would it be too far-fetched to say that the Chinese "software of the mind" is by itself more equipped for the capabilities needed for intercultural interaction?

A third possible part of the answer could be that the assumed paradigmatic contradiction between East and West are being perceived as less contradicting, or as less insurmountable by Eastern people than they are by Western people. Or put differently, that the Asian mind-set is better equipped for reconciling what appears to be contradicting than a Western mind-set since it is better fitting with the general cultural trait of fostering harmony and balance (China), or with oneness and a divine consciousness (India). For the latter, even though a country, India has all the characteristics of a continent with its people conversant with navigating its vast varieties—pluralism within India is larger than in the whole of the EU. The very fabric of India is polycultural; a single Indian is holding many simultaneous identities, and many Indians have more in common with foreigners than with other Indians (Manian and Naidu 2009). Empathy and perspective-taking does not need to be taught; it is ingrained.

A fourth part of the answers relates to the impact of *virtual* cross-cultural interaction from the 90s onward. A survivor of the Tsunami in 2004 stated that what kept him alive on his 'raft' was thinking of his favorite soccer team, Manchester United. Apparently the status of a game played by multinationals in a foreign country can serve as an inspiration for life at the other side of the globe. Values like individual freedom are being embraced across generations, and across nations, increasingly based on examples sourced through the internet (e.g. the recent revolt in Thailand). Western concepts of Eastern cultures are all too often too romantic, or simply out of date. Why would interculturally competent behavior not fit Asian cultures? Where does such a question actually come from?

Yet the most likely answer to the question how intercultural competence relates to Asian HRM is that we do not really know, since there is hardly such a category as Asian HRM. Granted, authors have written about Asian HRM in comparison to Western HRM as more "collaborative" as opposed to "adversarial" (with South Korea as the exception). Yet, in Bangladesh and Vietnam, the introduction of modern HR principles and practices is being crippled by power and corruption with as a key focal point the (low) cost of labor. Taiwan was more or less forced to embrace Western (international) HRM practices due to a prolonged period of high unemployment and pressure from MNEs and FDIs. South Korea had accepted individual performance and competencies as the core principles for HR management in order to become more flexible and cope with international competition—and successfully so. Singapore has been among the early adaptors of performance- and merit-based systems, promoting life-long learning and institutionalizing modern HR techniques. Japan, however, remains relatively slow in modernizing its HR practices even with an economy and demography demanding quick transitions for years in a row. China has only just started moving from traditional personnel management toward international HRM (not denying other immense changes in personnel relations that did occur over the past decades), while the Asian financial crisis and the political handover in 1997 had fuelled a massive transition in HR policies and practices concerning retention and compensation of staff in Hong Kong (Warner 2000).

Still there are common denominators in Asian HRM. In multiple Asian countries, the corporate world is seeking access to the required talents and skills, and starts to acknowledge that when this cannot be sourced, it will need to be actively developed. Likewise many MNEs accept that they will need to break with more traditional systems of employment, retention, and compensation, and will need to find a way of integrating performance and merit systems into their development, compensation, and promotion strategies in order to become or remain competitive in the global marketplace. Producing the required business leadership potential freed from, yet respecting, local governmental ties is another challenging HR topic in various Asian economies.

6 Conclusion

The overall conclusion, however, should be that Asian entrepreneurs meanwhile apply interculturally competent behavior (since effective and sufficiently appropriate) without using any conceptualization of the concept—leave alone conceptualization in Western terminology. Also, while intercultural competence is an emerging topic in International HRM, it is not at all a topic (yet) in Asian HRM. Meanwhile, Asian entrepreneurs do seem to act competently in cross-cultural environments. Where Western scholars have claimed that intercultural competence does not come naturally, the current success of Asian businesses in other cultural environments can be partly explained from the interculturally competent behavior of its international professionals that stem from the intrinsic and authentic Asian values aimed at "oneness" or "harmony": by actively seeking connection with the other prior to action. The Eastern mind-set is focused on relations prior to the tasks, and in West and East alike once a relationship has been established, the opportunities for collaboration will arise. By adhering to the principles of ancient philosophies, Asian entrepreneurs have pragmatically resolved conflicts of interest. This general Asian behavioral trait seems to reverse Allport's contact hypothesis that a shared goal and intergroup collaboration is required for improvement of the understanding of the other. What we witness is that once the technological and informational hurdles have been taken, adherence to authentic Asian behavioral guidelines forms a good starting point for effective international business. Asian HR may embrace this as a key USP for Asian corporate development.

References

Adler, N. J. (2008). *International dimensions of organizational behavior* (5th ed.). Mason: South-Western.
Allport, G. W. (1954). *The nature of prejudice: Unabridged*. 25th anniversary ed. Reading: Addison-Wesly.
Bennett, M. J. (2004). Becoming interculturally competent. In J. Wurzel (Ed.), *Toward multiculturalism: A reader in multicultural education* (2nd ed., pp. 62–77). Newton: Intercultural Resource Corporation.
Bennett, M. J. (2008). Transformative training: Designing programs for culture learning. In M. A. Moodian (Ed.), *Contemporary leadership and intercultural competence: Understanding and utilizing cultural diversity to build successful organizations* (pp. 95–110). Thousand Oaks: Sage.
Bennett, M. J. (2012). Turning cross-cultural contact into intercultural training. Paper presented at the Universidad 2012, 8th international congress on higher education, Havana, Cuba.
Bennett, M. J. (2013). *Basic concepts of intercultural communication: Paradigms, principles & practices* (2nd ed.). Boston: Intercultural Press.
Berger, P. L., & Luckmann, T. (1966). *The social construction of realilty*. New York: Anchor Books.
Briscoe, D., Schuler, R., & Tarique, I. (2012). *International human resource management: Policies and practices for multinational enterprises* (4th ed.). New York: Routledge.
Chen, G. M., & Starosta, W. J. (2003). Asian approaches to human communication: A dialogue. *Intercultural Communication Studies, 12*(4), 1–15.

Deardorff, D. K. (Ed.). (2009). *The SAGE handbook of intercultural competence*. Thousand Oaks, CA: Sage.

Kramar, R., & Seyd, J. (2012). *Human resource management in a global context: A critical approach*. New York: Palgrave Macmillan.

Lou, K. H., & Weber Bosley, G. (2012). Facilitating intercultural learning abroad: The intentional targeted intervention model. In M. Vande Berg, R. M. Paige, & K. H. Lou (Eds.), *Student learning abroad: What our students are learning, what they're not, and what we can do about it* (pp. 335–359). Sterling: Stylus.

Manian, R., & Naidu, S. (2009). India: A cross-cultural overview of intercultural competence. In D. K. Deardorff (Ed.), *The SAGE handbook of intercultural competence* (pp. 233–248). Thousand Oaks: Sage.

Offermann, L. R., & Phan, L. U. (2002). Culturally intelligent leadership for a diverse world. In R. E. Riggio, S. E. Murphy, & F. J. Pirozzoio (Eds.), *Multiple intelligences and leadership* (pp. 187–214). Mahwah: Lawrence Erlbaum.

Pettigrew, T. F., & Tropp, L. R. (2006). The meta-analytic test of intergroup contact theory. *Journal of Personality and Social Psychology, 90*(5), 751–783.

Rathje, S. (2007). Intercultural competence: The status and future of a controversial concept. *Language and Intercultural Communication, 7*(4), 254–266.

Spitzberg, B. H., & Changnon, G. (2009). Conceptualizing intercultural competence. In D. K. Deardorff (Ed.), *The SAGE handbook of intercultural competence* (pp. 2–52). Thousand Oaks: Sage.

Trompenaars, F., & Woolliams, P. (2009). Toward a general framework of competence for today's global village. In D. K. Deardorff (Ed.), *The SAGE handbook of intercultural competence* (pp. 438–455). Thousand Oaks: Sage.

Vande Berg, M., & Paige, R. M. (2009). Applying theory and research: The evolution of intercultural competence in U.S. study abroad. In D. K. Deardorff (Ed.), *The SAGE handbook of intercultural competence* (pp. 419–437). Thousand Oaks: Sage.

Warner, M. (2000). Introduction: The Asian-Pacific HRM model revisited. *The International Journal of Human Resource Management, 11*(2), 171–182.

Branding Trends in Asian Markets

Diederich Bakker

Abstract

This chapter examines current branding trends in significant Asian markets, namely Japan, South Korea, and India, with a special focus on one emerging branding nation, China. No generalizations towards the whole of Asia can be drawn from this research. However, research identified some aspects in the field of branding that have occurred in different Asian markets at different times. For example, the development of branding as a management strategy followed benefit-driven product management in both Japan and South Korea some decades ago. This development can now be witnessed in selected industries in China. Whether or not other Asian nations show similar developments (e.g. Indonesia) would be a topic for further investigation. Nevertheless, the following four Asian branding trends serve as the main outcomes of this research: extending the corporate brand into new fields of business, extending the corporate brand into diverse product categories, acquisition of Western brands by Asian investors and top-management support in brand building.

1   Introduction

The concept of branding has become a proliferated management strategy throughout the world since boardroom managers have long understood the value that brands can bring to an organization (Kapferer 2012). However, it is particularly the Western world where the concept of branding has started and from which the domain draws its leading principles and early success stories. For example, the fast moving consumer goods multinational Procter & Gamble from the USA, owner of numerous branded products, is widely believed to have first successfully

---

D. Bakker (✉)
International Business School, Hanze University OAS, Groningen, The Netherlands
e-mail: d.j.o.p.bakker@pl.hanze.nl

implemented a brand management system that helped the company to build market-leading brands in most of the markets it competes (Aaker 2013). At the same time the academic discussion and theoretical foundation on branding has been US- and Euro-centric, originating from marketing scholars such as P. Kotler, D. Aaker, K.L. Keller, and J.N. Kapferer, among others (refer to the main publications by these authors: Aaker 2002; Kotler et al. 2002; Keller 2008 and Kapferer 2012). Nevertheless, building strong brands is a global phenomenon in the eye of many boardroom managers and owning them is the aspiration for many consumers of all backgrounds. For example, particularly in Asia, Western luxury brands are highly regarded and sought after by consumers. Although still an exception, there are cases of successful brands that have derived from Asia and made their mark on a global scale. Here, Japan can be considered one of the key markets with many successful global brands in the technology and automobile sector. More recently, an array of strong global brands in similar domains have come forward from South Korea with household names such as Samsung, LG, and Hyundai, just to name a few. Other successful Asian companies that rely strongly on branding principles throughout their entire delivery are Singapore Airlines and Lenovo from China. Overall, however, the Asian representation of global brands still remains under represented.

As Table 1 illustrates, only ten Asian brands make it into the highly-cited Interbrand Best Global Brand ranking in 2013. Seven Japanese and three South Korean brands make it into the top-100 (Interbrand 2013c). This chapter examines the Asian branding landscape in some selected markets and aims to establish key trends in Asian branding. A special focus will be given to the Chinese branding

Table 1 Interbrand's Best Global Brands 2013 (Interbrand 2013c)

Rank	Company	Brand value ($m)	Country
1	Apple	98.316	USA
2	Google	93.291	USA
3	Coca-Cola	79.213	USA
4	IBM	78.808	USA
5	Microsoft	59.546	USA
6	GE	46.947	USA
7	McDonald's	41.992	USA
8	Samsung	39.610	South Korea
9	Intel	37.257	USA
10	Toyota	35.346	Japan
⋮			
20	Honda	18.490	Japan
35	Canon	10.989	Japan
43	Hyundai	9.004	South Korea
46	Sony	8.408	Japan
65	Nissan	6.203	Japan
67	Nintendo	6.086	Japan
68	Panasonic	5.821	Japan
83	Kia	4.708	South Korea

culture. This market still lags behind in branding issues but shows great potential for an emergence of strong brands. To establish reference points for brands in the selected markets, the above-mentioned ranking system from Interbrand Corporation will be applied. The methodology of Interbrand's brand valuation is straight forward. An actual money figure on any evaluated brand is the amalgamation of market, brand, competitor, and financial data (Rocha 2014). Overall, the brand valuation is meant as a tool to determine a brand's contribution to the company's business results. Table 1 shows the top ten of the Best Global Brand ranking and a selection of other global brands that includes all Asian brands in the ranking. Currently, Apple is the world's most valuable with a brand value of over 93 billion US$.

2 Branding and the Role of the Corporate Brand in Asia

Before the discussion towards "branding trends" can commence, the key terminologies of interest, i.e. "brand" and "brand management", must be specified. The course of action will also put the focus on the viewpoints towards theoretical perspectives that shall enable more targeted and generalizable outcomes of this research. Brands are the outcome of brand management efforts and therefore interrelate closely. Hence, trends in branding can be seen as the main results of brand management efforts, which represent the managerial or organizational perspective. On the other hand, brands are a relative concept mainly taking place in the customer's mind and who has to determine the meaning of any brand individually. Strong brands from both the customer's and corporate perspective possess a lot of brand equity (Kotler and Keller 2006). The main desirable outcome of brand management efforts should then foremost result in strong, equity-holding brands, a concept which will be touched upon later when discussing trends in branding.

Brand management is the design and implementation of marketing programs and activities to build, measure, and manage brand equity (Keller 2008). Successful brand management should consequently bring forward strong brands that possess the most possible amount of equity. Measuring this equity or value is therefore a task at hand to see where a brand stands in relation to the efforts put into it. The extant literature and business practice provide several methods to measure and determine the value of brands. One common practice is to put a monetary value on a brand (Feldwick 1996). Aaker's "Brand Equity Ten" are measures categorized into variables, such as customer loyalty, brand image, and brand awareness, which are meant to broaden the discussion to more intangible and consumer-driven valuation techniques (Aaker 2002). Finally, numerous brand consultancies have developed methodologies to evaluate the strength and value of brands. Here, Milward Brown's "Brandz" or Interbrand's "Best Global Brands" annual hit list are often referred to (Kapferer 2012).

Multi-product companies have to decide on the brand architecture they want to apply to their product portfolio. An important point of concern in this context is the number of brand levels that are used and the role and visibility of the corporate brand in the market offering (Kapferer 2008). The extant literature mentions two types of brand architecture that are opposite from each other; that is, at one end of the extreme is the corporate brand-dominant strategy "branded house" and at the opposite is the individual brand-dominated strategy "house of brands". A branded house structure uses a single master brand, often the corporate brand, to give coherence and lend common values to all offerings (Rajagopal and Sanchez 2004). The house of brands strategy, on the other hand, is characterized by independent and unconnected brands without an intentional connection to the corporate brand (Aaker 2004). In most Asian markets, a branded house strategy is most common (Kapferer 2012). It is currently the norm in Japan, South Korea, and China, to apply a "flexible umbrella strategy" to most diverse product categories (Kapferer 2012). For example, the Mitsubishi Corporation, known worldwide for its automobiles, sells cars, home electronics, real estate, and even food under the Mitsubishi brand name in its domestic Japanese market (Mitsubishi 2014). Many other large Asian companies keep similarly branded product portfolios. According to Kapferer (2012), one key advantage to applying the corporate name to many of the organization's products is that, in Asia, "the more powerful a group, the more it is respected". Manufacturing everything under the corporate umbrella brand name supports this goal (Kapferer 2012). Whether or not this typical Asian branding culture is still the norm in Asia and is, in particular, applied by the companies researched in this book will be an additional subject of investigation of this chapter. The following section will review and analyze the current branding landscape in selected Asia markets.

3 The Current Branding Landscape in Asian Markets

When it comes to naming famous Asian brands, most likely some Japanese brands such as Toyota, Sony, or Nintendo, for example, will come to mind. Catching up with the West in the post-World War II era quickly lead the country towards an export-oriented economy (Segers and Stam 2013). An outward focus and Japan's constant drive for quality and innovativeness may have been the grounds for professional development of brands that started several decades ago. Taking a further look at today's market-leading branded goods companies in Asian markets, the majority of companies have a Western background. As Table 2 shows, six of the top ten companies such as Coca-Cola, Unilever, and Nestlé are FMCG "giants" that all have their headquarters in either Europe or the USA. The remaining market-leading consumer goods companies in Asia are all from Japan.

The Asian consumer perspective generally reflects a Western brand preference as well. It is predominantly Western brands such as Coke, Nike, Apple, or BMW that Asian consumers usually nominate when asked about their favorite brands (Baladi 2011). Looking at the top ten best Chinese-brand list alone, there is only one consumer goods company (Mautai Alcohol) that made it into this ranking (Interbrand 2012). The other brands are all Chinese brands in either the finance or telecom sector, where a local dominance in these industries is obvious. Overall, it

Table 2 Asia's top ten consumer goods companies (adapted from McKinsey 2014).

Company	Market share (%)	Country
Coca-Cola	3.69	USA
Unilever	2.16	Netherlands/UK
Nestlé	1.85	Switzerland
Procter & Gamble	1.65	USA
Suntory	1.33	Japan
Kao	1.31	Japan
Pepsico	1.1	USA
Shiseido	1.01	Japan
Kraft	0.99	USA
Meiji and Lotte	Tied at 0.87	Japan

can be stated that hardly any of the leading local Chinese brands have any stake in broader international markets.[1] A different picture is evident in the South Korean brand landscape. According to Interbrand's best South Korean brands ranking list, four world famous brands made it into the top ten of this regional brand hit-list (Interbrand 2013a). Among these world market-leading companies are "heavy-weights" such as Samsung and LG (electronics) and Hyundai and Kia (automobiles). When taking a closer look at the top two brands in South Korea, e.g. Samsung Electronics at number one and Hyundai Motor Corp. as runner up, both companies are "off-springs" of large parent companies that maintain wider varieties of businesses that also made it into the 2013 Interbrand South Korean brand ranking. Both companies apply the branded house strategy which implies a brand architecture with common use of the corporate brand. However, the two companies execute the strategy differently. Samsung, on the one hand, uses one brand logo for all divisions and specifies the business area with a descriptor (e.g. Samsung Life Insurance). Only the number one South Korean brand Samsung Electronics does not use a descriptor for the business unit. Hyundai, on the other hand, uses the brand name for all its divisions but applies a unique corporate design for each of its market appearances, as can be observed by differently-designed brand logos (see Fig. 1). Similarly, both market-leading companies in South Korea make use of the brand strength of the corporate brand which reflects the common corporate strategy in many Asian markets as mentioned above. That brand equity also plays an important role in the future of corporate business is revealed in the following quote from Hyundai's homepage on its brand business: "Hyundai Corporation creates newer brand values by expanding the brand power of 'Hyundai', which has grown into a global brand, to home appliances and small power generators" (Hyundai 2014). Already a global brand, mainly due to its automobile business, the company clearly intends to make use of the corporate asset "brand" as a tool to grow into other fields of business and future growth markets. The practice of Asian corporations, which have achieved a certain global fame, to extend the

---

[1] "Lenovo", a leading maker of personal computers is the only world-known Chinese brand in Interbrand's top-50 Chinese brand ranking.

Fig. 1 Samsung's and Hyundai's South Korean Brand Portfolio (source: own and adapted from Interbrand 2013a)

(corporate) brand into new fields of business can be interpreted as a first trend in current Asian brand strategy.

Another notable market in Asia is India. It is the world's largest democracy and the size of the market, comprising of over 1.2 billion people, is massive (CIA 2014). The strongest brands in India are mainly the result of economies of scale reached by large and financially powerful organizations that have diversified businesses (Mishra 2013). A typical company and brand is "Tata". The brand is ranked as number one in India with a brand value of 10.907 million US$ (Interbrand 2013b). Just like many other famous Asian brands, Tata makes prolific use of its corporate brand name throughout its offering. From the over 60 marketed brands, more than 50 % bear the Tata name (Tata 2014). The use of the name across the range however is applied differently. In some cases, the product name is the corporate name plus a product category denomination such as Tata Automobiles, Tata Tea, or Tata Batteries. In other instances, the Tata name has more an endorsing role to the actual product name (e.g. i-Shakti food products) where it appears on the product packages in the form of the logo. Overall, it can be stated that the Tata brand name is stretched across a very diverse product range ranging from automobiles, food products, consumer electronics, heavy industry, financial services, telecommunication, and even home entertainment. This wide brand stretch into very diverse product categories is unusual in most Western markets, but can be considered a second Asian branding trend, as it has also been observed in other markets such as Japan and South Korea. This observation also confirms the above described "branded house" strategy typically applied in Asia after the examination of several markets up to this point. By taking a closer look at Tata's diverse brand portfolio, the company's automobile presence is obvious. Thirteen car brands can be accounted for that all follow an individual brand name strategy with evocative names such as Nano, Indica, Manza, or Aria. Next to these mainly Indian car brands, Tata can also call famous Western automobile brands its own. In 2008, Tata Motors purchased the Jaguar and Land Rover brands from Ford Motor Company and since then shows a presence in the global premium automobile market. The once struggling car brands have been turned around by Tata and are now turning in profits for the company (Jaguarlandrover 2013).

What happened to Jaguar and Land Rover has also been the fate of other formerly successful Western automobile brands that were acquired by mainly Chinese conglomerates. Volvo, Saab, and Rover are now all owned by Chinese holdings.[2] In addition to famous Western automobile brands acquired by Asian companies, the Chinese computer maker Lenovo purchased the personal computer unit from IBM including the world known ThinkPad brand name in 2005 (Lenovo 2004). The acquisition of Western brands by Asian and in particular Chinese companies can be considered an Asian branding trend.

The subject of the next section will be to make an assessment of the current Chinese branding situation and include an evaluation of recent Chinese foreign market entries by investments in foreign brands.

4   Branding in China

The Chinese economy ranks in top positions in many of the relevant criteria that can characterize a nation's economic power. It currently has the second largest GDP only trailing the USA by a shrinking margin (Segers and Stam 2013). Just the size of the population presently at 1.3 billion inhabitants makes China naturally an attractive market for many foreign and home grown brands. For instance, the mobile phone service provider China Mobile counted over 780 million customers, which makes the company "the world's largest mobile operator by subscriber base" (Zacks 2014). The sheer size of China's economy and its consumer base brings the possibility to this former developing country to take away significant influence from the West (Baladi 2011). This prediction provokes the questions as to whether or not Chinese brands are able to "conquer" world markets or whether or not Chinese consumers will favor them over Western rivals. As shown above in Sect. 2, only the personal computer maker Lenovo from China has a true global presence as the world market leader in PC sales (IDC 2013). With Huawei, another Chinese consumer electronics manufacturer is currently entering the world stage by gaining rapid market share in the mobile phone segment.[3] The company currently takes the number 3 spot in global smartphone market shares trailing only Samsung and Apple but surpassing former power houses such as LG and HTC (see Table 3).

---

[2] The MG Rover company was purchased by the Chinese Nanjing Automobile company who turned the Rover brand into "Roewe". The "Rover" brand name is now owned by India's Tata Motors.

[3] See also the company case study on Huawei in this book.

Table 3 Global smartphone market share (Strategy Analytics 2014)

Global smartphone vendor market share %	2012	2013
Samsung	30.4	32.3
Apple	19.4	15.5
Huawei	4.3	5.1
LG	3.8	4.8
Lenovo	3.4	4.6
Others	35.7	37.7
Total	100	100

Looking at Lenovo and Huawei, global consumers appear to accept the "Made in China" label on high-end consumer electronics products that have so far been exclusive to non-Chinese producers. It is notable that these two brands have also become household names in their local Chinese market.

This is also the case for Haier, a Chinese electronic appliances manufacturer which is the thirtieth most valuable Chinese brand in the domestic market according to Interbrand's best China brand ranking. The Haier Group has a dominating 27.2 % share of the appliance market in China and a considerable global market share of 9.6 % (Barris 2013). The brand is popular among Chinese consumers who often equip their kitchens and living rooms with Haier products fuelled by the Chinese push for urbanization. But the company and its brand must have global appeal, as the close to 10 % global market share may suggest. To compete overseas, Haier recently has increased its R&D spending to 4 % of revenues (Keller et al. 2012). With this strategy, backed by the company's CEO, Haier is even able to compete successfully in the USA where it was able to overcome cultural differences in the world's largest economy (Wu et al. 2011). The brand positions itself as a global brand in its foreign markets and stresses its global presence in production and product development. In the "About Us" sections on Haier's international homepages, no word mentions the company's Chinese roots or ownership. Instead, Haier praises its world market leadership and international facilities (Haier 2014).

A global brand-driven corporate strategy backed by top management has also been implemented successfully by Lenovo, the world market leader in personal computers. In a recent interview, Lenovo's CEO Yuanqing Yang emphasized the key role of innovation and branding for the company in becoming the world's leading PC manufacturer (Kirkland and Orr 2013). Although still the exception, it is noticeable that more and more Chinese CEO's of large companies are recognizing "branding" as a necessary strategy to gain consumer trust in domestic and international markets. This top management understanding of the brand's role for international expansion was a trend in South Korea decades ago that lead some of its at first obscure brands to global fame (Keller et al. 2012).[4] Now, in China, at least some companies are following suit and this can be considered as another trend in the

---

[4] South Korean automobile brands such as Hyundai and Kia, for example, first started out as good quality cars priced at the lower end and have now moved upscale into low- to mid-premium car brands.

Asian/Chinese branding culture. The similarities to some past South Korean brand life cycles are striking. Like many South Korean brands in the past, some notable Chinese companies tend to enter foreign markets by offering high quality products at very competitive prices targeting consumers of the leading competitors. The newly introduced flagship smartphone from Huawei for example has been labeled as "the iPhone killer" by product reviewers (NTV 2014a). The phone has the same or even better features and comes at a 40 % discount compared to its main quality rivals (NTV 2014a). The price discount is obviously also a sign of less brand value in the consumers eyes that Huawei has to account for in its pricing strategy. And while both Lenovo and Haier are already successful at the global stage, others are in the starting blocks. The aforementioned Huawei has an established presence in the global networking equipment market. Other notable Chinese brands outside "Red-China" include the athletic clothing and equipment maker Li-Ning and Tsingtao beer (Keller et al. 2012).

The foreign surge by Chinese companies is partly a function of the Chinese government's "Go Global" policy in 2000 that has led to a level of Chinese foreign direct investment in the recent past that has never been seen before (Wu et al. 2011). By this administrative initiative, up to 50 Chinese firms were meant to become "globally competitive" companies within a decade (Keller et al. 2012). And being global also resulted in Chinese corporations becoming multinationals and acquiring foreign assets. To illustrate the relevance of branding in this context is a quote from China's Commerce Minister Deming Chen in 2011 when he told parliament that the government would "encourage the best firms to acquire or build up overseas operations and to license or acquire famous global brands in order to obtain international recognition and improve the image and competitiveness of Chinese products" (Backaler 2012). Table 4 lists a selection of the recent and prominent brand purchases by Chinese firms.

Although such moves may have been the result of governmental policy, recent foreign direct investments by Chinese companies into brands can also be consumer demand driven, as the following example will illustrate.

"Made in China" does not essentially arouse feelings of high quality or high performance products among Western consumers and Chinese alike. Especially recent food scares have made Chinese consumers very suspicious of anything that is "produced in China and ingested into the human body" (Perkowski 2013). This consumer concern has recently culminated in the scandal of local baby milk powder that was made from milk adulterated with toxic chemicals in order to artificially augment the milk's protein amount (Giesen and Warmbrunn 2013). With sales of locally made baby formula coming to a near standstill, Western-made formulas are currently experiencing very high demands as Chinese consumers have been purchasing their products directly from German, French, or US shelves (Giesen and Warmbrunn 2013). Building on local distrust by Chinese consumers, Chinese national Steven Dai is now CEO and co-owner of IVC, an American-made vitamin supplements producer (see Table 4). With IVC's acquisition, the manager plans to export his vitamins to China because Chinese consumers "have the perception that 'US made' is a premium product, has high quality and high efficacy, is more

Table 4 Selection of foreign brand acquisitions by Chinese investors (source: author)

Foreign brand acquisition (year)	Chinese investor	Industry
Motorola Mobility Handsets (2014)	Lenovo	Mobile phones
Fisker Automotive (2014)	Wanxiang	Hybrid sports cars
Saab (2012)	NEVS	Automobiles
Volvo (2010)	Geely	Automobiles
IVC (2010)	Chinese private investors	Vitamin supplements
ThinkPad (2005)	Lenovo	Personal computers

trusted" (Giesen and Warmbrunn 2013; Hu 2013). It remains to be seen whether or not similarly motivated foreign brand acquisitions in the food and high-interest categories like the one with IVC will follow by Chinese companies. Certainly, many recent brand acquisitions have taken place in the automobile industry and tech sector (see Table 4). Famous car brands have been attractive targets for Chinese investors. Lenovo's investment into Motorola's mobile phone division, on the other hand, was especially directed towards the exploitation of the company's patents and, in particular, in a brand with global appeal and awareness (Kelly 2014).

To overcome the negative perceptions of the "brand China" both domestically and internationally, "Chinese firms must overcome negative perceptions including poor product quality and undercover political motivations" (Backaler 2014). One way Chinese firms can achieve this is by further acquisition of non-Chinese brands, which is expected to happen in the future. As an established branding trend above, the ongoing and possible future brand acquisitions out of China are expected to continue.

4.1 A Look at Chinese Customer Preferences

Why haven't more Chinese brands emerged to achieve global fame, given that they are coming from the world's second largest economy? This question is also fuelled by the 14 years that have passed since the Chinese government called for a corporate branding and foreign investment push ("Go global") in 2000. This section shall explore customer brand preferences within China and current practices in Chinese brand building for both internationally-famous companies and strong domestic companies. Firstly, primary data from a recent survey will be evaluated. The author of this chapter conducted a survey in April 2014 in Wuhan, Hubei province, China. The aim of the research is to assess consumer preferences of young Chinese adults aged 18–25 for Western/non-Chinese and domestic brands. The sample consisted of $n = 600$ and the interviews took place face-to-face by a self-administered questionnaire. Some preliminary results from the survey will be evaluated and discussed below.

As a starting question, the interviewees were asked to name their three favorite brands off the top of their heads. Table 5 exhibits the results of this question. Apple

Table 5 Favorite brands (source: author).

Rank	Brand	Percent	Industry	Country of origin
1	Apple	16.00	Mobile phones	USA
2	Samsung	10.40	Mobile phones	South Korea
3	Sony	9.13	Mobile phones	Japan
4	Pizza Hut	8.93	Fast Food	USA
5	Adidas	8.67	Sports/Athletics	Germany
6	McDonald's	8.20	Fast Food	USA
7	Nike	7.27	Sports/Athletics	USA
8	KFC	7.20	Fast Food	USA
9	Lamborghini	5.20	Automobiles	Italy
10	Laneige	4.33	Beauty Care	South Korea
11	Lancôme	3.73	Beauty Care	France
12	Ferrari	3.73	Automobiles	Italy
13	MAC	3.00	Personal Computers	USA
14	Mercedes-Benz	2.33	Automobiles	Germany
15	Uniqlo	1.87	Clothing	Japan

leads the brand ranking by a large margin followed by its main rival Samsung. In total five US brands were mentioned with German, South Korean, Japanese, and Italian brands also having multiple entries in this ranking. It is striking that no Chinese brand made it into the ranking. It is also notable that US fast food chains are popular among young Chinese adults. All of the mentioned brands have a strong presence in China. KFC, for example, operates more stores in China (4600) than in its home market in the USA (Yum 2013). McDonald's, on the other hand, is currently opening new stores in China and is planning to operate 2000 restaurants by year end (Yue 2014).

Another question from the survey that shall be discussed was the preference of those polled for Western/non-Chinese and Chinese brands. Table 6 summarizes the results and lists a total of ten industries or product categories. Overall, the results show that in most categories, non-Chinese brands are favored the most. The strongest preference is in automobile brands, which are preferred 92 % over their Chinese counterparts. Other strong product categories are mobile phones and watches, each at 84 %, and airlines (75 %). Soft drinks score about equal with only a small margin in favor of non-Chinese brands (51–49 %). This close call for Chinese brands despite the fierce competition in the domestic market from mainly famous US brands is due to the strong consumer focus on traditional Chinese flavors of soft drinks in China (Euromonitor 2013). Chinese brands are still quite popular in this category. The only category where Chinese brands can win over Western and non-Chinese brands is the refrigerator category. A 53 % majority of the sample favors a Chinese brand. It may be assumed that this result is due to the strong local Haier brand that has a market leading position in China.

According to these survey results, Chinese brands are mainly trailing Western brands and brands from either South Korea or Japan. For some industries and

Table 6 Preference between Western/non-Chinese and Chinese brands per industry (source: author)

Industry/product category	Western/non-Chinese brands in percent	Chinese brands in percent
Mobile phones	84.16	15.84
Automobiles	92.08	7.92
Clothing	57.64	42.36
Sportswear/athletics	55.00	45.00
Soft drinks	50.98	49.02
Personal computers	65.56	34.44
Airlines	75.00	25.00
Watches	84.00	16.00
TV's	59.82	40.18
Refrigerators	47.00	53.00

product categories, the results are not surprising. The automobile industry has been dominated by mostly Western and Japanese brands for decades and it will take time for Chinese auto makers to catch up. However, the first signs that Chinese car manufacturers are closing the gap are already visible. For example, the "Qoros 3", an automobile made by Chinese Qoros Auto Co. LTD, recently won the EuroNACP-Crash test beating out 30 other tested cars (NTV 2014b). And on top of this, safety is a product benefit that is traditionally owned by the Volvo brand, which is now also in "Chinese hands" due to the previously mentioned Chinese takeover of the Swedish car manufacturer.

Another dominant domain for non-Chinese brands in China is the mobile phone sector. Driven by Apple's "smartphone" invention and Samsung's prevalence with the very popular Android operating system, both brands have made it to global market leaderships and consumer preference—also in China. But, as mentioned before, Chinese smartphone makers such as Lenovo and Huawei are catching up both internationally and in the domestic market.

In summary, it appears that in most product categories, Western brands are still the norm and Chinese brands are left with a follower role. But as shown above, the incumbent role of market leadership and customer preference is not an exclusive right owned by non-Chinese brands. Selected industries and some product categories show strong signs of preferred status in the eye of Chinese consumers. The next section will highlight suggested reasons as to why the majority of Chinese firms still have weak brands. This excursion into Chinese branding insights will close with a brief case study on the Chinese internet industry to illustrate the branding dynamics on Chinese brand dominance in this sector.

4.2 Reasons for Weak Chinese branding

As the chapter headline suggests, Chinese brands can be, on a broad level, considered as weak. Most of the reasons for these weaknesses have been touched upon in the preceding discussions and findings of this chapter. In a recent post by the famous branding scholar David Aaker from Harvard Publishing, the same topic was discussed in detail (Aaker 2013). The main points of Aaker's opinion piece, on why Chinese firms have weak branding, will be highlighted and put into context in the following section.

Aaker's post was triggered by New York times writer David Brooks who claimed in his article that US firms still have a competitive advantage over Chinese firms due to their superior knowledge and skills in building and managing brands (Brooks 2013). Aaker supports this assessment but offers additional reasons for this competitive advantage of US and global firms. The **first** strength, or lack thereof by Chinese firms, is the availability of experienced brand managers in successful global firms that are fuelled by well-tested and applied brand management systems and processes. It is widely known that consumer goods multinationals such as Procter & Gamble and Unilever have been pioneers in establishing professional brand management systems from which many experienced brand managers have arisen (Keller et al. 2012; Aaker 2013). This long branding tradition does not yet exist in China and thus established branding systems and an abundance of well-trained branding specialists are still lacking. **Secondly**, China's businesses simply do not need branding in their corporate strategy just yet. According to Aaker, many of China's top firms are successors of state-owned companies that were able to operate without fearing too much competition (e.g. China Mobile). At the same time, Aaker states that due to the great growth in many Chinese markets, keeping up with manufacturing and distributing the goods have been the priorities over branding. With the recent slowing in Chinese growth and changes in the competitive landscapes, it is expected that branding will become more of a priority for Chinese companies in the future. Finally, Aaker brings forward a **third** reason for the slow development of branding as a corporate strategy in Chinese firms and that is the lack of support from the top management. Chinese top managers are not trained in marketing and focus more on operations, costs, and functional benefits (Aaker 2013). This performance focus also penetrates to much of China's brand communications as an expert and scholar in Chinese branding states.[5] Besides, most Chinese top managers lack international experience and maintain a domestic focus without having the global mind-set based on branding as a business model which American and other business leaders value (Aaker 2013).

In summary, branding as a business model still has a long way to go in China. Once growth potential must come from foreign markets, Chinese companies are expected to move along and will be required to play the "brand game" as it is

---

[5] Mentioned to the author of this article in a personal interview with Dr. Alison Lloyd on March, 20th, 2014.

currently perfected by mostly non-Chinese companies. That this is not "mission impossible" is demonstrated in the above-mentioned examples of companies such as Haier, Lenovo, and Huawei. In the meantime, the Chinese digital sector shows signs of marketing excellence and branding scale that is worth mentioning in more detail in the next section.

4.3 Digital Brands in the Chinese market

The Chinese market for online brands has been very dynamic and challenging over the past few years. Search engines like Google have been struggling and social media networks such as Facebook are even prohibited in the "Middle Kingdom". The ongoing global hype about the planned IPO for Chinese e-commerce company Alibaba will be used as an opportunity to examine China's digital big players. Alibaba Group Holding Ltd. is a Chinese e-commerce company that runs two popular shopping sites, namely "Taobao" and "Tmall". Together, both platforms have an 80 % stake in the Chinese online sales market and make more than 250 billion US$ in transaction volume by its estimated 500 million users (Osawa et al. 2014). Alibaba's sales are more than Amazon's and EBAY's annual sales combined (Osawa et al. 2014). To ease the payment process for millions of Chinese online shoppers, Alipay is the company's online payment service. Handling over 70 % of all Chinese online payment transactions, Alipay is the world's largest payment processor (Osawa et al. 2014). The majority of Alibaba is now owned by Yahoo Inc. and Japan's soft bank Corp. whilst the company's founder Jack Ma remains a minority shareholder.

Alibaba faces fierce competition from other successful online service providers in China. Tencent Holdings Ltd., which operates the popular Chinese "WeChat" mobile messaging service, has 300 million users of which 100 million are outside of China (Simcott 2014). Tencent recently bought a stake in the second largest Chinese online shopping portal JD.com (Carsten 2014). With this purchase, Tencent is expected to integrate its WeChat users into the shopping portal (Carsten 2014). Tencent also operates the Chinese social media platforms "RenRen" with nearly 200 million, mostly young, users and "Tencent Weibo" that can account for a user base of approximately 500 million users.

"Baidu" is China's most popular search engine. The NASDAQ-listed company operates countless other successful online based services such as travel booking sites, video platforms, and online dictionaries, just to name a few (IT Times 2014).

Six internet companies made it into Interbrand's "Best China Brands" ranking (Tencent # 8, Baidu # 13, Alibaba # 26). The examples listed above illustrate the dominance of local digital companies and their online brands in the Chinese market. The digital market in China illustrates a mix of the applied brand strategies. For example, both Alibaba and Tencent apply the typical Asian branded house strategy ("Alipay" or "Tencent Weibo"), but not exclusively. Most other brands in their portfolios bear a brand name where the corporate name does not appear (Alibaba's "Taobao" and Tencent's "WeChat", just to name a few). The reasons for the non-typical Asian brand strategy, in which the corporate brand generally is applied throughout the offering, could be manifold. For example, individual brand names for the products could be the result of mergers and acquisitions with inherited brand names. On the other hand, the digital market is "domain driven", i.e. the brand name is the name of the domain. Diversity in domain names for different e-commerce and online offerings seems logical and could be a reason for maintaining a house of brands strategy for Chinese digital marketing companies. This topic may require further investigation.

With the blocking of most foreign online domains, domestic companies have a clear advantage in the massive Chinese online market. Although the Chinese online and mobile market is highly competitive for the active players, it still offers great potential as new internet users will be entering the market for a longer time to come. But beyond the domestic market, Chinese digital companies, such as Baidu and soon Alibaba, are seeking financing in the foreign market place and run sites outside of their home territory. WeChat's 100 million users outside of China keep flocking towards the only serious WhatsApp competitor. Whether or not more Chinese digital brands will reach global appeal remains to be seen.

5   Conclusion

This chapter has examined current branding trends in significant Asian markets, namely Japan, South Korea, and India, and has dedicated a special focus to the emerging branding nation, China. It is obvious that no generalizations towards the whole of Asia can be drawn from this research. Like other geographical regions in the world, Asia consists of more than just four large economies. Asia offers an abundance of wealth in culture and there is no such thing as an "Asian way of doing business". However, the research identified some aspects in the field of branding that have occurred in different Asian markets at different times. For example, the development of branding as a management strategy followed benefit-driven product management in both Japan and South Korea some decades ago. This development can now be witnessed in selected industries in China. Whether or not other Asian nations show similar developments (e.g. Indonesia) would be a topic for further investigation.

Nevertheless, the following four Asian branding trends highlighted throughout this report will be briefly summarized and will serve as the main outcomes of this research. Their substantiation calls for further research and valorization.

Asian Branding Trend # 1: Extending the corporate brand into new fields of business

Successful global companies from Asia which predominantly apply a branded house brand architecture strategy are continuously putting emphasis on using the brand equity of the corporate brand for future business. This was illustrated with Hyundai that explicitly uses the "brand power" of its brand for product diversification. Similar approaches have been seen at Lenovo (personal computers, mobile phones), Huawei (networking technology, mobile phones), Samsung (across the board of all its services), Tencent (social networking), etcetera.

Asian Branding Trend # 2: Extending the corporate brand into diverse product categories

A wide brand covering very diverse product categories is typical, especially in Asian markets. Food and automobiles endorsed e.g. by the Mitsubishi brand in Japan is not unusual in Asia but is very unlikely in non-Asian markets. Many of the researched large Asian enterprises have built on their corporate brand and stretched it into diverse and fully unrelated product categories. A common culture where size and reputation matter most among consumers may be a key difference compared to Western markets where a large corporation may even be seen as an obstacle rather than an asset by consumers.

Asian Branding Trend # 3: Acquisition of Western brands by Asian investors

In the past years, Western brands in particular have been the target by Asian investors. The main purposes for these acquisitions remain manifold, whether to gain access to branding know-how, increase a reputation, improve product development capabilities, or off-set a lack of brand equity in domestic markets. The trust element in foreign brands remains a key motivation for Asian, and especially Chinese, consumers. As long as domestic brands are still seen as inferior, this branding trend is expected to continue.

Asian Branding Trend # 4: Top-management support in brand building

The examples of Japan and South Korea show that branding can play an important role in the corporate strategy, but that it needs the support of top-management if it is to be successfully applied to global markets. Some signs of this development have been revealed by this research in other Asian markets, namely China. In China, the majority of leaders are still focused inward without branding being on top of the agenda. Several successful Chinese global players have discovered the brand as a strategic item and the success stories of Lenovo and Haier will set the pace for others to follow. Driven by governmental policies, globalization of the brand as a concept will also proliferate in China and possibly other Asian markets.

References

Aaker, D. (2002). *Building strong brands*. London: Simon & Schuster.
Aaker, D. A. (2004). *Brand portfolio strategy: Creating relevance, differentiation, energy, leverage, and clarity*. New York: Free Press.
Aaker, D. (2013). *The real reasons Chinese firms have weak branding*. Retrieved June 6, 2013, from http://blogs.hbr.org/2013/06/will-china-catch-up-on-brandin/#disqus_thread
Backaler, J. (2012). *Viewpoint: Why Chinese firms buy Western rivals*. Retrieved February 28, 2012, from http://www.bbc.co.uk/news/business-17197907
Backaler, J. (2014). *Are Chinese companies ready to go west?* Retrieved February 25, 2014 from http://www.forbes.com/sites/joelbackaler/2014/02/25/are-chinese-companies-ready-to-go-west/#./?&_suid=13990212943550724519811333 2704
Baladi, J. (2011). *The brutal truth about Asian branding and how to break the vicious cycle*. Singapore: Wiley.

Barris, M. (2013). *Haier's stake sale a boost*. Retrieved February 10, 2013, from http://usa.chinadaily.com.cn/epaper/2013-10/02/content_17007490.htm

Brooks, D. (2013). *The romantic advantage*. Retrieved May 30, 2013, from http://www.nytimes.com/2013/05/31/opinion/brooks-the-romantic-advantage.html?_r=4&

Carsten, P. (2014). *Tencent-JD.com partnership goes straight for Alibaba's throat*. Retrieved March 10, 2014, from http://www.reuters.com/article/2014/03/10/us-jd-tencent-hldg-idUSBREA2902T20140310

CIA. (2014). *The World Factbook—South Asia: India*. Retrieved April 3, 2014, from https://www.cia.gov/library/publications/the-world-factbook/geos/in.html

Euromonitor. (2013). *Soft drinks in China April 2013*. Retrieved May 5, 2014, from http://www.euromonitor.com/soft-drinks-in-china/report

Feldwick, P. (1996). What is brand equity anyway, and how do you measure It? *Journal of Market Research Society, 38*, 85–104.

Giesen, C., & Warmbrunn, B. (2013). *Das Geschaumlft mit dem weiszligen Pulver*. Retrieved July 13, 2013, from http://www.sueddeutsche.de/panorama/babynahrung-in-china-das-geschaeft-mit-dem-weissen-pulver-1.1734790

Haier. (2014). *Über Haier*. Retrieved April 20, 2014, from http://www.haier.com/de/header/201108/t20110811_30679.shtml

Hu, H. (2013). *Vitamin maker IVC energized by Chinese investment*. Retrieved January 4, 2013, from http://usa.chinadaily.com.cn/epaper/2013-01/04/content_16081281.htm

Hyundai. (2014). *Brand business*. Retrieved April 5, 2014, from http://www.hyundaicorp.com/en/business/brand-business/

IDC. (2013). *Lenovo overtakes HP as the top PC vendor while U.S. shipments stabilize in the second quarter of 2013*. Retrieved July 10, 2013, from http://www.idc.com/getdoc.jsp?containerId=prUS24213513

Interbrand. (2012). *Best China brands ranking*. Retrieved March 10, 2013, from http://www.interbrand.com/de/knowledge/iq/2013/best-asian-brands/china/ranking.aspx

Interbrand. (2013). *The first official ranking of the best Korea brands*. Retrieved April 4, 2014, from http://www.interbrand.com/en/best-global-brands/region-country/best-korea-brands-2013.aspx

Interbrand. (2013b). *India's top 30 brands*. Retrieved April 1, 2013, from http://www.interbrand.com/de/best-global-brands/region-country/best-indian-brands/indias-top-30-brands.aspx

Interbrand. (2013c). *2013 best global brands: A deeper dive*. Retrieved February 2, 2014, from http://www.interbrand.com/de/best-global-brands/2013/BGB-Interactive-Charts.aspx

IT Times. (2014). *Baidu profitiert vom Mobile- und Online-Videoboom in China*. Retrieved May 6, 2014, from http://www.it-times.de/hintergrundbericht/baidu-profitiert-vom-mobile-und-online-videoboom-in-china-104291/

Jaguarlandrover. (2013). *Jaguar land rover FY14 Q2 results*. Retrieved November 8, 2013, from http://www.jaguarlandrover.com/gl/en/investor-relations/news/2013/11/08/jaguar-land-rover-fy14-q2-results/

Kapferer, J. N. (2008). *New strategic brand management: Creating and sustaining brand equity long term*. London: Kogan Page.

Kapferer, J. N. (2012). *The new strategic brand management*. London: Kogan Page.

Keller, K. L. (2008). *Strategic brand management: Building, measuring, and managing brand equity*. Upper Saddle River, NJ: Prentice-Hall.

Keller, K. L., Aperia, T., & Georgson, M. (2012). *Strategic brand management—A European perspective*. Harlow: Prentice Hall.

Kelly, G. (2014). *Lenovo was right to buy Motorola—Just look at ThinkPad*. Retrieved February 12, 2014, from http://www.forbes.com/sites/gordonkelly/2014/02/12/lenovo-was-right-to-buy-motorola-just-look-at-thinkpad/#./?&_suid=13993200409550814536981553 9187

Kirkland, R., & Orr, G. (2013). *Thriving in a 'PC-plus' world: An interview with Lenovo CEO Yang Yuanqing*. Retrieved June 2013, from http://www.mckinsey.com/insights/high_tech_telecoms_internet/thriving_in_a_pc-plus_world

Kotler, P., Armstrong, G., Saunders, J., & Wong, V. (2002). *Principles of marketing*. Harlow: Pearson.

Kotler, P., & Keller, K. L. (2006). *Marketing management.* Upper Saddle River, NJ: Pearson Education Inc.

Lenovo. (2004). *Lenovo to acquire IBM personal computing division.* Retrieved December 7, 2004 from http://www.lenovo.com/news/us/en/2005/04/ibm_lenovo.html

McKinsey. (2014). *Asia's top 10 consumer goods companies.* Retrieved March 18, 2014, from http://csi.mckinsey.com/knowledge_by_region/asia/rest_of_asia

Mishra, A. (2013). *Best Indian brands 2013—A definite guide to India's most valuable brands.* Retrieved April 9, 2014, from http://issuu.com/interbrand/docs/interbrand-best-indian-brands-2013?e=1175374/4238947

Mitsubishi. (2014). *Mitsubishi companies website search.* Retrieved March 20, 2014, from http://www.mitsubishi.com/php/users/category_search.php?lang=1

NTV. (2014a). *Huaweis neuer 'iPhone-Killer'—So sieht das Ascend P7 aus.* Retrieved April 30, 2014, from http://www.n-tv.de/technik/So-sieht-das-Ascend-P7-aus-article12748336.html

NTV. (2014b). *Sicherstes Auto ist ein Newcomer aus China.* Retrieved January 11, 2014, from http://www.n-tv.de/auto/Sicherstes-Auto-ist-ein-Newcomer-aus-China-article12049586.htm

Osawa, J., Mozur, P., & Winkler, R. (2014). Alibaba flexes its muscles ahead of U.S. stock filing. *Wall Street Journal Europe Edition, XXXII*(55).

Perkowski, J. (2013). Smithfield and Shuanghui: Is two pigs in a blanket? *Forbes Magazine.* http://www.forbes.com/sites/jackperkowski/2013/06/03/smithfield-and-shuanghui-two-pigs-in-a-blanket

Rajagopal, R., & Sanchez, R. (2004). Conceptual analysis of brand architecture and relationships within product categories. *Brand Management, 11*, 233–247.

Rocha, M. (2014). *Interbrand's brand valuation methodology.* Retrieved March 20, 2014, from http://www.interbrand.com/de/best-global-brands/region-country/best-indian-brands/interbrands-brand-valuation-methodology.aspx

Segers, R. T., & Stam, T. (2013). *Asia: Reshaping the global economic landscape.* Maastricht: Shaker.

Simcott, R. (2014). *Social media fast facts: China.* Retrieved February 7, 2014, from http://socialmediatoday.com/richard-simcott/2213841/social-media-fast-facts-china

Strategy Analytics. (2014). *Global smartphone shipments reach a record 990 million units in 2013.* Retrieved January 27, 2014, from http://blogs.strategyanalytics.com/WSS/post/2014/01/27/Global-Smartphone-Shipments-Reach-a-Record-990-Million-Units-in-2013.aspx

Tata. (2014). *Tata brands.* Retrieved April 9, 2014, from http://www.tata.com/brandshowcase.html

Wu, F., Hoon, L. S., & Yuzhu, Z. (2011). Do's and don'ts for Chinese companies investing in the United States: Lessons from Huawei and Haier. *Thunderbird International Business Review, 53*, 501–515.

Yue, L. (2014). *Can China rescue McDonald's?* Retrieved February 1, 2014, from http://www.chicagobusiness.com/article/20140201/ISSUE01/302019985/can-china-rescue-mcdonalds

Yum. (2013). *Yum! Financial data.* Retrieved MAY 2, 2014, from http://www.yum.com/investors/restcounts.asp

Zacks. (2014). *China mobile Q1 earnings fall, revs rise.* Retrieved April 29, 2014, from http://www.zacks.com/stock/news/131510/china-mobile-q1-earnings-fall-revs-rise

Part VII

Conclusion

Conclusions: Why and How Asian Businesses Will Conquer the World

Rien T. Segers and Filip Vedder

> The West in decline, Europe rampantly so. Some estimates suggest that by 2030 China could account for a third of global output and be twice the size of the US economy. American power would then be a pale shadow of what it is today.
> – Martin Jacques in Financial Times, 23 Oct 2014.

Abstract
When analyzing the company cases in this book, six similarities can be found: the corporate culture of the companies, their adaptability, the drive to internationalize, the Triple Helix as a facilitator of their success, the quality of the products, and finally, their competitiveness based on the combination of all these similarities. Obviously, there are many differences as well. These differences are a result of the way the companies try to realize the similarities. Broadly speaking, the differences are dependent on: (1) differences between countries (cultural identity) and (2) differences between companies (the specific character of entrepreneurs). The differences in the political-economic systems of Asian countries have a strong implication for the international drive of Asian companies. The implicit claim of most chapters in this book is that Asian companies will flock to the West in ever-increasing numbers. In the coming years, this concerns companies primarily coming from countries we have been dealing with in this book: China, India, Japan, South Korea and Vietnam. As an example we show the recent developments of Chinese outward foreign direct investment in the Netherlands.

R.T. Segers (✉)
International Business School, Hanze University OAS, Groningen, The Netherlands

Clingendael Netherlands Institute of International Relations, The Hague, The Netherlands
e-mail: m.t.m.segers@rug.nl

F. Vedder
International Business School, Hanze University OAS, Groningen, The Netherlands
e-mail: filip.vedder@gmail.com

1 Introduction

In the concluding section of this book, it is first of all necessary to analyze the similarities between the companies dealt with in this book. In this way, a picture will be constructed of "the" Asian company as the West will get to know it in the near future. In the second section, we will highlight six similarities between the companies.

Obviously, there are not only similarities but differences as well; they will be the subject of our analysis in the third section of the conclusions. Their differences are first of all based on the inevitable differences between the countries from which they come. Obviously, also Asian countries have their specific history, their own language and country-specific conventions leading to a clear-cut and cherished cultural and national identity. In addition to the similarities existing between Asian companies, there are numerous differences which will also be dealt with in this section.

In a concluding section of a rather extensive book on Emerging Asian Multinationals, the question should finally be posed as to what the future developments of these Asian companies will bring to the West. Here we single out a country whose companies at this moment are still met with fear as well as with admiration in the West. We will particularly concentrate on China's outward foreign direct investment to the Netherlands.

2 Similarities Between Asian Companies

In this section, we will focus on six similarities: the corporate culture of the companies, their adaptability, the drive to internationalize, the Triple Helix as a facilitator of their success, the quality of the products, and finally, their competitiveness based on the combination of all these similarities.

2.1 Corporate Culture

When looking at the corporate culture of the emerging Asian multinationals analyzed in this book, there are four points of similarity: a family-like atmosphere or structure; long term strategies over short-term gain; Japanese characteristics; and soft nationalism.

The *family-like atmosphere* and structure are a result of the cooperative Asian culture and serve to make the employee proud of, and therefore loyal to, the company. This can, for instance, be seen at the team building program for new employees at Alibaba. Also, Panasonic states in its code of conduct that employees should show a "challenging spirit", keep thinking and acting innovatively, and have a continuous drive for further development. Rakuten forced an "Englishnization" upon the company that was quite a culture shock for its Japanese employees.

The management is, likewise, willing to invest heavily in the employees of a company as evidenced by the many training opportunities that the companies in the book offer to their employees.

In addition, special insurance options for employees, as well as health and safety regulations that go beyond the laws of the country the company is from, are other examples of the commitment of the management. Panasonic even used to have a policy that they would not fire its employees during an economic downturn. However, the company had to stop this policy in order to restructure itself and stay competitive.

These structures do not mean that there is no incentive to innovate or work hard for the company. Some companies, for example, are organized into smaller units that can almost operate as separate companies (Alibaba, Haier). These smaller units can even compete with each other, meaning there will be a small-scale feeling for its employees, even if they work for a huge conglomerate. This encourages loyalty to the company as a whole, while not discouraging internal competition to deliver the best product or service. Other companies have chosen a more traditional top-down approach, like Uniqlo. Both types of companies, however, place a lot of value in incorporating the employees in their corporate culture and to make them feel part of a bigger team. The many training facilities of the bigger Asian companies are also meant to combat the lack of motivation and innovation that might be caused by the life-time employment system that is still often practiced in Asia.

Another defining characteristic of Asian corporate culture, is the focus on *long term strategies* of growth and market share instead of on short-term profit. This was originally caused by the Japanese-style ownership structures of cross shareholding between companies in conglomerates. However, it can also be seen in other Asian companies. Long term strategies based on market share, combined with the drive to internationalize, also lead to a lot of M&A activities. Alibaba's Big Bao Strategy and Tencent's partnerships are good examples of this. By either teaming up with, or buying, other companies, the market share can be extended.

Figure 4 in the chapter "Haier: A Case Study on How One of China's First Global Brands Keeps Expanding" shows how the company changed its strategy over the years. This step by step, long-term strategy was always aimed at making the company and brand grow. Obviously, every company (be it Asian or not) has a certain long-term strategy. However, for Asian companies, it is often more important to make the company grow than to get a short-term increase in revenues. In the case of conglomerate companies like Lotte or Panasonic, the revenues from the well-functioning parts can help to pay for temporary decreases in revenues from less well-performing parts of the company. Of course this does not mean that revenues are not important at all. Obviously, a company goes bankrupt if it doesn't manage to get good revenues. However, revenues are realized by building a large market share over time.

There are several reasons for this system. One reason is partly due to the cooperative Asian nature, which lead to the 'Japanese style' of ownership in large conglomerates where multiple businesses all hold shares of each other.

Another important reason for this way of doing business is the Asian financial crisis from 1997 and the lessons learned from that crisis. While the cause of the crisis was not directly related to business strategies, the reforms that were made under IMF guidance did have their influence. In the case of South Korea, the problem was that the chaebol were being built up too quickly. They needed more and more investment, and could not sustain themselves any longer. Eventually these chaebol were forced to close or sell underperforming parts of the conglomerate. The companies were also forced to contract direct ties with the government. These changes lead to stronger companies that were able to support themselves, but also kept intact the traditional cooperative and market share growth over revenues strategies. In other Asian countries, a similar evolution could be seen.

This does not mean, however, that cooperation between the business world and government was completely halted. The triple helix remained an extremely important part of the Asian way of doing business, as we will discuss later. As the worldwide financial crisis of 2008 has taught, the Asian long-term strategies can be much more versatile than the Western short-term ones. Not only were Asian countries and companies less affected, they also recovered a lot faster. Immediately after the crisis, the exports to Western markets decreased. However, this was quickly negated by exporting to developing markets, as well as by offering their lower-price products to Western consumers, who were seeking to cut costs. They were able to do this due to their varied strategies and businesses, which made them flexible and able to adapt quickly. This lead to the paradoxical situation where the long-term oriented Asian companies could adapt to the crisis faster and more efficiently than the Western ones with their short-term strategies.

Many of the Asian company characteristics have a *Japanese origin*. Why did Japan have such a strong influence on business in Asia? Japan was the country that lead the first wave of 'Asianization' (1975–1990), and was and still remains an important example for other Asian countries looking for innovation, economic growth and internationalization. This also means that companies from these countries copied many Japanese best practices and therefore use many Japanese characteristics. An obvious example would be the South Korean chaebol like Lotte: giant conglomerates that consist of many subsidiaries and are active in a wide variety of markets. This has many similarities with the classic Japanese keiretsu such as Mitsubishi. In fact, many similarities between Asian companies can be traced back to Japan.

The "kaizen" (good change) principle that was first implemented by Japanese companies after World War II, for instance, is also widely-spread among other Asian companies. The kaizen principle means that everybody who works for the company, from the lowest assembly worker to the CEO keeps working on personal improvement for the benefit of the company. It does not only apply to the employees of the company, but the production process as well. These many small improvements add up and allow the company to function much more efficiently. The many training and teambuilding facilities that Asian companies offer to their employees are instrumental to this.

The working ethos of Asian employers and employees, all in for the company, is also something that could first be seen in Japanese companies. They had to work long days, and while the Japanese economy was booming in the 1970s and 1980s, they accepted pretty modest wage increases. This meant that the companies could grow in a spectacular manner. We can see a similar attitude in most of the companies analyzed in this book. Companies expect a maximum of dedication from their employees. At the same time, the employees show a lot of drive to do their best for the company and are proud to work for it.

Not only are Asian workers proud of their company, they are proud of their country as well. They apply their strong sense of *soft nationalism* to the company they work for. This is especially apparent in China where CEOs do not only want to expand their business, but also want to prove that China is more than a low-quality manufacturer. A good example is Huawei, whose name already means 'China can'. The name Alibaba has association with the phrase "open sesame", which could be interpreted as opening the doors between China and the world.

This attitude is not limited to China. We see a similar strong motivation in other Asian countries. The aforementioned modest wage increases in Japan were accepted because it was for the good of the country as a whole. In the other countries mentioned in this book (India, South Korea and Vietnam), the multinationals from their own soil are also a source of national pride. While the term "nationalism" has a negative connotation for most people in the West, it can also be a source of inspiration, innovation and dedication. Of course, the governmentally-promoted nationalism in these countries can also negatively influence political relations in the region as could be seen during the recent border disputes between China and Japan. Seen from a purely business or employee attitude perspective, however, this soft nationalism has increased productivity and made people accept sacrifices that would allow the company, and in turn the country, to profit as a whole.

Soft nationalism is related to the Triple Helix influence. For example, Huawei management has close ties with the Chinese government. This implies that many foreign governments, especially the USA, are highly suspicious of double agendas because of this. These suspicions hinder the international impact of Asian companies. Therefore, it is important for these companies to show that they have only positive intentions.

While the border disputes between China and Japan led to much political turmoil and protests and calls on the streets for boycotts, Chinese and Japanese companies took a very pragmatic stance. They are too intertwined and dependent on each other for their supply chains and production processes to go along with the nationalistic sentiments of many citizens.

It is, in other words, important not to look at the soft nationalism of Asian CEOs as feelings of superiority over other countries. It is simply the pride of one's country, and the ability to help the country to become more influential on the world stage. It also means that these companies are sometimes active in local communities and charity work. Good examples are Vinamilk's program to provide school children in remote places of Vietnam with milk for free, or Panasonic's "sacred task" to help society and eliminate poverty. The reasons for this soft nationalism are, again, mostly cultural and political. Asian governments have often tried to stimulate soft nationalism, either to make it easier to implement certain policies or to distract citizens from internal scandals. This endeavor, combined with the already present "groupism" had its influence on society as a whole. It was even further motivated by the desire to catch up with the West (or with Japan) and to show the world that the country deserves the same respect as any developed economy. Even in the current age in which individualism is on the rise, even in Asia, there remains a strong conviction to do one's upmost for the country.

2.2 Adaptability

Despite, or maybe even because of, the focus on long-term strategies, Asian businesses have proven to be very adaptable. This can be seen in both recently- and well-established companies. The new companies, often from developing economies but also from more established economies, are expanding abroad, mostly (but not exclusively) towards the West. Established companies are forced to adapt to these new competitors.

The Chinese companies analyzed in this book are good examples of the first category of companies. Alibaba, which was founded in 1999 and had the largest IPO in history in 2014, started on the large Chinese home market. However, there had always been the ambition to go international; the name was even specifically chosen to be usable on non-Chinese markets. Alibaba's internet colleagues from Tencent were originally purely focused on the PC market. From 2006 onwards, however, mobile internet started growing in China and eventually became much more prevalent than internet access via a computer. The company responded by shifting its focus from PC applications to mobile apps. The gigantic success of WeChat in Asia is a demonstration that Tencent could successfully and quickly adapt to this important change in the internet market. The overall strategy of the business did not change, but it was able to quickly adapt to the new internet platforms and to stay an important and large player in the field.

Car manufacturer Geely showed a similar ability to quickly adapt. Its first cars, released at the end of the 1990s, were made to be as affordable as possible. This sole focus of price led to a comparatively low quality car and consumers on the Chinese market did not buy many of them. From 2005 onwards, the company improved the quality of its cars, and also started exporting them. This strategy was more successful, but from 2010 onwards it was changed again. Now the company follows a multi-brand strategy, were it manufactures cars in many price ranges. Due to this strategy it was able to compete very well with not only other Chinese manufacturers, but also with established international brands.

Haier is another Chinese company that has shown some excellent adaptability. When CEO Ruimin Zhang took over from his predecessor in 1984, the company was nearly bankrupt. But by the end of the decade it had become one of the leading refrigerator brands in China. A quick, radical change in company culture and corporate strategy were the corner stones for this success. Throughout the 1990s, Haier took over multiple poorly-functioning companies and brought about the same changes in them. This strategy lead to both quick growth and more diversity. The next step was to internationalize; the company started exporting and eventually even opened manufacturing plants abroad.

Huawei, a company that is very active overseas, has shown a strong adaptability in bridging the cultural gap between China and the West. In order to better understand the Western market, Western executives have been hired. The company claims to have adapted a Western professional management style and combined this with Eastern culture. Thanks to this hybridity, the company can be successful in both regions: in the East as well as in the West. This is even reflected in the pronunciation of the company name, which is officially different in each market.

The Indian companies analyzed in this book are similarly adaptive in their expansion strategies. Dr. Reddy's overall strategy is to produce medicine that is no longer under patent, meaning it can be offered for a very low price. These products were branded in India (and Russia), but the company adapted a generic brand strategy for regulated markets. Meanwhile, Dr. Reddy's also opened a research lab in the US to develop specific medicine aimed at Western markets. In other words, the company is willing to invest heavily to adapt and become more prominent on these markets. In another important foreign market for Dr. Reddy's, Russia, the company could face potential problems due to new legislation that does not allow medicine to be sold that was manufactured outside the country. Therefore, Dr. Reddy's announced that it would start production in Russia itself.

Infosys was ranked by Forbes as one of the most innovative companies in the world. It could not have achieved this without a strong sense of adaptability. Long before its international expansion, Infosys already had a corporate culture to not give in to the corruption that was prevalent in the Indian economy at that time. Due to this practice, it could internationalize easier and was able to build up a trusted name worldwide.

In Japan (and to a smaller extent South Korea), the situation is somewhat different as compared to the other countries in this book. Japan was the first Asian economy to rival Western economies. Many current Japanese companies are very old and therefore face other problems than their emerging competitors. Panasonic, for instance, had to adapt to changing market circumstances continuously. After the initial international expansion, the company had to adapt to new competitors, first from South Korea and currently from other emerging Asian countries as well, mainly China. As mentioned in the chapter about Panasonic, the only constant factor in its history is change. Fortunately for its success, the company is not afraid to keep changing and adapting to the new market circumstances.

Rakuten, which is a younger company from Japan, has shown its adaptability in the internet market. In order to be able to compete internationally, the company changed its official working language to English. Because this came as a culture shock for its, mostly Japanese, employees, the company had to intervene and offer active support. Due to these quick reactions, it was able to keep on expanding.

Clothing manufacturer and retailer Uniqlo has also faced some cultural problems during its expansion. Fashion is inherently different in every world region. By teaming up with well-known German designer Jil Sander, the company can provide clothes that fit Western tastes while holding on to its strategy of offering affordable clothing not based on the most recent trend.

The South Korean company Lotte shows a development similar to Japanese companies (it was even originally founded in Japan). Lotte's strategy was to expand and diversify as much as possible. The adaptability from chaebol such as Lotte comes from simply expanding into other, profitable, markets, while at the same time protecting less performing activities with the revenue from others, so that Lotte is able to make the necessary changes to become profitable on a larger basis than before.

2.3 The Drive to Internationalize

As has become apparent from the previous section, many Asian companies show their adaptability by expanding to, and performing exceptionally well in, foreign markets. This is because, for these companies, expanding to foreign markets is not only a way to increase profits, but sometimes almost a goal in itself. The entrepreneurs running these companies have a very international outlook. Performing well in Western markets is not only good for the profitability of the company, but also gives prestige to both the company and the home country of the company. This can be a strong motivation especially in countries with a developing economy. The drive to internationalize goes hand in hand with the adaptability of the Asian companies. While not all companies in the book are international household names (yet), they certainly have the drive to become a household name. It must have been a painful decision for Huawei to leave the US market (and perhaps that was the reason they have backtracked on the decision since) after all the spying suspicions. Fortunately for the company, it could remain in Europe.

For an older, more established company such as Panasonic, these new emerging multinationals form a huge risk, because they can often profit from lower labor costs while delivering high quality products. Therefore, the older Japanese (and South Korean) companies are also forced to reconsider their international strategies. Regardless of motivation, there are two possible ways in which Asian multinationals could establish themselves in new markets. The first is "greenfield" investment: setting up a completely new office, factory or daughter in the new market. The second is M&A: mergers and/or acquisitions with existing companies. Since the border between a merger and an acquisition is not always clear (sometimes takeovers are being communicated as mergers), we will view this as a similar category.

Within the companies discussed in the book, M&A activities are the most prevalent. Alibaba's "Big Bao Strategy" is a classic example of the M&A approach to expansion, although it is currently mostly aimed at the Chinese market. The Geely takeover of Volvo is probably one of the most well-known M&A activities by a Chinese company discussed in the book. The company was able to realize the takeover because it had lots of cash while Volvo was in crisis. Thanks to the acquisition, Geely can not only profit from Volvo's brand, prestige and focus on safety, but also from their technological knowledge, which would enable it to perform better in competition with its international competitors. This, combined with the diverse brand strategy, was of great importance for Geely's success.

Huawei used a combination of greenfield and M&A methods by first starting a joint venture together with Symantic, and later buying all the stakes of this jointventure. Lenovo's takeover of IBM's PC division is comparable to Geely's Volvo takeover. In one swoop, the company secured a well-known and trusted brand, as well as the technological knowledge of the company. In a similar vein, they took over part of Motorola's business. This fits into Lenovo's overall strategy to take over companies that match their basic interests as well as extend their portfolio.

Tencent also follows this strategy. In markets were the Tencent product fails to take over share from a competitor, the company teams up with another smaller competitor. In practice these strategic partnerships look more like takeovers. Abroad, Tencent has bought many shares of South Korean game developers, and more recently, shares of some US game developers as well. However, in Tencent's case, this was mostly done to expand the business on the domestic market, which is still the most important one for the company.

The takeovers by Geely and Lenovo in particular have come as a surprise for most Western consumers. However, as this book has shown, both companies did not just appear out of thin air, but already had a longer history. The takeover of foreign firms was simply part of their international expansion strategy. The Indian Infosys also expands by acquiring foreign companies. Several companies (including some from Australia and Switzerland) were bought up by and incorporated into Infosys.

For Japanese companies, M&A activities have always been an important strategy. This can also be shown by the companies analyzed in this book. While Panasonic has halted its M&A activities a bit in recent years due to cost-cutting and restructuring, we can see the classic pattern within Rakuten. After the Japanese market lost most of its growing potential, the company started to look abroad. The fastest way to get a foothold abroad were to look for M&A opportunities. Now, over 50 companies are part of Rakuten. The South Korean chaebol Lotte has also expanded and diversified its business by M&A activities, including the takeovers of foreign companies. Examples of this are its acquisitions in the Belgian and Polish food industries.

However, Asian companies are not afraid for the "hard" way of foreign expansion either. Greenfield activities can be done both with a (foreign) partner, or by the company itself. We can see that many Asian companies open up manufacturing and R&D projects on foreign markets. These R&D projects often (but not exclusively) take place in developed markets, while manufacturing plants are often (but again, not exclusively) opened in developing markets. Greenfield investment also includes the opening of local offices for management of supplies, customer support and PR. While these investments are often of much lower value than M&A activities, they can be very profitable in the long run for the receiving country. Not only will a new office require employees, and thus directly create jobs and tax revenue, there will also be a spillover effect for surrounding businesses and the possibility of further foreign investment.

2.4 Triple Helix as a Facilitator

All of the previously mentioned similarities between Asian companies have an important facilitator: the Triple Helix of government, business and education. The Triple Helix system concerns the close cooperation between these three cornerstones of society. In most Asian countries, the government is very strong and leading. This is most obvious in China, where the implementation of the "go global" policy resulted in a surge of internationalization amongst Chinese companies.

The governmental support does not necessarily happen directly. Alibaba and Tencent, for example, profited from the liberalization of the internet and advertisement markets, as well as from government programs, to increase the amount of people with internet access.

Since the opening up of the country in 1979, the Chinese government has slowly but surely increased the possibilities of Chinese companies to go global and started with more active encouragement since the turn of the century. The current M&A wave from Chinese companies is a direct result of this government policy. The liberalization tendency, however, does not imply a less important role of the Triple Helix. In practice, liberalization often means less direct involvement of the government. But in the Chinese case, it can be seen that, while markets have been liberalized, the government still plays a very active role, not only as a regulator, but also as an encourager.

In India, the case is similar to China. The government has been liberalizing the market while also heavily investing in necessary development such as infrastructure, healthcare and education. This created an environment in which companies such as Dr. Reddy's and Infosys could grow. Vietnam is still in the earlier stages of the same development.

Japan has a much more developed economy than China and India, and therefore has another role for the government. However, the interaction between business cycles and government is still very important. The interaction between the keidanren (the Japanese Business Federation) and the Japanese government was and is very important for the policy making process. The "amakudari" process, in which politicians retire early to join an important business, shows how closely linked the Japanese political elite is with big business.

In South Korea, the government also has a firm grip on the economy. In order to make the South Korean economy more resilient for the future, it has started to encourage diversification and a loosening of the strict rules on (inward) foreign investment. It actively promotes high-tech and green industries, in which it sees the biggest growth potential.

The third part of the Triple Helix, education, is by no means the least important in Asia. Education is instrumental in the processes of innovation and adaptability which are needed to perform well in today's world economy. Educational institutions not only provide businesses with well-educated employees and board members, they can also actively work together in fields like R&D. Many Asian companies invest heavily in education (both in their own company as well as in public or private institutes) for this particular reason. The government, of course, also has a role in providing, stimulating and improving education.

2.5 Quality Products

In the minds of many Western people, Asia is still a place where low-quality manufacturers make cheap copies of Western products. While such companies certainly exist, the analyses in this book have shown that Asian multinationals are quite different. They produce high quality goods for a competitive price. This is caused by a combination of low manufacturing costs, large scale production and well-done market research, adaptability and a strong drive for high quality. A car-manufacturer like Geely produces a wide variety of different models for different consumers, but they all combine high quality with affordable prices compared to their direct competitors. Haier is another example. It offers a variety of products for a very competitive price, without compromising on quality. Not only are its products themselves of high quality, the company also has a high standard of service.

This service-oriented approach was very important for the early growth of the company, as well as for building trust amongst consumers. Huawei is another company that singles out customer service as an important focus point. Panasonic still bases its business practices on the writings of its founder, who viewed it as his "sacred task" to eliminate poverty and improve people's lives. This approach also leads to a focus on affordable high quality products as well as customer care and support. Lenovo offers its products in both the middle and high end markets. Price-wise, they are not the cheapest, but still offer a product of higher quality than their direct competitors.

For internet based companies such as Alibaba, Tencent and Rakuten, customer service is even more important than for manufacturers of physical goods. Alibaba and Rakuten mostly have other companies as customers instead of individual consumers. However, in the C2C market, in which Alibaba is also active and where fraud is often a point of concern, measures were taken to increase the quality of the product by combating fraud. Trust is very important in the internet business, and that is why Rakuten has both high quality standards and tight regulation of its platforms. This increases trust among consumers using the platform, which in turn makes it more attractive for merchants to use the platform as well.

Tencent has a somewhat different approach than most of the other companies analyzed in this book because of their unique revenue model. Their products are of comparable quality to those of their competitors, but they are offered for free with optional add-ons that users can pay for. Therefore, it is very important for the company to know what is popular with their users. Dr. Reddy's, meanwhile, produces high quality medicines, but is able to sell them for very affordable prices because they are patent-free. Their R&D departments improve the quality of existing products and in this way the company can offer products with high standards for a comparatively low price. For Uniqlo, founded during the Japanese "first lost decade" of slow economic growth, offering high-quality, affordable products is in its blood. By focusing on more "timeless" clothing, instead of the latest trends like their competitors, the company can profit from economics of scale and is able to offer a cheaper product, while still coming up with very high quality. Vinamilk offers products for various income groups, but all with high-quality standards, ensured by its continuously improving R&D department.

A unique aspect of Asian products is the way the branding of their products works. There is an important difference in "branding culture" between Asia and the West. Where Western products often have individual brand names, in Asia it is much more common that a big company uses its name to brand all of their products. Lotte has both hotels and aluminum manufacturers, but with the same company name (although they do not rename their acquisitions). Yamaha produces both keyboards and motorcycles under the same brand name. Of course, this difference could lead to problems when Asian countries are internationalizing and also enter markets where such branding concepts are perceived differently.

Therefore, Asian companies have found a variety of solutions for this problem. For some companies, there is no real need to change their branding strategy. In the internet industry, for instance, using a single brand name is pretty common (Google, for example). Alibaba specifically choose its name because it refers to a tale that is known worldwide. Tencent mostly operates with two brand names (QQ and WeChat) that are used for a wide variety of products, but are also linked together in various ways. The company name returns also in some products (Tencent Weibo). Other companies buy up foreign competitors in order to get hold of a trusted and well-known brand name. Geely bought Volvo, for instance, and Lenovo IBM Thinkpad. Buying a brand is the easiest way of brand-building, but can also be expensive and does not necessarily mean that the new owner can keep up the prestigious name of the brand.

Rakuten has bought many foreign competitors and uses a combination of the company name and the original name (Rakuten's Play.com) to both build brand awareness for itself as well as to profit from customer loyalty to the original company. Huawei has built up a good reputation in the professional telecom market, and is now also entering the consumer market under its own brand name. Slowly the name is becoming more well-known among the general public outside of China. Haier has three distinctive brands which focus on different markets. The main brand remains Haier, but there is also Casarte and Leader for different uses. Dr. Reddy's sells its products under a generic no-brand name on the Western market, but uses distinctive brand names elsewhere. Panasonic is more traditionally Asian in its branding strategy, although this way of branding was only chosen relatively recently. Before 2003, Panasonic operated a variety of different brand names. For all these different approaches, these companies have one goal in common: they want to build well-known and trustworthy brands for the international market.

2.6 Competitiveness

Based on all characteristics mentioned so far, the final similarity between emerging Asian multinationals is their competitiveness. There are many fears in the West for the "yellow peril". Whether these fears are justified or not, the question remains: how did these companies manage to become so competitive? The answers have already been provided above and are summarized below. The emerging Asian multinationals have:

- A strong corporate culture that is based on long-term growth strategies.
- The ability to quickly adapt to different markets and different market circumstances.
- A strong drive to internationalize.
- Excellent products for competitive prices.

These four points are facilitated by the fifth characteristic: the Triple Helix. All of these factors together create very competitive companies that are ready to conquer the world.

The competitiveness of the emerging Asian multinationals leads to both challenges and chances for the EU and the USA. Western companies might have a hard time to compete with the Asians. On the other hand, Asian companies are not necessarily hostile. They often seek cooperation with local companies and are willing to invest heavily. Because they prefer long-term growth strategies over short-term profit making, they are also often reliable and loyal partners. Western governments and educational institutions should also actively be involved when dealing with these companies. Not only because the Triple Helix system has been so successful in Asia, but also because Asian companies expect some form of governmental presence when investing abroad.

3 Differences Between the Asian Companies

The analysis of the similarities between emerging Asian multinationals has made clear that there are many differences as well. These differences are a result of the way the companies try to realize the similarities. Broadly speaking, the differences are dependent on: (1) differences between countries (cultural identity) and (2) differences between companies (the specific character of entrepreneurs).

3.1 Differences Between Countries

Asia is a huge continent which houses 60 % of the world's total population and has a history that goes back for thousands of years. Obviously, this means that there are large differences in the identity, political-economic situation and history of Asia. In turn, these huge cultural differences have a direct impact on the corporate culture of the companies from these countries. They influence how they can do business. In this section, we will focus on the countries of the companies we have analyzed in this book.

There are roughly three different ways of political-economic decision making. The first is the strict top down model:

This model is the Chinese model (Fig. 1). There are strict orders from the top towards the bottom with little or no room for discussion. This is in line with China's idea of a "socialist market" system. The government is not only the strongest part of the Triple Helix in this model, it is also the sole leader and decision maker.

The complete opposite of the model is the Western model, which is also practiced in post-bubble Japan (Fig. 2):

In this model, there is interaction between "top" and "down" as well as interaction between the business sector and the educational institutions. While the government can still play a very prominent role in this model, it is not the only decision maker. The influence from "down" to "top" can be in the form of participation via

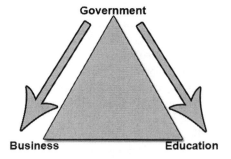

Fig. 1 Chinese model of political-economic decision making

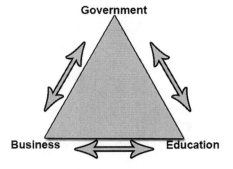

Fig. 2 The Western model of political-economic decision making

Fig. 3 The Asian (Japan, South Korea, Taiwan) model of political economic decision making

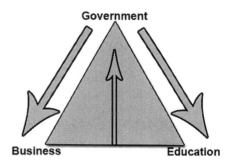

elections, a strong lobby, or otherwise. The three parts of the Triple Helix are much more balanced as far as their power is concerned.

The most prominent model in Asia, however, is a mix between the first two models:

This is the "old Japanese" model (1970–1990), which is also practiced in countries like South Korea and Taiwan (Fig. 3). While the interaction is mostly top-down, the top is still open for feedback. There is a strong, leading role for the government, but other voices also have influence. While the government is the strongest party of the Triple Helix, business and education play an important role as well, not only as receivers of orders, but also for feedback towards the government.

This strong leading role of the government in Asia can be both helpful and harmful for domestic companies. On the one hand, a strictly-regulated economy is often protectionist, which makes it easier for domestic companies to compete with big foreign multinationals in their own market. But on the other hand, it can also hinder their international expansion. Most Asian governments realize the importance of internationalization, which is most obvious in China's "go global" policy. But even then, a strong governmental influence can be a disadvantage. Take for instance Huawei, which has an excellent relationship with the Chinese government. In the USA and Australia, however, these warm ties were perceived as a national security risk eventually leading to Huawei (temporary planning on) leaving the US market completely.

Companies from less regulated markets like Japan do not face these risks, even though the political and business elite in Japan often consist of the same people. Of course, the view of China and Japan as a whole also plays a role here. Since World War II, Japan has been seen as an ally of the West while China, on the other hand, has been seen as an adversary. These historical differences between countries also play an important role in their business cultures. Not only the perception the West has constructed of these countries is important. In fact, the view Asian countries have of each other, is probably even more important. Japan in particular is perceived negatively because of its role before and during World War II. Many Asian nations feel that Japan has not made enough apologies for what happened. At the same time, the Japanese feel that World War II has become a wild card for other countries in the region to be pulled out arbitrarily in unrelated diplomatic disputes.

But the history since World War II has also had its impact on the economic situation. China became a communist nation, while Japan was guided towards a free market parliamentary democracy under the American occupation. Korea split in two after the Korean War, with a capitalist South and a communist North. After a similar conflict in Vietnam, the country was eventually united under communist rule. India meanwhile, became a democratic, federal republic after its independence from the UK, where the socialist party constructed a strong government. While in recent years there has been a similar movement towards more liberalization in all of the countries mentioned above (except North Korea), the old ideologies are still important. In countries like China and Vietnam, the government plays a much more leading role than in South Korea and Japan, as discussed earlier. This of course has its consequences in how business is conducted. Local regulations are important for emerging multinationals especially where overseas M&A and greenfield activities are concerned.

The overall differences in cultural identity between the Asian countries are another point of interest. For example, China has a much more extrovert culture, compared to the more introvert Japanese. Conventions in China are easy-going and a contract can be signed fast, but can also change unexpectedly. In Japan, protocols are strict and the decision-making process is long, but contracts are rock solid. South Korea, meanwhile, is somewhat halfway between introvert and extrovert, has stricter conventions than China, but flexibility and fast sales are deemed more important than a contract. And, while for the outside observer the culture of these countries may seem a bit similar, Chinese, Japanese and South Koreans view themselves as completely different. In other words: Western policy makers should not only make general "Asian strategies" to deal with companies from this continent, but country-specific ones as well. Therefore, a deep understanding of the different cultures and motivations of Asian countries is highly necessary.

3.2 Differences Between Companies

Obviously, companies from the same country in most cases do not have the same corporate culture. For instance, in Japan we can see a divide between the traditional Japanese-style, giant corporation and newer US-style startups. This is caused not only by the specific character of the entrepreneur, but also by time. It is, after all, not impossible for a small startup to grow into a big conglomerate. We can already see such a development from Chinese internet companies such as Alibaba and Tencent. They started in a very specific market, but kept expanding into different markets abroad and taking over (or starting new) companies.

We discussed the similarities in corporate culture between emerging Asian multinationals. They have a family-like atmosphere, a focus on long-term strategies and many Japanese characteristics, and in addition their entrepreneurs, are often motivated by soft nationalism. But even these similarities manifest themselves in different ways. Take for example the groupist structures. The similarity here is that the company expects that its employees give their best for the company and show a loyalty that often goes beyond what we are used to in the West. For some companies (Uniqlo, for instance), this means that all employees should follow company directions without hesitation and that there is little room for individual initiatives.

This is the traditional view many people have of big Asian companies. However, there are other companies that specifically stimulate internal competition in order to get the best out of people. A good example is Haier. While it is a massive company active in many markets, it has split its 80,000 employees into 2000 "zi zhu jing ying ti" (ZZJYTs, self-managed teams). These ZZJYTs function basically as smaller, separate companies. This environment stimulates innovation and initiative. It creates the somewhat paradoxical situation where competition between several parts of a company is good for the company as a whole. It also shows that the political-economic system of a country cannot always be directly related to the corporate culture of multinationals from this country. That would underestimate the influence CEOs have on business. The Chinese political system might be strictly top down and the Chinese economy might be a socialist state-lead market economy, but there is definitely still room for excellent entrepreneurship. The founders of Alibaba and Tencent became billionaires without direct state support, thanks to their market knowledge and entrepreneurship.

This is true in other Asian countries as well. Compare, for example, Rakuten with Panasonic and Uniqlo. While Rakuten follows the typical M&A pattern of foreign expansion for Asian companies, the corporate culture is incomparable to that of the much more traditional Panasonic and Uniqlo. This is partly due to the different markets in which the companies operate, but also because of the vision, character and structure of their CEOs. When Rakuten founder Hiroshi Mikitani left a good banking job to start a new venture, his family was shocked. For many Japanese at that time (and this is largely still the case), the best way to success is to start working for a large, well-established and prestigious company and work your way up over the course of your life. Perhaps because of his exposure to the view of entrepreneurship in the US, or perhaps because of what he experienced after the Kobe earthquake, he decided to leave this path and start his own company. Regardless of his exact motivation, a step like this shows Mikitani's determination and his will to leave the traditional path of Japanese culture.

Perhaps it also a sign of changing times. As has been discussed in detail in the chapter about Asian HR in this book, the traditional Western perception of Asian societies might be based on outdated preconceptions. The Japan of 2015 is not the same as the Japan from 1970, and the same is true for other Asian countries as well. In this perspective, people like Mikitani might not be the exception to the rule of their countries, but the pioneers of a new style of Asian entrepreneurship. This view is reinforced when we look at the Chinese outward foreign direct investment in the Netherlands over the past 10 years. The vast majority of these Chinese companies investing in the Netherlands are not giant corporations, but smaller and younger companies. The new Asian style companies combine traditional values and attitudes with Western entrepreneur styles, creating a hybrid-style of corporate culture which is very successful.

At the same time the more traditional, conglomerate-style companies, also remain active on the world stage and are reforming themselves to be able to compete with their new competitors. They mainly try to do this by focusing on new markets with growth potential. An example is Panasonic's recent investment in sustainability and green fields. While these companies operate differently as opposed to the new generation of Asian companies, their role is in no way played out. Therefore they should certainly not be underestimated.

The above analysis certainly suggests how we in the West should react to Asian companies. A sound analysis and deep knowledge of not only the Asian region as a whole, but also of individual countries and individual companies is of utmost importance. Currently this knowledge is sparse and diffuse in the West. Political policymakers, academic experts and business leaders should consult each other more frequently and centralize their knowledge and experiences. Only in this way will we be prepared for the Asian future.

4 Future Developments

The differences in the political-economic systems of Asian countries have a strong implication for the international drive of Asian companies. In the case of the strongly top-down Chinese model, this implies that after the implementation of the "go global" policy (2001) there is an enormous increase of outward foreign direct investment (OFDI) from China. The implicit claim of most chapters in this book is that Asian companies will flock to the West in ever-increasing numbers. In the coming years, this concerns companies primarily coming from countries we have been dealing with in this book: China, India, South Korea and Vietnam. In the case of Japan, there will be primarily a focus on mergers and acquisitions.

Obviously, this is not to say that in recent years companies from the countries involved have not been active in the West: on the contrary! As an example of this tendency, we could testify to the recent Chinese activities worldwide. Even in the future these activities in all likelihood will increase to a significant extent. Therefore, some specialists ask the questions: is the West still relevant? Is China buying the world? (Nolan 2012).

Over the last decade, China has quickly developed itself into a global economic superpower. Many Western countries view this as both an opportunity (a big potential market with increasingly wealthy customers) and a danger (ranging from Chinese foreign buying sprees to espionage and other national security issues). This is especially evident in the Outward Foreign Direct Investment (OFDI) activities of Chinese companies. On the one hand the increasing investments from China are a welcome addition to the national income, but on the other hand there are severe concerns. Many Chinese investors are state-owned companies and therefore seen with distrust. Telecom company Huawei, for instance, wanted to even completely leave the US market, because it was unable to complete deals due to espionage concerns.

In this part of the conclusion, we will briefly examine some of the trends in Chinese OFDI, both worldwide and in the Netherlands in particular, to examine whether these concerns are well-grounded. Are the Chinese really buying up the world? The section concludes with an overview of some Chinese OFDI activities in the Netherlands over the past 4 years, both greenfield projects and M&A activities. These examples are by no means meant to give a definitive overview of all relevant Chinese OFDI in the Netherlands in this period. Official figures are hard to come by and many activities did not receive much media coverage, if at all. Companies are often not very keen on disclosing the value of their deals either. Therefore, some of the larger OFDI projects have been selected, together with some smaller examples. This should give an adequate overview of the specific kind of recent OFDI activities of Chinese companies in the Netherlands. Because Hong Kong, while an autonomous part of China, is regarded separately in most statistics, the focus will be exclusively on companies from mainland China.

4.1 Chinese Foreign Direct Investment Worldwide

In this section, we will take a look at the overall Chinese OFDI flows and stock since 2004 and their geographical spread. Following the definition by UNCTAD, OFDI flows are: "For associates and subsidiaries, [...] the net sales of shares and loans (including non-cash acquisitions made against equipment, manufacturing rights, etc.) to the parent company plus the parent firm's share of the affiliate's reinvested earnings plus total net intra-company loans (short- and long-term) provided by the parent company. For branches, [O]FDI flows consist of the increase in reinvested earnings plus the net increase in funds received from the foreign direct investor" (UNCTAD 2014b). Stock is "for associate and subsidiary enterprises, [...] the value of the share of their capital and reserves (including retained profits) attributable to the parent enterprise (this is equal to total assets minus total liabilities), plus the net indebtedness of the associate or subsidiary to the parent firm. For branches, it is the value of fixed assets and the value of current assets and investments, excluding amounts due from the parent, less liabilities to third parties" (UNCTAD 2014b).

Since the formalization of the "go global" policy in 2001, the Chinese government is actively supporting outward FDI (Segers and Stam 2013). After 2004, the Chinese OFDI really took off. There is an explosive grow between 2007 and 2008. A slight stop in 2008 is followed by an increase in flows which continues at a constant rate until 2013 (Fig. 4) (UNCTAD 2014a).

Chinese OFDI stock, on the other hand, has been on a constant exponential rise since 2005 (Fig. 5).

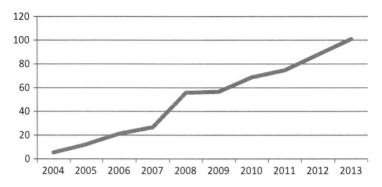

Fig. 4 Chinese OFDI flows 2004–2013 in billion US$ (UNCTAD 2014a)

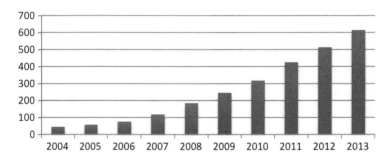

Fig. 5 Chinese OFDI stock 2004–2013 in billion US$ (UNCTAD 2014a)

This enormous growth in both OFDI flows and stocks has caused China's fast rise on the international investor lists. Where China was the 24th largest investor (measured in OFDI flows) in 2004, by 2013 the country had become the third largest investor, only behind the USA and Japan. In OFDI stocks, China is not quite there yet, but rapidly approaching the top as well. The country rose from 26th place in 2004 to 12th place in 2013 (UNCTAD 2014a).

Geographically, Asia was and continues to be, the greatest destination of Chinese OFDI flows. In 2012, 78 % of all Chinese OFDI flows went to Asia (National Bureau of Statistics of China 2014). These Asian flows mostly go to the autonomous region of Hong Kong, where many Chinese companies have subsidiaries for their outward investments. This is a result of the fact that Hong Kong had a stock exchange long before Shanghai (Segers and Stam 2013). Figures 6 and 7 show the geographic distribution of the Chinese OFDI flows with and without Asia in percentages.

An interesting observation is that the OFDI flows towards Europe have overtaken those towards Latin America in 2012, which used to be the predominant destination of Chinese OFDI outside of Asia. The sharp rise of OFDI towards North America between 2011 and 2012 is also remarkable, as well as the sudden peak of OFDI towards Africa in 2008.

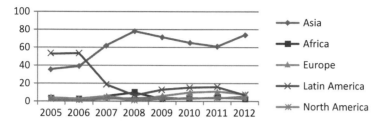

Fig. 6 Geographical distribution of Chinese OFDI flows per continent (National Bureau of Statistics of China 2014)

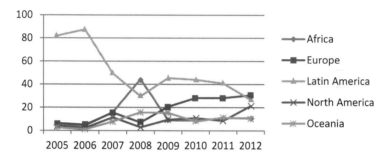

Fig. 7 Geographical distribution of Chinese OFDI flows per continent without Asia (National Bureau of Statistics of China 2014)

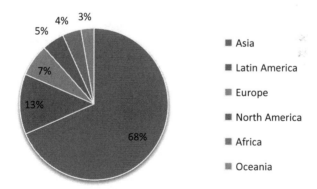

Fig. 8 Geographical distribution of Chinese OFDI stock in 2012 (National Bureau of Statistics of China 2014)

The concentration of OFDI stock shows a similar distribution. Asia has by far the largest share, followed by Latin America. Europe had a slightly larger share than North America, Africa and Oceania (Fig. 8). This also means that a trend has been broken, since historically China used to have a larger percentage of its OFDI stock in Africa than in Europe or North America (Segers and Stam 2013).

4.2 Chinese Foreign Direct Investment in The Netherlands

Segers and Stam (2013) mention, based on figures from 2010: "Chinese companies have not prioritized investment in Europe over the years because the international investment agenda was mainly focused on acquiring natural resources and energy to fuel Chinese industrial production. As the Chinese domestic economy is currently restructuring and laying more emphasis on technological advancement and the development of the services sector, the prospect of intensified Chinese investment flows in Europe is very likely". The recent OFDI flow and stock trends as shown in the previous section seem to indicate that indeed Europe has become a more important place of investment for Chinese companies.

Unfortunately, there are no recent official figures concerning Chinese OFDI flows and stock in the Netherlands. The Chinese Ministry of Commerce (MOFCOM), published its most recent English Statistical Bulletin in 2011. De Nederlandse Bank (DNB, the Dutch central bank) also tracks inwards FDI, but has figures that are incomplete (2012 is missing) and which differ from the official Chinese ones, so the two sets cannot be combined.

The MOFCOM figures show some ups and downs in OFDI flows towards the Netherlands, as can be seen in Fig. 9 (please note that the data from 2005 and 2006 do not contain financial OFDI, so in reality these values are higher).

The figures of DNB show different Chinese OFDI flows. This is probably the result of using different currencies during calculations and different definitions. These figures also show a spectacular explosion of Chinese OFDI flows towards the Netherlands in 2013 (DNB is missing figures from 2012). This might have been caused by the HNA Group deal (Fig. 10) (see the next section).

According to MOFCOM figures, in 2010 the Netherlands was, with 64.53 million US$, the sixth largest receiver of Chinese OFDI flows in the EU, behind Luxembourg (3207.19 million US$), Sweden (1367.23 million US$), Germany (412.35 million US$), Hungary (370.1 million US$) and the UK (330.33 million US$). In the same year, the Netherlands was at fifth place stock-wise, with 486.71

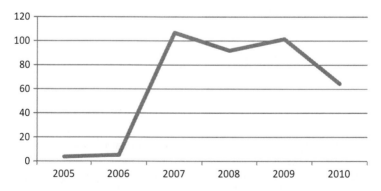

Fig. 9 Chinese OFDI flows towards the Netherlands 2005–2010 in US$ millions, according to MOFCOM (MOFCOM 2011)

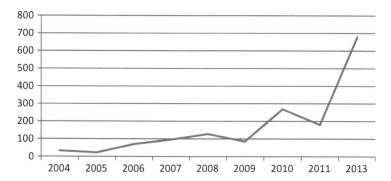

Fig. 10 Chinese OFDI flows towards the Netherlands 2004–2013 in € millions, according to DNB (DNB 2014)

million US$, behind Luxembourg (5786.75 million US$), Germany (1502.29 million US$), Sweden (1479.12 million US$) and the UK (1358.35 million US$). Between 2007 and 2010, Chinese OFDI stock in the Netherlands more than tripled, from 138.76 million US$ to 486.71 million US$ (MOFCOM 2011). These figures show that, compared to other EU countries, the Netherlands is at the sub-top as far as receiving Chinese OFDI goes.

This position of the Netherlands also matches with statistics from the European Commission (Clegg and Voss 2012). At the end of 2013, Dutch Prime Minister Mark Rutte was in China for a short official visit. There, he stated he welcomed more Chinese investment and also stressed the fact that in the EU, the Netherlands is the third largest receiver of Chinese OFDI behind Germany and the UK (People's Daily 2013).

Chinese OFDI stock in the Netherlands is mostly concentrated in the services sector, but there is also a considerable amount in the manufacturing sector (Clegg and Voss 2012).

Another way of measuring the interest of Chinese companies in the Netherlands is the amount of projects the Netherlands Foreign Investment Agency (NFIA) has acquitted over the past years. These figures are of course not necessarily representative of all Chinese investments in the Netherlands as a whole, but they give a good indication of OFDI trends. Over 2013, the NFIA reported 26 Chinese investment projects. This makes China by far the largest Asian investor. However, when measured by amount of jobs created, China ranks third (after India and Japan), implying that most Chinese investments were relatively small scale (NFIA 2014). An overview of all the NFIA acquisitions since 2004 can be found in Fig. 11. It is important to note that the NFIA opened its first office in mainland China in 2004 (Shanghai), followed by two additional offices in 2006 (Guangzhou) and 2008 (Beijing). This extended presence in China might explain the increases after 2004 and 2006.

These figures show a similar trend to the aforementioned ones: Chinese investment in the Netherlands is gradually increasing. While there are ups and downs in

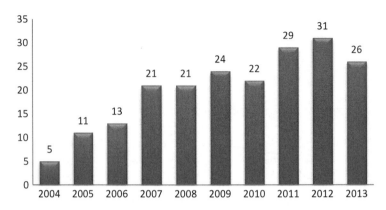

Fig. 11 Chinese acquisitions by the NFIA, 2004–2013 (NFIA 2007, 2009, 2010, 2011, 2012, 2013, 2014)

the OFDI flows, the overall direction is certainly upwards. Both Chinese OFDI flows and stocks have increased dramatically since 2004 and there are no signs of a cooling down.

At the same time, other countries in the EU have managed to attract a lot more Chinese OFDI than the Netherlands. It is worth mentioning that Luxemburg saw the Chinese OFDI stock increase from 122.83 million US$ to 2484.38 million US$ between 2008 and 2009, and that Sweden saw an increase from 111.89 million US$ to 1479.12 million US$ between 2009 and 2010. This considerable increase was the result of large scale takeovers, such as Geely's takeover of Volvo in Sweden. At the same time, Luxemburg is often used as a gateway for investments elsewhere in the EU, so OFDI entering the country does not necessarily end up there (Clegg and Voss 2012).

When compared to other countries, OFDI flows from China to the Netherlands so far play a small part in the total breakdown. According to De Nederlandse Bank, in 2013, China was the 31st biggest investor in the Netherlands. If Hong Kong were to be included, China would still only end up at 18th place. To put this into perspective, the total OFDI flows of China and Hong Kong to the Netherlands is only 5 % of the OFDI flows of the USA towards the Netherlands in the same year. The largest Asian investor in the Netherlands in 2013, Japan, had OFDI flows that were three times as big as those of China and Hong Kong combined (DNB 2014).

4.3 Some Examples of Chinese Foreign Direct Investment in the EU: the case of the Netherlands

The following lists ten recent examples of Chinese OFDI: it concerns ten Chinese companies over the last 4 years;

1. 2011, March: Landwind Motors Company Europe (Helmond)

   Landwind is an automobile brand from Jiangling Motors Holding (JMH). JMH, one of the largest automobile manufacturers of China, is a public company founded in 1952. Their Landwind CV9 was the first Chinese car which got through the European approval tests and marked their entry into the European market (Landwind 2014). This car was partly developed in Helmond. On the high tech campus there, Landwind established an office from which it planned to start R&D activities together with the research institutions TNO in the Netherlands and Tüv in Germany. The R&D focuses on research and test programs in the fields of emission, safety and electric cars. It will also take over some tasks previously done by Jiangling itself. In the future, it is planned to give the Helmond office a larger role in the development of European models for Jianling. Marketing and sales activities are also done from the Helmond office (Automotive 2011). Later in 2011, there were also rumors that Jiangling Motors wanted to manufacture cars at Nedcar, a Dutch car manufacturing company which previously did manufacturing work for Mitsubishi. However, this seemed to be based on a misunderstanding: Nedcar was only in contact with the Dutch Landwind importer to store the cars on Nedcar terrain (Autoweek 2011).

2. 2011: NavInfo: Mapscape (Eindhoven)

   NavInfo is the largest digital map provider in China and the fourth largest in the world. It was established in 2002, but originated from the Navigation Department of China Siwei Surveying and Mapping, which was founded in 1997 (NavInfo 2014). Mapscape was founded in 2007 and is the market leader in production services for navigation display maps. The maps compiled by Mapscape are used for GPS systems in consumer cars. Customers are companies like Audi, BMW, Volkswagen, NAVTEQ and Tele Atlas (Telematicsnews 2011). According to the company, "Mapscape joined NavInfo to ensure sufficient financial support to build the next generation of digital map ecosystems and telematics services. For NavInfo, this merger also makes strategic sense as it gives the company access to the high-tech tool chain and quality processes of Mapscape. Cooperation between Beijing and Eindhoven is close and frequent. The combination of NavInfo and Mapscape is important to Asian and European customers, as automotive manufacturers today are global players with global customer management processes. The merger therefore results in a powerful combination of creativity, reliability, scalability, continuity, efficiency and a global view on business" (Mapscape 2014). One hundred percent of Mapscape's assets were bought by NavInfo for around seven million €. This money was excess from its initial public offering (Telematicsnews 2011).

3. 2011, July: Beijing Hainachuan Automotive Parts Co., Ltd (BHAP): Inalfa Roof Systems Group B.V. (Inalfa) (Venray)

   BHAP is a leading automotive parts manufacturer founded in 2008. It is a subsidiary of the Beijing Automotive Group CO., Ltd. Inalfa designs, develops and manufactures vehicle roof systems. It is one of the biggest companies in its field and supplies to car manufacturers worldwide. Some of its customers are BMW, Daimler, Chrysler, Ford, General Motors, Geely and Volkswagen (Autonews 2011). Inalfa has been active in China since 2006 and opened a factory in Iantai in 2007. It considers the deal with BHAP as an opportunity to increase its activities in Asia, where it expects to generate 45 % of its revenue. For BHAP, Inalfa will be a means to access the European and North American markets, where it did not have subsidiaries yet. BHAP has taken over Inalfa completely, but the Inalfa headquarters, as well as R&D and production facilities, will stay in Venray. The management of Inalfa would remain in their positions as well (Automobielmanagement 2011). While the amount of money involved in the deal has not been disclosed, it is estimated to be one of the largest, if not the largest, investments from mainland China in the Netherlands up to 2011 (Volkskrant 2014). Inalfa will be able to function mostly independent, showing that Chinese investments are not only meant to quickly buy Western knowledge, as is often feared.

4. 2011, July: Ausnutria Dairy Corp Ltd's: Hyproca Dairy Group B.V. (Ommen)

   Ausnutria is a leading company in the Chinese diary market. It produces, distributes and sells high quality milk products in mainland China. Hyproca Dairy dates back to 1897, and is "a professional dairy factory which not only produces own brand products but also supplies various large international companies with top-quality dairy ingredients" (Ausnutria-Hyproca 2014). Ausnutria paid 10.4 million € for an additional 31.6 % stake in the company, which would mean that it had a combined stake of 51 %. This takeover was the result of a lack of trust from Chinese consumers in domestic milk products. During 2008, there was a huge scandal with tampered milk. In order to make the milk appear more protein rich, it was laced with melamine. This resulted in almost 300,000 sick children throughout China as well as six deaths. After the scandal came to light, Chinese consumers started buying foreign brands in droves. Chinese dairy companies, including Ausnutria, are looking for foreign partners in the hope of improving their products and winning back trust from the domestic Chinese consumers (China Daily 2011). Another example of this were the plans to build a milk factory of Scepter Brands Company in Assen. However, this idea was ultimately canceled (DVHN 2013).

5. 2011, November: Lepu Medical Technology: Comed (Bolsward)

   Lepu is a manufacturer of coronary artery intervention equipment founded in 1999. Comed started in 2000 as a trading and service company. According to their website, in 2011 they "achieved to build up [their] own product portfolio in interventional cardiology, structural heart disease, peripheral vascular, critical care and IVD by integrating European needs and quality requirements with Chinese manufacture advantages to provide the best technology and solution to the WW health care system" (Comed 2014). Initially Lepu invested 5.5 million € to set up a Dutch branch, together with its subsidiary Tiandi Hexie Technology. This Dutch branch of this Chinese company would acquire 40 % of Comed for 1.39 million € and invest another 3.47 million € into the company afterwards. This would result in an indirect 70 % share for Lepu. The goal of Lepu was to further expand in the Dutch and European markets (Research in China 2011).

6. 2011, November: China Hi-Tech Group Company (CHTGC): GINAF Trucks Nederland B.V. (Veenendaal)

   CHTGC is a state-owned company that was established in 1998. It operates in three fields: textile machinery, textile and trade and commercial vehicles (CHTGC 2014a). GINAF is a manufacturer of trucks, which had financial trouble during 2011 and eventually went bankrupt. It could continue to exist thanks to CHTGC, which bought the company at the end of 2011. According to GINAF, "the primary goal is to continue with GINAF as a brand according to current standards, both on the national and international level. The Netherlands remains the focus, with its loyal customers and specific legislation. This is almost identical to the already set course of GINAF" (GINAF 2011). Unfortunately, not much information can be found behind the reasoning of the takeover. However, earlier in 2011 CHTGC also bought some automotive companies and formed a group consisting of companies in Germany, Austria and Italy (CHTGC 2014b). Presumably the company wants to enter the European market or wants to acquire innovation, since GINAF was known as an innovative manufacturer.

7. 2012, June: LiuGong (Almere)

   LiuGong is a machinery manufacturer originally founded in 1958. It has establishments all over the globe. Its mission statement is "to provide global customers with excellent construction equipment and services" (LiuGong 2014). LiuGong established its first overseas division in Australia in 2004, followed by North and Latin America in 2008 and finally Europe, Pacific Asia, the Middle East and South Africa in 2010 (LiuGong 2014). In 2012, the company decided to open its new European headquarters in Almere. This location was chosen for its proximity to Amsterdam and its excellent infrastructure and nearby main ports. According to Chairman Xiaohua Wang, "This new office will strengthen our presence as a top construction equipment manufacturer brand, and to service our dealers and customers in the whole European market. Our staff will be able to interact more closely with our customers in Europe, and gain a deeper knowledge and understanding of the needs of each local market. Not only will this allow us to react to customers more effectively, it will also help us develop products that will better meet the local requirements". The company expects the new headquarters to become one of the most vital overseas bases of LiuGong (LiuGong 2012).

8. 2013, October: HNA Group Company Limited (HNA): TIP Trailer Services Group (TIP) (Amsterdam)

   HNA is a holding company founded in 2000, whose subsidiaries are mostly active in air transportation services, but also in "tourism, airport management, logistics, hotel management, retailing, finance, and other related businesses" (Businessweek 2014). TIP was founded in 1968, and is the biggest renter of trailers in Europe (Volkskrant 2014). Xiangdong Tan, the vice-chairman and president of HNA, said about the deal: "The acquisition of TIP into our portfolio is a good strategic fit, complementing our existing investments in world-wide aircraft leasing, marine container leasing and ship leasing. We are very pleased to be acquiring an excellent GE management team whom we fully support. We continue to strengthen our transportation finance and services capabilities internationally, and we intend to grow TIP Trailer Services during the coming years" (Business Wire 2013). According to HNA chairman Chen Feng, they deserve an award from the Dutch government for the deal, in which they completely bought TIP for the sum of "a few hundred million euros" (Volkskrant 2014). TIP was taken over from the American GE Capital.

9. 2014, March: COFCO: Nidera (Rotterdam)

   COFCO is a state-owned food-processing holdings company from Beijing. It was founded in 1949. It is on the 401st place on Fortune's Global 500 list (Fortune 2014). Nidera was founded in Rotterdam in 1920, and trades in grain, oilseeds, vegetable oils, specialty oils, biofuels and oilseed meals. It is active all over the world, including Latin America. This deal fits in the trend of China spending lots of money to acquire food assets overseas, especially in Latin America. Other important markets for Nidera, Eastern Europe and Russia, are also of special interest to the Chinese. The growing wealth in China makes the demand for food higher, leading to more imports. In 2011, the country became a net importer of rice (WSJ 2014). COFCO bought a 51 % stake in Nidera. The amount of money paid for the deal was not disclosed by the companies, but the China Global Investment Monitor 2014 estimates it at 1.2 billion US$ (Heritage 2014). This would mean an enormous boost of Chinese OFDI flows and assets in the Netherlands for 2014, comparable to the Geely takeover in Sweden. It is also most likely the largest investment from (mainland) China done in the Netherlands. In this case, access to markets elsewhere made the deal attractive for the Chinese party, not necessarily the Netherlands as a location.

10. 2014, July: United Vansen: ADO Den Haag (The Hague)

    While most Chinese takeovers or investments go by without the media taking much notice, it was quite different when Chinese lawyer and entrepreneur Hui Wang, owner of United Vansen, bought the Dutch professional football club ADO Den Haag. Most reactions to the news sounded like panic: does this Chinese guy even know what he is doing? Will China eventually buy up all teams in the Dutch first league (Eredivisie)? This was not helped by interviews in the Dutch press, where Wang did not recognize the mascot of the club. However, the millionaire has great plans for the club. Within 5 years, ADO Den Haag should reach the Europa League and the stadium should be extended to accommodate 30,000 supporters instead of the current 15,000. Wang wanted to buy a football club for a long time and eventually choose ADO because it had been profitable in the past 3 years (something that even the biggest football clubs have trouble with), it had relatively moderate costs and a great prospect for improvement (in results on the football field). He stressed that the club should stay "Hague-ish" and that he would not touch the "DNA" of the club. In total, Wang paid around eight million € for the club (NRC 2014) when the deal was finalized at the end of January 2015. This amount makes it a relatively small fry compared to some of the other M&A deals in this section, but of course the fact that this was a well-known football club from the first league of Dutch football gave it much more media attention.

5 Conclusions

Asian OFDI is certainly on the rise. On a global scale, China has become one of the biggest investors and, with the continuing economic growth in the country, can be expected to become even bigger. Furthermore, Europe is becoming an increasingly-important destination for Chinese companies. Where previously Chinese OFDI was mostly concerned with securing raw materials and food for Chinese use, the investments are now also rapidly spreading to other areas.

This raises the question, should the West be afraid of Asian and especially Chinese companies buying up the companies and even the countries of the West? There is no reason for panic just yet. Let us take the example of the Netherlands vis-à-vis Chinese OFDI. First of all, Chinese OFDI there, while growing and while individual deals are getting more and more capital-intensive, is still behind OFDI in, for instance, the UK or Germany. While the NFIA claims that the Netherlands is the third largest receiver of Chinese OFDI in the EU, the figures from De Nederlandse Bank and the European Commission seem to disagree. This raises another point: there are many institutions, both in the Netherlands and elsewhere, which track Chinese OFDI, but their figures vary wildly. Perhaps efforts should be made for a more integrated cooperation between these institutions to get a better overall view of Chinese OFDI stock and flows in the Netherlands. In any case, it can be concluded that in the Netherlands, Chinese OFDI is still relatively marginal compared to the OFDI coming from the USA, for example.

Part of the reason for the above situation is that most Chinese establishments in the Netherlands are relatively small-scale and don't employ a lot of people. This also implies that they do not cost a lot of money, although we have shown some examples of deals in the multiple hundred million €. When one thinks of Chinese companies, one normally thinks of gigantic state-owned institutions, while a lot of the Chinese companies in the Netherlands are actually small or medium-sized businesses which like the Dutch entrepreneurial climate. They often feel that the Chinese government does not take them seriously because they are too small, while the Dutch government, on the other hand, is very helpful (Akemu 2013; People's Daily 2013). It is not very likely that these smaller companies will form a security risk for the country, but at the same time they are of course not capable of huge investments.

Asian investment in the Netherlands shows roughly two trends. The first is to gain access to different markets and the second is to acquire knowledge or innovation. This is in line with the trends noted by Segers and Stam (2013). When looking at our examples, it is remarkable that often the smaller companies specifically choose for the Netherlands because of its location, while the bigger companies are often interested in market entrance to other countries. Examples of the latter category would be Changhong, which bought Sterope in order to acquire a South Korean company, or the megadeal of COFCO with Nidera in order to gain access to Latin America. Chinese companies that are looking for knowledge often start R&D centers in the Netherlands; there are many more Chinese R&D centers in the Netherlands than the ones mentioned here, for example those of Goodbaby, a company specialized in juvenile products which has an R&D center in Utrecht. These companies view the Netherlands as a good R&D base to eventually strengthen their presence in the entire European market (Akemu 2013).

Should the Netherlands try to attract more Asian OFDI? This is a rhetorical question. It is of the utmost importance that the Netherlands should develop stronger business connections with Asia that will more and more determine the rules of the (business) game. In addition, the Netherlands is in need of creating job possibilities, low and high paid. If the Netherlands doesn't enhance its efforts to attract Asian OFDI, the Asian companies will flock to bigger countries, which have a brand name in Asia, e.g. Germany and the UK. After all, companies like GINAF would have closed down completely where it not for an interested Chinese investor.

What is valid for the Netherlands is also valid for other countries as well. That means that a severe competition has started between many countries in the EU to attract as many Asian companies as possible.

The view of Chinese companies buying up a country is, in any case, unfounded. Following that logic, the Netherlands, for example, would already be completely owned by the USA or Japan, both countries having much larger OFDI flows and stock in the Netherlands. And, while most establishments are still small, they still have great potential. A distribution center might grow if the company gets more successful on the European market and will also provide jobs to other companies near it. The policy implications mentioned by Segers and Stam (2013) still hold true: attract both gateway companies and potential future market leaders. The spillover effect from these types of companies will be the most profitable in the long run. At the same time the Netherlands should not be afraid of acquisitions from Chinese companies. In many cases, the Chinese investor did not relocate the acquired company (and the jobs it provided) to China, but heavily invested in it. Why would a Chinese company even relocate jobs from the Netherlands when its goal was to gain access to the European market? Companies acquired by Chinese partners have often been successful, even when they were struggling previously (Akemu 2013).

In conclusion, there is no reason to be afraid of Asian or Chinese OFDI. On the contrary, the Netherlands or any other country might actually try to attract more Asian investors to not lose out to other EU countries like Germany or the UK. By attracting more Asian investors, the overall business climate of any country will improve, there will be more money put into the economy and, perhaps most importantly, more jobs will be created, especially in the long run.

References

Akemu, O. (2013). Chinese investment in Netherlands – The real story, October 25, 2013. Retrieved from http://www.slideshare.net/onajomoakemu/chinese-investment-in-netherlands-the-real-story.

Ausnutria-Hyproca. (2014). *History*. Retrieved August 22, 2014, from http://www.ausnutria-hyproca.com/about-us/history/.

Automobielmanagement. (2011). Chinese BHAP neemt zonnedakfabrikant Inalfa over, April 27, 2011. Retrieved from http://www.automobielmanagement.nl/nieuws/auto-economie-buitenland/nid11427-chinese-bhap-neemt-zonnedakfabrikant-inalfa-over.html.

Automotive. (2011). Landwind naar Helmond, March 3, 2011. Retrieved from http://www.automotive-online.nl/home/8472-landwind_naar_helmond.html.

Autonews. (2011). Beijing firm buys Inalfa Roof Systems, May 4, 2011. Retrieved from http://europe.autonews.com/article/20110504/ANE/110509983/beijing-firm-buys-inalfa-roof-systems.

Autoweek. (2011). Geen Chinese klant voor Nedcar, April 13, 2011. Retrieved from http://www.autoweek.nl/nieuws/16445/geen-chinese-klant-voor-nedcar.

Business Wire (2013). *HNA Group Completes Acquisition of TIP Trailer Service Group*, October 23, 2013. Retrieved from: http://www.businesswire.com/news/home/20131023006642/en/HNA-Group-Completes-Acquisition-TIP-Trailer-Services

Bloomberg Businessweek. (2014). *Company overview of HNA Group Co., Ltd*. Retrieved August 21, 2014, from http://investing.businessweek.com/research/stocks/private/snapshot.asp?privcapId=9124352.
China Daily. (2011). Ausnutria buys stake in Dutch dairy firm, July 22, 2011. Retrieved from http://usa.chinadaily.com.cn/business/2011-07/22/content_12961223.htm.
CHTGC. (2014a). *About CHTC*. Retrieved August 22, 2014, from http://www.chtgc.com/n150/n289/n353/index.html.
CHTGC. (2014b). *History*. Retrieved August 22, 2014, from http://www.chtgc.com/n150/n289/n359/index.html.
Clegg, J., & Voss, H. (2012). *Chinese overseas direct investment in the EU*. Retrieved August 20, 2014, from http://www.chathamhouse.org/sites/files/chathamhouse/public/Research/Asia/0912ecran_cleggvoss.pdf.
Comed. (2014). *About Comed*. Retrieved August 22, 2014, from http://www.comedbv.com/about_comed/Abou.htm.
De Nederlandse Bank (DNB). (2014). *Betalingsbalans en extern vermogen*. Retrieved August 18, 2014, from http://www.statistics.dnb.nl/betalingsbalans-en-extern-vermogen/index.jsp.
Dagblad van het Noorden (DVHN). (2013). Chinese fabriek niet naar Assen, December 6, 2013. Retrieved from http://www.dvhn.nl/nieuws/drenthe/chinese-fabriek-niet-naar-assen-10383343.html.
Fortune. (2014). *Fortune global 500*. Retrieved August 21, 2014, from http://fortune.com/global500/cofco-401/.
GINAF. (2011). Doorstart GINAF een feit!, November 30th, 2011. Retrieved from http://www.ginaf.nl/index.php?id=48&tx_ttnews[tt_news]=123&tx_ttnews[backPid]=24&cHash=2b3e1217f4.
Heritage (The Heritage Foundation). (2014). *China global investment tracker 2014*. Retrieved August 20, 2014, from http://thf_media.s3.amazonaws.com/2014/xls/China-Global-Investment-Tracker-2014.xls.
Landwind. (2014). *Landwind in Europa*. Retrieved August 22, 2014, from http://www.landwind.eu/.
LiuGong. (2012). LiuGong opens new European headquarters in Almere, June 27, 2012. Retrieved from http://www.liugong.com/en_sa/news/7001_for_companynews_text.htm.
LiuGong. (2014). *Our company*. Retrieved August 22, 2014, from http://www.liugong-europe.com/about.
Mapscape. (2014). *History*. Retrieved August 21, 2014, from http://www.mapscape.eu/about/history.html.
MOFCOM (Ministry of Commerce). (2011). *2010 Statistic bulletin of China's outward foreign direct investment*. Retrieved August 18, 2014, from http://hzs.mofcom.gov.cn/accessory/201109/1316069658609.pdf.
National Bureau of Statistics of China. (2014). *National Bureau of Statistics of China database*. Retrieved August 18, 2014, from http://www.stats.gov.cn/english/Statisticaldata/AnnualData/.
NavInfo. (2014). *Official website*. Retrieved August 21, 2014, from http://www.navinfo.com/en/.
NFIA. (2007). *Breakdown of results Netherlands Foreign Investment Agency over 2004 to 2006*. Retrieved August 19, 2014, from https://zoek.officielebekendmakingen.nl/kst-30800-XIII-39-b1.pdf.
NFIA. (2009). *NFIA results 2006–2008 in # projects by country of origin*. Retrieved August 19, 2014, from www.nfia.nl/files/pdf/2006-2008_country.pdf.
NFIA. (2010). *Resultaten 2009*. Retrieved August 19, 2014, from http://www.rijksoverheid.nl/documenten-en-publicaties/jaarverslagen/2010/03/16/nfia-resultaten-2009.html.
NFIA. (2011). *NFIA results 2010*. Retrieved August 19, 2014, from www.nfia.nl/files/publications/NFIA_results2010_A4_Eng_LR_def.pdf.
NFIA. (2012). *Resultaten 2011*. Retrieved August 19, 2014, from http://www.rijksoverheid.nl/documenten-en-publicaties/jaarverslagen/2012/02/09/nfia-jaarresultaten-2011.html.
NFIA. (2013). *Resultaten 2012*. Retrieved August 19, 2014, from http://www.rijksoverheid.nl/documenten-en-publicaties/rapporten/2014/03/17/resultaten-nfia-2013.html.

NFIA. (2014). *Resultaten 2013*. Retrieved August 19, 2014, from http://www.rijksoverheid.nl/documenten-en-publicaties/rapporten/2014/03/17/resultaten-nfia-2013.html.

Nolan, P. (2012). *Is China buying the World?* Cambridge: Polity.

NRC (NRC Handelsblad). (2014). De rode kapitalist van ADO, August 2, 2014.

People's Daily (Online). (2013). Dutch PM: Netherlands is ready for more Chinese investment, November 15, 2013. Retrieved from http://english.peopledaily.com.cn/90883/8457343.html.

Research in China. (2011). Lepu medical technology expands into The Netherlands, November 15, 2011. Retrieved from http://www.researchinchina.com/news/NewsInfo.aspx?Id=26137.

Segers, R. T., & Stam, T. (2013). *Asia: Reshaping the global economic landscape*. Maastricht: Shaker Publishing.

Telematicsnews. (2011). China: Navinfo to acquire Holland's Mapscape for $9.35 million, January 17th, 2011. Retrieved from http://telematicsnews.info/2011/01/17/china-navinfo-to-acquire-hollands-mapscape-for-935-million_j2171/.

UNCTAD. (2014a). *UNCTADSTAT*. Retrieved August 18, 2014, from http://unctadstat.unctad.org/wds/ReportFolders/reportFolders.aspx.

UNCTAD. (2014b). *Sources and definitions*. Retrieved September 11, 2014, from http://unctad.org/en/Pages/DIAE/FDI%20Statistics/Sources-and-Definitions.aspx.

Volkskrant (De Volkskrant) (2014). Chinese tycoon neemt geruisloos Nederlandse transportgigant over, February 6, 2014. Retrieved from http://www.volkskrant.nl/vk/nl/2680/Economie/article/detail/3591405/2014/02/06/Chinese-tycoon-neemt-geruisloos-Nederlandse-transportgigant-over.dhtml.

Wall Street Journal (WSJ). (2014). China's Cofco to buy 51 % of Grain Trader Nidera, February 28, 2014. Retrieved from http://online.wsj.com/news/articles/SB10001424052702304071004579409933990686414.